Lingering Bilingualism

Judaic Traditions in Literature, Music, and Art

Harold Bloom and Ken Frieden, *Series Editors*

Other titles in Judaic Traditions in Literature, Music, and Art

Bridging the Divide: The Selected Poems of Hava Pinhas-Cohen
Sharon Hart-Green, ed. and trans.

Early Yiddish Epic
Jerold C. Frakes, ed. and trans.

Letters to America: Selected Poems of Reuven Ben-Yosef
Michael Weingrad, ed. and trans.

My Blue Piano
Else Lasker-Schüler; Brooks Haxton, trans.

Rhetoric and Nation: The Formation of Hebrew National Culture, 1880–1990
Shai P. Ginsburg

Social Concern and Left Politics in Jewish American Art: 1880–1940
Matthew Baigell

The Travels of Benjamin Zuskin
Ala Zuskin Perelman

Yiddish Poetry and the Tuberculosis Sanatorium: 1900–1970
Ernest B. Gilman

Lingering Bilingualism

Modern Hebrew and Yiddish Literatures in Contact

NAOMI BRENNER

Syracuse University Press

First Edition 2016
16 17 18 19 20 21 6 5 4 3 2 1

For a listing of books published and distributed by Syracuse University Press, visit https://press.syr.edu.

ISBN: 978-0-8156-3423-2 (cloth) 978-0-8156-3409-6 (paperback)
978-0-8156-5343-1 (e-book)

Library of Congress Cataloging-in-Publication Data
Brenner, Naomi, author.
Lingering bilingualism : modern Hebrew and Yiddish literatures in contact / Naomi Brenner.
pages cm. — (Judaic traditions in literature, music, and art) Includes bibliographical references and index.
ISBN 978-0-8156-3423-2 (cloth : alk. paper) — ISBN 978-0-8156-3409-6 (pbk. : alk. paper) — ISBN 978-0-8156-5343-1 (e-book) 1. Yiddish literature—History and criticism. 2. Hebrew literature—History and criticism. 3. Jews—Languages. 4. Yiddish language. 5. Hebrew language. 6. Bilingualism. 7. Languages in contact. I. Title.
PJ5120.5.B67 2015
839'.109003—dc23 2015036237

The authorized representative in the EU for product safety and compliance is Mare Nostrum Group B.V, Doelen 72, 4831 GR Breda, The Netherlands.
gpsr@mare-nostrum.co.uk

For Ari

Contents

Illustrations

Acknowledgments

AS A COLLEGE STUDENT, I had my first whiff of the joys, along with the sneezes, of research while turning the pages of musty old periodicals, finding stories and poems nestled alongside agricultural reports and advertisements for aspirin and shoe polish. The process of reading these literary texts and reading around these texts has been inspired, guided, and immeasurably assisted by many people. I would like to thank my teachers Robert Alter and Chana Kronfeld, who taught me how to read literary texts with precision, creativity, and sensitivity. Daniel Boyarin and Naomi Seidman were always generous with their time and ideas, engaging in thought-provoking conversations from the theoretical to the practical. I was transformed as a reader, writer, and human being while sitting with them in Berkeley offices, cafés, and living rooms. I am grateful to the many scholars and friends who have helped me develop and revise this project: Robert Adler Peckerar, Maya Barzilai, Vitaly Bergelson, Alisa Braun, Robert Chazan, Jordan Finkin, Dan Laor, Tamara Mann, Avraham Novershtern, Shachar Pinsker, Allison Schachter, and David Shneer. I have presented sections of several chapters at the annual conferences of the Association for Jewish Studies, the American Comparative Literature Association, and the National Association of Professors of Hebrew, and I appreciate the comments and the conversations that ensued. I also want to thank Syracuse University Press's anonymous readers for their suggestions.

At The Ohio State University, I am grateful for the support of my colleagues in the Department of Near Eastern Languages and

Cultures and the Melton Center for Jewish Studies, especially librarian and bibliographer extraordinaire Joseph Galron-Goldschläger. In Israel, the librarians and archivists at the National Library of Israel, Gnazim Institute, and Tel Aviv University's E. Sourasky Central Library provided access to a wide variety of texts, including many periodicals hiding on dusty shelves and in microfilm cabinets. The University of California, Berkeley, Wexner Foundation, National Foundation for Jewish Culture, Lucius N. Littauer Foundation, Rothschild Foundation/Hanadiv Fellowship, and The Ohio State University have generously supported my work over the years. Syracuse University Press staff, particularly acquisitions editor Deborah Manion and project editor Brendan Missett, have guided this book through the publication process with great care and enthusiasm. Leslie Rubin helped polish it with her attention to detail.

I would like to acknowledge the Modern Languages Association for permission to quote from Stephen Greenblatt's "Racial Memory and Literary History," *PMLA* 116 (2001); the E. Sourasky Central Library at Tel Aviv University, which provided access to the magazines *Milgroym* and *Rimon* and their vivid images; the Abraham Nahum Stencl Archive (PP MS 44) at the SOAS Library for permission to reprint the poem "Vider un vider"; Rutie Eshel-Shlonsky, for permission to reprint sections from "Amal" and "Le-aba-ima"; the Gnazim Institute in Tel Aviv for permission to quote from Rachel Feygenberg's correspondence; the University of California Press, for permission to reprint excerpts from Benjamin and Barbara Harshav's translation of "Good Night, World," published in *American Hebrew Poetry* (1986); and Helit Yeshurun, for permission to reprint Avot Yeshurun's "Duleshoniyut." I am grateful for permission to reprint earlier versions of sections from chapters 1 and 2 that appeared in "*Milgroym*, *Rimon* and Interwar Jewish Bilingualism," *Journal of Jewish Identities* 7, no. 1 (2014): 23–48 (reprinted by permission of the *Journal of Jewish Identities*); and "A Multilingual Modernist: Avraham Shlonsky between Hebrew and Yiddish," *Comparative Literature* 61, no. 4 (2009): 367–87 (reprinted by permission of Duke University Press).

Finally, I want to thank the community of friends and family who have cheered my progress from the very beginning, offering their assistance, encouragement, and company along the way. At the top of a very long list are my most willing readers and staunch supporters, my parents Dean Brenner and Merle Brenner, and my siblings Yoni and Michelle, Dani and Sara, and Bean Brenner. My daughters, Maya and Noa, have lived this project from beginning to end, contributing their perspectives on language and life and helping keep everything in perspective. Nadav made his welcome appearance during copyediting. And most of all, thank you to Ari, who has been a constant source of strength and laughter. None of this would be possible without you.

Lingering Bilingualism

Introduction

> Language is the slipperiest of human creations; like its speakers, it does not respect borders, and, like the imagination, it cannot ultimately be predicted or controlled.
>
> —Stephen Greenblatt

"CEGLANA STREET WAS, it seems to me, my first literary incubator," bilingual Hebrew-Yiddish writer Zalman Shneour (1886–1959) reminisced.[1] "I was drawn to it in the bloom of my youth, to warm myself in the light of famous writers and soon-to-be famous writers."[2] One of many to describe the Jewish cultural scene in Warsaw at the very beginning of the twentieth century, Shneour recalled the good old days when Yiddish and Hebrew writers lived "in peace and harmony."[3] Yitzhak Leyb Peretz, the doyen of Jewish literary life in Warsaw, lived at 1 Ceglana Street and welcomed up-and-coming writers to weekly gatherings in his home. In late 1902, Yosef Klausner, the newly appointed editor of the Hebrew monthly *Ha-shiloach* (published 1896–1926), moved into a house down the street and started hosting his own Saturday-evening gatherings. Young writers such as Sholem Ash, H. D. Nomberg, Avrom Reyzen, Yitzhak Katznelson, Ya'akov Fichman, Y. D. Berkovitz, and Shneour himself frequented these and other literary gatherings around town, some preferring the Polish conversation at the Peretz household, others gravitating toward the Russian-speaking crowd at the Klausners.[4] Like Shneour, Berkovitz also fondly remembered his visits to Ceglana Street: "Those were days of fraternity and amiability between the two languages, of renewed Jewish creativity, which enjoyed a new abundance of youthful powers."[5] These Warsaw literary salons were just two of the many meeting places for Hebrew and Yiddish and their writers in the early years of the twentieth century, reflecting the unique circumstances of the two languages of Eastern European Jewry at this historical moment. Sketching an idyllic portrait of a bilingual Jewish culture, Shneour wrote years later: "We lived in peace. It is a shame that this brotherly-peace is no longer known or understood these days among our writers' associations in Hebrew and Yiddish."[6]

Shneour's memoirs span a remarkable trajectory from what he represents as peaceful linguistic and cultural symbiosis to contentious split, from the concentration of Jewish life in Eastern Europe to its dispersion across Europe, the Americas, and pre-state Palestine. In 1902, when Shneour came to Warsaw and published his first Hebrew and Yiddish poems, ambitious young writers flocked from Jewish towns and villages to the cultural centers of Warsaw, Odessa, and Vilna to seek their fortunes. *Ha-shiloach* was just one of many Hebrew and Yiddish periodicals available to aspiring writers, who chose to write in one—or often both—of the languages of Eastern European Jewish life. Inspired by S. Y. Abramovitsh's sly and satirical narratives, Peretz's elegant prose, and Chayim Nachman Bialik's rich and varied poetry in both languages, these writers saw both Yiddish and Hebrew as viable literary languages for the growing audience of readers in Jewish communities across Eastern Europe and beyond.

Hebrew had long been considered the more prestigious of the two Jewish languages by virtue of its biblical and scholarly tradition. But modern Hebrew was a literary language in construction, lacking a spoken register, a modern vocabulary, and, most of all, a significant readership. Yiddish, by contrast, was the vernacular of the majority of Jews and Jewish writers from Eastern and Central Europe but was stigmatized as *zhargon*, a "jargon" for the masses not suitable for literature or culture. However, Yiddish's expressive capacities had greatly improved by the beginning of the twentieth century thanks to its writers' literary innovations. While Hebrew was still well-established as the language of Jewish intellectual pursuits, Yiddish was increasingly seen as a viable and, for some, a preferable literary language for the Eastern European Jewish masses.

By 1959, when Shneour published his recollections, Eastern European Jewish life had been transformed in ways unimaginable decades earlier: battered by intense periods of violence, from the 1905 revolution and its ensuing pogroms to World War I and the Russian Revolution; polarized by the rise of ideological and political movements; spread across Europe, North and South America, and Palestine; and devastated by the Nazi genocide. Jewish-language literature, too, had undergone major changes. Writers in both languages had experimented with stylistic trends like romanticism, realism, impressionism, expressionism, and surrealism in quick succession. Yiddish literature, variously allied with communism, autonomism, and socialism, thrived in the active cultural spheres in interwar Poland and the Americas. In the young Soviet Union, Yiddish had been declared the language of the Jewish minority but later was suppressed by Soviet authorities. Hebrew literature, with its strong ties to Zionism, had migrated east to Palestine, though writers in Europe and the United States continued to publish Hebrew poetry and prose. By the postwar period, the Jewish literary bilingualism that had defined the literary gatherings on Ceglana Street had virtually disappeared, as Hebrew was ensconced as the language of the young state of Israel and Yiddish was scattered throughout postwar Jewish communities in Europe and the Americas.

This book traces the paths of Hebrew-Yiddish bilingualism—its writers, readers, and institutions—across the first half of the twentieth century, from the intimate quarters of Warsaw's literary salons to the many mid-twentieth-century sites of Jewish-language literature. Peretz's home, in which Hebrew and Yiddish writers gathered together to read, declaim, and debate, was replaced by a variety of other points of literary contact across the expanding geographical and ideological maps of Jewish culture. The face-to-face encounters that had been commonplace in homes, on street corners, and in cafes in places like Warsaw, Odessa, and Vilna became increasingly rare with the political polarization of Jewish life and the emigration of both writers and readers from the Jewish cultural centers of Eastern Europe. Intersections between the two Jewish languages of Eastern Europe continued on the pages of periodicals, within literary oeuvres, and between translated texts. The terms of engagement between Hebrew and Yiddish were negotiated and renegotiated in Moscow, Berlin, Paris, Tel Aviv, New York, and many other sites of early twentieth-century Jewish culture. The literary bilingualism that had defined nineteenth-century Eastern European Jewish culture and the gatherings on Ceglana Street gave way to different modes of literary-linguistic contact between World War I and World War II.

The aim of *Lingering Bilingualism* is neither to idealize the Hebrew-Yiddish bilingualism that once defined Eastern European Jewish culture nor to recount the "language war" that challenged it. Rather, this book argues that continued Hebrew-Yiddish literary contact was critical to the development of each literature, cultivating literary experimentation and innovation through language and, often, in between languages. In contrast to historians and critics who have stressed the imperatives of Zionist and Yiddishist politics, the consolidation of a Hebrew national culture and the emergence of a self-sufficient Yiddish culture, *Lingering Bilingualism* takes a closer look at the bilingualism that was denied, negated, or believed to be left behind in Eastern Europe. Focusing on a series of encounters between Hebrew and Yiddish writers and texts, it analyzes how literary works resisted the demands of monolingualism and moved between the languages of early twentieth-century Ashkenazi Jewish life.

Yet this book is more than just a glimpse into a disappearing world of Hebrew-Yiddish bilingualism. Historically, bilingual writers became an endangered species during the interwar period, marginalized by the geographic upheaval and ideological polarization of Jewish culture. But the writers and editors who persisted in their efforts to sustain Hebrew-Yiddish bilingualism offered alternative visions for Jewish culture that rejected the inevitability of a single national literary language and created space for multiple languages and multiple voices within Jewish-language literature. The unique circumstances of Jewish literary bilingualism shaped a compelling vision for a modern translingual culture, one that was realized for fleeting moments, but never in full.

A Tale of Two Languages

Shneour's retrospective account provides a good starting point not only because it fondly evokes the halcyon days of a bilingual past but also because it calls attention to several key elements in the trajectory of Hebrew-Yiddish literary bilingualism. First and foremost, his narrative reveals the complex linguistic map of Jewish Eastern European society. Born into a traditional Jewish family in the Belorussian town of Shklov, the young Shneour wrote in both Hebrew and Yiddish and spoke enough Russian and Polish to function comfortably in both Peretz's Polish salon and Klausner's Russian one. Shneour describes a group of similarly multilingual young writers who pursued their interests in Hebrew and Yiddish up and down Ceglana Street. These multilingual writers were not merely exceptional individuals; their linguistic repertoires were products of the multilingualism that defined Ashkenazi Jewish life in Eastern Europe.

Eastern European Jewish communities had long maintained what Max Weinreich calls "external bilingualism," using different languages to interact with Jews and the surrounding non-Jewish environment. Ashkenazi Jewish society also cultivated internal bilingualism, what has been called "functional diglossia," in which the traditional Jewish sacred tongue, Hebrew (or, as Weinreich specifies, *loshn koydesh*, a fusion of Hebrew and Aramaic), was complemented by the Yiddish vernacular. Yiddish was the *mame-loshn,* the mother tongue and language of daily life, encompassing everything from mothers' lullabies to rabbis' sermons. Hebrew, the *fotershprakh* (father tongue), was the written language of the Bible, rabbinic texts, and, increasingly, of Jewish enlightenment texts that circulated in Eastern Europe over the course of the nineteenth century.[7]

By the time Shneour and his fellow writers were congregating in Warsaw, the traditional symbiotic relationship of the languages, with its clear division of labor, had been challenged by a new generation of writers, thinkers, and ideologues. The written-oral distinction between Hebrew and Yiddish had never been complete or absolute; Yiddish texts date back to at least the thirteenth century, and a variety of religious, historical, and imaginative works circulated within an ever-growing population of Yiddish readers over subsequent centuries.[8] By the second half of the nineteenth century, Jewish writers were producing both mass-market and literary texts for eager Yiddish readers, from the wildly popular chapbooks and novels of Ayzik Meyer Dik and Shomer (Nokhum Shaykevitch) to the satirical portraits of shtetl life of S. Y. Abramovitsh. Jewish writers—often some of the same writers—were also writing stories, novels, and memoirs in Hebrew intended to chronicle sweeping changes in Jewish life and inspire modern interest in the holy tongue. Other Jewish writers turned to non-Jewish languages, whether Russian, Polish, German, or other languages in multilingual Eastern and Central Europe. As a result, one of the key components of what Benjamin Harshav calls the "modern Jewish revolution" that began in the last decades of the nineteenth century was "the flourishing of a polyphonic literature and textual culture in 2+1 languages: Yiddish, Hebrew and the languages of state and culture."[9] From Samuel Beckett to Vladimir Nabokov, critical approaches to modern literary bilingualism have focused on the exceptionalism of the bilingual writer and associated difficulties with writing in a nonnative tongue.[10] But at the beginning of the twentieth century in the Jewish cultural centers of Eastern Europe, it was hard to find a writer who had not tried his or her hand at both Hebrew and Yiddish, not to mention Russian or Polish.[11]

Shneour's nostalgic account demonstrates the coexistence of Hebrew and Yiddish and the rivalry that emerged between the two. On the one hand, Shneour recalls a time when Hebrew and Yiddish writers "lived in peace and harmony."[12] On the other hand, his description of the literary scene is filled with binaries: Warsaw (Peretz) or Odessa (Klausner); Polish (Peretz) or Russian (Klausner); and, implicitly, Yiddish (Peretz) or Hebrew (Klausner). In early twentieth-century Warsaw, these boundaries could still be traversed, both conceptually and literally, by a short walk up and down Ceglana Street. Hebrew and Yiddish writers and readers were still bound together by their geographic proximity and widespread bilingualism. However, subsequent decades transformed the geographical, ideological, and cultural maps of Eastern European Jewish life and, with it, Hebrew-Yiddish bilingualism.

Shneour, like many others, blamed the "fall" of Hebrew-Yiddish bilingualism on the First Yiddish Language Conference, held in Czernowitz, then the capital of the Austrian crown province of Bukovina (now Chernivtsi, Ukraine) in 1908. Hebrew and Yiddish coexisted peacefully, Shneour insisted, until the fateful conference: "Only after the Czernowitz Conference was the 'breach' widened by the writer Peretz himself. He added to Yiddish the definite article *hey,* [making it] *the* national language. Opinions were divided and hearts were distanced from each other. And the literary *torah* was made into two *torahs*, each one opposing the other."[13] The conference, convened by the writer Nathan Birnbaum, ideologue Khayim Zhitlovski, and Yiddish novelist Dovid Pinski, was intended to discuss issues such as Yiddish orthography and grammar and the economic status of Yiddish writers and actors. But with an audience full of Yiddish and Hebrew loyalists, it was dominated by debates surrounding the tenth and final proposed agenda item: recognition for the Yiddish language.[14] With a play on the Hebrew word "breach" (*perets*), Shneour blames Peretz for cultural incitement and couches the demise of Jewish bilingualism in terms of Jewish tradition. Rabbinic theology is predicated on the idea of the dual Torah, written and oral scripture that together represent divine revelation. Importing this foundational belief into the literary sphere, Shneour represents the Czernowitz Conference as a heretical split of the literary canon into two opposing rather than traditionally complementary camps. But Shneour misrepresents Peretz's involvement in the conference: Peretz, along with conference organizers Birnbaum and Zhitlovksi, pushed for a compromise on the concluding resolution concerning the status of Yiddish in Jewish culture. Avoiding the pressure of both those who wanted to declare Yiddish as *the* national Jewish language and those who upheld Hebrew as the eternal national Jewish language, the conference's final resolution proclaimed Yiddish *a* national Jewish language, incurring the wrath of all parties. Shneour invokes Czernowitz not as a tempestuous, disorganized conference that occurred in a sleepy Austro-Hungarian town in 1908 but rather as the mythic site of the rupture between Hebrew and Yiddish literature.

But the Czernowitz Conference had little practical effect on Jewish cultural production in Eastern Europe. The conference concluded with no plan of action or organizational structure and even the minutes of the proceedings were soon lost. Reactions in the Yiddish and Hebrew press ranged from disinterest to denunciation, both from Hebraists, who vehemently disagreed with Yiddish's "encroachment" on Hebrew, and from Yiddishists, who felt the conference's resolution did not go far enough.[15] Rather, Czernowitz became a symbol: for some, a symbol of the legitimacy and rising profile of Yiddish; for others, like Shneour, a symbol of the unnecessary and traumatic split between Yiddish and Hebrew.[16]

More significant, at least in practical terms, were the effects of World War I and the Russian Revolution. The war ravaged Jewish cities and towns across the Pale of Settlement and in the Austro-Hungarian Empire, where battles raged between German, Austro-Hungarian, and Russian forces. European Hebrew literature had developed in a geographic milieu that promoted circulation and exchange among a relatively small audience of writers and readers spread across the Russian and Austro-Hungarian Empires, precisely the area that was irrevocably altered by World War I. In Dan Miron's words: "The fronts tore the 'Hebrew space' of Eastern Europe to pieces and rendered communication within it impossible. This space was never to be truly stitched together, since the war would be followed by civil wars and pogroms of unprecedented magnitude; then, the victorious Bolshevik regime, which would . . . eliminate all public Hebrew activities in the Soviet Union."[17] Yiddish, Miron argues, was less severely affected by the war because it relied less on long-distance communication and transportation.[18] But the violence and massive dislocation not only brought Eastern European Jewish culture to a virtual standstill but also redrew the boundaries in which it had thrived. Before the war, the majority of European Jewry had lived in the Russian and Austro-Hungarian

Empires, with thriving literary centers in Vilna, Warsaw, Odessa, and Kiev (Russia) as well as in smaller cities like Cracow, Lvov, and Czernowitz (Austria-Hungary). After a devastating war, these Jewish communities found themselves spread among eight different states, with thousands of stateless Jewish refugees.[19] Meanwhile, growing centers of Jewish culture in Berlin, London, New York, and Tel Aviv were compelling alternatives to an Eastern European landscape in shambles. The traditional center of bilingual Hebrew-Yiddish Jewish culture was in disarray, never to regain its former glory.

Even Warsaw's Ceglana Street as a microcosm of Jewish literary bilingualism would never be the same: Peretz moved to a house on Jerozolimskie Street and died in 1915; Klausner returned to Odessa in 1906 and then moved on to Palestine in 1919. Young writers who once had gathered to debate Hebrew and Yiddish literature and life on Ceglana Street had spread across the modern Jewish diaspora: by the mid-1920s, Ash, Reyzen, and Berkovitz were in the United States, Shneour was in Paris, and Fichman was in Palestine; only Nomberg and Katznelson remained in Poland. In interwar Warsaw, Yiddish writers congregated at 13 Tlomackie Street, the headquarters of the Association of Jewish Writers and Journalists, while their Hebrew colleagues created their own Association of Hebrew Writers and Journalists in Poland and gathered half a mile away at 11 Orla Street.[20] As Ashkenazi Jewish literary horizons expanded beyond Warsaw and the Eastern European Jewish heartland, the nature of Hebrew-Yiddish literary intersections changed dramatically.

Lingering Bilingualism

Not surprisingly, World War I has been cited as a pivotal point in the history of Hebrew-Yiddish bilingualism and language more generally. The years surrounding World War I, George Steiner argues, coincided with a language revolution in Western culture, marked by new approaches to linguistics, philosophy, psychology, and poetry. "A striking aspect of this language revolution," Steiner states, "has been the emergence of linguistic pluralism or 'unhousedness' in certain great writers."[21] Early twentieth-century Hebrew and Yiddish literatures shared in this sense of "unhousedness" given the interwar upheaval. But for Hebrew and Yiddish writers, the decades following World War I represent not the emergence of linguistic pluralism but the transformation of traditional Jewish bilingualism.

Itamar Even-Zohar, whose polysystem theory has been influential in the study of Jewish culture, locates a major change in the relationship between Hebrew and Yiddish literatures in the years surrounding World War I. Even-Zohar argues that the long-standing arrangement in which Hebrew was the vehicle of Eastern European Jewish high culture, and Yiddish satisfied the lower cultural stratum, fell apart by World War I.[22] Hebrew, he argues, became the spoken language in prestate Palestine, and Yiddish was replaced by local languages in Eastern Europe and the United States. Yet Even-Zohar notes that linguistic transfer between the languages, such as the direct use of Yiddish in Hebrew, continued long after the dissolution of the Hebrew-Yiddish polysystem.[23] Lingering intrasystemic and growing intersystemic elements—or more simply put, lingering norms of traditional Hebrew-Yiddish bilingualism and negotiations of alternative literary-linguistic arrangements—make the dynamics of the interwar years crucial to understanding Jewish-language literature.

However, it was not just the cultural norms that were changing in the years surrounding World War I. Dan Miron narrates a similar account of the Hebrew-Yiddish split with a focus on the writers involved: "When World War I broke out, and actually already before then, it became obvious that the bilingual option was imaginary and the erstwhile bilingual writers could no longer evade the linguistic choice that had been inherent in their work even before they acted on it. Thus Sholem Ash, Hersch Dovid Nomberg, Avraham Reysen, and other writers, who had made bilingual debuts at the beginning of the twentieth century, became one hundred percent Yiddishists. Others, like Ya'akov Shteinberg or Aharon Reuveni and later Greenberg, all of them upcoming Yiddish or Hebrew-Yiddish young writers, left their Yiddish past behind them once they made aliya and became committed Hebraists. . . . Essentially all writers had to make a choice, which was interpreted as a vote of confidence, whether they meant or did not mean it as such."[24] Miron argues not only that Hebrew and Yiddish writers followed separate paths after World War I but also that Hebrew-Yiddish bilingualism had never really been a viable option, despite its many practitioners at the beginning of the twentieth century. Focusing on individual writers rather than a larger system or relationship, he stresses that writers were compelled to choose between the languages by ideology (becoming Yiddishists = choosing Yiddish) or geography (immigrating to Palestine = choosing Hebrew).

Yet there was a third choice available to interwar writers, virtually all of whom had grown up in the multilingual world of Jewish Eastern Europe: the choice to continue writing in Hebrew and Yiddish. Despite the radical transformations of the Eastern European world in which traditional Jewish bilingualism had thrived, individual bilingualism remained a viable option for a small subset of writers. The Hebrew-Yiddish literary bilingualism most famously practiced by S. Y. Abramovitsh was increasingly marginalized in the 1920s, but writers like Shneour, Berkovitz, Uri Zvi Greenberg, Eliezer Shteinman, and Aharon Zeitlin continued to publish in both languages. For many of these writers, literary success and canonization were elusive; bilingualism was not an ideologically popular choice in a highly ideological time. Chana Kronfeld points to the Zionist Yiddish literature of poets like Rikuda Potash and the non-Zionist Hebrew writing of David Fogel to make the case that "it is a mistake to assume an automatic correlation between language choice and ideology, a correlation expressed by the purported equation Hebrew = Zionism."[25] Bilingual writers further confused the language-ideology correlation by repeatedly traversing the boundaries erected between Hebrew and Yiddish. Their ability to do so reflects not only the potentially subversive nature of bilingual writing but also the gaps between statements of language ideology and actual literary-linguistic practice during the interwar years. Literary bilingualism may have been waning but it was far from imaginary.

Beyond the shrinking pool of active bilingual writers, individuals continued to traverse the two languages in a variety of ways. The popular Yiddish novelist Ash wrote solely in Yiddish after early literary attempts in Hebrew, but he worked on an institutional level to reconcile American Yiddish and Hebrew writers, visiting the Yishuv and Israel several times between 1908 and 1957. Hebrew poet Bialik lectured to Jewish audiences in Hebrew and Yiddish throughout the United States during his 1926 speaking tour. Yiddish poet Dovid Hofshteyn spent a year in Tel Aviv and published in Hebrew periodicals before returning to Kiev in 1926. Translation also played an increasingly prominent role, whether in individual writers' translations or larger-scale translation projects, as writers like Ya'akov Shteinberg and Aharon Reuveni spent years translating their Yiddish prose into Hebrew in the early 1920s. One of the best representatives of the complex literary-linguistic dynamics of the time was Uri Zvi Greenberg. Greenberg dramatically renounced Yiddish in 1923, embraced Hebrew, and moved to Palestine. By the mid-1930s, however, he returned to Poland as a spokesperson for the Revisionists and, like medieval Jewish writers in Iberia who wrote their prose works in Arabic and their poetry in Hebrew, published essays in Yiddish and poetry in Hebrew. Thus even writers who championed Yiddish or Hebrew continued to move between the languages. After generations of ingrained internal Jewish bilingualism, the extensive linkages between Hebrew and Yiddish did not disappear overnight.

Individual bilingualism, however, was not the only link between Hebrew and Yiddish literatures. Naomi Seidman has examined the gendered social, historical, and cultural connections between the two languages of Jewish Eastern Europe. Hebrew and Yiddish, she argues, were understood in terms of the masculine/feminine opposition of Ashkenazi gender structures: "the full range of potential linguistic and sexual relations, from harmonic complementarity to violent conflict, have found their expression in the long history of the Hebrew-Yiddish sexual-linguistic system."[26] Seidman's analysis of Hebrew and Yiddish literature and early twentieth-century Jewish history demonstrates the way in which connections between the languages were not simply or strictly linguistic or literary but embedded in established social structures. Still, Seidman affixes an endpoint to this sexual-linguistic system, several years after Even-Zohar marks the end of the Hebrew-Yiddish polysystem. In 1927, Bialik pronounced Hebrew and Yiddish as "a marriage made in heaven" as part of a longer speech about the venerable relationship between the two Jewish languages. As we will see in chapter 2, Avraham Shlonsky sparked a bitter controversy in prestate Palestine by forcefully rejecting Bialik's marriage metaphor. Seidman identifies this public debate as the final dissolution of the Hebrew-Yiddish sexual-linguistic system.[27]

Instead of marking the demise of Hebrew-Yiddish bilingualism, I argue that the interwar period was a time of profound transition in Jewish-language literature, as Ashkenazi Jewish culture expanded beyond Eastern Europe to new sites in Palestine, Western Europe, and the Americas. Hebrew and Yiddish literatures were, in Allison Schachter's words, "enmeshed with each other, but not necessarily equivalent."[28] The precise terms of engagement were being negotiated in pragmatic, conceptual, and literary terms among the different agents of Jewish culture in Hebrew and in Yiddish. Fewer writers were actively bilingual, but many maintained extensive contacts with their Hebrew and Yiddish colleagues, engaged an overlapping readership, and shared the experiences of modern Jewish life. The sexual-linguistic system no longer functioned in the emerging centers of Jewish-language literature, but the two languages still coexisted in different configurations across the expanding map of Jewish culture. In Poland, for example, readers could choose among competing Polish, Yiddish, and Hebrew books and periodicals; in Berlin, Hebrew and Yiddish were both minor languages with respect to German cultural trends; in New York, Yiddish dominated the Jewish-language cultural scene, relegating Hebrew to small coteries and isolated writers; and in Tel Aviv, Hebrew was the language of the Zionist enterprise and Yiddish ostracized as the language of the diaspora. In each of these sites, writers, editors, critics, and publishers sought to reconceive the relationship between Hebrew and Yiddish literary cultures.

From Literary Bilingualism to Translingualism

Lingering Bilingualism contends that the interwar period represents a new phase in the long history of Hebrew-Yiddish literary contact. Throughout the nineteenth century, the symbiotic relationship between Hebrew and Yiddish was knitted into the fabric of Eastern European Jewish-language culture, exemplified by writers such as Yosef Perl (1773–1839), whose anti-Hasidic satire *Megale temirin* (Revealer of Secrets, 1819) was published in Hebrew but widely circulated in Yiddish; and Yitzhak Ber Levinson (1788–1860), who wrote the majority of his Enlightenment works in Hebrew, but tried to reach more Eastern European Jewish readers with Yiddish dramas like *Di hefker velt* (The Lawless World, 1888).[29] Even as the Haskalah movement, the Jewish Enlightenment, sought to reinvigorate Hebrew and substitute state languages like German, Russian, or Polish for lowly regarded Yiddish, *maskilim* (enlighteners) like Perl, Levinson, and many others continued to use Yiddish to communicate with the Jewish masses.[30] Hebrew was entrenched as the high language of scholarly and literary production and Yiddish was considered the low, vernacular language of the Jewish masses. Functionally, Hebrew and Yiddish literature complemented each other within the cultural logic of Jewish Eastern Europe.

Toward the end of the nineteenth century, a different bilingual model emerged as writers like S. Y. Abramovitsh produced literary texts in Hebrew and Yiddish by writing and rewriting their own texts. Bilingual individuals like Levinson and Perl had written in both languages, but until Abramovitsh, few had engaged systematically in both modern Hebrew and Yiddish literary production. Abramovitsh's earliest works were published in Hebrew in the 1850s. In 1864 he switched to Yiddish in search of a suppler stylistic medium and a broader audience, but from the 1870s onward he wrote extensively in both languages, publishing his literary texts in parallel Hebrew and Yiddish versions.[31] Abramovitsh was not the sole practitioner of this kind of literary bilingualism. Peretz, Nomberg, Shneour, Berkovitz, Perets Hirshbeyn, and Devorah Baron can also be counted among the many bilingual writers at the beginning of the twentieth century. In 1908, Yiddish literary critic Bal Makhshoves argued that Hebrew and Yiddish comprised a single literature because of the many professional Jewish writers who published in both Hebrew and Yiddish.[32] Bilingual writing was reputable, thanks to Abramovitsh's status, and also potentially lucrative as writers attempted to reach both the small but prestigious Hebrew market and the much larger Yiddish audience in Eastern Europe. At the same time, this individual bilingualism demonstrated the extent to which Hebrew and Yiddish were both emerging as modern literary languages, dispensing with earlier functional divisions and increasingly competing with each other.

Reeling from the intrinsic developments epitomized by the Czernowitz Conference and the extrinsic effects of war and revolution, Hebrew and Yiddish literatures entered a new phase in the 1920s characterized by changing modes of linguistic and literary contact. Both cultural and individual bilingualism were declining in response to interwar geographical dispersion and the ideological polarization of Jewish-language literature. Even Bal Makhshoves, an outspoken proponent of Jewish literary bilingualism, registered these changes by appending a new section to his essay "Tsvey sphrakhn—eyneynsike literatur" (Two Languages—A Single Literature) in 1918. While he had focused on bilingual writers in 1908, Bal Makhshoves stressed ideological imperatives ten years later, arguing that Hebrew and Yiddish together had to preserve extraterritorial national identity and reach both the Jewish intelligentsia and *folk*.[33] In this respect, he was in the minority. He employed the tropes of survival, identity, *folk*, and nationalism that were rife in interwar Zionist and Yiddishist discourse but to very different ends, trying to sustain the prewar status quo in the face of changing discursive practices. Despite his advocacy for national-spiritual bilingualism, interwar Hebrew-Yiddish bilingualism shifted inward, either encapsulated within a single literary text—what Rainier Grutman calls "heterolingualism"—or the movement between texts, what I call "translingualism."[34]

In adopting the term "translingualism," I emphasize the movement across languages, that is to say, the movement of people, ideas, and institutions across linguistic boundaries.[35] Steven Kellman defines translingual writers as those "who write in more than one language or at least in a language other than their primary one."[36] Though he mentions what he calls "ambilinguals," writers who write significant works in more than one language, his examples overwhelmingly focus on those writing in nonnative tongues, such as Joseph Conrad and Mary Antin. Hebrew-Yiddish bilingualism complicates this equation by pointing to problematic assumptions about such "primary languages." Was Shneour's native tongue the Yiddish spoken in his parents' home or the Hebrew he learned to read and write as a young boy in school? Was Shlonsky's primary language the Russian he spoke with his mother, the Hebrew he spoke with his father, or the Yiddish that he spoke at home and with many of his neighbors? The extensive external and internal bilingualism of Eastern European Jewish culture confounds simplistic divisions between primary and secondary languages, demanding a more fluid understanding of interlingual commerce. Translingualism, I argue, provides a more precise way of describing and understanding profound shifts in Jewish-language culture during the interwar period from Hebrew-Yiddish bilingualism toward other translingual cultural forms.[37]

Rather than viewing translingualism as the process of writing in a nonnative tongue, I understand literary translingualism as the cultural politics and poetics of language-crossing. A focus on translingual dynamics shifts attention away from bilingualism—as the possession of or competence in two or more languages—to the movement between two or more languages on individual, textual, institutional, and social levels.[38] Bilingualism becomes a subset of broader translingual practices, an intense form of translingual contact but not the only way in which languages intersect. In contrast to the prefixes *bi-* or *poly-*, Aihwa Ong suggests that *trans-* stresses a series of new and dynamic potential relations: "*Trans* denotes both moving through space or across lines, as well as changing the nature of something. Besides suggesting new relations between nation-states and capital, transnationality alludes to the *trans*versal, the *trans*actional, the *trans*lational, and the *trans*gressive aspects of contemporary behavior and imagination that are incited, enabled, and regulated by the changing logics of states and capitalism."[39] Reading translingually is not simply a matter of tracking the movement of early twentieth-century European Jewish writers, readers, and texts between Hebrew and Yiddish. Rather, it spotlights the literary transversals, transactions, and translations between these two languages that give rise to a range of new relations between Jewish literatures. Literary translingualism can be manifested in a single text that incorporates more than one language; multiple texts in a given writer's oeuvre or published in a shared framework like a literary journal or anthology; and translations and other interlingual negotiations between texts. Linguistic difference has often delineated national, cultural, and hegemonic borders. Translingual contact challenges these boundaries and contends that cultural spheres are far more fluid and interconnected than has typically been acknowledged.

The prevalence of translingualism in interwar Jewish culture was at odds with the growing ideological emphasis on monolingualism. Monolingualism was an ideological construct of eighteenth-century Europe, spurred by Johann Gottfried Herder's claim that language, community, and territory were interconnected and Friedrich Schleiermacher's insistence on the organic nature of the mother tongue.[40] The ubiquitous movement between languages in the work of writers like Charles d'Orléans, John Donne, and John Milton was replaced by the conviction that national identity was predicated on one language and that each individual possessed a single native tongue.[41] The relatively late emergence of Jewish nationalist movements at the end of the nineteenth century set into motion a similar shift in Eastern European Jewish culture. Israel Bartal writes: "[T]he ending of a bilingual state of affairs and the presentation of monolingualism as normal was a complete innovation on the part of modern nationalism."[42] As Eastern European Jewish intellectuals sought to transform Hebrew and Yiddish into full-fledged modern literary cultures based on European models, traditional Jewish bilingualism came to be regarded as unnatural or old-fashioned because it failed to adhere to nationalist ideologies of language. Interwar Zionism was closely tied to Hebrew, representing it as the only suitable framework for a new national culture and as a vehicle for both individual and social transformation. As Chana Kronfeld explains, "Indeed the official literary historiography that mainstream literary historians, critics, school curricula, and other interpellated hegemonic discourses have provided for the development and periodization of modern Hebrew literature gives the impression that modern Hebrew literature could have reached modernity—and aesthetic maturity—only by becoming monolingual."[43] Yiddish writers shared this faith in monolingualism, as Soviet and Bundist Yiddishists distanced Yiddish from Hebrew to build a national culture defined by language.[44] These efforts to eradicate Hebrew-Yiddish bilingualism in order to create national literary cultures obscured translingual dynamics but did not eliminate them.

Given the powerful monolingual currents in modern Jewish culture, it is not surprising that bilingualism waned during the early decades of the twentieth century. However, literary bilingualism was replaced by other forms of translingual contact: twin Hebrew and Yiddish periodicals; Hebrew poetry suffused with Yiddish sounds and allusions; stories that captured the movement between languages; and a wide variety of translations. Translingual writing was not unique to early twentieth-century Hebrew and Yiddish literatures, but it was integral to them during the reconfiguration of Jewish life and culture between the world wars. It is this translingual rather than bilingual contact that came to define Hebrew and Yiddish literature by the early 1940s.

My goal in delineating different phases in the relationship between Hebrew and Yiddish literatures is not to provide a rigid historiographic model for Ashkenazi Jewish literary bilingualism, but rather to place interwar Jewish-language literature on a continuum with earlier literary-linguistic practices. Elements of sociocultural bilingualism and the sexual-linguistic system lingered, as did aspects of individual bilingualism. Literary translingualism did not simply replace earlier forms of bilingualism in the interwar period but coexisted with them as part of a broad spectrum of Hebrew-Yiddish contact. Despite changing literary-linguistic dynamics, the essential fact of this continued contact has significant implications for both Hebrew and Yiddish literatures. For generations, the two Ashkenazi Jewish-language literatures had been defined with respect to one another, coupled together in a symbiotic relationship. Even with the disintegration of that strong sociocultural bilingualism, the two Jewish literatures continued to define themselves through interlingual contact. Debates over the rapprochement of Hebrew and Yiddish literature in Palestine in the 1920s concealed deeper questions about the geographical locus of Hebrew language and literature: Hebrew was the language of the Yishuv, but what was its role in the Jewish diaspora? Public exchanges about the necessity and desirability of translations between Hebrew and Yiddish pivoted on the needs of each literature as much as their sense of mutual responsibility. The question of language and specifically the relationship between Jewish languages preoccupied Jewish writers and critics throughout the first half of the twentieth century.

One of the consequences of Hebrew and Yiddish literatures following different literary, ideological, and geographical trajectories was that, as Max Weinreich argues, "a new equilibrium was in the making to replace the old one that had been disturbed."[45] Individual writers, periodicals, political parties, and cultural institutions were all involved in efforts to envision a new linguistic status quo in this time of profound cultural flux. Their interactions and intersections are not merely expressions of an outdated cultural paradigm or random incidents of linguistic convergence. Nor are they evidence of a single bilingual Jewish literary tradition or a unified modern Jewish culture. Individually, they demonstrate the fluidity and variability of Jewish cultural production in multiple languages, both traditionally Jewish (Hebrew, Yiddish) and not (Russian, German, Polish, English, and more), during this transitional period. Collectively, they point to a dynamic process of linguistic and literary change during which Hebrew and Yiddish traveled in different directions, both literally and figuratively, but maintained significant points of contact. By World War II, a new equilibrium between Hebrew and Yiddish had not been achieved. Jewish-language literature was in transition, shifting from the proximity that had defined Eastern European Jewish culture to a heterogeneous postwar cultural field, from literary bilingualism to other forms of literary translingualism. The bilingualism that defined Shneour's Ceglana Street no longer existed, in Warsaw or anywhere else, in the newly expanded map of Jewish culture. But plenty of cultural agents—texts, writers, and institutions—moved between Hebrew and Yiddish, creating a rich set of collaborations, competitions, transfers, and other modes of contact.

Literatures in Contact

It is far from accidental that Uriel Weinreich, Yiddish linguist and the son of Yiddish scholar Max Weinreich, pioneered the study of internal and social aspects of linguistic contact, laying the foundations for modern sociolinguistics.[46] Contact linguistics, as explicated by Weinreich and expanded upon by linguists like Donald Winford, René Appel, and Pieter Muysken, proceeds from the basic premise that language contact orchestrated by various historical and sociocultural factors has significant and quantifiable impacts.[47] Linguistic scholarship has demonstrated the effects of different aspects of linguistic contact on both Yiddish and Hebrew. From Ber Borochov to Max Weinreich to Dovid Katz, Yiddish has been well documented as a fusion language that incorporates elements from Semitic, Germanic, and Slavic languages.[48] More recently, linguists like Ghil'ad Zuckermann have challenged narratives of the revival of Hebrew and argued that modern Hebrew, or what he calls "Israeli Hebrew," is also a fundamentally hybrid language, with primary contributors Hebrew and Yiddish along with secondary contributions from Russian, Polish, German, Ladino, and more.[49] But what can contact linguistics, with its emphasis on spoken language, contribute to the study of written language?

Contact linguistics resonates for the study of literature precisely because the early twentieth century saw a transition from literary texts ensconced in an Eastern European Jewish society, in which bilingual speech was the norm, to those that sought to compensate for the disappearance of that linguistic bilingualism. Arguing that contact is best understood "in a broad psychological and socio-cultural setting," Weinreich insists that the study of linguistic contact must pay close attention to linguistic as well as cultural and social aspects of contact.[50] Shifting from linguistic contact to literary contact, this book enlists linguistic, literary, and sociocultural analysis in making sense of changes in Yiddish and Hebrew literatures. Weinreich also proposes contact linguistics to supplement rather than replace other approaches to linguistic study. Thus a contact-driven approach to Hebrew and Yiddish literature does not insist that Hebrew and Yiddish comprise one single literature or two separate ones, but rather that literary bilingualism is one of multiple historiographical narratives. I argue that by focusing on a series of literary collisions between Hebrew and Yiddish we can discern a dynamic cultural field in which these literatures were constantly negotiating and renegotiating their terms of engagement. Finally, by following Weinreich's model in which a constituent feature of Jewish language is part of a broader linguistic framework, I demonstrate how Hebrew and Yiddish as literatures in contact can change the ways in which we think about literary-linguistic intersections more generally.

Lydia Liu also sees linguistic contact as a key element in her analysis of literary discourse. Focusing on cross-cultural collisions between East and West, Liu proposes the term "translingual practice": "Broadly defined, the study of translingual practice examines the process by which new words, meaning, discourses, and modes of representation arise, circulate and acquire legitimacy within the host language due to, or in spite of, the latter's contact/collision with the guest language."[51] Interlingual contacts, she argues, give rise to specific discursive practices that in turn affect the conditions of translation. Translation, as the preeminent form of linguistic contact, "becomes the very site of such [political and ideological] struggles where the guest language is forced to encounter the host language, where the irreducible differences between them are fought out, authorities invoked or challenged, ambiguities dissolved or created, and so forth, until new words and meanings emerge in the host language itself."[52] Liu envisions a combative arena for linguistic contact, in which a confrontation between guest and host languages creates new modes of representation.[53]

The concept of translingual practice is useful for the Hebrew-Yiddish case because it links literary contact to linguistic, discursive, and representational changes within a particular ideological context. While Weinreich provides a framework that focuses on linguistic and social exchanges between two languages in contact, Liu calls attention to the discursive and representational implications of linguistic contact. Liu's work demonstrates how translation, often seen as an area of study unto itself or a peripheral literary task, can be central to cultural and literary practice. As important as translation, however, are the conditions of translation, as Liu focuses on the process set in motion by interlingual contact as much as the linguistic and literary results. Contact, then, becomes a mechanism by which a language and accompanying literature constitutes itself. By combining elements of contact linguistics and translingual practice, *Lingering Bilingualism* analyzes changing means and modes of literary-linguistic contact in the context of the dramatic changes in Jewish culture across the early decades of the twentieth century.

Unlike the East-West dynamic that Liu examines, however, Hebrew-Yiddish contact confounds clear distinctions between guest and host and between one culture and another. In the early decades of the twentieth century, the translingual movement between Hebrew and Yiddish was bidirectional; when Y. D. Berkovitz translated Sholem Aleykhem's Yiddish prose into a stylized Hebrew, Hebrew was the host language; but when he translated his own early Hebrew short stories into a realistic, psychologically probing Yiddish, Yiddish was the host language. The continual translation between Hebrew and Yiddish necessitates a rethinking of translingual practice to allow for more dynamic interlingual movement in which the guest and host trade places, repeatedly. The implications of these collisions may affect just one language, as for example Berkovitz's translations, which crafted a definitively Hebraic voice for Sholem Aleykhem and helped establish linguistic standards for subsequent Hebrew translations. But they may also intervene in both languages, such as Berkovitz's self-translations of his own short stories between Hebrew and Yiddish.

In this respect, the peculiarities of Hebrew and Yiddish expand the concept of translingual practice. Liu states that her goal "is to reconceptualize the problematic of 'language' in a new set of relationships that is not predicated on some of the familiar premises of contemporary theories of language, which tend to take metropolitan European tongues as a point of departure."[54] Even as Hebrew and Yiddish aspired to become more like those metropolitan European languages, their intersections add a different kind of linguistic contact to Liu's East-West dynamic, an intracultural exchange that destabilizes notions of native and nonnative tongues, guest and host languages, and fixed national-linguistic borders. Given the changes in Jewish-language translingual practice across the first half of the twentieth century, Hebrew and Yiddish literary collisions also call attention the dynamics of the literary arena, in which linguistic and associated discursive practices can undergo major changes within a relatively short period of time.

Hebrew and Yiddish Literatures in Contact

Lingering Bilingualism puts literary-linguistic contact at its very center, analyzing intersections between Hebrew and Yiddish literatures across modernist and nonmodernist prose and poetry and across diasporic and national texts. Rather than focusing on a particular geographic location, genre, or style, it highlights two recurring elements that facilitate literary contact: translation as a recurring means of contact, and periodicals as frequent sites of contact. This broad scope allows each chapter to highlight literary-linguistic movement between texts and between geographical and ideological positions. If face-to-face encounters between Hebrew and Yiddish writers had once defined Eastern European Jewish literature, later intersections between the literatures are far more varied. In some cases, personal contact spurred literary contact, like the 1927 visit of Yiddish writers to Palestine. In others, texts brought together individuals who were highly unlikely to have sought out each other's company, whether in the Berlin periodicals *Rimon* and *Milgroym* or in anthologies of

Yiddish prose and poetry translated into Hebrew. These literary junctures underscore the extent to which questions of language permeated all facets of early twentieth-century Jewish literary creation. By focusing first and foremost on literary-linguistic contact, this book examines a broad cross-section of literary production in Hebrew and Yiddish and identifies ways in which translingual dynamics defined interwar Jewish literary production.

Both literary bilingualism and translingualism are most frequently registered as forms of translation. Translation, once regarded as a derivative art form or second-order representation, has more recently garnered attention as a mechanism of literary change (Itamar Even-Zohar), a means of establishing literary value (Pascale Casanova), a process of literary manipulation (André Lefevere), and an interpretive art (Lawrence Venuti).[55] In Hebrew and Yiddish literature at the beginning of the twentieth century, the individual writer was most commonly the locus of translation, writing and then rewriting his or her own texts in Hebrew and Yiddish, in some order. The prevalence of self-translation challenges fundamental assumptions about the translator as a mediator and the translated text as being transported across cultural boundaries. When Shneour published a Hebrew version of his Yiddish novella *A toyt* (A Death, 1910), it was not because Hebrew readers could not have read the Yiddish version. Nor did his Hebrew readers need culturally specific references to be explicated or glossed, as the Yiddish-speaking world in which Shneour's protagonist details his suicidal impulses was the same world inhabited by the Hebrew reader. Hebrew-Yiddish translation was primarily an intracultural literary-linguistic exercise with aesthetic and ideological implications rather than the transposition of a text into a different culture.

In response to changes in Jewish life over subsequent decades, translation between Hebrew and Yiddish became more necessary and more conventional, registering the literary-linguistic changes underway in Jewish culture. Functional Jewish bilingualism was disappearing in the United States and prestate Palestine with the rise of English education and English speakers among American Jews and staunch

Hebraism in Palestine. By the 1940s, it was no longer safe to assume Hebrew readers could read Yiddish literature, nor that Yiddish readers could read Hebrew literature. Hebrew-Yiddish translation also became more conventional in the sense that it became increasingly intercultural. When Dov Ber Malkin wrote an introduction to his 1943 anthology, he saw Hebrew translations of Yiddish short stories as introducing a new generation of readers not only to Yiddish literature but also to Yiddish life in the diaspora. Some of Malkin's potential readers in Palestine probably still could have read the work of Yona Rozenfeld, Rokhl Korn, and Isaac Bashevis Singer in Yiddish. But the conditions of translation were radically different in the early 1940s than they had been forty or even twenty years earlier; the possession of shared languages and shared cultures could no longer be assumed. While translation had once been evidence of Hebrew-Yiddish literary bilingualism in the person of the self-translator, the chapters that follow trace how translation increasingly became a means for sustaining Jewish literary contact.

One of the most productive cultural spaces for intersections between Hebrew and Yiddish throughout the first half of the twentieth century was the periodical. With virtually no institutional support for modern Jewish culture in Eastern Europe—no modern seminaries, restricted access to universities—periodicals were surrogate homes for Eastern European Jewish intellectuals.[56] The Hebrew-language *Ha-shiloach*, for example, founded by Hebrew intellectual Achad Ha-am and first published in 1896, saw itself as a new intellectual forum for Jewish culture, as its opening statement explains: "We are not founding a study house for scholars to sit and debate with each other at length and come up with new interpretations so as to expand Torah and wisdom for its own sake; rather we turn our hearts to the entire people, who will find in this periodical suitable nourishment for its spirit and things important to know so as to repair its breaches and to build its ruins."[57] Achad Ha-am envisioned *Ha-shiloach* as the modern replacement of the defining institution of religious Jewish society, the *beit midrash* (study house). Rejecting the central rabbinic value of *torah li-shma*, studying the Torah for its own sake, he ambitiously aimed to educate and nourish the Jewish people and to repair what he saw as their decaying culture—all via a monthly periodical. As David N. Myers writes, "the journal served simultaneously as a forum for scholarly inquiry, intellectual debate and ideological polemic, as well as an arbiter of literary taste and a source of financial subvention."[58] Smaller groups of Hebrew and Yiddish writers also founded their own short-lived journals, especially during the early decades of the twentieth century, to showcase their literary sensibilities and ideological persuasions.[59] Sarah Abrevaya Stein argues that "Jewish newspapers were both a manifestation and a mechanism of change" in the Russian and Ottoman Empires.[60] While literary periodicals like *Ha-shiloach* had much smaller audiences than the popular press Stein examines, they also saw themselves as agents of cultural change. As Ashkenazi Jewish culture and its writers spread throughout Europe, North America, and Palestine in the early decades of the twentieth century, periodicals remained a critical forum for intellectual exchange across the modern Jewish diaspora.

Reading literary texts and critics' debates on the pages of periodicals reveals textual exchanges and intersections that have often been overlooked. Sean Latham and Robert Scholes insist that "we have often been too quick to see magazines merely as containers of discrete bits of information rather than autonomous objects of study."[61] Periodicals as autonomous objects highlight the work of literary intermediaries like publishers and editors and the ways in which their work affects the circulation and reception of texts. Stamped with a specific date and place of publication, periodicals anchor texts in a particular historical moment even as they are designed to disseminate ideas across long distances. As collaborative texts, periodicals are also sites of contact between texts produced by different writers, between different genres, and, depending on circulation, different audiences. Thus periodicals were the front lines for early twentieth-century Hebrew and Yiddish literatures: places for literary innovation, political screeds, and ideological performances; arenas for cultural controversies; vehicles for transmitting texts and ideas across the far-flung Jewish culture;

and, pragmatically, sources of financial support for legions of writers. In some of the following chapters, periodicals provide the basis for literary encounters. In others, periodicals register the impact of literary contact that originates in other cultural spaces. But in each of the literary intersections analyzed in this book, periodicals feature Hebrew and Yiddish texts and the complex negotiations that surround these texts' composition, translation, and reception.

Periodicals, specifically two related arts-and-letters magazines, the Hebrew *Rimon* and the Yiddish *Milgroym*, provide a platform for one vision of a modern bilingual Jewish culture, the subject of chapter 1. In the years immediately following World War I, Eastern European Jewish intellectuals flocked to Berlin, eagerly soaking up the avant-garde cultural scene and seizing upon publishing opportunities made possible by the Weimar Republic's hyperinflation. Among the many Hebrew and Yiddish publications that appeared in Germany in the early 1920s were *Rimon* and *Milgroym*, exquisitely designed twin magazines published by Mark Wischnitzer and Rachel Wischnitzer Bernstein. The magazines' editors contended that a single Jewish artistic tradition could transcend linguistic difference and political debates by treating the two modern Jewish languages as equals. Yet that equality proved fleeting in the magazines, as both Yiddish and Hebrew contributors challenged the belief that Jewish culture could or should transcend language and ideology. With their artful layouts and wide range of texts, *Milgroym* and *Rimon* exhibited instead a periodic bilingualism, one in which Yiddish and Hebrew literatures intersected at times and diverged at others.

Chapter 2 shifts the scene to the Yishuv, the Jewish community in Palestine, where the local Association of Hebrew Writers' reception to honor visiting Yiddish writers Sholem Ash and Perets Hirshbeyn erupted into a fierce debate about Hebrew-Yiddish bilingualism in 1927. In the Yishuv, there was no pretense that Hebrew and Yiddish were equal or even equally valid languages of the Jewish people; Hebrew was essential to the very core of the Zionist enterprise. But at the reception for Ash and Hirshbeyn, prominent Hebrew writers pronounced an end to the Language War, encouraged reconciliation between the languages, and proposed models for the continued contact between the two literatures. What might have been a polite but forgettable reception, however, exploded into a clamorous controversy, splashed on the pages of the Hebrew press, thanks in large part to the efforts of Eliezer Shteinman and Avraham Shlonsky. Styling themselves as representatives of the new generation of Hebrew writers, they brashly renewed the war on Yiddish in the pages of the literary journal *Ketuvim* and rejected any suggestion of Hebrew-Yiddish rapprochement. Surprisingly, both writers maintained extensive bilingual and translingual contacts with Yiddish literature even as they denounced Yiddish as a threat to Hebrew Zionist culture. The gaps between public pronouncements and implicit poetics demonstrate deep ambivalence about Hebrew-Yiddish bilingualism even at the emerging center of Hebrew literature in Palestine, where literary-linguistic practice did not necessarily follow cultural ideology. Despite their rhetoric, Shteinman and Shlonsky's literary work from the 1920s suggested that there could be a place for Yiddish within Hebrew culture as long as writers followed strict ideological parameters.

Yet there were writers who had no interest in adhering to the expectations of Hebrew culture in the Yishuv or those of Yiddish culture in the United States. Zalman Shneour and Yitzhak Dov Berkovitz, the central figures of chapter 3, were two such writers who scorned any intimation that they could no longer fully participate in both Hebrew and Yiddish literatures. When they began writing in the early years of the twentieth century, the prevalence of Hebrew-Yiddish self-translation reflected the ease at which individual writers could move between the two literatures. Despite the growing ideological, geographic, and stylistic distances between Hebrew and Yiddish literature, Shneour and Berkovitz continued to participate in both literatures via their self-translations into the 1930s. However, they and their texts were marginalized in ideological climates that had little interest in accommodating their literary bilingualism. Confronted by literary establishments increasingly hostile to the old bilingual paradigm, they each pursued different translingual strategies in their self-translations in hopes of situating their work in the Jewish-language literary cultures in Tel Aviv and New York.

Ultimately, it was Hebrew-Yiddish translation rather than self-translation that came to represent the future of Jewish literary-linguistic contact. Chapter 4 traces major changes in translation between the two languages and compares two translation projects that sought to facilitate literary-linguistic contact at the end of the interwar period. One of the projects, Rokhl Feygenberg's Ha-me'asef Press, used translation as a tool to promote Hebrew in the Yishuv and to acquaint Hebrew readers with the decline and corruption of Eastern European Jewish life. The other, the American anthology *Achisefer*, enlisted translation in order to sustain cultural bilingualism. Although they articulated distinct visions for the future of Hebrew-Yiddish contact, both translation projects appeared at a time in which the discourse of cultural preservation dominated that of cultural building. Produced in the shadow of World War II and the Holocaust, Ha-me'asef and *Achisefer* became translingual repositories for Yiddish literature rather than vehicles of monolingualism or bilingualism.

At first glance, these literary encounters appear to be failures or cultural dead-ends: periodicals that collapsed after a mere two years; literary reconciliation that devolved into a vicious public debate; rising literary stars who lost their direction and fame; ambitious translation projects that faltered. However, each of these endeavors reimagined Jewish bilingualism for new cultural circumstances. Some proposed ways in which the two literatures could continue to exist within a bilingual framework, either by sustaining older models or creating new ones. Others sanctioned translingualism within particular ideological and geographical contexts. These episodes do not constitute a full history of Hebrew-Yiddish bilingualism in the interwar period, nor do they offer a comprehensive view of Jewish literary contact, which would include intersections among Hebrew, Yiddish, Russian, Polish, English, Arabic, and German, just to name a few. But as these chapters explore vital instances of literary-linguistic contact, they demonstrate how bilingual and translingual practices can exist alongside and inside monolingual literary cultures. If Hebrew and Yiddish were, as Bialik famously claimed, joined by a marriage made in heaven, their union did not survive the interwar period. But its dissolution was not so much a stormy divorce as complex and fitful negotiations of a new relationship between long-intimate companions.

1

"Only a World War Could Bring Us Such Elegance"

Milgroym, Rimon, *and Periodic Bilingualism in Berlin*

IN THE YEARS FOLLOWING WORLD WAR I, Eastern European Jewish intellectuals flocked to Weimar Germany. The war exacted a heavy toll on Germany, yet its destructiveness also obliterated many social and artistic conventions in German society, setting the stage for the Weimar period, "with its heady enthusiasms, its artistic experimentation, its flaunting of sexuality and unconventional relations, its vibrant, kinetic energy."[1] Like their non-Jewish counterparts, Jewish writers and artists were drawn to Berlin's vibrant intellectual life—its cafés, galleries, libraries, and lectures—even in the midst of the young republic's political and economic crises. Weimar culture, as Peter Gay describes it, was a potent mix of creativity and anxiety, experimentation and fear, "the creation of outsiders, propelled by history into the inside, for a short, dizzying, fragile moment."[2]

Within the broader German culture existed a distinct Jewish subculture that encompassed communal and educational institutions as well as literature, theater, art, and more—what Franz Rosenzweig called a modern-day *Zweistromland* (land of two rivers), in which the modern Jew was nurtured by German humanistic culture and Jewish religious and spiritual heritage.[3] A smaller coterie of Jewish émigrés and refugees from Eastern Europe who were dedicated to writing and performing in Yiddish and Hebrew also thrived within this cross-cultural *Zweistromland.*[4] Some of those residing in Germany, like Yiddish writers Dovid Bergelson and Moyshe Kulbak and Hebrew poet Chayim Nachman Bialik, sought refuge from postwar devastation in Poland, pogroms in Ukraine, and the Soviet crackdown on the Hebrew language in Odessa. Others, like artist Henryk Berlewi and Hebrew writer S. Y. Agnon, were enticed by exciting literary and artistic developments in Germany. Still others, like Hebrew writers M. Y. Berdichevsky and Shaul Tchernikhovsky, had settled more or less permanently in Germany after studying in German universities. Thanks to this convergence of Jewish cultural figures, Weimar Germany became a fulcrum of Jewish creativity in Yiddish and Hebrew in the early 1920s, propelled by interactions among intellectuals with different backgrounds, languages, and ideologies.

For the remarkable number of Hebrew and Yiddish writers settling in Berlin or passing through, Germany was neutral linguistic ground during a time of linguistic schism. Though the competition between modern Hebrew and Yiddish literatures had steadily intensified since the late nineteenth century, wartime destruction of Eastern European Jewish communities and subsequent political transformations accelerated fundamental shifts in Jewish culture. The traditional Hebrew-Yiddish bilingualism that had defined Eastern European Jewish culture was increasingly contested from all sides. Further east, the new Soviet Union endorsed Yiddish as the language of its substantial Jewish minority and suppressed Hebrew; Polish was a compelling alternative for Jews seeking opportunities in newly independent Poland; and in British-administered Palestine, the Zionist establishment promoted Hebrew as the language of the new Hebrew society being built and rejected Yiddish along with diaspora life. But in cosmopolitan Weimar Germany, Yiddish and Hebrew were merely two of many languages circulating within an effervescent cultural environment. Berlin, in particular, became an enclave of Jewish modernism in which Yiddish and Hebrew writers interacted with each other, as well as their counterparts writing in Russian and German—Jewish and non-Jewish—in a thoroughly multilingual cultural milieu.[5]

Whether at the tables of the Romanisches Café or on the pages of the books and periodicals rolling off German presses, Berlin brought Hebrew and Yiddish writers and their texts into contact in new and surprising ways. Neither East nor entirely West, neither Hebrew nor Yiddish, Berlin's cultural and geographical liminality facilitated a range of Jewish-language experimentation and innovation. New illustrated books, theatrical performances, and periodicals were simultaneously products of the dynamic Weimar environment and participants in an increasingly transnational modern Jewish culture that stretched from the Soviet Union to North and South America.

Among the most interesting of these experiments were the belletristic magazines *Rimon* and *Milgroym* (Pomegranate), published in Hebrew and Yiddish, respectively. Periodicals had long been one of the primary forums for intellectual exchange in European Jewish culture, compensating for the lack of institutions in which modern Jewish-language writers came into contact and facilitating the transnational circulation of new texts and ideas. Early twentieth-century modernist writers in Yiddish and Hebrew were particularly enamored with literary journals, often creating personal platforms for their manifestos, poems, and prose. The Berlin-based *Milgroym* and *Rimon* entered a cultural arena filled with competing literary journals in both Yiddish and Hebrew that debated the present and future of Jewish culture, Jewish literatures, and Jewish languages. From their inaugural issues, however, they were distinctive in both their high-quality production aesthetics and their attempts to transcend ideological schisms in modern Jewish life, particularly the polarization between Hebrew and Yiddish literatures. Treating Hebrew and Yiddish as functionally equivalent, these unusual magazines were designed to disseminate a shared Jewish artistic tradition that transcended Jewish linguistic difference. In contrast to other Hebrew and Yiddish periodicals of the time, *Milgroym* and *Rimon* demonstrate the contact between Yiddish and Hebrew writers and texts that not only continued after World War I but also took on innovative and increasingly translingual forms.

Reading *Rimon* and *Milgroym* Together

Rimon and *Milgroym* represent a fruitful union of primarily Eastern European Jewish editors and writers and German intellectual ideals, catalyzed by cultural and economic circumstances in Weimar Germany. First issued in 1922, the magazines were part of a remarkable surge in Hebrew and Yiddish publishing in Berlin during the early 1920s. In the years following World War I and the Treaty of Versailles, the Weimar Republic's staggering hyperinflation gave Jewish publishing houses, bankrolled by American and European readers' foreign currency, access to top-notch German printing facilities at remarkably low cost.[6] The Rimon Publishing Company, founded by historian Mark Wischnitzer (1882–1955) and art historian Rachel Wischnitzer Bernstein (1885–1989), his wife, took the opportunity provided by the weak German economy to create visually stunning periodicals in both Hebrew and Yiddish that featured high-quality art reproductions and illustrations along with essays on art, theater, and music translated into both languages in the shared art sections, and original and translated literature in separate Hebrew and Yiddish literary sections.[7] While the precise financial details of the expensive dual publications are unclear, Wischnitzer Bernstein reports that Leopold Sev, a personal friend and onetime editor of the St. Petersburg Jewish newspaper *Novy Voskhod*, was intrigued by the idea of publishing an arts and letters magazine, and enlisted the financial support of businessman Ilya Paenson.[8] With Paenson's backing—at least for the first two issues[9]—and the cheap cost of publication in Weimar Germany, six issues of each magazine were published at irregular intervals between 1922 and 1924 and distributed by bookstores in Berlin, New York City, London, Toronto, and Buenos Aires. Reader subscriptions in the West, particularly American readers' dollars, were critical for the viability of the enterprise. By 1924, with attempts to stabilize the German mark succeeding, Wischnitzer Bernstein wrote that "the dollars we received for copies sold in the U.S. [were] losing their astronomical value, the magazines had to be discontinued."[10]

Within this brief period, the Wischnitzers and several literary editors published issues averaging forty to fifty well-designed pages and featuring carefully chosen typefaces and color illustrations. The magazines presented a variety of approaches to Jewish visual and textual culture as they documented the large number of Hebrew, Yiddish, and German Jewish artists, writers, and scholars in Germany during the early 1920s. Their oversized pages shared the same wide-ranging articles on art, theater, and music that were edited by Wischnitzer Bernstein and translated into Hebrew and Yiddish as needed. But each magazine maintained its own distinct literary section filled with literary and critical texts.[11] So while the magazines' impressive format resembled that of expatriate Russian art magazine *Zhar-Ptitsa* (Firebird), whose editor Alexander Kogan helped Wischnitzer Bernstein produce the first issue, its contents were carefully aimed at prospective Jewish audiences in Yiddish and Hebrew.[12] In their survey of Yiddish publishing in the Weimar Republic, Leo and Renate Fuks comment on *Milgroym*: "The journal can be considered the highlight of Yiddish publication in Germany, combining the talent of the writers and artists with the technical know-how and skill of German printing."[13]

Milgroym and *Rimon*, however, were unique precisely because they showcased not only Yiddish publication but also Hebrew publication in Germany. Both Hebrew and Yiddish culture flourished in Germany during a brief period in the early 1920s, spurred by radical transformations of Eastern European Jewish life after World War I and amid Weimar Germany's vibrant intellectual climate.[14] But there is little consensus on the extent to which Yiddish and Hebrew writers interacted in this multilingual metropolis. Joseph Sherman, surveying Hebrew and Yiddish literary developments, emphasizes that "the worlds of Yiddish and Hebrew rarely overlapped" in Berlin, while Shachar Pinsker argues that during the early 1920s Hebrew and Yiddish literature were created side-by-side in Berlin, sometimes literally at adjacent tables at the Romanisches Café.[15] One clear site of Hebrew-Yiddish overlap is on the pages of *Milgroym* and *Rimon*. The magazines attest to this Jewish literary convergence in Germany and provide a tangible representation of the coexistence of the two Ashkenazi Jewish languages in Berlin, with varying degrees of creative contact. They also provide a glimpse of the complexity of this cultural moment, in which a cast of primarily Eastern European Jewish intellectuals, writers, and artists could produce dual-language magazines in Berlin for readers across Europe, the Americas, and Palestine.

While Berlin was a gathering point for Hebrew and Yiddish writers in the early 1920s, few of *Milgroym* and *Rimon*'s readers lived in Germany. As Michael Brenner points out, there was virtually no audience in Germany for cultural products in either of the two Jewish languages.[16] Large-scale Jewish immigration to Germany immediately after World War I made Jews, and specifically *Ostjuden*, Eastern Jews, more visible in Germany society. But most of these immigrants were far removed from both the cultural elite involved in producing the magazines and the readers with disposable income who were purchasing them. *Milgroym* and *Rimon*, evident from the international list of bookstores and distributors at the beginning of each issue, were produced primarily for export across the expanding map of modern Jewish culture. Though they owed their high-quality production and many of their contributors to a fortuitous historical moment in Berlin, the magazines were designed less as attempts to participate in German or German Jewish culture in Berlin than as efforts to educate and galvanize a diverse transnational readership about the present and future of Jewish culture. They were simultaneously products of Weimar Germany and participants in ongoing debates about tradition and modernity and the value of modernist art that unfolded on the pages of other Hebrew and Yiddish periodicals from Poland, the Soviet Union, the United States, and Palestine.

The divergent paths of Hebrew and Yiddish literary cultures in the interwar period have led critics and scholars to read either *Milgroym* or *Rimon*, not both.[17] With rare exceptions, critics have elected to discuss their preferred half of the twin publications, hewing to the traditional boundaries between the distinct and ideologically charged fields of Yiddish and Hebrew literary scholarship.[18] These magazines, however, provide a rare example of a bilingual publishing project, one that sought to swim against the powerful ideological currents of the time with alternative ideas about Jewish culture and language. Reading *Rimon* and *Milgroym* together affords a better understanding of these unique periodicals and a different perspective on the prickly relationship between Yiddish and Hebrew literatures in the early 1920s.

For a reader paging through *Milgroym* or *Rimon*, the magazine would have appeared to be monolingual; all articles were written or translated into Yiddish or Hebrew, respectively. It is only by reading them side-by-side that a peculiar kind of bilingualism comes into view. Multilingualism, Benjamin Harshav explains, "is the knowledge of more than one language by a person or a social group and the ability to switch from one language to another in speech, in writing or in reading."[19] The locus of multilingualism, in this case bilingualism, was the publication itself, which switched from one Jewish language to the other. Harshav further specifies three primary types of multilingualism: personal multilingualism of an individual; social multilingualism of a nation, tribe, or other social group; and intersubjective multilingualism, in which the use of multiple languages was widespread but not obligatory within a given society.[20] *Milgroym* and *Rimon* are subsets of the intersubjective multilingualism of interwar Jewish culture, but they offer a rare case of what could be called "periodic bilingualism." Periodic bilingualism relies on the unique features of periodicals, namely their serial and collaborative format, to provide periodic manifestations of language switching and other translingual contact on the pages of magazines and journals. Shifting the emphasis from spoken language to the published word, it recognizes the ways in which periodicals participate in broader Jewish multilingualism and—in the case of *Milgroym* and *Rimon*—propose cultural alternatives to the status quo.

The magazines' periodic bilingualism was part of their editors' ambitious attempts to realize a holistic Jewish culture through linguistic, literary, and stylistic multiplicity. *Milgroym* and *Rimon*'s editors pursued a new linguistic relationship that transcended traditional boundaries, seeing the two Ashkenazi Jewish languages as companions in their cultural enterprise: coextensive rather than diglossic, equal partners in Jewish culture rather than competitors for national-linguistic superiority. El Lissitzky, chronicling his prewar expedition in search of Eastern European synagogue paintings in the third issue of the magazines, asks: "Who are we? Where do we belong among the nations of the world? What is the nature of our culture, and what kind of art do we want to create?"[21] For Lissitzky and the magazines more generally, "our culture" transcends linguistic difference. Lissitzky's searing questions, posed in Yiddish and translated into Hebrew, resonate throughout both *Milgroym* and *Rimon*. These are precisely the questions that the editors sought to address in the magazines, offering an implicit program that was radical in its essence if not always in its articulation: to disseminate modern and modernist Jewish culture predicated on visual art in a bilingual framework to a transnational Jewish readership.

The periodic bilingualism of *Milgroym* and *Rimon* from the magazines' first issues in 1922 to their abrupt suspension in 1924 offers an alternative vision for European Jewish culture and serves as a metaphor for the changing relationship between Yiddish and Hebrew. The magazines challenge both the argument that Hebrew and Yiddish comprised a single, bilingual Jewish literature, most often associated with Bal Makhshoves, Shmuel Niger, and Dov Sadan, and the contention that they were separate literatures, endorsed by many critics from Yosef Klausner to Dan Miron.[22] Instead, *Rimon* and *Milgroym* provide an unusual example of what we could call a middle ground: the languages were still linked together but outside of the traditional symbiotic relationship. They both participated in a shared vision for modern Jewish culture, but they did so in distinct manners. Though short-lived, their dual publication mirrors the situation of the European Jewish languages themselves, which were historically and culturally linked together but were in the process of creating new terms of engagement, outside of the hierarchical traditional relationship that valued Hebrew as the literary language and Yiddish as its vernacular complement.

The magazines modeled a new paradigm of contact in which the languages were in close proximity but no longer enmeshed in the cultural framework of Jewish Eastern Europe. During the interwar period, writers in emerging Jewish cultural centers throughout Europe, the Americas, and Palestine were considering the future of modern Jewish-language culture and renegotiating what relationship, if any, might still exist between the two Ashkenazi Jewish languages. Berlin, as one of the first stops on many writers' immigrant journeys, provided geographical and symbolic distance from the Eastern European Jewish society in which both Hebrew and Yiddish had emerged as modern literary languages still enmeshed within traditional hierarchies of value. Associations of Hebrew with the study house and Yiddish with daily life, or Hebrew with men and Yiddish with women, had been challenged further east but still lingered. These sorts of distinctions between the two Jewish languages were rendered obsolete in the crowded cafés and busy presses of this thoroughly modern metropolis. Despite the many differences between the languages, in cosmopolitan Berlin, Hebrew and Yiddish were both minor languages in relation to German or even German Jewish culture.[23] Thus the Rimon Publishing Company's bilingual venture challenges arguments for both a single bilingual Jewish literature and independent Hebrew and Yiddish literatures; *Milgroym* and *Rimon* are neither one single magazine nor two separate ones. Rather, these periodicals traveled across a broad spectrum of literary-linguistic possibilities, at times virtually identical, at others completely distinct. Read together, they represent an ambitious project to disseminate a bilingual vision for modern and modernist Jewish culture that, despite its attempt to transcend ideology, had to contend with the political and cultural fragmentation of the time.

As periodicals, *Milgroym* and *Rimon* were well suited to capture this dynamic cultural moment. Throughout the early decades of the twentieth century, small groups of Hebrew and Yiddish writers founded an impressive number of cultural journals, many of them short-lived, to showcase their literary sensibilities and ideological persuasions. Alan Mintz points out that "it is exactly the provisional and impermanent qualities of the periodical—its fluid, combinable, and uncanonical makeup—that put it in the position to broker the piecing together of new cultural formations."[24] Periodicals such as *Milgroym* and *Rimon* not only brokered emerging Jewish cultural formations but themselves are pieces of a changing cultural and linguistic landscape. Unlike books or monographs that may carry a publication date tucked away in the prefacing pages, periodicals have a date and location prominently stamped on their masthead, anchoring them chronologically and geographically. Published in Germany in the years following World War I, the magazines and their contributors were keenly aware of lingering postwar trauma as well as modernist trends. As with most periodicals, *Milgroym* and *Rimon* included material that varied greatly in genre and quality. But it is precisely this fluidity and changeability that make the magazines valuable sources on the changing relationship between Yiddish and Hebrew. In a crowded field of Jewish periodicals, these magazines' impact is not simply a matter of their longevity or the quality of their texts and writers. Rather, their periodic bilingualism offers an alternative to the monolingualism of contemporaneous periodicals and showcases a range of interactions between the two languages, from almost complete separation in the inaugural belletristic sections to identical art sections. A closer look at *Milgroym* and *Rimon*—their colorful covers, essays, poetry, stories, and more—reveals both the potential and the pitfalls of literary bilingualism at this transitional historical moment.

"Only a World War Could Bring Us Such Elegance"

Perhaps the first hint of the magazines' unique aesthetic and linguistic arrangement is their visually arresting covers: two separate images designed by the same artist, German Jewish graphic artist Ernst Boehm.[25] In contrast to the utilitarian type on the covers of Hebrew journals such as the long-running *Ha-shiloach* (1896–1926) and the newly founded *Dvir* (1923–1924, Berlin), *Rimon*'s cover is visually striking.

1. Cover of *Rimon* 1, no. 1 (1922). Courtesy of E. Sourasky Central Library, Tel Aviv University.

It features the gated city of Jerusalem crowned by the Temple and surrounded by mythical creatures, foliage, and, of course, a pomegranate. The cover's deeply red background and profuse forms recall painted synagogue ceilings from Poland and Ukraine, with their intense but flat coloration and horror vacui, thus anchoring it to the Jewish artistic tradition. The mythical dragon-like creatures that guard the walls gesture toward traditional Jewish art forms as seen in the thirteenth-century illuminated manuscript of *Machzor Worms* and the eighteenth-century synagogue painting of the Gwoździec wooden synagogue.[26] At the same time, the animal figures and the nonnaturalistic shading also bring to mind Jewish avant-garde art, such as *Fantastic Animals* from Natan Altman's book *Evreiskaia Grafika* (Jewish Graphic Art) (1923), with its stylized reinterpretation of the same mythical creatures that grace *Rimon*'s cover; and El Lissitzky's 1919 *Chad Gadya* (One Little Goat) and its combination of avant-garde and folk elements.[27] Thus *Rimon*'s cover envelops the magazine in a vivid representation of the Jewish past that incorporates modernist elements.

Milgroym's cover depicts a different scene but shares the same visual aesthetic. In contrast to *Rimon*'s small, peripheral pomegranate, here the pomegranate is placed at the center of the image. Both covers showcase visual metaphors for the riches promised within, but *Rimon*'s zealously guarded temple is replaced by *Milgroym*'s seductively open pomegranate. Like *Rimon*, the cover image strives for balance rather than symmetry with its flat, organic forms. But replacing the deep red with a neutral background calls greater attention to the vibrant red pomegranate and the complementary green bird pecking at its seeds. Though far from the linocuts featured in Yiddish modernist periodicals like *Yung yidish* (Young Yiddish, 1919, Łódź) and *Albatros* (Albatross 1922–1924, Warsaw-Berlin), *Milgroym*'s pomegranate conveys a dynamic sense of Jewish tradition newly exposed and revealed to the bird or, perhaps, to a modern audience.

In both instances, the colorful cover images communicate the magazines' financial resources as well as their attempts to encompass both traditional and modern Jewish art. More subtly, they suggest

2. Cover of *Milgroym* 1, no. 1 (1922). Courtesy of E. Sourasky Central Library, Tel Aviv University.

the relatedness of the two periodicals and their respective languages. The titles and the covers are different, but their details are dwarfed by similarities in the subject matter, font, layout, and alphabet. Here and throughout the magazines, visual representation conveys as much or more than the written texts.

If the covers of *Rimon* and *Milgroym* call attention to visual art, the nearly identical short textual introductions printed at the beginning of both magazines further emphasize format and design: "The magazine is published bimonthly in the format of this issue, printed on the choicest paper and with a full-color cover. It is dedicated to art, music and theatre, particularly Jewish art of the past and present.[28] Each issue will include approximately twenty-five pictures, some in color, and numerous other images and decorations. The literary section includes stories and poems, literary criticism, and articles about literature, art and scholarship from the best writers."[29] The introduction foregrounds the magazine's format, high-quality paper, and illustrations. It also emphasizes its dedication to art, particularly visual art. Though earlier periodicals, most notably the Berlin-based *Ost und West* (East and West, 1901–1923) and the short-lived *Makhmadim* (Precious Ones, Paris, 1912), had featured visual art, *Milgroym* and *Rimon* were part of a wave of Jewish modernist journals that viewed art as a critical aspect of the modernist enterprise. Inspired by periodicals such as the German *Die Aktion* (The Action) and *Der Blaue Reiter* (The Blue Rider) and the Polish *Zdrój* (Fountainhead), which championed visual art and expressionism, several Yiddish journals appeared from 1919 onward, notably *Yung-yidish* in Łódź, *Ringen* in Warsaw, and *Albatros* in Warsaw and later in Berlin.[30] This combination of visual and textual art was not limited to periodicals; several art books appeared in the 1920s that integrated verbal and visual expression, like *Troyer* (Grief, 1922), a collaboration between Yiddish poet Dovid Hofshteyn and artist Marc Chagall; and *Vilna* (1924), which featured Zalman Shneour's Hebrew long poem alongside Hermann Struck's woodcuts.[31] Visually oriented periodicals were less common in Hebrew, likely because of closer connections between Jewish visual artists and Yiddish writers, particularly in Eastern Europe and the Soviet Union. Still, a number of single and multivolume Hebrew modernist collections, such as Odessa's *Masu'ot* (Torches, 1919) and Warsaw's *Kolot* (Voices, 1923–1924), were published around the same time with more modest artistic efforts. Like their Anglo-American counterparts, these "little magazines" were small-budget operations that published experimental works for a limited readership. In the context of postwar and postrevolutionary upheaval, these periodicals sought to articulate a new modernist culture in Yiddish or in Hebrew; *Milgroym* and *Rimon* broke the mold with their extravagance and bilingualism.

The only visually oriented periodical comparable to *Rimon* and *Milgroym* was Uri Zvi Greenberg's *Albatros.* The avant-garde journal was similarly dedicated to art and literature but, unlike *Milgroym* and *Rimon*, it was deeply ideological, first in its aggressive expressionism (issues 1 and 2) and later in its opposition to Jewish "exterritorialism" and validation of practical Zionism.[32] *Rimon* and *Milgroym*, by contrast, were silent on ideology, eliding ideological questions of the time in favor of essays on Jewish art and culture. This deliberate detachment—which, as we will see, earned the magazines a great deal of criticism in the highly ideological circles of Yiddish and Hebrew culture—was in many ways characteristic of Weimar Berlin, where unlike Warsaw or Moscow, politics and culture were "to an unusual extent independent and irrelevant to each other."[33] In the highly ideological field of interwar Jewish culture, periodicals were defined by their choice of language and political affiliation; *Milgroym* and *Rimon* were anomalies.

Perhaps what is most striking about the prefacing page that accompanies each issue of *Rimon* and *Milgroym* is that language is not mentioned. In *Rimon*, the Hebrew description, as well as the list of participants in the Hebrew magazine, are featured on the top half of the page, while the text is repeated in Yiddish along with the list of Yiddish contributors on the bottom half of the page. In *Milgroym*, the text remains the same but the order is reversed, with the Yiddish statement preceding the Hebrew.

Nothing on this page or subsequent pages remarks on the magazines' systematic bilingualism. There is no editorial commentary or

מילגרוים

צייטשריפט פאר קונסט און ליטעראַטור

די צייטשריפט גייט ארויס איינמאָל אין צוויי חדשים אין פאָרמאַט פון דעם העפט, אויף קונסטדרוקפּאַפּיר מיט אַ פאַרביגן שער־בלאַט. זי איז געווידמעט פאַר קונסט, מוזיק און טהעאַטער, דער עיקר דער יידישער קונסט אין עבר און איצט. יעדעס העפט האט אנ׳ערך פינף און צוואנציג בילדער, אַ טייל פון זיי פאַרביג, און אַ סך שוואַרצווייסע צייכנונגען. אין ליטע־ראַרישן טייל קומען דערציילונגען, שירים, קריטיק און ארטיקלען וועגן ליטעראַטור, קונסט און וויסנשאַפט פון די בעסטע שרייבער.

עס נעמען אנטייל י. אפּאַטאָשו, דר׳ מאיר באלאבאן, ד״ר חוגא ביבער, דוד בערגעלסאָן, מאכס בראָד, ד״ר מ. גאסטער, ד״ר נ. מ. געלבער, ר. האפּשטיין, ד״ר מ. ווישניצער, רחל ווישניצער־בערנשטיין, ד. י. זילבערבוש, ד״ר רפאל וועליגמאן, וואלדעמאר ושארוס, מלך חמעלניצקי, פּראָפ. א. י. טויבלער, פּראָפ. ס. לאנדסבערגער, ווי. לאצקי־בערטאלדי, מ. ליוושיץ, א. לעווינסאָן, ד״ר ג. מארצינסקי, י. מייער־גרעפע, רער נסתר, ד״ר מ. סאלאווייטשיק, ד״ר ווי. פרענגער, סטעפאן צווייג, ל. קוויטקא, ד. קיגען, זלמן רובאשאוו, ד״ר א. ז. שווארץ, ד״ר מיכאל שווארץ, נחום שטיף (בעל רמיון), ד״ר י. שיפּער און אנדערע.

רמון

מאסף עתי עברי לאמנות ולספרות

המאסף יוצא אחת לשני חדשים בגודל החוברת הנוכחית. נדפס על־גבי נייר מן המובחר ומעוטף במעטפה מצוירת בשלל צבעים. המאסף מוקדש לאמנות, לנגינה ולתיאטרון, ביחוד לאמנות הישראלית שבעבר ובהוה. בכל חוברת באים כעשרים וחמשה ציורים, קצתם בשלל צבעים, והרבה תמונות וקישוטים. החלק הספרותי מכיל ספורים ושירים, בקורת־ספרים ומאמרים על נושאים ספרותיים, אמנותיים ומדעיים מטובי הסופרים.

משתתפים א. צ. אידלזון, ח. נ. ביאליק, ד״ר חוגו ביבר, ד״ר מאיר בלבן, ש. בן־ציון, מכס ברוד, ד״ר ש. ברנפלד, ד״ר מ. גאסטר, מרדכי גולדנברג, שמשון דובנוב, ד״ר ש. א. הורודצקי, ש״י איש הורוויץ, צבי וויסלבסקי, ד״ר מ. ווישניצר, רחל ווישניצר־ברנשטיין, דוד ישעיהו זילברבוש, ד״ר רפאל זליגמן, מ. א. דיק, וולדמר ושרוש, פרופ׳ א. י. טויבלר, מ. ד. לאנגר, א. לוינסון, י. ליכטנבוים, פרופ׳ ס. לנדסברגר, יוליוס מאיר־גרפה, ד״ר ג. מרצינסקי, ד״ר מ. סולובייציק, אריה סימון, ש. י. עגנון, א. פוזנאנסקי, א. פירשטיין, יעקב פיכמאן, ד. א. פרידמאן, דוד פרישמאן, ד״ר ש. פרלמן, וו. פרנגר, סטיפאן צווייג, ד״ר יחזקאל קויפמאן, פרופ׳ א. קלישר, יעקב קופליביץ, ד״ר יעקב קלאצקין, משה קליינמאן, יצחק קצנלסון, ברוך קרופניק, זלמן רובשוב, ד״ר א. ז. שווארץ, מיכאל שוורץ, יעקב שטיינברג, ד״ר י. נ. שמחוני ועוד.

IV

3. Preface, *Milgroym* 1, no. 1 (1922). Courtesy of E. Sourasky Central Library, Tel Aviv University.

programmatic statement, no opening manifesto or concluding note that reflects on the decision to publish simultaneously in Hebrew and Yiddish. But as the prefacing statements demonstrate, there is also no attempt to hide the dual publication. The coexistence of the two languages on the introductory pages is itself an editorial statement, an implicit assertion of the interrelatedness of the two magazines and, by extension, Yiddish and Hebrew.

Why did the Rimon Publishing Company decide to publish versions of the same periodical in both languages? A few years after *Milgroym* and *Rimon* had folded, art editor Rachel Wischnitzer Bernstein explained this curious choice as a reaction against the politicization of modern Jewish culture in a brief article in Berlin's German Jewish periodical *Soncino-Blätter*: "Neither *Rimon* nor *Milgroym* are party or clique organs. The equality of both languages was intended to completely dispense with the language debate."[34] Wischnitzer Bernstein, a scholar deeply engaged with questions of Jewish tradition, culture, and continuity, evinces surprisingly little interest in the "language question" that preoccupied early twentieth-century debates on Jewish culture. Wischnitzer Bernstein spent formative years before World War I in St. Petersburg, with its Russified Jewish circles and their trilingual approach to language (Russian-Hebrew-Yiddish).[35] But instead of publishing in a "neutral" language like Russian or German, the Rimon Publishing Company pursued a policy of language equality in the guise of publishing equality, which served as an expedient way of avoiding the question altogether. The content of *Milgroym* and *Rimon* reflects this fundamental disengagement with the ideological dimensions of language choice. Perhaps the best example of this linguistic disconnect is the work of Wischnitzer Bernstein herself: she was both founding art editor and one of the most frequent contributors to *Milgroym* and *Rimon*, yet all of her essays were written in German and translated into Hebrew and Yiddish.

Years later, Wischnitzer Bernstein revisited the establishment of *Rimon* and *Milgroym* in her 1979 memoirs but responded to the language question differently. "The first question we had to face," she writes, "was the question of language . . . We realized that German, the language of Goethe, Schiller, and Moses Mendelssohn was, after World War I, no longer the unifying cultural vehicle of the Jewish intelligentsia. We wanted to reach out to cultural groups in America and the growing Jewish community in Palestine. Yiddish and Hebrew seemed to be indicated. There were to be two companion magazines, each with a literary and an art section."[36] Writing in English, Wischnitzer Bernstein focuses on geography more than ideology. The desire to reach Jewish readers in North America and Palestine motivates the decision to publish in both Yiddish and Hebrew and reflects a significant reorientation of Jewish culture. Like many scholars, Wischnitzer Bernstein identifies a fundamental change in Jewish language after World War I. But in her narrative, Yiddish and Hebrew together become the solution to the displacement of German as the language of the Jewish intelligentsia, pragmatic substitutes for a Jewish culture no longer bound to eighteenth-century Jewish Enlightenment ideals and their initial language of expression. In contrast to Wischnitzer Bernstein's earlier account, language is a vehicle for the magazines' cultural program rather than an entity linked to a particular political party. Though the magazines and Wischnitzer Bernstein herself were based in Berlin, the retrospective account written from her longtime home in New York identifies the Yiddish-speaking American Jewish community and the Hebrew-speaking Palestinian Jewish community as target audiences for the magazines' program of arts education and as lucrative customers who would pay in foreign currency. Wischnitzer Bernstein's memoirs not only dismiss a German readership but also make no mention of potential Eastern European readers. Language, for Wischnitzer Bernstein, was first and foremost a cultural vehicle, preferably one that could unify Jews scattered to the far edges of the Atlantic and Mediterranean.

In addition to her comments about the languages themselves, Wischnitzer Bernstein's retrospective accounts reflect on the magazines' belletristic sections. In her earlier remarks, she explains that each magazine sought original literary texts, as *Rimon* published the work of Agnon and *Milgroym* published the work of Bergelson. But her later memoirs suggest a more complicated arrangement.

"We published poems, stories and literary essays only in the original language, so that David Bergelson appeared only in the *Milgroym*, while Bialik and Agnon were to be found only in the *Rimon*. Shaul Tchernikhovsky, a leading Hebrew poet, gave us a poem, 'Black was the Night,' in Yiddish. It was published in the *Milgroym*, while his Hebrew essay on Bialik and his Hebrew translation of the 'Hymns of Akhnaton' appeared in the *Rimon*."[37] Wischnitzer Bernstein confuses this linguistic-based division of literary labor with the example of the poet Shaul Tchernikhovsky, a friend and fellow student at the University of Heidelberg. Tchernikhovsky, one of the few Hebrew writers of the renaissance generation who did not write in Yiddish, contributed a Hebrew poem in A. Reynen's Yiddish translation to *Milgroym* and ancient Egyptian poetry in his own Hebrew translation to *Rimon*. Consciously or unconsciously, her reference to Tchernikhovsky highlights the prominence of translation and the value of translated texts, contradicting her assertions that literary works were published "only in the original language." The magazines' reliance on translation, both the artistic translations of Tchernikhovsky as well as the more prosaic translations of editors Barukh Krupnik and Moshe Kleinman, reveals the growing distance between Yiddish and Hebrew. Fifteen years earlier, it would have been easy to fill a periodical with Eastern European Hebrew-Yiddish writers. By the early 1920s, the number of bilingual texts had dwindled.[38] While the magazines' literary sections were conceived as monolingual, they in fact reflect a widespread translingualism in *Milgroym* and *Rimon*, with texts and not necessarily individual writers crossing between the two languages.

Milgroym and *Rimon*'s introductory texts assert that a modern perspective on Jewish culture should transcend interwar politics and linguistic difference. Contrary to contemporary periodicals, the magazines' vivid covers, conceived by Wischnitzer Bernstein and realized by Boehm, invited Yiddish and Hebrew readers to immerse themselves in politically disengaged art, a sensibility that owes more to a Romantic appreciation of aesthetics than the ideological imperatives of the early twentieth century. Ironically, in their desire for Jewish culture to transcend political and linguistic ideology, the magazines' editors laid the foundations for undoing the very cultural vision they sought to advance. Their attempts to educate their readers about Jewish art and culture at large were consistently undermined by their own contributors, who voiced dissonant notions of Jewish art, culture, and history. So while *Milgroym* and *Rimon* succeeded in creating a new and different forum for Jewish culture, what Susanne Marten-Finnis and Igor Dukhan have aptly termed "a laboratory for implanting new Jewish art,"[39] from the first issues of the magazines it was clear that in these magazines, as in Jewish cultural debates more broadly, there was no consensus on the nature of this new Jewish visual and textual art.

Unity or Fragmentation? Modern Jewish Culture in Hebrew and Yiddish

Wischnitzer Bernstein may have conceived of Yiddish and Hebrew as equal linguistic partners in this cultural enterprise, but the first issues of *Milgroym* and *Rimon* were far from identical. Though they shared an art section and a single design and layout, their respective literary sections comprised strikingly different texts that reflect many of the differences between Yiddish and Hebrew literatures in the early 1920s. At first glance, the arts-and-letters magazines have split personalities: simultaneously one "arts" magazine and two "letters" magazines.

The magazines begin with an essay that proposes cultural unity as a shared point of departure. Presented in lieu of an editorial statement, Wischnitzer Bernstein's essay "Ha-omanut ha-chadasha va-anachnu"/"Di naye kunst un mir" (The New Art and Us)[40] surveys the relationship between Jewish artists and major trends in art history from the Middle Ages to the present. She celebrates what she sees as newfound harmony between Jewish and modern art. "The art of today breathes the same hot air that the Jew breathes, and creates rhythms that ring in his ears. . . . She [art] fights for expression and he [the Jew] fights for expression of his essence."[41] This statement hints at several important principles behind the magazine's art and literary sections. First of all, it embraces the modern without explicitly identifying with a particular modernist stream. The "hot air" shared by modern art and the modern Jew is a familiar modernist identification of the exceptionality of this historical moment. The "fight for expression," however, borrows the language of German Expressionism that in its broadest conceptions championed subjectivity, passion, and rebellion.[42] In Wischnitzer Bernstein's description, the fight for expression against repressive sociocultural conditions of the early decades of the twentieth century, primarily though not exclusively expressionist in form, resonates with the specifically Jewish fight for political and cultural expression.

Wischnitzer Bernstein's statement also stresses the magazines' focus on the relationship between art and the Jew, or in broader terms, between Western culture and Jewish culture. The work of modern Jewish expressionists like the Russian Jewish painter I. B. Ryback, she emphasizes, is successful because it is grounded in Jewish tradition. Wischnitzer Bernstein's essay inscribes Jewish artists within the Western art tradition as important participants in European Expressionism, but it also situates them within a specifically Jewish context, conceptually and visually linking images from medieval manuscripts and expressionist paintings. In this essay and throughout the magazines, art is an essential dimension of Jewish unity, one that links Jewish artists across time: "In the hearts of the young artists of our generation this spirit [of national unity] is also living and breathing. The spirit of connection to the past, to the Israelite past stirs within them. With pained sweetness and bitter, hurried courage they feel the shared present, that we are one nation with one fate for us all. And from this spirit their artwork is so important and so convincing and its personal tone is so strong. Because our generation of sorrow and anguish is thirsty for expression. Our generation is cleaved from its restrained emotions, the froth and love held back, which demand expression. The Jew battles for himself and others."[43] In this short passage, Wischnitzer Bernstein mixes key modernist concepts with a fervent belief in the power of Jewish unity. She does not advocate for the kind of creative reconstruction of the past that Martin Buber called for as early as 1901 in *Ost und West*, but rather a rediscovery of the creative Jewish past paired with an appreciation of the artistic present.[44] The ways in which Wischnitzer Bernstein tries to present a compelling Jewish artistic tradition as a precursor for modern Jewish art resonates with other indigenizing tendencies within early twentieth-century Jewish culture. In the decades before and after World War I, Bialik used his considerable cultural influence to preach "a strategy of recasting the indigenous traditions of Judaism as a secular-national patrimony."[45] Shifting her focus to visual art, Wischnitzer Bernstein argues that there exists a Jewish artistic tradition that could similarly serve as national-cultural inspiration for modern Jewish artists. It is this "spirit of connection to the past" that is intended to unify Jewish artists and provide the foundations for the Jewish art, both visual and textual, that is featured in *Milgroym* and *Rimon.*

Although Wischnitzer Bernstein concentrates primarily on visual art in this essay, her remarks resonate for the magazines' literary sections as well. The Hebrew and Yiddish versions of the essay invoke the postwar vocabulary of modernism that fills the work of Yiddish and Hebrew poets such as Hofshteyn, Perets Markish, Greenberg, and Avraham Shlonsky with the keywords "generation of sorrow" (*dorenu ha-dvay/oysgepaynigter dor*), "cleaved or torn" (*mitbake'a/tserinsener*), and "thirsty for expression" (*tsame le-bitui/zukhn . . . an oysdruk*). By focusing on visual art rather than literature, she avoids specifying a single language and instead draws upon a shared language of modernism. Notably, neither Wischnitzer Bernstein nor the magazines incorporate modernist trends in the 1920s that blur distinctions between the visual and the textual, such as micrography, avant-garde typographies, and the Constructivist stylization of the text. Hewing to more traditional genres of painting and medieval manuscripts, Wischnitzer Bernstein proposes an artistic identity predicated on a common history and spirit that transcends chronological, stylistic, and, presumably, linguistic boundaries. Here and throughout the essay, Wischnitzer Bernstein argues about the relevance of modern art to "us" and "our generation," that is to say, to the imagined community of these periodicals, Yiddish and Hebrew readers across Europe, the Americas, and prestate Palestine, a readership that was usually divided among many different Hebrew and

Yiddish politically oriented publications. The consistent use of the first-person plural in this essay seeks to create a shared stake in the vision of Jewish culture expressed in the magazines.

Yet the literary sections that follow Wischnitzer Bernstein's essay seem to undermine her thesis, emphasizing modern fragmentation rather than cultural unity, particularly in Yiddish. *Milgroym*'s inaugural literary section is best represented by Dovid Bergelson's work, which sets a thoroughly modernist tone in the short story "Onheyb kislev 1919" (Early Kislev 1919) and the reflection on contemporary Yiddish poetry, "Der gesheener afbrokh" (The Recent Eruption).[46] Yiddish coeditors Bergelson (1884–1952) and Der Nister (Pinkhes Kahanovitsh, 1884–1950) were prominent members of the Yiddish literary community in Berlin in the early 1920s, Bergelson known for his stylistic and thematic innovations in Yiddish prose and Der Nister for his stylized, fantastic Yiddish tales.[47] Though Der Nister's fantastic-symbolist story, "Afn grenits" (At the Border), showed the wide range of Yiddish modernist prose in *Milgroym*'s first issue, Bergelson's essay celebrates modern and modernist fragmentation in the work of Russian Yiddish poets such as Arn Kushnirov, Leyb Kvitko, and Hofshteyn. Writing in exuberant expressionist prose of this "revolutionary time," Bergelson cautions his readers: "Do not search for any wholeness among the young generation of poets, no polished shoes, no juggling tricks of a fashionable dandy."[48] Unity of style, of national spirit, and of language are a far cry from Bergelson's expressionist aesthetic, which celebrates revolutionary and modernist fragmentation. Like so many European modernists, Bergelson insisted that modern Yiddish literature had to consciously break with the Jewish past. While Wischnitzer Bernstein argued that the Jewish artistic tradition should provide the foundation for modern Jewish art, Bergelson sought radical Jewish cultural transformation through modernist art.[49]

The poetry of *Milgroym*'s first issue shares the modernist passion of Bergelson's essay. Poet Dovid Hofshteyn's avant-garde "Dos lid fun mayn glaykhgilt" (Song of My Indifference), for example, features lines filled with slant rhymes and sound play, crosses and church steeples.

איך בין מיד שוין
פֿון שוועבן,
פֿון שווינדלען,
פֿון שווימען
פֿון ווייקן אין וואסערן פֿרעמדע . . .[50]

I am tired already
Of hovering,
Of swindling,
Of swimming
Of soaking in strange waters . . .

Hofshteyn, who published a longer version of the same poem in the first issue of the Soviet Yiddish literary journal *Shtrom* (Stream, 1922), conveys a restless ennui in his short lines, as his expressionist "indifferences" resonate both within the Bergelson/Der Nister–edited literary section in *Milgroym* and the Moscow-based *Shtrom*. Other poems in *Milgroym*'s first issue also experiment with modernist innovations like metrical variety, free verse, irregular strophes, and, particularly suited to *Milgroym*, creative visual layout. Kulbak's "In a vald a yadlavn" (In a Forest of Firs) alternates between stillness and movement, silence and sound, in its depiction of a forest scene, conveyed in fragmented lines with irregular rhymes.[51] Kulbak's poem, however, is paired with the color image that crowns the same page, part of an Italian illuminated *ketubah* (Jewish marriage contract) from 1727. Here and throughout the magazine, the coexistence of past and present is not necessarily within a single work, as Wischnitzer Bernstein envisions, but often a function of the publication's layout. Yet the juxtaposition of an eighteenth-century painting of Jerusalem, a gold-tipped temple at its center, with Kulbak's poem and its uneven, broken lines is less a harmonious continuation of the past than an odd disconnect between a traditional Jewish art form and a modernist Yiddish poem or, in *Milgroym*'s terms, between Wischnitzer Bernstein and Bergelson.

In contrast to *Milgroym*, *Rimon*'s first literary section is uneven in style and quality. *Rimon* offers virtually no sense of postwar urgency or newness, none of *Milgroym*'s ravaged landscapes and soul-searching poetics in its poetry and prose. Ya'akov Kopelevitz, both an early contributor and critic, complained that the journal showed "no clear spiritual or conceptual-cultural direction—the essence of its character was simply aesthetic, and thus it would accept whatever material came to hand, without any principled selection."[52] Kopelevitz's comment rings true for the first issue's Hebrew texts, including his own short poem. Ya'akov Shteinberg's story "Al chof ha-desna" (On the Banks of the Desna), for example, chronicles the rocky relationship between two female cousins, one polished and urbane, the other provincial and passionate. Ironically, *Rimon*'s first short story was originally written in Yiddish during Shteinberg's prolific Yiddish period (1909–1914) and later translated by the author into Hebrew. Shteinberg deftly captures the women's complex emotions, but his story pales in comparison to Bergelson's expressionist fragments or Der Nister's atmospheric prose in Yiddish. The first issue's poetry follows suit, reflecting the presiding Romantic poetics in Hebrew rather than recent developments in Hebrew modernism. Yitzhak Katznelson, for example, a Hebrew poet best known for his later participation in the Warsaw Ghetto Uprising and his Holocaust poems, contributes a lilting set of rhymed quatrains titled "Halakh-nafesh" (Mood), which recounts the enchanting qualities of a special flower that casts its spell over the queen with few linguistic, formal, or thematic innovations. Lacking any literary or critical work comparable to Bergelson's Yiddish contributions, no unifying style or ideological perspectives, and drawing extensively on prewar writing, *Rimon*'s literary section communicates little about the state of Hebrew literature in Berlin or beyond.

While the magazines share a nearly identical set of essays on art and art history, their literary sections are surprisingly different: modernism is pervasive in *Milgroym* and absent in *Rimon*. Thanks to the guiding hands of Bergelson and Der Nister, there is a clear sense of poetic direction among this group of young Yiddish modernists, as well as internal cohesion that is a product of shared literary and ideological sensibilities. This coherence was not accidental; in 1918

Bergelson and Der Nister established the journal *Eygns* (Our Own) to publish the modernist Yiddish literature of writers associated with the Kiev Group. Reflecting the optimism of the months immediately after the revolution, this collection featured many of the same writers whose work appeared several years later in *Milgroym*, including the then-unknown poets Hofshteyn and Kvitko, as well as editors Bergelson and Der Nister.[53] This first issue is simultaneously a new Berlin-based cultural project and the next step of the Kiev Group in the wake of the devastating 1919 pogroms in Ukraine. A comparable sense of cohesion had not yet emerged among Hebrew modernist writers: Avraham Shlonsky, Yitzhak Lamdan, and Avigdor Ha-me'iri were in Palestine, pursuing different political and poetic directions; others, like Gershon Shofman and David Fogel, were writing urbane prose and minimalist poetry in Central and Western Europe.[54] Hebrew modernist factions would coalesce over the course of the 1920s, but Bialik's poetics still dominated the Hebrew poetry scene in Berlin, even as Bialik himself was focusing on a variety of other literary projects, not writing new poetry. Despite Wischnitzer Bernstein's emphasis on the unity of Jewish art regardless of language, the first issues of *Milgroym* and *Rimon* emphasize the differences between Hebrew and Yiddish literatures at this historical moment as they testify to their geographical coexistence.

Yet we cannot conclude that Yiddish and Hebrew were proceeding in separate aesthetic and ideological directions based only on the inaugural issues. Subsequent issues underscore the kaleidoscopic nature of the periodical; initial impressions can shift dramatically over time because of the magazines' fragmentary nature and changing cast of contributors. *Rimon* included a greater variety and higher quality of literary work in Hebrew, including the texts of Ha-me'iri and Agnon. Conversely, the stylistic and ideological coherence of *Milgroym*'s first literary section unraveled after a precipitous change in editors, leading to a far more eclectic set of literary contributions. The serial nature of the periodicals also affected the content, particularly in the case of *Milgroym*, as decidedly negative reviews catalyzed major changes in the magazine.

The Critics Speak

Word of the new arts and culture magazines spread quickly throughout the Yiddish and Hebrew press, with announcements of the publication soon followed by reviews. Critics in both languages tended to focus on the place of publication (Berlin) as much as the publication itself, seeing the magazines first and foremost as German products despite their primarily Eastern European editors and contributors. While these reviews demonstrate the different literary and ideological contexts in which each magazine circulated, they also reveal surprising convergences in the critiques of *Milgroym* and *Rimon*.

Hebrew critics in two of the main literary journals of the time found *Rimon* lacking in aesthetic and ideological terms. Writer and critic Asher Barash sardonically praised the new magazine in the Tel Aviv-based journal *Hedim* (Echoes): "The world catastrophe . . . brings blessings upon our literature. Germany, with skilled workers and open doors, is now being utilized as a giant factory for several nations and grants Hebrew some fine gifts. *Omanut*, *Moriah*, *Klal*, *Einot*, and now added to them *Rimon*, an illustrated collection of art and literature. . . . Its elegance—like a miracle for our literature, which now compensates its external nakedness. Only a world-war could bring us such luxury."[55] Barash adds *Rimon* to a growing list of Hebrew texts churned out by German printing presses, recognizing the irony of this "gift" left by an enormously destructive war. Barash promoted the work of young writers in Hebrew, more open than most contemporary critics to emerging modernist trends, but his appreciation of the aesthetics of this German "luxury" did not extend to its contents. Barash writes that the colorful cover lacks convincing "Hebrew interiority" but comes across as vaguely Slavic, and that the literary section is "deficient, as in any publication like this."[56] *Rimon*, he concludes, may add polish to Hebrew literature but contributes little in terms of substance. In contrast to *Hedim*, which sought to nurture young Hebrew writers and cultivate new literary styles, Barash found *Rimon*'s first literary section lacking innovation, sophistication, and, most of all, ideologically engaged Hebrew culture.

Like Barash, Ya'akov Kopelevitz took issue with *Rimon*'s contents in his review in *Ha-shiloach*. Though Kopelevitz himself had contributed a poem to the first issue, he harshly critiqued the magazine's focus on visual art, the quality of its translations, its eclecticism, and what he saw as its expressionist proselytizing. Kopelevitz argued that *Rimon* lacked Jewish content; rather than promoting harmonious and classical Jewish art based on form, he found it espoused dangerous external influences like expressionism and Bolshevism. In the context of *Ha-shiloach*, a representative of the old guard of Hebrew literature, *Rimon* was dismissed as not sufficiently Hebraic and Jewish in its content.

While Yiddish reviewers of *Milgroym* were as critical as Barash and Kopelevitz, their comments came from very different geographical and ideological vantage points. Yiddish artist Yoysef Tshaykov's (Iosif Chaikov) 1922 review in the Soviet *Shtrom* shares Kopelevitz's critique that the magazine lacked internal coherence, but links that observation to his overall assertion that *Milgroym* was elitist and moribund, a grave-inscription "dead and created for the dead."[57] Tshaykov's socialist politics undergird his wide-ranging critical fury, from his dismissal of the art essays written by degree-adorned professors to his claim that *Milgroym* was entirely deaf to the burning questions on art of the time and blind to contemporary plastic culture. For Tshaykov, *Milgroym* was too Jewish, exemplifying "the national bigotry of the eternal unity of the Jewish people."[58]

Yiddish modernists Perets Markish and Melekh Ravitch also inveighed against *Milgroym*, castigating Yiddish writers fleeing tough times in Moscow for the bourgeois comforts of Berlin cafés.[59] Writing in his personal literary journal *Di vog* (The Scale), Ravitch railed against the steady stream of "new, elegant, truly European-dressed book[s]" whose magnificent covers conceal "their empty nakedness."[60] Ravitch's words are strikingly similar to Barash's criticism in *Hedim*. Both critics fault the magazines for their lack of aesthetic and ideological substance: Barash lauds *Rimon*'s impressive exterior but suggests that the magazine's interior falls short of its visual elegance, while Ravitch mentions the "empty nakedness" within colorful exteriors. Despite the many differences between this Zionist Hebrew critic and socially engaged Yiddish writer, their comments share a similar suspicion of Berlin-based publications. For Barash and his fellow Hebrew critics, Berlin represents a seductive visuality, decadence, and foreign expressionism. For Ravitch and his Yiddish peers, Berlin's bourgeois capitalism goes against the revolutionary spirit of expressionism. Neither Barash nor Ravitch reflected on the bilingual nature of the magazines; like the other critics, they considered them entirely within their respective literary spheres. Yet the fact that prominent Yiddish and Hebrew writers bothered to comment on *Milgroym* and *Rimon* suggests that the magazines were part of the cultural landscape, periodicals that were read seriously and critically by a cross-section of the Yiddish and Hebrew literary establishments. The linguistic and ideological neutrality that made Germany an ideal location for an ambitious publishing project like *Milgroym* and *Rimon* also exposed the magazines to harsh criticism from all sides.

Critical reviews, even harsh ones, do not necessarily have much of an effect. But on the page after Tshaykov's review of *Milgroym*, the editors of *Shtrom* printed a letter from Bergelson and Der Nister: "We would like to inform our colleagues, whom we have invited in conversation or in writing to work with us in *Milgroym,* that we no longer have a relationship with the editorial board of the aforementioned journal nor are we among their contributors."[61] In their terse letter, also sent to the Berlin-based *Unzer bavegung* (Our Movement), Der Nister and Bergelson do not explain why they severed all ties with *Milgroym* after the publication of the first issue. In *Di vog*, Ravitch speculated that it must have been for ethical reasons, some sort of difference of opinion with the publisher or editors.[62] Perhaps the gap between Wischnitzer Bernstein's belief in a new unity of Jewish art predicated on shared tradition and Bergelson's endorsement of a Yiddish poetics of newness and fragmentation, expressed in the first issue of *Milgroym*, made it impossible for art and literary editors to coexist. Delphine Bechtel suggests that the highly critical reaction to their participation in the bourgeois magazine led to their break with *Milgroym*.[63] Both Bergelson and Der Nister remained in Berlin, the former until 1934 and the latter until 1926.

In the wake of the sudden departure of Bergelson and Der Nister from *Milgroym*'s editorial staff, the magazine's literary section floundered. Instead of boasting some of the most recognizable names in Yiddish prose alongside rising stars of Yiddish poetry, *Milgroym* was left scrambling for a new literary editor as well as contributors. In typical *Milgroym* and *Rimon* style, the magazine made no announcements about its changing editorial staff. *Milgroym*'s masthead merely omits the mention of literary editors in the second issue and then, just as subtly, lists Dr. M. Wischnitzer and M. Kleinman at the top of the third issue in both Yiddish and Hebrew.

While Moshe Kleinman may have been a natural choice for *Rimon*, he was radically different from his *Milgroym* predecessors. Both Bergelson and Der Nister came to *Milgroym* as acclaimed writers and prominent figures in Yiddish culture. Kleinman, who left Soviet Odessa for Berlin with Bialik in 1921, was a prolific writer and editor at the World Zionist Organization's journal, *Ha-olam* (The World), and a strong proponent of both Zionism and Jewish bilingualism.[64] An established editor, he was an arbiter of literary taste, selecting which works to publish in *Ha-olam*, but lacked the literary cachet possessed by his Yiddish predecessors. Though Kleinman's Zionist views were not foregrounded in *Milgroym* or *Rimon*, the roster of participants shifted away from those affiliated with the Yiddish left and toward Yiddish and Hebrew writers based in Germany, the United States, and Palestine: S. Y. Agnon, Yoysef Opatoshu, and Moshe Stavski. Under Kleinman, the two magazines became similarly eclectic in style and tone, with occasional moments of literary contact, one facilitated by translation and the other by a shared literary sensibility. These intersections between Yiddish and Hebrew literary texts in the related magazines exemplify the shift underway from early twentieth-century Hebrew-Yiddish literary bilingualism to translingualism.

Textual Convergences

The third issues of *Milgroym* and *Rimon*, both edited by Kleinman, feature a moment of Yiddish-Hebrew bilingualism mediated by Chayim Nachman Bialik. Bialik, then living in Germany, had been listed as a contributor in both *Milgroym* and *Rimon* from the first issue, but his sole textual contribution to the magazines was a letter that narrates his encounter with fledgling Jewish writer Yisrael Vakser in the spring of 1919 in Odessa.[65] Bialik recalls how impressed he was by Vakser's Yiddish stories and praises their breathtaking imagination, confidence, and honed style. As he recounts in the letter, Vakser was killed by Ukrainians during the Civil War shortly after his brief meeting with Bialik. Bialik concludes his elegy for the young writer with a request to publish Vakser's work, first in the magazines and eventually as a stand-alone collection.[66] Not surprisingly, two of Vakser's tales, "The Last Tear" and "In Seven Days," follow, printed in the original Yiddish in *Milgroym* and in Hebrew translation in *Rimon*.[67] Both stories feature princes and princesses who meet gruesome fates in stylized faux-folktales.

Vakser's stories are evocative but unremarkable, particularly in *Rimon*, where they are eclipsed by Agnon's intricately crafted story "Yatom ve-almanah" (Orphan and Widow) in the same issue. However, the publication of Vakser's stories in both magazines foregrounds translation between Hebrew and Yiddish in the magazines. Earlier issues of *Milgroym* and *Rimon* had not concealed the necessity of translation into Hebrew and Yiddish; translators were credited in small type at the bottom of each issue's table of contents. However, for a reader flipping through the Hebrew or Yiddish text, very little in *Rimon* or *Milgroym* marked these texts as anything but Hebrew or Yiddish, much less bilingual, aside from the brief literary-cultural chronicle that listed Hebrew and Yiddish books, exhibits, and cultural events worldwide.

In the third issue, however, Bialik, Vakser, and their texts explicitly move between Hebrew and Yiddish. Vakser approached Bialik as the arbiter of both Hebrew and Yiddish literary taste, and Bialik stresses Vakser's commitment to both Hebrew and Yiddish: he had been a skilled Hebrew teacher and a promising Yiddish writer. The Hebrew-Yiddish bilingualism shared by Bialik and Vakser is registered by *Milgroym* and *Rimon* in a way that no monolingual periodical could approximate. In *Milgroym*, Bialik's letter was printed in Kleinman's

Yiddish translation, along with an explanatory paragraph at the beginning, followed by Vakser's original Yiddish stories. In *Rimon*, not only were Vakser's stories printed in translation, but Bialik's Hebrew letter also addressed the potential drawbacks of the translated versions. Bialik explains that these stories were not necessarily Vakser's best, but rather they were two that had been translated from Yiddish to Hebrew and thus suitable for *Rimon*. This represents a rare moment in which the magazines show the movement of texts between Yiddish and Hebrew. The dual publication of the stories in *Milgroym* and *Rimon* also serves Bialik's goal of promoting Vakser's work, as he concludes his letter with the hope that Vakser's stories would be published in Yiddish and Hebrew editions.[68] In Bialik's view, Vakser's Yiddish prose was worthwhile for both Yiddish and Hebrew readers, asserting a shared literary inheritance from this Jewish martyr.[69] It is far from accidental that the catalyst for this convergence of Yiddish and Hebrew literature was Bialik; few other figures had the cultural authority in both languages to promote the posthumous work of an unknown writer. The dual publication of Vakser's stories presents the magazines as an ideal forum for the bilingual circulation of these texts. At the same time, the way in which Bialik situates these stories in the context of the Ukrainian Civil War contrasts Vakser's work with Bergelson's reflections on that same violence in *Milgroym*'s first issue. Vakser's folkloric fantasies fit more comfortably with the magazines' aesthetics, though Bergelson's vivid expressionism was more in tune with early twentieth-century Jewish and European cultural responses to war.

In the context of *Milgroym* and *Rimon*, this instance of explicit literary bilingualism is notable because of its rarity. These magazines were the only bilingual publishing venue of the time, and could have featured far more Hebrew-Yiddish bilingual writing, either from the dwindling ranks of bilingual writers like Uri Zvi Greenberg and Y. D. Berkovitz or via translation. While Vakser's stories demonstrate the bilingual platform that the magazines could provide, they also show that the majority of the time the magazines' editors did not advocate for literary bilingualism. With their "separate but equal" approach to bilingualism, the magazines sought not to replicate literary texts in both languages but to integrate both languages within a common artistic framework. Their periodic bilingualism sought to promote Jewish art broadly construed, not Hebrew-Yiddish bilingualism.

A Shared *Hefker*

Although Vakser's stories are the only literary texts that appeared in both *Milgroym* and *Rimon*, the magazines' sixth issues demonstrate another kind of literary convergence, thematic and stylistic rather than textual. *Milgroym*'s final issue includes two short poems by the Yiddish poet Avrum Nokhem (A. N.) Stencl (1897–1983), while *Rimon* features a Hebrew long poem by Uri Zvi Greenberg (1896–1981). If the first issues of the magazines highlighted the many differences between Yiddish and Hebrew literatures, and Vakser's stories showed their bilingual potential, these poems point to a shared Yiddish-Hebrew language of expressionism and a poetics of wandering.

Like many other writers, A. N. Stencl left his home in Poland for cosmopolitan Berlin in 1921, where he became a prolific Yiddish modernist poet, a habitué of the Romanisches Café as well as an "ardent admirer" of the German Jewish poet Else Lasker-Schüler.[70] The second of Stencl's two poems in *Milgroym* invokes the language and rhythms of expressionism:

ווידער און ווידער
שטורעם און לעצטער שטראַלן אָטעם
און איך בין הֶפְקֵר-

אַ געקרויצטער וועג-ווײַזער
אויף קרומע וועלטן ראָגן![71]

Again and again
Storm and last rays of breath
And I am *hefker*—

A crucified way-pointer
On crooked world corners!

The untitled poem plunges immediately into the breathless storm that surrounds its first-person speaker, who announces his existential state with one of the keywords of Yiddish poetic expressionism, *hefker*. The Hebrew rabbinic term refers to ownerless property that is found unclaimed and, by extension, licentiousness or libertinism. But in Yiddish modernism *hefker* becomes a new mode of poetic identity that at once celebrates and suffers from this lack of belonging, combining a sense of freedom and homelessness.[72] Stencl's third line echoes Perets Markish's lines, "I am nobody's, I am *hefker* / Without a beginning, without an end" (kh'bin keynems nit, kh'bin hefker, / on an onheyb, on a sof).[73] The celebration of *hefker* is pervasive in Eastern European Yiddish modernist poetry. Bergelson, in the first issue of *Milgroym*, uses *hefker* to try to capture the essence of expressionist poetry: "And let loose, let loose [*hefker*, *hefker*], like the million-crashes of all the exterminated individual worlds, the new poem has fired a shot."[74] In contrast to Bergelson and Markish's freedom and movement, Stencl's *hefker-yung* is no free modernist spirit, but rather a crucified Jesus, nailed at the crossroads.

Stencl, like many early twentieth-century Yiddish poets, uses Jesus as a charged poetic figure and powerful symbol.[75] In contrast to H. Leyvik's "Yezus" (1915), which depicts Jesus as a universal figure of suffering abandoned by the world, and Moshe Leyb Halpern's "A nakht" (A Night, first published 1916), which links Jesus' crucifixion to Jewish historical suffering, Stencl's poem neither Judaizes Jesus nor particularly dramatizes his suffering. The words *gekroytster* (crucified) and *genogelt* (nailed) are repeated, emphasizing the identification of the poetic speaker with Jesus. But it is the word *hefker*, repeated in the ninth line, that characterizes this Yiddish Jesus:

ווײַיז אויף צָפון
ווײַיז אויף דָרום
און בלייב גענאָגעלט
הֶפְקֵר צו אַרְבַּע־רוּחות וועלט . . .[76]

Pointing north
Pointing south

And remaining nailed
Abandoned [*hefker*] to the four-winds of the world . . .

The poem, its language, and its form all revolve around the contradiction between the movement inherent in an intersection and the utter stasis of the crucified Jesus-speaker. While the repetition of the verb *vayz* (pointing or showing) suggests action, it merely provokes action on the part of others, sending people on their various directions while the speaker remains paralyzed on his perch. With *hefker* as the speaker's defining quality, the poem is stripped of all religious claims, portraying a Jesus who is neither identifiably Christian nor Jewish. In a Nietzschean world in which God no longer plays a part ("And God— / he we have already devoured!"),[77] all this poetic speaker can do is to wait and watch those who pass in front of him.

Stencl's "Vider un vider" (Again and Again) finds an intriguing counterpart in "Al derakhim ba-ma'arav" (On Paths in the West), Uri Zvi Greenberg's Hebrew poem featured in the last issue of *Rimon*.[78] Although Greenberg published his poems widely in the Yiddish and Hebrew press, during the early 1920s he invested most of his efforts in the Yiddish *Albatros*, with its strident manifestoes, unrestrained criticism, and expressionist poetry and art.[79] Readers may have been surprised to come across a poem by Greenberg in *Rimon* rather than *Milgroym*. During his brief sojourn in Berlin (November 1922–August 1923), Greenberg embraced the city and its culture.[80] Like Stencl, he frequented the Romanisches Café and spent time with Lasker-Schüler. While in Berlin, Greenberg published the combined third and fourth issues of *Albatros* that boldly rejected European society and culture and endorsed Zionism in poetry, prose, and visual art.[81]

Greenberg's "Al derakhim ba-ma'arav" dramatically rejects Jewish life in Europe. Similar in style and spirit to its Yiddish predecessors, the poem's "ecstatic expressionism"[82] diverged from most of the Hebrew poetry published in previous issues of *Rimon*. The long poem, which consists of four sections, renounces Europe and European culture in favor of the land of Israel. Initially, this rejection is placed in the context of a shared Christian and Jewish disillusionment with the

West, drawing on sunset imagery prevalent in European culture with a nod to Spengler's *Der Untergang des Abendlandes* (Decline of the West).[83] But before the poetic speaker can take leave of Europe, he wrestles with its history of Jewish suffering and pain using the language and imagery of Christianity, like so many of Greenberg's Yiddish poems of the early 1920s. With "eyes that have sorrowed / from seeing the crosses," Greenberg's speaker bids farewell to Jesus, who, in the poem's most radical move, is transformed from Christian savior into another Jewish victim.

אָח מוּקָע לִי אֶחָד,
אָח גְלִילִי הַתּוֹלֶה
עַל כְּלוֹנָס דָּלוּחַ,
עַל אֶבֶן בֵּין שִׂיחִים . . .

הוּא הַפְקֵר בְּבָשְׁתּוֹ
לְעֵינֵי הָעוֹלָם —

וּבְטֶרֶם אֶעֱזְבוֹ וּבָא עָלָיו לַיִל
לְכַסּוֹת מַעֲרֻמָּיו —

לְהַגִּיד לוֹ שִׂיחִי הַצּוֹרֵב אֶתְיַצֵּב
לְרַגְלָיו הַדָּווֹת —
שֶׁאוֹתָן לֹא אֶשַּׁק.[84]

I have this condemned brother,
A Galilean brother who hangs
On a turbid post,
On a stone between the bushes.

He abandons in his shame
To the eyes of the world—

And before I leave him and night comes upon him
To cover his nakedness—

To address him with my biting words I will stand
At his sorrowed feet—
That I will not kiss.

Jesus's poetic appearance is by no means unusual in Greenberg's poetry. As in the work of Stencl and so many other expressionist poets, Jesus comes to represent a universal figure of humanity, at once a victim who cannot save himself and the lover of suffering humanity.[85] But Greenberg's lines also emphasize the Jewishness of this "condemned brother," referring to him repeatedly as not just a brother in human suffering, as he does in earlier poems like "La-arba ha-ruchot" (To the Four Winds), but as a fellow Jew, a Galilean. As in the Yiddish "In malkhus fun tseylem" (In the Kingdom of the Cross), the poetic speaker is careful to distinguish between the historical Jesus, a Jew, and the theological Jesus of the Christian Church.[86] The speaker states that he will stand at Jesus' crucified feet, visiting a "sick" relative as it were, but he will not kiss them because his Jesus is not the holy figure of Christian theology. Matthew Hoffman explains "this distinction makes it possible for him to portray the depravity of the Christian world as it mocks its own god, while simultaneously presenting Jesus as a symbol of Jewish suffering at the hands of the Christians."[87]

As in Stencl's poem, the word *hefker*—here, the infinitive construct *hafker* rather than nominal form *hefker*—is critical, at once a bridge between Greenberg's Yiddish and Hebrew poetry and an expressionist proclamation. This Jesus *hafker be-voshto* (abandons in his shame), publicly renders himself ownerless. Though he shares the modernist spirit of ownerlessness and alienation, this more active sense of giving up the self summons the allusive strata of Hebrew. In a Talmudic discussion of freeing slaves, Rabbi Yochanan ben Zakai is quoted as saying, "when a person declares his slave ownerless [*ha-mafkir avdo*]."[88] Like Greenberg's *hafker*, the Talmud's *mafkir*—he who declares property ownerless—is derived from the same root as *hefker* but calls attention to the action being performed, to what is and is not accomplished in this speech act. The slave is not freed but rather declared ownerless, a status that contributes to the ambivalence of *hefker*, with its shades of freedom and alienation. Greenberg's Jesus assumes this paradoxical role for himself, ownerless but, given his position nailed to the cross and the Talmud's additional requirement of a letter of emancipation (*get*), neither physically nor existentially free.

The noun *hefker* and its verbal variations link together the poem's different sections as it connects Greenberg's Hebrew text to Yiddish modernism. Earlier in the poem, the lyric speaker declares: "I am a son of *hefker* / the grandson of those same ancient exiles, / whose golden prayer shawl never fell from their shoulders."[89] This self-identification as *ben-hefker* (son of *hefker*) rather than the ontological *ikh bin hefker* (I am *hefker*) reflects an important distinction between the speakers in Greenberg's and Stencl's poems. To be *hefker* is to renounce all ties of ownership and belonging, and, in Stencl's poem, to become a fixed object encountered by others at the European crossroads. To be the son of *hefker* adds a paradoxical element of family ties, of belonging to a fellowship of the ownerless and abandoned that links Greenberg's speaker to previous generations of Jewish exiles with their yearnings for the East. So while Greenberg embraces this *hefker* identity in his Hebrew work, the term undergoes significant grammatical and conceptual revision.

In the second and fourth poems in the cycle, the poem plays with different forms of *hefker* as it approaches the crucified Jesus and, later, bids farewell to a corrupt European culture. First the speaker imagines the questions his fellow Galileans will ask him about their famous brother in the diaspora: "Does he still abandon [*mafkir*] his naked torso to the winds / to the rain / to the sun / and to the mouths of creations / to be kissed?"[90] In another variation of *hefker*, firmly within the bounds of Hebrew grammar, Greenberg's speaker describes Jesus' physical self-sacrifice, not for redemption but rather for adoration. Does Jesus still endure the physical and meteorological torment of being on the cross in Europe, when he could be enjoying the fragrant fruits and pleasant weather of the land of Israel? Or, in other words, is Jesus too stuck in this mode of self-abandonment, of making himself *hefker*, to find the obvious Zionist alternative? In the fourth and final section, Jesus' European world is also implicated in this pervasive *hefker*-ness. Greenberg's speaker ponders an appropriate parting gift for the "concubine of the cross," namely European culture:

בְּיַרְכְּתֵי דְרָכִים חָפַרְתִּי לָךְ בֶּאֱרוֹת דָּמִים,
אַתְּ הַפְקֵר קָרָאת לְכָל עוֹבֵר אֶל מִשְׁתֵּה הַלַּיְלָה:
כַּד יַיִן מִזְרָחִי מְשֻׁמָּר שְׁאַב מִן הַבְּאֵר פֹּה לְשַׁבֵּר צִמְאוֹנֵךְ.[91]

At the edge of the paths I dug for you wells of blood,
You called abandon [*hafker*] to all who passed on their
way to the night feast:
A jug of Eastern sanctified wine drawn from the well here
to shatter your thirst.

The active abandonment—here the concubine's call to all passersby to abandon themselves to the nighttime revelry, fueled by Jewish blood—again criticizes European society rather than celebrating *hefker* as modernist ontology. Even as *hefker* links together the poetic persona ("son of *hefker*") and Jesus ("*hafker* in his shame"), its expressionist connotations are progressively replaced by a critique of European culture.

Greenberg's *hefker* clearly connects him to Yiddish poets like Stencl and Markish and the expressionist spirit Bergelson celebrates in the first issue of *Milgroym*, but it also alludes to Hebrew poetry. Bialik's 1901 poem "Lo zakhiti ba-or min ha-hefker" (I Have Not Found Light in the Unclaimed) uses *hefker* in a very different poetic context: "I have not found light in the unclaimed [*hefker*] / Nor has it come to me as an inheritance from my father, / rather from my stone and my rock have I gouged it / and hewed it from my heart."[92] Bialik's poet-prophet sacrifices himself to his readers in this metapoetic text, insisting that his inspiration is neither inherited nor easily claimed from unknown or foreign sources—European poetic trends, perhaps—but painstakingly hewed from within.[93] Unlike Bialik, Greenberg writes his poetic speaker into a modernist *hefker* but he, too, repudiates external influences, here conceived as European Christian norms. Greenberg renounces Europe and its possessions in the fourth section in a manner that runs contrary to the presiding cultural spirit of *Rimon*. The last lines proclaim this final break:

לֹא נִשְׁאַר לִי דָבָר בִּרְשׁוּתִי רַק רוּחַ הַקּוֹדֶשׁ
וְהָאֵמוּן בִּדְבַר אֱלֹהִים אֲשֶׁר נִגְלָה לַנְּבִיאִים—
וּשְׁתֵּי סְגֻלּוֹת אֵלּוּ מַה שָּׁווֹת לָךְ הֵן אַחַר לֶכְתִּי.[94]

Nothing remains in my possession only the holy spirit
And faith in the word of God revealed to the prophets—
And what are these two talismans worth to you after my departure.

The lyric "I" claims that he leaves Europe with nothing other than what his ancestors had brought with them into exile centuries earlier. If Bialik's poem had refuted European influences on his literary work, here Greenberg's poem denies that anything has survived the flames of European anti-Semitism. Writing in one the most tolerant cultural climates Germany had offered its Jewish residents, Greenberg's text is absolute in its dismissal of precisely the kind of Jewish-European exchange that *Rimon* cultivated, particularly in Rachel Wischnitzer Bernstein's essays. Yet the poem makes its claims in poetic lines that are fundamentally a fusion of Hebrew language, Yiddish stylistics, and the German Expressionism prevalent both in Berlin and in the magazines.

Both Stencl's Yiddish "Vider un vider" and Greenberg's Hebrew "Al derakhim ba-ma'arav" represent a moment of contact between *Milgroym*'s Yiddish and *Rimon*'s Hebrew, as the poems share the language of *hefker* as well as the centrality of Christian symbols. However this is not, strictly speaking, bilingualism. Both texts share the rabbinic Hebrew word *hefker* but they do not switch from one language to the other, as Harshav defines bilingualism.[95] Rather, as modernist versions of this existentialist Jewish *hefker* rendered in two different Jewish languages, they represent the fluidity of linguistic boundaries or, in other words, the translingualism of modernist Yiddish and Hebrew poetry. Each text crosses the Hebrew-Yiddish border linguistically and conceptually to craft distinct reflections on modern European Jewish culture.

As the final literary voices in their respective magazines, these poems point to different directions for Yiddish and Hebrew literature.

Stencl's poem and its Jesus are anchored at a crossroads in the European geographical and cultural landscape, not unlike the poet himself who stayed in Berlin until 1936, long past the Nazi rise to power in 1933. Greenberg's poem, however, published in *Rimon* after the poet had already left Berlin for Palestine, is constantly moving within the Western world as it anticipates immigration to the East. Stencl fixes his Yiddish poem within European cultural discourse, while Greenberg uses that discourse to pronounce his rejection of European language, geography, and ideology. Here we see the simultaneous convergence and divergence of Stencl and Greenberg and the literatures they come to represent. The juxtaposition of Stencl and Greenberg in *Milgroym* and *Rimon* demonstrates that the magazines share more than just the art section; these poems represent translingual Jewish cultural production, combining expressionist poetics with uniquely Jewish inflections of *hefker* that move between Hebrew and Yiddish. They, like their respective literary spheres, are connected thematically and stylistically but are linguistically and ideologically distinct.

Assessing *Milgroym* and *Rimon*

True to form, the sixth and final issues of *Milgroym* and *Rimon* offered no warning of their impending closure. With the Weimar government's anti-hyperinflation measures of late 1923, the Rimon Publishing Company's foreign revenue could no longer support the magazines' lavish format nor the company's other publishing endeavors. Like many other Jewish publishing ventures, *Rimon* disappeared virtually overnight. Hebrew and Yiddish writers continued to pass through Berlin, but the locus of Jewish literature moved to other geographical locations: Bialik uprooted himself and his many projects for Palestine in 1924, and Tchernikhovsky followed suit a few years later in 1931. Many Yiddish writers returned east to the Soviet Union over the course of the ensuing decade, including Kvitko (1925), Der Nister (1926), and Bergelson (1934). Others, like Stencl, continued west to England and the United States; editors Mark Wischnitzer and Rachel Wischnitzer Bernstein stayed in Berlin until 1938 before fleeing to Paris and, eventually, New York. Within just a few years of the magazines' collapse, few traces remained in Berlin of *Rimon*, *Milgroym*, or their many contributing writers.

What, then, is the significance of these periodicals? Six issues of each magazine were published over two years despite their supposedly bimonthly format, reflecting the meteoric rise and precipitous decline of Yiddish and Hebrew culture in Weimar Berlin. Arthur Tilo Alt concludes that *Milgroym* "has passed into Yiddish literary history as little more than a footnote to the Yiddish modernist moment that began and ended in the Ukraine and Poland."[96] Gershon Shaked dismisses Germany as a "temporary refuge" for Hebrew literature, with Berlin and *Rimon* meriting merely a footnote in his discussion of Hebrew literary centers between the wars.[97] Yet footnotes and failures of this sort have the potential to reorient our reading of this complex and dynamic time in Jewish culture and specifically the changing relationship between Hebrew and Yiddish. In fact some of the most innovative and influential periodicals were similarly fleeting: Sholem Aleykhem's *Yiddishe folksbibliotek* and Wyndham Lewis's *BLAST*, Tristan Tzara's *Dada* and Yonatan Ratosh's *Alef*. The ephemeral nature of the magazines and Yiddish and Hebrew culture in Berlin do not compromise their historical and cultural significance. Rather, the two magazines showcase the sophistication of early 1920s Jewish-language culture and publishing as well as the many cultural and ideological fault lines that made difficult any concerted effort to envision modern Jewish art, even in the relative cultural neutrality of Berlin.

Milgroym and *Rimon* were part of a brief but immensely productive episode of Jewish cultural production in Germany, and they exemplify both the strengths and weaknesses of this cultural moment. Linking art, literature, theater, and music in their finely designed pages, the magazines highlight immensely productive intersections of German and Jewish scholarship, of modernist and Jewish art, and, at moments, of Hebrew and Yiddish literature. Relying heavily on translation between German, Hebrew, Yiddish, and Russian, to name just a few languages, these magazines insisted on both the relevance and translatability of Jewish culture. Linguistic fluidity becomes a textual manifestation of the transnationalism that characterized life in

Berlin for this small group of writers and intellectuals. The impressive list of contributors not only catalogs the many Hebrew and Yiddish intellectuals who passed through Berlin during this brief period but also demonstrates the magazines' remarkable ability to attract writers, artists, and scholars who were unlikely to come in contact in other periodicals or cultural institutions. Color and black-and-white images, ranging from illuminated manuscripts and ancient glass art to modern lithography and contemporary Russian Jewish art, provide glimpses of the German printing resources available during the brief inflationary period and, more significantly, the dynamic Jewish artistic scene in Berlin. The periodicals represent a moment of creative possibility in Jewish languages in a European cultural center that may, at first glance, seem unlikely. Thanks to their eclecticism, *Milgroym* and *Rimon* succeeded in bringing disparate aspects of modern culture together on their pages: Why not publish belletristic magazines simultaneously in Hebrew and Yiddish? Why not feature Walther Rathenau, Vladimir Korolenko, Leonardo da Vinci, and Hippolyte Taine, among others, in Yiddish and Hebrew?

Together, these magazines contended that a new cultural environment necessitated a new linguistic arrangement, one that neither duplicated the premodern Hebrew-Yiddish symbiosis nor reiterated the early twentieth-century politicization of language. Wischnitzer Bernstein and her coeditors shaped an alternative model of periodic bilingualism, a creative contiguity in which Hebrew and Yiddish "united" at moments (the art section) and "divided" at others (the literary section). But this division of linguistic labor was blurred by recurrent textual and stylistic intersections, translingual moments in which the two Jewish languages crossed the boundaries established by the magazines themselves, with monolingual, bilingual, and translingual elements. By featuring separate literary sections, *Milgroym* and *Rimon* suggested that their respective literatures were distinct and self-contained entities. Yet in the context of a shared artistic framework, both divergences and convergences between the two languages become visible. Published at a time in which other periodicals emphasized the separation of Hebrew and Yiddish, *Milgroym* and

Rimon demonstrated the extent to which the two languages were still in vital and productive contact with each other. The magazines set aside arguments for a single literature or two separate literatures in favor of an ambitious attempt to present a modern and modernist Jewish culture that balanced past and present, visual and textual. In the process, Yiddish and Hebrew coexisted, albeit briefly, as equal partners within the Jewish cultural landscape represented in *Milgroym* and *Rimon*.

Yet the magazines' attempts to disseminate a new approach to Jewish art encountered opposition as they circulated among the politicized centers of interwar Jewish culture. The linguistic and cultural parity imagined by the editors proved fleeting. Only the magazines' art section, controlled by Wischnitzer Bernstein, realized the cultural agenda that she promoted in "Di naye kunst"/"Ha-omanut ha-chadasha," which valorized a selectively constructed artistic tradition and modern art. From Bergelson to Greenberg, the two literary sections were defined first and foremost by their eclecticism and differences, not by their unity. Wischnitzer Bernstein's desire for "the equality of the languages" as a means of transcending cultural and linguistic politics encountered a reality in which Yiddish and Hebrew literary cultures were deeply polarized along geographical and political lines. On their finely designed pages, *Milgroym* and *Rimon* showcased not only the creative convergences of Yiddish and Hebrew in Berlin but also the difficulty of sustaining those cultural contacts.

The magazines' periodic bilingualism is unique—it was not adopted by later periodicals. But the dynamics of this periodic bilingualism anticipate a broader shift away from traditional bilingualism, exemplified by texts like Vakser's short stories, and toward other modes of translingual contact, as in the case of Stencl and Greenberg's *hefker*. Read together, *Milgroym* and *Rimon* demonstrate the range of literary-linguistic contact that existed between Hebrew and Yiddish literature: from the separation of the first issues' literary sections to their convergence in the texts of Bialik and Vakser; from similarities between the realistic sketches of Ya'akov Shteinberg in Hebrew and Yoysef Opatoshu in Yiddish to contrasting uses of a single shared word, *hefker*. This spectrum of literary-linguistic contact continued to define Hebrew and Yiddish literatures in the interwar period even after *Milgroym*, *Rimon*, and their editors' visions of Jewish linguistic parity disappeared.

While the circumstances that gave birth to *Milgroym* and *Rimon* in Berlin were in many ways unique, the translingual dynamics at work in the magazines were not limited to this brief cultural moment in Weimar Germany. Elements of literary bilingualism and translingualism surfaced even in the highly ideological atmosphere of the Jewish community in prestate Palestine. In Berlin, Hebrew and Yiddish writers circulated in related émigré communities and often found themselves face-to-face in the same cafés. In Tel Aviv, visiting Yiddish writers initiated a very different kind of literary collision, a debate about the relationship between Hebrew and Yiddish that raged on the pages of Hebrew newspapers and was watched from afar by Yiddish papers. But behind the grand rhetoric and public drama, individual writers like Eliezer Shteinman and Avraham Shlonsky continued to move between Hebrew and Yiddish. Literary-linguistic practice, even at the emerging Zionist center, proved far more dynamic than its ideological framework would suggest.

2

Breathing Hebrew with Both Lungs

Hebrew and Yiddish in Palestine

BY THE MIDDLE OF THE 1920S, many of the Hebrew writers in Germany had relocated to prestate Palestine, joining colleagues in the rapidly growing Zionist center of Hebrew culture. Still, writers based in Palestine maintained a variety of contacts with colleagues they had encountered in places like Warsaw and Berlin or read on the pages of Hebrew and Yiddish periodicals. In May 1927, Bialik, Greenberg, and other prominent Hebrew writers and intellectuals welcomed visiting Yiddish novelist Sholem Ash, Yiddish playwright Perets Hirshbeyn, and Yiddish poet Esther Shumiatsher, Hirshbeyn's wife, at a reception in Tel Aviv's Zionist Club.[1] The reception in honor of Ash and Hirshbeyn was not unusual; the Association of Hebrew Writers regularly convened to welcome guests or discuss issues related to Hebrew literature in the Yishuv, the Jewish community in Palestine. Yet this reception proved to be more memorable than most because it provided a public opportunity for representatives of Hebrew literature in the Yishuv to reflect on the present and future of Yiddish and Hebrew culture.

The event featured a veritable who's who of Hebrew culture in the Yishuv, with speakers ranging from Bialik to Berl Katznelson, labor leader and editor of the daily paper *Davar*. Most of the speakers turned to metaphor to encapsulate the relationship between the two Jewish languages. Poet and writer Ya'akov Fichman insisted that Hebrew and Yiddish were "two literary branches of a single tree" and encouraged his Hebrew colleagues to build bridges between the organically related languages.[2] Katznelson employed a familial analogy when he described the Hebrew-Yiddish encounter as "a meeting of brothers who had each followed his own path to seek his own fortune."[3] Several speeches later, Perets Hirshbeyn, speaking in Yiddish, returned to the brotherly metaphor: "We are brothers, but not [identical] twins."[4] Though Katznelson and Hirshbeyn both foregrounded the family relationship that linked the two languages together by virtue of their shared parentage and heritage, the first emphasized the different choices each "man" had made, while the second stressed the essential differences between the two. These metaphors distill the central message of the speeches offered in honor of this encounter between representatives of Hebrew in Palestine and Yiddish in the diaspora: Hebrew and Yiddish shared inherent features as Jewish-language literatures, even as they pursued different ideological and cultural paths.

The most famous of the metaphors presented at what might have been an otherwise forgettable literary gathering was voiced by Chayim Nachman Bialik. Bialik spoke eloquently of the long coexistence of Hebrew and Yiddish: "These two languages are a match made in heaven that cannot be separated. The two breathed together, lived together one alongside the other, the two were nourished from a single source."[5] Bialik refined his conception of this relationship a few lines later when he described Yiddish in the service of Hebrew, but his comments and, most of all, his metaphor ignited an explosive debate about Hebrew-Yiddish bilingualism. In public demonstrations and in the Hebrew press, prominent writers and politicians weighed in on the question of the proper relationship between Hebrew and Yiddish culture in the Yishuv and in the diaspora.

This "Yiddish Affair," one of several skirmishes over Yiddish in Palestine, epitomized the strong emotions and incendiary rhetoric spurred by literary-linguistic contact in the mid-1920s. Although Zionist ideology rejected Yiddish as part of its overall rejection of Jewish diasporic life, the unfolding of this drama demonstrates the continued relevance of Yiddish in the emerging center of Zionist

Hebrew culture. At the same time, the cultural tempest obscured the widespread literary bilingualism and translingualism of writers in the Yishuv, ranging from writers who actively published in both Hebrew and Yiddish to those who moved between the languages in more subtle ways. Hebrew was the uncontested language of the Zionist enterprise in prestate Palestine, but tensions between Yishuv Hebrew and diasporic Yiddish and between public rhetoric and personal literary practice show the extent to which literary-linguistic dynamics in Palestine were still being contested.

Hebrew, Speak Hebrew!

Not surprisingly, attitudes toward Hebrew-Yiddish literary bilingualism in Palestine were very different from those in Weimar Germany, where Hebrew and Yiddish were both marginal languages with respect to the dominant German-language culture. In the Yishuv, Hebrew was a critical element of the Zionist project to shape a new secular identity in the land of Israel, a cultural ideology that became dominant during the Mandatory period.[6] David Ben-Gurion, in a 1924 speech, designated Hebrew culture as the "glue" in creating a Hebrew national identity.[7] Yiddish was viewed as the language of the diaspora, representing all that Zionism sought to negate about Jewish existence in the diaspora. But as Yael Chaver has demonstrated, the actual place of Yiddish and Yiddish culture in Palestine was far more complicated: "The view that by the late 1920s Yiddish had disappeared is an example of a Zionist myth . . . The flourishing of Yiddish in the Yishuv was problematic, an anomaly that needed to be integrated into the national narrative."[8] The ongoing presence of Yiddish as a spoken and literary language within the Yishuv, as well as the flourishing of Yiddish culture in Europe, the Americas, and the Soviet Union, meant that Yiddish remained a force to be reckoned with.

The hullabaloo surrounding Ash and Hirshbeyn's trip to Palestine was a key transitional moment in the changing relationship between Hebrew and Yiddish. First, as Arye Leyb Pilowsky argues in his detailed history of the controversy, it set an important precedent in which the question of language became a literary issue rather than a political issue in the Yishuv.[9] Zohar Shavit, surveying literary life in the Yishuv, focuses almost entirely on the literary dimensions of this controversy, arguing that it served as a pretense for a bitter brawl between literary generations, as Hebrew writers Avraham Shlonsky and Eliezer Shteinman led the young modernist charge against Bialik and his supporters.[10] But reading the Yiddish dimension out of this episode removes this battle for literary succession from its historical and cultural context. As Naomi Seidman suggests, "the internal poetic struggles of Hebrew literature and the larger linguistic conflict intersected."[11] Seidman identifies this episode as the final moment, the "stormy divorce," of the Hebrew-Yiddish sexual-linguistic system that she traces from the *Tsenerene* until the 1920s: "For the Zionist modernist writers who left family and mother tongue behind, the Hebrew culture of Palestine was the clearest expression of the rupture of history, in its personal as well as national dimension. The furious outbreak that followed the Tel Aviv reception for the Yiddish writers cannot be understood outside this sense that Hebraism required the rejection of earlier codes."[12] Seidman sees the responses of Shlonsky and other Hebrew writers to Bialik's comments as both reactions against traditional Hebrew-Yiddish bilingualism and the end of this bilingualism. If it is in fact an endpoint, however, what comes next? That is to say, what follows this "divorce"?

This chapter analyzes the Yiddish Affair not as a bitter end to Hebrew-Yiddish literary bilingualism but rather as part of ongoing negotiations of the terms of engagement between Hebrew and Yiddish cultures. This is by no means the only such negotiation within the Yishuv, but close attention to the substance of this often-vicious debate—reading behind and beyond the metaphors—exposes different visions for Jewish culture, literature, and language. These conflicting visions were articulated, attacked, and defended by the many participants in this public drama, played out primarily on the pages of the Hebrew press in Palestine. Though Ash and Hirshbeyn were quickly forgotten in the textual furor and in later analyses, their encounter with Hebrew literary colleagues put Yiddish at the center of a defining episode for Hebrew literature in the Yishuv. Furthermore, a closer look at the literary work of two key participants in the debate, Avraham Shlonsky and Eliezer Shteinman, reveals that the linguistic and cultural battle lines were far more vexed than they appear in the rhetorical flourishes of this debate. As much as Hebraists wanted to imagine that Yiddish had no place in the Yishuv, this instance of literary-linguistic contact makes clear that Yiddish and Hebrew were still interacting in substantive ways in the public sphere and in literary texts. Within the self-consciously monolingual national Hebrew culture lurked a variety of approaches to Jewish bilingualism and translingualism.

Literary Ambassadors? Visiting Cousins?

At first glance, Ash and Hirshbeyn's trip to Palestine in 1927 resembles other transcultural literary "missions" common in the early decades of the twentieth century. The years after World War I were a time of geographical mobility, not only for the thousands displaced by the war but also for cultural and intellectual figures. Cities like Berlin, Paris, London, Vienna, New York, and Chicago attracted migrants of all kinds and became hotbeds of new political and cultural activity.[13] In addition to this transnational circulation of intellectuals, a different kind of mobility was evident in writers' trips to foreign countries, either as individuals or as participants in cultural delegations.

During the 1920s, perhaps the most frequent destination for these cultural "fact-finding missions"—part reportage, part glorified tourism—was the Soviet Union. Readers across the ideological spectrum were fascinated by the transformation of the Russian Empire into a new communist society. Soviet leaders saw tourism as an effective form of propaganda aimed at public opinion abroad and encouraged visitors to tour sights that epitomized the new social order—factories, power plants, collective farms, prisons, and schools—and to report their (positive) impressions.[14] Daniel Soyer, examining travelogues in the American Yiddish press, argues that prominent intellectuals' journeys, and particularly their reports in the Yiddish press, had far greater effect on the home culture than the society that had been visited.[15] In the popular New York Yiddish daily *Forverts*, editor-in-chief Abraham

Cahan's travelogues were used not only to entertain readers but also to reorient editorial policy. Cahan's trips to Palestine (in the fall of 1925) and to the Soviet Union (in the summer of 1927) were highly publicized in the paper and were chronicled in detail, one part of a major shift in the influential paper's stance on Zionism and the other providing rejoinders to Soviet propaganda.[16]

These expeditions also had the potential to affect the "host" culture as much as the "home" culture. Bertrand Russell, for example, traveled to Russia as part of a British delegation sent to investigate the effects of the Russian Revolution in 1920. Later the same year, he traveled to China to lecture in Beijing and tour the country. After both journeys, Russell recorded his impressions of the nations and cultures that he visited, published as *The Practice and Theory of Bolshevism* (1920) and *The Problem of China* (1922). While accounts like Russell's reveal as much about the traveler as his destination, the texts also represent key moments in transcultural and, in Russell's case, translingual contact. Lydia Liu, analyzing Russell's comments on the "Chinese character" and their prompt translation into Chinese, demonstrates how a traveler's assessment can provoke debate within the "host" culture. In Russell's case, his encounters with Chinese writers show that the myth of national character was shaped in part by coauthorship, combining the perspectives of outsiders like Russell and the ways in which they were rendered in Chinese. This physical-turned-conceptual contact precipitated the development of a Chinese discourse on national character that Liu examines.[17]

Though the circumstances of Ash and Hirshbeyn's trip were quite different from Russell's expedition, the Yiddish writers' presence in Palestine raised similar questions of transcultural and translingual contact. Russell visited China as an outsider, a representative of the "West" encountering the "East." The contact brought about by Ash and Hirshbeyn's trip to Palestine, however, was more complicated. During the early decades of the twentieth century, Hebrew and Yiddish writers traveled throughout the expanding map of Ashkenazi Jewish culture. In the years after World War I, Ash visited Lithuania, Weimar Germany, and Palestine in official and unofficial capacities while living in New York and Warsaw; Hirshbeyn and Shumiatsher's trip to Palestine was one stop on their round-the-world expedition, which Hirshbeyn detailed for the Yiddish press; Bialik, as he mentions in his speech at the 1927 reception, had returned from a trip to England and the United States only a few months earlier. The travels of these writers, as well as many of their colleagues, were covered by the Jewish press, recounted in speeches and first-person articles, and often republished as books.[18] These trips and especially the narratives that surrounded them reflect the strong centrifugal forces at work in interwar Jewish culture, as there was no longer any single site or cluster of sites that stood as the cultural center.[19] At the same time, certain centripetal forces—both ideological and pragmatic—continued to bring Jewish writers together, often through these sorts of cultural trips: shared audiences; personal acquaintances (often formed in places like Odessa, Warsaw, Vilna, and other Eastern European cities); fundraising (particularly in the United States); and tourism (especially in Palestine).

Should we understand these trips in the context of transcultural "missions," not unlike Russell's trip to China, or as translingual "family vacations"? In other words, was Ash's third trip to Palestine in 1927 an intercultural journey of a would-be Yiddish ambassador to the emerging center of Hebrew literature? Or was it an intracultural visit of one high-profile Jewish writer to his Jewish colleagues, virtually all of whom had once interacted in the Jewish cultural centers in Eastern Europe? Different factions in the controversy provoked by Ash and Hirshbeyn's visit answered this question differently. Their responses call attention to one of the fundamental points of contention, a familiar question that percolated within the larger debate: Were Hebrew and Yiddish part of a single Jewish culture or two separate language-based cultures? In Berlin, the editors of *Milgroym* and *Rimon* responded to this question by producing two separate magazines with a shared artistic core and cultural vision, asserting that Jewish art could transcend the divisions between Hebrew and Yiddish and that the languages could be functionally equivalent. In the Yishuv, Hebrew's primacy as the language of the national project was well established by the middle of the 1920s. But what contact should the Hebrew literary establishment in Palestine maintain with Jewish cultural institutions—the majority of which relied on Yiddish—in Europe, the Soviet Union, and the Americas? Were proponents of modern literature in Hebrew and Yiddish bound together by virtue of their common roots in Eastern Europe, or had the communal and geographical ties of Eastern Europe dissolved with the migration of Jewish-language culture to the West and the Middle East? Just as Russell's delegation to China and his ensuing written account prompted debate within Chinese intellectual discourse, Ash and Hirshbeyn's visit as quasi-ambassadors of the Yiddish diaspora triggered debates about the past and future of Hebrew-Yiddish literary bilingualism and the essence of Hebrew literature.

At the Reception

The reception for Ash and Hirshbeyn consisted of a series of speeches in Hebrew by prominent intellectual figures in the Yishuv and speeches in Yiddish by the visiting writers, reported by all of the major Hebrew papers and several Yiddish ones. Within the predictable welcomes, tributes, and clichés, two primary approaches to the relationship between Hebrew and Yiddish emerged: some speakers viewed the two languages as two interdependent components of a shared Jewish culture and therefore a single bilingual culture; others saw them as historically related tongues that had pursued distinct geographical, ideological, or cultural paths, thus constituting functionally separate cultures. These distinctions, however, were obscured in the debate that erupted after the reception and focused far more on the speeches' rhetorical flourishes than their substance.

Fichman, speaking in Hebrew, welcomed the two writers in the reception's first speech as representatives of Yiddish culture. Adopting a conciliatory tone, he emphasized the distance between Hebrew and Yiddish even as he expressed regret over the consequences of the language war: "It is important for writers in the land of Israel to extend a bridge between Hebrew creation and the spoken language of the people. A great loss, spiritual and social, is caused by this unnecessary war between the two cultures, which could in fact and perhaps will in the future join together and greatly influence each other for the better."[20] Initially, Fichman invoked the historical relationship between Hebrew, the literary language, and Yiddish, the spoken language of the Jewish people. But he quickly made clear that he saw contemporary Hebrew and Yiddish as separate cultures, though he expressed his hope that they might cooperate in the future. "Most Hebrew writers," he continued, "who truly value Hebrew culture are not fighting against Yiddish literature, and men of culture and truth in Yiddish literature are not attacking the rights of the Hebrew language."[21] Pronouncing an end to the "stupidity" of the Language War, Fichman validated the importance of Yiddish and insisted that it could coexist in a mutually beneficial, transcultural relationship with Hebrew.

Not all of the evening's speakers agreed with Fichman's suggestion that Hebrew and Yiddish were distinct cultures. Bialik, the last of the gathering's Hebrew speakers, described a different relationship between the two. Though Bialik's famous metaphor that Hebrew and Yiddish were "a match made in heaven" received the most attention, the broader context of his speech did not represent the two languages as equal partners: "These two languages are similar to Naomi the noble Hebrew and Ruth who chanced upon her in the diaspora of Moab and returned with her to the land of Israel. From this match came David the son of Jesse. In what context? When Ruth was faithful to Naomi. When the urge to separate stirred within her, she condemned herself to death. When she tosses us a writ of divorce—she is not ours, she will be considered a hated and bitter enemy."[22] With his biblical analogy, Bialik curbed the suggestion that the languages existed in harmonious partnership by depicting a contingent relationship: the foreign-born Yiddish (Ruth) is only Jewish as long as "she" remains loyal to Hebrew (Naomi). Hebrew and Yiddish, in Bialik's terms, could not be conceived as separate cultures because that separation would render Yiddish no longer Jewish. Returning to the marriage metaphor, the partners cannot separate because their divorce would in effect cast out Yiddish. Thus it follows that Bialik praised the two Yiddish writers as "eternal servants of Hebrew, unknowingly," without inquiring about their political views.[23] By virtue of their visit to Palestine, he suggested, they still saw themselves as partners within this shared Jewish enterprise and, by implication, as subjects of the eternal Hebrew tongue. Invoking yet another familial metaphor, he welcomed them to Palestine as brothers, assured them that "no one persecutes languages here" (*en rodef kan leshonot*), and expressed his hope that they would convey this message to others after they left Palestine.[24] For Bialik, this encounter was strictly between two different languages, not between two different cultures.

A similar transcultural/translingual dichotomy surfaces in the speeches of the guests themselves. Most accounts of the Yiddish Affair ignore Ash and Hirshbeyn, since they played little part in the controversy triggered by their presence. However their Yiddish speeches were part of the unfolding of this drama. Ash, speaking immediately after Bialik, opened his remarks in Hebrew and assured his listeners that he had not come "to do business, advertise or demonstrate on behalf of Yiddish."[25] Switching to Yiddish, which needed no translation in the Yishuv, Ash stressed the urgency of uniting together against the threat of assimilation: "Why have we come here: because we are Jews. There is no language question that divides us, no war between Hebrew and Yiddish, but rather a war against destruction. Between us—brotherly unity, but we have a war against the sea of assimilation and estrangement that encircles the entire Hebrew nation."[26] Invoking first and foremost Jewish unity, Ash replaced the divisive Language War with a joint war against Jewish assimilation in the diaspora, which he saw as an equal threat to both Yiddish and Hebrew in Poland. If Jews cannot agree on a strategy, he warned, there will be no Yiddish or Hebrew schools left in Poland. To Ash, this threat of assimilation impelled Hebrew and Yiddish intellectuals to bond together as Jews to protect a shared Jewish culture that transcended language. Ash mentioned, perhaps in response to Bialik's comments, that Yiddish had long been nourished by Hebrew and had to continue this connection, but he was far more concerned with external threats than with internal language politics. He spoke to his audiences as equal participants in a single, translingual Jewish culture, asking them to work together with their Yiddish peers to tackle the uncertain cultural future in the diaspora. Little did he know that the relationship between Yiddish and Hebrew in the diaspora would become one of the flashpoints of the debate that followed.

While Ash appealed to a shared sense of Jewish identity and shared responsibility for Jewish culture in Poland, Hirshbeyn framed his remarks in Yiddish as an outsider. Speaking in Yiddish, Hirshbeyn mourned the damage that had been wrought by the Language War, but in no way suggested that the rift had been bridged or repaired as implied by most of the speakers who preceded him. Rather, he concluded the evening's speeches by wishing the Hebrew crowd well: "that everything of yours will grow and will sprout in the light, your souls, and sun."[27] With his second-person plural address, Hirshbeyn excluded himself from his audience and their national project. Yiddish, his remarks suggest, played no part in this new culture being cultivated under the Middle Eastern sun. Like Fichman, Hirshbeyn viewed Yiddish and Hebrew as distinct cultures, each defined by language and geography. But rather than building bridges, Hirshbeyn surveyed this new cultural landscape as a tourist—as a transcultural expedition not unlike his encounters with the Maori in New Zealand.

Despite the congenial atmosphere of the reception, these speeches demonstrate the different ways in which the participants construed the relationship between Hebrew and Yiddish. Conceiving of Hebrew and Yiddish as separate cultures, Fichman optimistically envisioned an eventual reconciliation, while Hirshbeyn acknowledged past damage and wished Hebrew well on its separate path. Maintaining that Hebrew and Yiddish were part of a single culture, Bialik insisted that Yiddish could not sever itself from Hebrew and remain Jewish, while Ash set aside the past in hope that the two languages could unite to protect a shared cultural future. Perhaps the only point they all agreed upon was that the Language War had ended and that a new destiny awaited Hebrew and Yiddish. Yet it quickly became clear that not even that consensus would remain unchallenged.

Contesting Views

Two weeks after the reception for Ash and Hirshbeyn, the Warsaw Yiddish daily *Haynt* reported that the Yiddish writers' visit had provoked *a shtikl tumel*, "a bit of an uproar," in Palestine.[28] *Ha'aretz* editor Moshe Glikson was not quite as restrained in his description of ensuing events: "our little world is astir, as if we did not have other true 'worries' apart from some expressions or banquet speeches."[29] Initially, the Yiddish writers' audacity in speaking Yiddish in public provoked protests, spearheaded by members of the Brigade of Defenders of the Language (*gdud meginei ha-safa*), a group of primarily young men dedicated to fighting against any perceived threats to Hebrew in the Yishuv. But attention soon shifted from the language to the content of the speeches given at the reception. These attacks and ensuing counterattacks in the Hebrew press disputed the reception's consensus that the Language War had been settled, showing that the relationship between Hebrew and Yiddish was still being actively contested in the Yishuv. The diversity and intensity of reactions to Ash and Hirshbeyn's reception demonstrate the continued relevance of Yiddish, not only in the linguistic sphere but also in highly ideological literary debates.

Initial protests commenced during the reception itself: Brigade members, most of them high school students or recent graduates, forced their way into the reception prepared to disrupt any public speaking in Yiddish. Their protest, according to the Warsaw-based paper *Der moment*'s account, was staved off by Bialik's assurance that Yiddish speeches would be translated into Hebrew.[30] Since its establishment in 1923, the Brigade had advocated, at times violently, for the Hebrew language and against all other languages within the Jewish community in prestate Palestine. Its predominantly young members protested against signs written in languages other than Hebrew, pressured publishing companies not to print in Yiddish, and warned theaters not to allow non-Hebrew performances and lectures. The Brigade also intimidated people who did not speak Hebrew in the streets, distributing pamphlets with their beliefs and slogans such as

Ivri daber ivrit! (Hebrew, speak Hebrew!)[31] But in this case, their campaign against speaking anything other than Hebrew, soon to resurface in protests against Martin Buber's lecture in German at the Hebrew University, was transformed into protests against the idea of Yiddish. According to *Davar*, some 800 people gathered in Tel Aviv a week and a half after the reception to rally against Bialik's suggestion that Hebrew and Yiddish were intimately connected, which ran contrary to their belief in linguistic purity.[32] The *gdudniks*, as they were affectionately known, were treated by most commentators with paternalistic fondness: though A. Z. Ben Yishai criticized their impudence in showing up at the reception uninvited, Y. Ch. Ravnitsky, M. Glikson, and even S. Pietrushka, writing in Yiddish for *Haynt*, viewed the protesters as "good lads," well-intentioned but a bit overzealous in their efforts to promote Hebrew.[33] Their objections to Yiddish were familiar business in the Yishuv by 1927, part of political discourse—political theater, even—that was not taken particularly seriously by the cultural establishment in the Yishuv.

What was taken seriously, however, was a five-pronged attack on Bialik and his remarks about Yiddish that was published in the Association of Hebrew Writers' weekly journal *Ketuvim*. On May 11, 1927, a week after the reception and the Brigade protests, a group of highly regarded Yishuv writers led by *Ketuvim* editor Shteinman and poet Shlonsky launched a salvo of attacks on Bialik and, in participant Asher Barash's words, "the division of the kingdom" between Yiddish and Hebrew.[34] In short pieces filled with pugnacious rhetoric, Barash, Shlonsky, poet Yitzchak Lamdan, Ya'akov Rabinovitz, and Shteinman challenged Bialik's statements and the conciliatory views toward Yiddish voiced at the reception. The group included both more established writers who had immigrated to Palestine before World War I (Barash, Rabinovitz) and younger, more modernist-inclined writers who had arrived in Palestine after the war (Shteinman, Lamdan, Shlonsky). Shlonsky's fiery response has attracted the most attention, but all five contributors rejected both the translingual model of cultural dependency articulated by Bialik and Ash and the transcultural view set forth by Fichman and Hirshbeyn. First and foremost, they argued that Hebrew could not cede the diaspora to Yiddish, or in other words, that the Language War was still being fought outside of Palestine. The *Ketuvim* Five regarded the diaspora as far more essential to the future of Hebrew in the Yishuv than many of their colleagues, who were willing to concede the dominance of Yiddish outside of Palestine.

Reports on the precarious state of Hebrew in Europe had been featured in *Ketuvim* for months. Shteinman, for example, castigated Polish Jews for not sustaining a Hebrew newspaper, while Ben-Zion Dinur (Dinaburg) detailed the repression of Hebrew publishing, schools, and writers in the Soviet Union.[35] Rabinowitz's *Ketuvim* essay continues this concern, as he furiously responded to Ash's warning about the dangers of assimilation facing Eastern European Jews: "You expelled Hebrew from the newspapers, you expelled it from libraries and school, and also from personal letters, you expelled it from all of the public and private offices."[36] Rabinowitz railed against the injustices "you" have perpetrated against Hebrew in Poland and the USSR, conflating Yiddishists, the Central Bureau of the Jewish Section of the Communist Party (*Evseksiia*), and Yiddish writers more generally. In his essay, Lamdan explicitly connected the speeches at the reception and the persecution of Hebrew writers in the Soviet Union by situating the Yishuv's warm welcome for Yiddish writers "only a few short days after we heard the cries of our comrades in Russia violently choked by the prohibiting hand that covers their mouths."[37] For Rabinovitz and Lamdan, the suppression of Hebrew in the Soviet Union necessitated not a reevaluation of the animosity toward Yiddish in the Yishuv, but rather an intensification of the battle for Hebrew's linguistic and cultural superiority in the diaspora.[38]

In addition to their indignation over the persecution of Hebrew in the Soviet Union, the *Ketuvim* writers attacked the old guard in Hebrew literature and their views on Hebrew-Yiddish bilingualism. Shlonsky contested Bialik's statement that Hebrew and Yiddish were a "match made in heaven" and what he saw as Bialik's overall message of rapprochement with Yiddish: "We have not agreed to the matchmaking of languages as a match made in heaven, therefore we shall not rejoice with the groomsman nor shall we expect some Rabbi Gershom with a rabbinic prohibition that forbids the multiplicity of languages. Our entire anguished existence is this prohibition!"[39] Shlonsky rejected Bialik's "special relationship" between the Ashkenazi Jewish languages by invoking a key rabbinic figure of early Ashkenaz, the tenth-century Rabbi Gershom ben Yehuda. Famous for prohibiting polygamy, Rabbeinu ("our rabbi") Gershom's enactment also prohibited a man from divorcing his wife against her will.[40] Rejecting the nuptial metaphor, Shlonsky unilaterally divorced Hebrew from Yiddish and explicitly cast off linguistic matrimony in favor of Hebrew's free interaction with the languages of the world.[41]

Shlonsky's caustic rejection of Bialik's marriage metaphor has been understood more as a personal attack on Bialik and his poetics than as a polemical refutation of Hebrew-Yiddish bilingualism.[42] But it was not accidental that Shlonsky chose bilingualism to launch his intergenerational literary offensive. Shlonsky countered Bialik's portrait of Hebrew-Yiddish marital harmony with his own metaphor for bilingualism: "We view this catastrophe of bilingualism as we would view tuberculosis, gnawing away at the lungs of the nation. We want Israeli breathing to be *completely Hebrew*, with both lungs!"[43] Alluding to S. Y. Abramovitsh's famous comment that writing in Hebrew and Yiddish was like "breathing through both nostrils," Shlonsky shifted the metaphorical debate from matchmaking to the vital realm of breathing. Rather than seeing Hebrew-Yiddish bilingualism as a customary feature of traditional Jewish society (an arranged marriage, perhaps, or a preordained one), bilingualism becomes in Shlonsky's image a cultural scourge, a dangerous remnant of Eastern European poverty and disease. Only a total reinvention of the diasporic Jew as the new Hebrew could cure this deadly disease: "A land of Israel that is Hebrew, labors for the people, loves her creators and culture—that is the 'Society for the War on Tuberculosis.'"[44] The Yishuv, in Shlonsky's metaphorical language, had to be the bulwark against Hebrew-Yiddish bilingualism.

Lamdan also stressed the gap between literary generations on the issue of bilingualism and offered his own metaphor. Bilingualism,

Lamdan insisted, was a remnant of the Eastern European past, something foreign to the new generation of Hebrew writers that had to be eradicated in the land of Israel. Like Ya'akov Fichman, who described Hebrew and Yiddish as two branches on the same tree, Lamdan turned to botany to speak on behalf of the younger generation: "And with the discerning power of this instinct we see this blurring in our midst as couch grass [*yablit*] that is liable to injure the roots of our essence. The decree for such blurring [*tishtush*] is, then, just as the decree for couch grass!"[45] Lamdan argued that only the younger generation could perceive the danger of bilingualism, here rendered as "blurring" between Hebrew and Yiddish. This danger is represented as an invasive weed, *Cynodon dactylon* or couch grass (*yablit*), native to Palestine. A notoriously tenacious weed, *yablit* bedeviled the Hebrew settlers, as its deep roots were extremely difficult to eradicate. For Lamdan, the process of eliminating bilingualism was akin to the backbreaking physical labor of the early settlers; both farmers and writers had to uproot their respective *yablit* so that they could sow the fields for future productivity. Much like Shlonsky, who saw bilingualism as an incurable disease that threatened the health of the new Jewish nation, Lamdan identified bilingualism as a pernicious growth that threatened the future of Hebrew society. However, Lamdan clearly structured this cultural analogue to Zionist labor along generational lines. He claimed that only the younger generation was able to clearly discern the dangers of this cultural blurring.

In contrast to the Brigade protests, Shlonsky and Lamdan's essays did not object to Yiddish per se, but to Hebrew-Yiddish bilingualism. Yet when read in concert, the five *Ketuvim* essays sought to rekindle the Language War with their inflammatory rhetoric. Physical contact, in this case the reception of the two Yiddish writers, provoked renewed literary-linguistic conflict. Shteinman emphasized this point in his concluding essay: "These articles serve as a proclamation of our mobilization as Hebrews, who must strengthen themselves and redouble their strength and desire for our Hebrew movement and set out for a new and renewed attack on all of the systems that oppose us, on near and far fronts. . . . No, brothers in this land and other lands, we have not yielded! We shall not yield!"[46] Shteinman incited readers to launch a new offensive against the enemies of Hebrew. In this debate as a whole, it is remarkable how the rhetoric remained focused on the relationship between Hebrew and Yiddish and ignored the fact that Jews were increasingly turning to other languages, such as Russian, Polish, and English. Despite the concern they expressed for Hebrew in the diaspora, the *Ketuvim* writers saw Ash's worries about assimilation as limited to Yiddish and ignored, for example, the fact that young Polish Jews were abandoning both Jewish languages in favor of Polish. The cultural politics of the Language War, even before the Czernowitz Conference, had pitted Hebrew against Yiddish and left no room for other competing languages. In renewing the battle cry against Yiddish, Shteinman maintained this cultural myopia as he targeted "all of the systems that oppose us" but named only Yiddish and Yiddishists as threats.

Reactions against the *Ketuvim* essays came fast and furious in the Hebrew press. The next issue of *Ketuvim* featured a scathing response by Ya'akov Fichman, who ridiculed the accusations that were made by the five *Ketuvim* contributors, arguing that they epitomized all that was wrong with Hebrew literature, all show and no substance. "I am not so naïve to think that the tragic question of language can be solved by a nice conversation at a reception," Fichman wrote. "But we thought we had the opportunity to inform both camps that there is no need for fanaticism or madness."[47] Moshe Glikson agreed that Bialik's remarks had been overly conciliatory, but scolded both Brigade leaders and *Ketuvim* writers for going too far, insisting, "We do not fight against Yiddish, we negate Yiddish."[48] Ultimately it was *Ketuvim* writers' attacks on Bialik, not their denunciations of Hebrew-Yiddish bilingualism or the mission to rescue Hebrew in the diaspora, that provoked the biggest controversy.

The Yiddish press also reported on the furor in Palestine, though in a surprisingly circumspect manner. Both *Haynt* and *Literarishe bleter*, published in Warsaw, rationalized the Brigade's "encouragement" of speaking Hebrew in the Yishuv. However, *Haynt*'s Tel Aviv correspondent Sh. Pietrushka pointed out that compelling people who did not know modern Hebrew to speak the language was ridiculous, while *Literarishe bleter* implored Hebrew writers to intervene so that such extremism would not continue unchecked.[49] *Der moment*'s Tel Aviv correspondent Y. L. Wohlmann provided a far more sarcastic perspective, describing the events as an alarming "paper war" (*papirene milkhome*).[50] Ash and Hirshbeyn, who both published extensively in the Yiddish press, declined to comment publicly on the aftermath of the reception, though Hirshbeyn published a highly critical article about the poor state of Hebrew and the repression of Yiddish in Palestine several months later in *Literarishe bleter*.[51]

Counter-counterattacks followed the counterattacks, as the *Ketuvim* Five defended their criticism as well as their right to criticize and other voices weighed in. The May 25 issue of *Ketuvim* shows the rhetorical escalation of the ongoing debate. Its front cover foregrounded a letter from the Hebrew scholar and critic Yosef Klausner, who depicted himself as a longtime warrior against Yiddish and insisted "that *zhargon* is more dangerous to us than any other foreign language precisely because it is not so foreign to us."[52] Immediately following Klausner's piece was another letter, this one from Sholem Ash himself. Writing in a stiff Hebrew, Ash thanked the people of the land of Israel for their warm welcome and commended their efforts to build the land. He thanked the Zionist leadership, the General Federation of Labor (*Histadrut*), and finally the great Ch. N. Bialik and—without any apparent irony—the Association of Hebrew Writers "for the love that you showered upon me."[53] It is hard to imagine that Ash could have been unaware of the protests that accompanied his visit, but he chose to ignore the controversy, both in this parting gesture in the Hebrew press and in his reports published in the Yiddish press. By juxtaposing his note of thanks with Klausner's polemical case against Yiddish, *Ketuvim*'s editor insinuated that Ash's sentiments were yet another example of the insidious threat Yiddish posed to the future of the Zionist project.

The debate over Hebrew-Yiddish bilingualism in the press was more than a pretense for literary generational struggle or an outpouring of vitriol against Yiddish. Rather, it reveals distinct constituencies within the Hebrew cultural establishment that were distinguished by their views on the relationship between the growing Jewish community in prestate Palestine and the diaspora, and between the traditional Eastern European centers of Ashkenazi Jewish culture and the emerging centers in the Yishuv and the United States. The many metaphors for the literary-linguistic relationship between Hebrew and Yiddish in fact camouflaged a fundamentally metonymic approach to language that underlies this debate and Hebrew discourse more generally at this time. Yiddish, and specifically Yiddish culture, stood in for the entire Ashkenazi Jewish diaspora, while Hebrew was part and parcel of the nationalist project. Initially, the "Language Question," as articulated at the Czernowitz Conference, had been about which Jewish language should be the national language of the Jewish people. But in the Yishuv, that question had been answered: Hebrew was *the* language of the Jewish people and the Zionist national project. That answer was accepted by virtually all of the participants in the debate and enforced by the Brigade of Defenders of the Language. This debate, however, was prompted by a revised version of that question: Which Jewish language should ensure the Jewish future in the diaspora? As Klausner points out, both Hebrew and Yiddish writers were aware of the fact that the majority of Jews were not in the Land of Israel, a status quo that seemed unlikely to change from the vantage point of 1927. The *Ketuvim* group and its supporters attacked Bialik's metaphorical representation of the relationship between Hebrew and Yiddish, but in fact they were contesting the metonymic truce that had been tacitly agreed upon at the reception for Ash and Hirshbeyn.

Given the scholarly consensus that the Hebrew-Yiddish polysystem had collapsed by the early 1920s, it is important to stress that both the confrontational camp (*Ketuvim* Five) and the conciliatory camp (Bialik et al.) in this debate conceived of the Yishuv as part of a larger Jewish cultural system that encompassed the Ashkenazi Jewish diaspora. Cultural developments in the Soviet Union, for example, were of immense interest and concern for these Hebrew writers. Similarly, speakers at the reception were highly attuned to the messages that they were sending to Yiddish speakers and readers in Europe and the United States. Conceived alternately as transcultural or translingual, this was a debate over the future of Jewish language and literature: the continuation of Hebrew-Yiddish literary bilingualism or the triumph of Hebraic monolingualism.

Literary-Linguistic Ambivalence

This episode, with its grand rhetoric and public pronouncements, revolves around a series of linguistic and cultural binaries in the Yishuv: the old guard, products of the traditional literary bilingualism of Eastern European Jewish centers, versus the young bucks, casting off the bilingual strictures and structures of the past; Hebraists versus Yiddishists; the Yishuv versus the Jewish diaspora. The situation, however, was far more complex that its polemical representations would suggest. Polemical speech tends toward the vivid metaphor and the call to arms, both of which were evident in responses to the Ash-Hirshbeyn reception. A closer look at the main participants in the public drama demonstrates both the inconsistencies in literary practice and the ambivalence toward language that were submerged within the cultural polemic.

On the pages of Hebrew papers, one story unfolded: two prominent Yiddishists were warmly welcomed by the reigning Hebrew national poet, who was attacked by an ideologically driven cadre of young writers. But the story is not quite so simple. Neither Ash nor Hirshbeyn were official emissaries of any Yiddish cultural institutions, much less representatives of the Yiddishist camp. They were prominent writers who published regularly in the Yiddish press, but they did not speak for Yiddish literature as a whole, nor did they represent the Yiddishist ideological vanguard. Similarly, Bialik was represented as defending Yiddish though he had clearly asserted the supremacy of Hebrew.[54] But it is in the cases of Shteinman and Shlonsky, leaders of the *Ketuvim* insurrection, that literary-linguistic inconsistencies are most surprising and most significant. Despite their ferocious attacks on Hebrew-Yiddish bilingualism, both Shteinman and Shlonsky were still deeply engaged with Yiddish in their literary work.

One of the key terms that recurred in arguments surrounding the Yiddish Affair was the danger of *tishtush*, the blurring between Hebrew and Yiddish and the historical, social, and ideological boundaries between them. In *Ketuvim*, Shlonsky faulted the "blurring and concessions" at the gathering for being dangerous and irresponsible.[55] Lamdan, too, railed against this pernicious blurring, insisting that it was impossible for a writer to straddle the Hebrew-Yiddish border.[56] Klausner pronounced, "it is an unforgivable sin to blur [*le-tashtesh*] the principled, historical, and deep opposition between Hebrew and Zhargon."[57] But the literary work of both Shteinman and Shlonsky reveals precisely the kind of blurring of literary-linguistic boundaries that they and their allies denounced on the pages of *Ketuvim*. Shteinman fulminated against the Yiddish establishment's treatment of Hebrew in Poland and the Soviet Union as he published regularly in the Warsaw Yiddish paper *Der moment*. Shlonsky's 1927 campaign against Bialik and his condemnation of bilingualism was accompanied by his publication of a Hebrew poetic collection infused with Yiddish words and associations. While Shteinman and Shlonsky appeared publicly antagonistic toward Hebrew-Yiddish bilingualism, lingering linguistic associations and contemporary realities led to far more ambiguous attitudes toward language in literary practice.

Between Warsaw and Tel Aviv

In the midst of the commotion surrounding *Ketuvim*, Hebrew writer Avigdor Ha-me'iri ridiculed these new Hebrew zealots, Shteinman in particular: "Shteinman with his protests and his jealousy on behalf of Hebrew—this, my friends, is pure caricature: Shteinman the professional *zhargon* correspondent, who plies his art and livelihood to this very day in newspapers in Warsaw and America—Shteinman fights the fight for the Hebrew language . . . Shteinman who protests against Yiddish—in fact profits from Yiddish. In others' hands, the Yiddish language is vermin; but in his own hands, a tasty roast. *Bon appetite*!"[58] Ha-me'iri accuses Shteinman of hypocrisy for simultaneously campaigning against Yiddish in Palestine and publishing in Yiddish in Poland. Not only was the editor of *Ketuvim* and self-appointed champion of the Hebrew language publishing regularly in Yiddish, but apparently that fact was well known among his colleagues.[59] Certainly anyone who read *Der moment*, one of the major Yiddish dailies in Warsaw with a circulation of over 20,000 copies per day in the 1920s, would have come across Shteinman's Friday columns.[60] Ha-me'iri's barbed comments, however, stopped neither Shteinman's Yiddish writing nor his zealous defense of Hebrew. Despite the fact that he published columns in Yiddish within days of the Yiddish Affair, Shteinman did not see himself as a bilingual writer. His bifurcated literary production—Hebrew in the Yishuv, Yiddish in Poland—demonstrates that the Hebrew-Yiddish bilingualism contested in the Hebrew press in 1927 was both a very real phenomenon at the time and subject to interpretation.

Like many of his colleagues, Shteinman (1892–1970) started publishing at a young age in both Hebrew and Yiddish Eastern European periodicals. His memoirs chronicle encounters with Abramovitsh, Bialik, Peretz, and especially David Frishman, for whom he worked for several years as an assistant, and depict an Eastern European cultural scene in which it was natural for a young writer to compose in both Jewish languages.[61] From 1920 until 1930, however, two aspects of his career remained constant as he moved from Odessa to Warsaw to Tel Aviv: Shteinman wrote passionately about the significance of Hebrew language and culture, and he published regular columns in Yiddish in *Der moment.* In early 1920s Warsaw, such bilingual publishing was far less common than it had been fifteen years earlier, but it still existed. Writers like H. D. Nomberg, Ash, and Hirshbeyn had all started writing in Hebrew but switched to Yiddish within a few years of publishing in Eastern European Jewish periodicals. Similarly, writers like S. Y. Agnon, Ya'akov Shteinberg, and Aharon Reuveni shifted from writing in Yiddish or Yiddish and Hebrew to writing exclusively in Hebrew over the first two decades of the twentieth century, typically after immigrating to Palestine. Despite many examples of writers' transitions from literary bilingualism to monolingualism, Shteinman was far from the only writer still publishing in Yiddish and Hebrew in the early 1920s: Uri Zvi Greenberg had been publishing his expressionist poetry in Hebrew and Yiddish since 1912, Aharon Zeitlin was writing lyrical and mystical poetry in both languages, and, as we will see in chapter 3, Y. D. Berkovitz and Zalman Shneour published extensively in both languages.[62]

In contrast to Greenberg and Zeitlin, however, Shteinman maintained a clear distinction between his work in Hebrew and Yiddish, evident from the beginning of the 1920s. In Hebrew, Shteinman's early novel *Esther Chayot* (1922) anticipated key features of his evolving modernist prose. Toward the beginning of the novel, the narrative follows Esther's thoughts during a relatively rare moment of peace in a busy household: "At these hours when silence reigned there were times when Esther Chayot's eyes were opened wide; her powers of discernment would become clear and her mind would catch things that had stymied her at first. It is clear that a lie, a giant one, loomed over life. All of the years of youth, all of the tender soul's quivering, all of the spirit's burdens, the heart's throbbing, virginity's grief and the whispers of the willows and lovers in the moonlight and all of the hopes amounted to nothing more than an opening to a certain something small and weak, a speck of pleasure, whose vital power escapes and is proven false in the span of a minute."[63] Shteinman's narrator delves into Esther's psyche, tracing her alienation from the world surrounding her and her frustrated passions. The narrator, like many of Shteinman's characters, resembles the unmoored protagonist Ulrich of Robert Musil's *The Man without Qualities*, while Esther shares characteristics with Henrik Ibsen's Nora from *A Doll's House*, namely her intense, contradictory desires. While uprooted, alienated men fill the early-twentieth-century Hebrew prose of writers like M. Y. Berdichevsky, Uri Nissan Gnessin, and Y. H. Brenner, Shteinman's *Esther Chayot* and the later *Zugot* (Couples, 1930) feature female protagonists, situating these women between the stultifying atmosphere of provincial Eastern European towns and the often unattainable promises of the city, with a generous dose of Strindbergesque spiritual contemplation and Freudian psychoanalysis.[64]

Shteinman's linguistic and formal choices, however, differentiate him from his literary colleagues. In the above passage from *Esther*

Chayot, narrative description shifts into psychological reflection verging on philosophical contemplation. Rather than simply explaining the great lie that dominates her life, one overwrought image is stacked on top of the next, from the tender soul to the burdened spirit to the throbbing heart and beyond, using clichés to evoke precisely the youthful naïveté that is being deflated. Yisrael Zmora, a critic associated with Shteinman and Shlonsky's *Ketuvim* group, praised Shteinman as a "master of abundance" thanks to his wide-ranging topics and genres and his unique approach to the Hebrew language.[65] Shteinman's Hebrew prose is full of adjectives, neologisms, parables, and other linguistic games, often breaking apart idioms and creating new ones, at times strangely at odds with the generally somber tone of his prose. When describing Esther's psychological state, the text slyly emphasizes *koach chayuto*, the vital power, of this disappointingly small "speck of pleasure" rather than the imagined grand passion. The word *chayut*, vitality, is a homograph of *chayot*, animals, which is also Esther's last name. The wordplay emphasizes Esther Chayot's search for vital life forces and animal passions. As he explained in the essay "Ha-lashon al ha-ovnayim" (Language on the Potter's Wheel), the task of the writer was to "expand and create breaches in language" provided such breaches were spiritually necessary.[66] His modernist approach to language matched his efforts, starting in the 1920s and continuing through the 1930s, to find a distinctly modernist way of writing in Hebrew. "Can there be a modern story?" Shteinman asked at the beginning of a 1936 essay.[67] Shteinman rejected realism, telling his readers at the beginning of the novel *Duda'im* (Tel Aviv, 1931), "I will not deal much with events, accidents, adventures and the like in the unfolding of my story. Not mine and not others."[68] He insisted that the time demanded an "internal plot" freed from conventional plotting and narration.[69] This resistance to realism, as well as the fragmentation of his prose and the foregrounding of a spiritually inclined, reflective omniscient narrator emerge full force in his modernist fiction in the 1930s.

The Yiddish Shteinman looks quite different from the Hebrew Shteinman. Shteinman's *Ukraine veynt* (Ukraine Cries, 1923), published a year after *Esther Chayot*, is a topical novel, chronicling the violence against Jews during the Ukrainian Civil War in 1919. It narrates the life of a *shtetl* rather an individual, and registers the effects of brutal events on the town and its inhabitants. When one of the characters tries to raise his listeners' spirits about the uncertainty caused by the revolution, for example, there is a collective, not an individual, reaction: "The doom and gloom in the *shtetl* became even thicker, like a threatening cloud, full, ready to pour itself out, and enveloped the *shtetl*."[70] Though there are glimpses of Shteinman's propensity for stringing adjectives together and his verbose Hebrew, his Yiddish prose concentrates on describing this small town, not on penetrating the psyches of its characters. In contrast to Bergelson's expressionist story "Beginning of Kislev 1919" in *Milgroym*, Shteinman's literary description of the slaughter of Ukrainian Jews is presented in realistic prose, set in a Ukrainian town populated with a range of Jewish characters. He uses Yiddish primarily to memorialize those killed, and only secondarily as a literary or philosophical tool. Beyond *Ukraine veynt*, Shteinman published relatively little fiction in Yiddish. Yiddish, his bibliography suggests, was the language for essays and other topical subjects; Hebrew, for literature.

In Yiddish, Shteinman is a fine essayist: clear and readable with deft humor, persuasive without being strident, varied in his topics and approaches. Sharing *Der moment*'s pages with frequent contributors such as Hillel Zeitlin, Rokhl (Rachel) Feygenberg, and Zalman Shneour, Shteinman reflected on the challenges of being a Jewish writer, Jewish refugees, film technology, and other topics.[71] From late 1924, Shteinman became one of the paper's unofficial correspondents in Palestine, posting a series of columns about his journey to the land of Israel in 1924 and often focusing on Palestine-related topics, reporting in detail on the July 1927 earthquake in Palestine, publishing a multipart expose on the exploitation of Eastern European Jewish immigrants on their journeys to Palestine, and musing about the Palestinian climate. Gershon Shaked criticizes Shteinman's Hebrew prose for staying mired in Eastern Europe, for lacking any ideological perspective, and for being overly psychological, a "European voice in the Zionist desert."[72] Ironically, Shteinman's Yiddish essays remedy each of these perceived problems: they focus on Palestine, not Poland; they are strongly Zionist; and, for the most part, they eschew psychological analysis in favor of providing European readers glimpses of life in the land of Israel. Thus Shteinman of *Der moment* is distinct from Shteinman the Hebrew novelist.

However, there are texts that bridge the divide between Shteinman's Yiddish and Hebrew writing. In *Tsu mentsh un folk* (To Man and Folk, 1922), a collection of Yiddish essays on the state of Jewish culture, there are glimpses of Shteinman the modernist and Shteinman the Hebraist that would not have suited the pages of *Der moment*. Writing in a Yiddish filled with vivid images and rampant adjectives, Shteinman insisted that he turned to Yiddish out of necessity given the deteriorating state of Jewish life after World War I: "In the Yiddish language I have written about and esteemed the power of the toiling folk . . . But my ardor, my flame, my Hebrew fire were in *golus* [diaspora]."[73] Here and throughout his Yiddish prose, Shteinman emphasized his commitment to Zionism and the Hebrew language. Like S. Y. Abramovitsh and Sholem Aleykhem, who justified their "conversions" to Yiddish by the need to reach the Jewish masses, Shteinman aimed to reach Yiddish readers in the diaspora in order to promote Jewish culture. But unlike the classic Yiddish writers, Shteinman saw Yiddish as a cultural duty, his personal diaspora. Hebrew, as he makes clear in the essay "Hebraists" later in the same volume, is the ancient, spiritual, and lofty tongue.[74] In *Kolot* (Voices, 1923–1924), a monthly Hebrew journal he founded and edited, Shteinman used a similarly ardent Hebrew to profess his dedication to the language:

> We, who view all existence in its entirety through the twenty-two Hebrew letters.
>
> We will continue the tradition.
>
> The Hebrew, the dreamer-fighter, the believer, brother please come meet us
>
> Hear!
>
> Help!
>
> Love![75]

In both Hebrew and Yiddish prose, Shteinman employed dramatic repetition, vivid images, and copious adjectives to make his case not just for Hebrew but for the continued relevance of Hebrew in the diaspora.

Shteinman, living in Warsaw at the time, had no objections to writing in Yiddish, especially when Yiddish was enlisted on Hebrew's behalf. He did, however, object to bilingual writing, lashing out at bilingual writers in another Hebrew essay from the early 1920s entitled "Ki kin'at betkha akhaltani" (Because Zeal for Thy House Hath Consumed Me). As part of his argument that Hebrew writers had to create their own writers' association in Warsaw, Shteinman rejects Hebrew-Yiddish bilingualism: "There are writers like these, who serve both languages and both literatures. They are torn [*kruʿim*]. They carry the tear in their hearts. But it is impossible to create an association from the beginning with this tear. It is impossible to sew a garment from shreds."[76] Invoking Romantic views of language as the inner essence of a people, Shteinman argues that any writer who tries to serve more than one literature corrupts the necessary interiority of literary language and is consequently incapable of producing worthwhile literature in either language. His argument against literary bilingualism—anticipating his comments in *Ketuvim* in 1927—is part of his rejection of the claim that Yiddish and Hebrew writers could continue to coexist as part of a single Association of Jewish Writers and Journalists in Warsaw.

Shteinman's comments on the impossibility of Hebrew-Yiddish bilingualism suggest that he did not consider himself a bilingual writer. Instead, Shteinman subscribed to an older symbiotic view of Eastern European Jewish bilingualism in which the languages and their literatures complemented rather than competed with each other. Shteinman did not see himself as serving two languages and literatures, but rather promoting Hebrew literature and ideology while writing in both Hebrew and Yiddish. This differentiation makes sense in the context of the linguistic logic that long defined Eastern European Jewish culture: Hebrew was the indisputable high language of literature, Yiddish was the language of the masses. Simultaneously writing in Yiddish and disparaging the language, Shteinman followed in the footsteps of *maskilim*, Jewish enlighteners, who saw their Yiddish prose as a necessary evil or, in some cases, a secret pleasure. But as Ha-me'iri pointed out, Shteinman's rickety rationalization was at odds with his bilingual writing during the 1920s.

Shteinman was unusual because he maintained this differential bilingualism, writing different kinds of texts in each language, well beyond its cultural heyday. At the beginning of the twentieth century, the differential bilingualism of writers like M. Y. Berdichevsky, who used distinct styles and genres in Hebrew, Yiddish, and German, coexisted with a more integral approach, represented by S. Y. Abramovitsh's rewriting of most of his literary texts in Hebrew and Yiddish.[77] Thanks to Abramovitsh, bilingual writing was regarded not just as a way for a Jewish writer to finance his literary endeavors but as a literary achievement in its own right. By the 1920s, both differential and integral approaches to literary bilingualism were declining as a result of the politicization and geographic dispersion of Eastern European Jewish culture, setting Shteinman apart from his contemporaries. In Poland, Shteinman's Yiddish colleagues in the Jewish Writers and Journalists Union would have strongly objected to his categorization of Yiddish as a language whose primary purposes were either to uplift the masses or to subsidize Hebrew literary pursuits. In Palestine, many of his Hebrew colleagues would have similarly objected to the implication that Hebrew was effective primarily for "high" literature.

Whether conceived as hypocritical (à la Ha-me'iri) or routine (Shteinman himself), Shteinman's combination of fierce anti-Yiddish rhetoric and frequent Yiddish publication highlights the transitional nature of this literary-linguistic moment. Shteinman's 1927 attacks on Yiddish and Yiddish writers in *Ketuvim* only make sense if he considered himself a Hebrew writer who published in Yiddish, not a bilingual Hebrew-Yiddish writer. His distinction, however, is more than mere semantics; he defined bilingualism not as the ability to write in two different languages, an ability possessed by the majority of early twentieth-century Hebrew and Yiddish writers born in Eastern Europe, but the equal commitment to both languages and literatures, a premise he vociferously rejected. Yet shared features in Shteinman's Hebrew and Yiddish prose complicate this distinction. Though he wrote fiction almost entirely in Hebrew, Shteinman's narrators often sound very much like his essayistic persona in both Hebrew and Yiddish: keenly interested in psychology; reflective, often spiritual; loquacious, or, as Zmora would say, "abundant." Even his insistence—in both Yiddish and Hebrew essays—that the modern Hebrew writer must endure the profound loneliness of writing in the "eternal tongue" resonates with the lonely and socially isolated characters in his Hebrew fiction. Thus a parallel, if not identical, Shteinman is recognizable in both Hebrew and Yiddish. His attempts to suppress Hebrew-Yiddish bilingualism, denying his own bilingual output and criticizing that of others, do not signify the death knell of literary bilingualism but rather affirm the stubborn presence and relevance of Yiddish in the Yishuv.

The Language of *Aba-Ima*

Like Shteinman, Avraham Shlonsky (1900–1973) vigorously expressed his opposition to Hebrew-Yiddish bilingualism in *Ketuvim*. But in contrast to Shteinman, Shlonsky was not a bilingual writer: he published many Hebrew works and Hebrew translations from Russian, French, and Yiddish, but he did not publish in Yiddish. Immigrating to Palestine as a young adult, Shlonsky established his literary career in the Yishuv, part of a post-Czernowitz generation.[78] Writers like Shlonsky embarked upon their careers in the wake of the political and cultural politicization of language represented by the Czernowitz Conference and after World War I and the Russian Revolution had left the centers of Eastern European bilingualism in disarray. Shlonsky had been too young to knock on Peretz's door and gather with fellow Hebrew and Yiddish writers or to experience the vibrant literary life of prewar Odessa. Instead, he joined the revolutionary ethos of the Third Aliyah, draining the swamps and cultivating the wilderness in Palestine, though in Shlonsky's case, only for a few months before returning to the relatively urban Tel Aviv. An ardent socialist, he inscribed himself in the Zionist narrative of the Hebrew pioneer in the poetry collection *Ba-galgal* (In the Whirlwind, 1927), seeking to create a resolutely new and modernist Hebrew literature in the Yishuv. That is why the Yiddish that surfaces in another collection of Shlonsky's poetry published in 1927 is so surprising. In Shlonsky's *Le-aba-ima* (To Papa-Mama, 1927), Yiddish echoes within the Hebrew lyric poetry, a textual translingualism that contrasts with Shteinman's literary bilingualism.

The controversy surrounding Ash and Hirshbeyn's visit was not the first time that Shlonsky had targeted Bialik in the context of Jewish multilingualism. In early 1923, Shlonsky participated in an issue of the literary journal *Hedim* dedicated to Bialik on the occasion of his fiftieth birthday. In the familiar company of Ya'akov Rabinovitsh, Asher Barash, and Yitzchak Lamdan, who sing Bialik's praises in short essays, Shlonsky formally and thematically broke ranks. Shlonsky's piece, "Le-yovel Bialik" (For Bialik's Jubilee), incongruously draws Bialik into the harsh pioneering life: "To lie in a tent and feel its canvas: 'Will the rain seep in?' And go back to reading the most modern of modern books under a coarse gray standard-issue blanket, or to wail: '*beladi! beladi!*' [my hometown! my hometown!] and to think: 'a twig alighted on a fence—and dozed' and to think: there, far away in Europe—falling leaves . . . Beneath the gray coarse blanket they will lug the scythes beneath the tin roof of the 'kitchen,' and feet threshing, stomping, dancing: '*di mame kokht varenikes—un ikh bin fleyshig*' [Mama's cooking dumplings—but I ate meat]."[79] Shlonsky established himself as a pioneering modernist in this short piece, a collage of images and words. As his speaker huddles in his tent in the cold rain of a Palestinian winter, his narrative darts between the land of Israel and Europe, between fragments of Bialik's poetry and disjointed modernist phrases, between Hebrew, Arabic, and Yiddish. A critical dimension of this text is its language: the exuberant, fragmented modernist language and the different languages. Shlonsky's neologistic Hebrew is situated between the sounds of this new land: the Arabic *beladi* (my country, my hometown), phrases from Bialik's European-inflected Ashkenazic Hebrew, and the first line of a Yiddish folksong, *di mame kokht varenikes—un ikh bin fleyshig* (Mama cooks milk dumplings—but I ate meat).[80] The juxtaposition of these linguistic fragments creates a masterful effect of dislocation in this pioneering camp, at the mythologized moment of territorialization. The plaintive Arabic cry ironically recalls the European home that has been left behind, while the Yiddish expression of thwarted desire is literalized in the makeshift kitchen mired in the Palestinian mud. Shlonsky's text simultaneously valorizes and undermines the figure of the heroic pioneer, sardonically mapping Bialik's poetry onto the "new pioneering reality" but revealing the speaker's linguistic and emotional yearning for the past represented by both Bialik and Yiddish.

This text's evocation of the quintessential pioneering experience is thoroughly multilingual, as the language of past (Yiddish), present (Arabic), and future (Hebrew) lands intermingle. Thus even as it questions the relevance of previous literary paradigms—Bialik's poetry—to this new Hebrew space, it acknowledges the translingualism of this new Hebrew man and his text. Ideological or cultural transformations are not accomplished instantaneously or by fiat; rather, the Palestinian landscape coexists with a remembered Eastern European landscape, the Arabic heard in Palestine mixes with the Yiddish of childhood.

While Shlonsky effectively used a Yiddish phrase to evoke the modernist dislocation of the pioneer in "Le-yovel Bialik," Yiddish played a more sustained role in his poetry from the mid-1920s. Shlonsky's early poetry is filled with neologisms and linguistic virtuosity, as his texts transform modern Hebrew into a supple instrument of poetic rhyme, rhythm, and sound. Yiddish is not central to his poetics in *Dvay* (Distress, 1924), though he shared aspects of his modernist aesthetics with Yiddish Expressionists like Perets Markish and Introspectivists like A. Leyeles.[81] But one of Shlonsky's best-known poems, or more precisely, the concluding section of a poetic cycle, "Halbishini, ima kshera" (Clothe Me, Dear Mother), first published in 1924 and later included in both *Le-aba-ima* (1927) and *Bagalgal* (1927), further develops the tension between Yiddish and the pioneering spirit evident in "Le-yovel Bialik."[82] That tension, however, is not necessarily apparent from an initial reading of the poem, with its images and allusions:

הַלְבִּישִׁינִי, אִמָּא כְּשֵׁרָה, כְּתֹנֶת פַּסִּים לְתִפְאֶרֶת
וְעִם שַׁחֲרִית הוֹבִילִינִי אֱלֵי עָמָל.

עוֹטְפָה אַרְצִי אוֹר כַּטַּלִּית,
בָּתִּים נִצְּבוּ כַּטּוֹטָפוֹת,
וְכִרְצוּעוֹת תְּפִלִּין גּוֹלְשִׁים כְּבִישִׁים, סָלְלוּ כַּפַּיִם.

תְּפִלַּת שַׁחֲרִית פֹּה תִּתְפַּלֵּל קִרְיָה נָאָה אֱלֵי בּוֹרְאָהּ.
וּבַבּוֹרְאִים — בְּנֵךְ אַבְרָהָם,
פַּיְטָן סוֹלֵל בְּיִשְׂרָאֵל.

וּבָעֶרֶב בֵּין הַשְּׁמָשׁוֹת יָשׁוּב אַבָּא מִסִּבְלוֹתָיו
וְכִתְפִלָּה יִלְחַשׁ נַחַת :
הֲבֵן יַקִּיר לִי אַבְרָהָם,
עוֹר וְגִידִים וַעֲצָמוֹת —
הַלְלוּיָהּ.

הַלְבִּישִׁינִי, אִמָּא כְּשֵׁרָה, כְּתֹנֶת פַּסִּים לְתִפְאֶרֶת
וְעִם שַׁחֲרִית הוֹבִילִינִי
אֱלֵי עָמָל.[83]

Clothe me, dear mother, in splendor in a coat of many colors
And with the dawn lead me to toil.

My land is wrapped in light like a prayer shawl,
Houses stand like frontlets
Roads stream like phylactery straps, paved by many palms.

Here the lovely city recites morning prayers to its creator.
And among the creators—your son Avraham,
Poet-paver in Israel.

In the evening twilight father will return from his travails
And like a prayer whisper slowly:
My dear son Avraham,

> Skin and sinews and bones—
> Hallelujah.
>
> Clothe me, dear mother, in splendor in a coat of many colors
> And at dawn lead me
> to toil.

The lyric speaker focuses on the male body that will be clothed in parental love and then toil on the land. As he creates a secular-sacred poem-prayer that weaves together glimpses of the newly built homeland with traditional religious imagery, Shlonsky's lyric persona identifies himself as "your son Avraham / Poet-paver in Israel." The avant-garde celebration of labor, with its vivid imagery and expressionist rhythms, continually refers to the speaker's family; from the opening apostrophe to the mother to the father's whispered prayer, it alludes to a parade of biblical sons, from Abraham and Isaac's early morning journey (Genesis 22) to Jacob's gift of a coat of many colors to Joseph (Genesis 37). At the same time, it provides an exalted, almost ecstatic view of the new land. Leah Goldberg attempts to reconcile these dimensions into a synthetic whole, reading this poem biographically as a bridge between the Jewish diaspora and the Zionist experience, the two sides of the poet's life: "This is the bridge upon which the poet stood above the river of his life, one bank—the tradition of the Jewish nation, papa and mama, who belong to the tradition of Jewish diaspora more than the poet's actual personal biography, and the Hebrew language, the language of prayer in its essence; and the other bank—roads being paved and houses being built in a steamy old-new land, and that same Hebrew language, beginning to call objects by name."[84] Goldberg suggests that "Halbishini" bridges the Jewish past and future, the diaspora and the land of Israel, a sacred and a secular Hebrew. But in representing the poem as a link between these dichotomies, Goldberg—a contemporary of Shlonsky and fellow participant in the first generation of Hebrew modernists, the *moderna*—obscures a different linguistic duality that is built into the poem and reflected in its curious publication history.

First published in 1924, "Halbishini" appeared as the last section of the poem "Amal" (Toil), a poetic representation of the manual labor that culminates with the houses and freshly paved roads of "Halbishini." "Amal" was included in the "Gilboa" section of Shlonsky's collection *Ba-galgal* (1927), a showcase for the young, canonical Avraham Shlonsky, from the modernist satire of "Honolulu" to the images of revolution in "Srak" (Bareness) and the celebration of land and labor in "Gilboa." From its beginning, the full poem focuses on the working body of its lyric protagonist:

כַּף יָד לָנוּ קְטַנָּה וְאֶצְבָּעוֹת חָמֵשׁ לָהּ,
אֶצְבְּעוֹת-שַׁעֲוָה דַקּוֹת לְהִשָּׁבֵר,
בְּרֵאשִׁיתָן הוֹלֵם דֹּפֶק וּבִקְצֵיהֶן — צִפָּרְנַיִם.
הָהּ מַה נַּעַשׂ לָאֶצְבָּעוֹת בַּיּוֹם שֶׁיְּעֻבַּד בָּן?[85]

We have a little hand and it has five fingers,
Wax-fingers delicate enough to break
At one end beats a pulse and at the other—fingernails.
Oh, what shall we do to the fingers when they are put to
work?

These first lines focus on the hand, detailing its component parts: first the fingers, then the fingernails. But even before the collective "we" reveals the body that owns these hands, they are consecrated to manual labor, as the poem looks forward to the day when—not if—they begin to toil. Shlonsky deftly rewrites a verse from the Song of Songs to express the inevitability of this labor: "We have a little sister, and she has no breasts. What shall we do for our sister when she is spoken for?"[86] Shlonsky's poem replaces the little sister with the poetic speaker, as her absent breasts are transformed into the speaker's childish hands. Just as this girl will mature sexually, these delicate fingers will be dedicated to manual labor. The hands plunge the poem into an exaltation of labor through the glorification of the male body: its fingers gripping a sickle, sweat dripping from a high forehead over hairy flesh, fists on the sand. The feminized little hands of the yeshiva student are transformed into the new worker's hands, hairy and callused.

The poet-paver Avraham in "Halbishini," the fourth and final section of the poem, becomes an extension of the masculine Jewish body. The concluding poem immediately evokes this body, summoning the mother figure to "clothe me in splendor in a coat of many colors," and soon after, mapping the landscape of Mt. Gilboa onto a different male body, that of a man garbed with accoutrements of prayer. The poem reverses a traditional biblical metaphor, turning the land-as-sexualized-woman into the land-as-worshipping-man to inscribe a new religion of labor. In the context of the preceding sections of the poem, written in free verse, these lines also read as free verse in the new Israeli pronunciation. The repetition of words that evoke this landscape under construction, such as toil (*amal*), houses (*batim*), town (*kirya*), and road (*kvish*), knit together the different sections of the poem with the language and the rhetoric of labor Zionism. The speaker's declaration, "we are going to toil," is echoed at both the beginning of the full poem and at the end of "Halbishini," as the speaker enjoins his mother, "lead me to toil," stressing and sanctifying this labor.

"Halbishini," however, was also published in Shlonsky's slim collection of poetry, *Le-aba-ima. Le-aba-ima* is very different from *Ba-galgal*, with lyrical poems that repeatedly invoke the mother and father and mix images of a new land with memories of childhood and biblical allusions. Shlonsky's language is redolent with Yiddish calques and overtones from the title on, as the Hebrew phrase *le-aba-ima* (to papa-mama) is a transparent rendering of the common Yiddish phrase *tate-mame* (lit., papa-mama, referring collectively to parents). Avraham Hagorni-Green suggests that Shlonsky wanted to give his readers a more personal-experiential set of poems that they could identify with after the experimental and somber *Dvay*, while Hagit Halperin contends that this collection was Shlonsky's gift to his parents, a poetic diary of sorts.[87] Either way, the differences in language, tone, and overall atmosphere are astonishing given the fact that all but two of the *Le-aba-ima* poems were reprinted in *Ba-galgal*, revised and scattered throughout the larger collection's different sections. Instead of concluding the poema "Amal," as it does in *Ba-galgal*, "Halbishini" is the last section of the poem "Le-aba-ima." In the context of *Ba-galgal*, "Halbishini" participates in the labor Zionist dream of building the land, with physical hardship dedicated to reviving a national splendor. In *Le-aba-ima*, the poem is surrounded by and infused with images of an Eastern European childhood and echoes of Yiddish. Doubly inscribed in these collections, "Halbishini" registers the poet's affiliations with both the Yiddish of the old parental world and the Hebrew of the new land.[88]

In "Le-aba-ima," feet replace the callused hands of "Amal" and the sweaty, toiling body is replaced by a nostalgic child:

רַגְלַיִם קְטַנּוֹת הָיוּ לָנוּ
(אֶפְרוֹחֵי-אֱלֹהִים! הוֹי, נַחַת אִמָּא-אַבָּא)[89]

We had little feet
(God's chicks! Oh, parents' pride and joy)

Opening with a childlike perspective, this poem first focuses on "little feet" that have taken the poetic speaker far from the world of his parents. The second line immerses the reader in the Yiddish language of *tate-mame*, as the exclamation *efrochei-elohim* (God's chicks) imports the Yiddish endearment *oyfele* (little chick), commonly used to refer to a baby, as well as the parents' *nachat/nakhes* (joy) from their child. As the final poem in the cycle, "Halbishini" reads as a valedictory address to the parental figures, blending a weary self-sacrifice with the ethos of labor, Hebrew with Yiddish. The first line, *ima kshera* (dear mother), is a calque of the Yiddish phrase *koshere mame*, a colloquial endearment that tenderly evokes the generic mother figure of Yiddish folksongs. Similarly, the father is explicitly Yiddishized when he returns from his work and slowly whispers his blessing; the Hebrew word *nachat* is used here as an adverb (slowly, leisurely), but by omitting the preposition typically affixed to the adverb (*be-*) Shlonsky simultaneously elevates his Hebrew and calls to mind the related Yiddish term, *nakhes fun kinder*, a parent's delight in his or her child. This single word encapsulates the complicated linguistic and cultural relationship between the two languages: the Yiddish *nakhes* comes from the Hebrew expression *nachat ruach* (satisfaction), but acquires a new meaning in Yiddish, a parent's pride and delight in a child, which then returns to modern Hebrew with its Yiddish connotations intact. Shlonsky's poem, however, transforms the set phrase *nakhes fun kinder* into *nachat ima-aba*, infusing this parental pride with a reciprocal child's pride and a child-centric view. Here and throughout the collection, parents and children are diffused through the poetic speaker's language. This *nakhes* also knits the larger poem together, appearing three times in the full text: in the second line, as part of the speaker's exclamation of parents' joy in their child: "Oh, a parent's delight" (*hoy, nachat aba-ima*); in the fourth section, as the speaker's brother describes his young daughter: "and leisurely recounts her wisdom" (*vi-ysaper nachat chokhmoteha*); and at the very end of the poem, the father's pride in his laborer-son in "Halbishini." Thus the Hebrew word powerfully evokes Yiddish family and linguistic dynamics, stressing the lyric persona's identity as a Yiddish son.

The poem's linguistic layers are complicated by intricate poetic form, weaving together different meters and rhythms. Though the scansion is not regular, Jordan Finkin points out that there are significant sections that can be read in meter in the Ashkenazic pronunciation characteristic of the Eastern European Hebrew of Shlonsky's poetic predecessors. This Ashkenazic scansion, however, is often disrupted visually by the layout of the lines, which has led most readers to assume that it was written as free verse in the new "Sephardic" or "Israeli" pronunciation adopted in Palestine.[90] Shlonsky, a key figure in the adoption and implementation of a radically different pronunciation scheme in modern Hebrew, was experimenting with the poetic possibilities of both pronunciations in the middle of the 1920s, a period of transition reflected in *Le-aba-ima* as well as in *Ba-galgal.* But interestingly enough, Shlonsky himself suggested that the poem be read in the Ashkenazic pronunciation. In the list of poems at the end of *Le-aba-ima*, Shlonsky differentiated between poems written in the Ashkenazic pronunciation and the new pronunciation, illustrative of his own poetic evolution in the early 1920s. "Le-aba-ima," he tells us, was written with the traditional Ashkenazic stresses.[91] Even the famous middle line, "a poet-paver in Israel," ironically enough scans close to an Ashkenazic trochaic tetrameter: *PAY-tan SOY-lel be-yiz-ROY-el*, a Palestinian poet-paver with a distinct Eastern European flavor.

The strong Yiddish resonances that emerge in the poem "Le-aba-ima" permeate the collection as a whole. *Le-aba-ima* begins with the poem "Tishre," which features a *paytan*, a poet, without the *solel*, the paver, attached. As in "Halbishini," this melancholy poet identifies himself as a son in the first stanza: "the son wants to return / to the lullaby, papa-mama." The lyric speaker wants to return not to some universal state or place, but to the language of childhood. The speaker as poet traces his work and his poetic desires back to a Yiddish point of origin, marked by the recurring phrase *aba-ima* and the invocation of *shir eres*, the lullaby. While some lullabies had been written in Hebrew during the late nineteenth century, a far better known corpus of songs existed in Yiddish.[92] As the vernacular language of Eastern European Jewish communities, Yiddish had typically been the language in which parents would sing their children to sleep, with songs that feature familiar themes, like the distant father. In this poem, however, the son in Palestine is geographically and temporally distant from his parents, reversing the conventional circumstances of early Hebrew lullabies, with their dreams of the Holy Land, and well-known Yiddish ones, with mothers singing songs about absent fathers. Here the lullaby becomes a manifestation of linguistic and personal distance, an intertextual marker of the lost parental world. Shlonsky's speaker is figured as both poet and son in a thoroughly poetic universe, living between his most recent poem and the remembered lullabies. This emphasis on the Eastern European Yiddish roots of the poet inflects the poet-paver of "Halbishini." Throughout *Le-aba-ima*, Yiddish words, rhythms, and references to a Yiddish-speaking childhood seep into Shlonsky's modern Hebrew, creating a translingual poetic collection.

Shlonsky's two 1927 collections, published before and after the controversy surrounding Ash and Hirshbeyn's visit, represent two poetic personas. The first, *Le-aba-ima*, features the homesick *oyfele* (chick) of "Le-aba-ima" in a Yiddish-inflected Jewish tradition, one that infuses "Halbishini" with a remembered childhood Yiddish. The second, *Ba-galgal*, focuses on the canonical laborer-poet of "Amal" in a thoroughly Hebrew evocation of land and labor, one better suited to the nationalism and hostility to Yiddish and Hebrew-Yiddish bilingualism expressed in *Ketuvim*. The poetry of *Le-aba-ima*, as epitomized by "Halbishini," is by no means bilingual: like all of Shlonsky's poetry from the 1920s, it is written in an evocative Hebrew filled with neologisms and vivid imagery. But it is translingual: it summons Yiddish in its vocabulary, rhythmic structure, and themes.

The Hebrew-Yiddish translingualism of *Le-aba-ima* seems to contradict Shlonsky's statements about Yiddish and Hebrew-Yiddish bilingualism in *Ketuvim*. Yiddish, he railed, was a threat to the future of Hebrew literature and a plague on the nation. Shlonsky was far from the first Hebrew writer to integrate Yiddish elements into his Hebrew literary work. But in contrast to writers like Abramovitsh, Bialik, and Yosef Chayim Brenner, who incorporated Yiddish in various ways, Shlonsky's literary assimilation of Yiddish is surprising in view of his simultaneous cultural campaign against the "catastrophe of bilingualism." Not unlike Shteinman's continued bilingual writing, Yiddish within a proper aesthetic context—literally inside of Hebrew poetry—was not perceived as a threat. In Shlonsky's "Le-yovel Bialik," Yiddish is a remnant of the old world that the pioneer struggles to reconcile with the Palestinian present. In *Le-aba-ima*, Yiddish is the resonant language of the parental home, a fond reminder of childhood, but ultimately dedicated to the new Zionist homeland. Yiddish lingers in the poet's idiolect as a translingual marker of the past within a firmly Hebraic present. Despite their combative rhetoric, Shteinman and Shlonsky did not seek to eradicate Yiddish in their writing so much as they sought to situate Yiddish within the Hebraic cultural sphere. In this respect, their uses of Yiddish are updated versions of Bialik's vision for Yiddish in the service of Hebrew culture. As a practitioner of a particular kind of literary bilingualism, Shteinman essentially redomesticated Yiddish, using his Yiddish prose in service of Zionist goals in a manner that had been practiced since the nineteenth century. Shlonsky, by contrast, mixed Yiddish into his Hebrew poetry, a particular kind of translingual literary practice in which Yiddish existed within modern Hebrew expression.

Translingual Politics and Poetics

When Ash and Hirshbeyn arrived in Palestine in 1927, few would have anticipated the literary debate that was provoked by the visit of two popular Yiddish writers. But their physical presence in Palestine pitted several competing discourses against each other: literary, with a young group of Hebrew writers' modernist poetics mobilized against a Hebrew literary establishment still dominated by Bialik; cultural, questioning whether Hebrew and Yiddish comprised a single culture or two distinct cultures; political, spanning the politics of language in the Yishuv, where Hebrew was an integral part of Zionism, the Soviet Union, where Yiddish was the officially sanctioned language of the Jewish population, and the rest of the diaspora, where Yiddish and Hebrew were competing for a dwindling number of readers; and historical, looking backward to the traditional symbiosis between the languages and the Language War and forward toward an uncertain future. From speeches at the reception to pages of Hebrew newspapers to rallies in the street, reactions to Ash and Hirshbeyn's visit combined aspects of these literary, cultural, political, and historical dynamics. In his welcome to the Yiddish writers, Bialik emphasized the historical and cultural bonds between the two languages of Eastern European culture. Ash addressed the future of Jewish culture in Eastern Europe, a future that he saw threatened by contemporary assimilation. Protesters from the Brigade of Defenders of the Hebrew language focused almost entirely on the language politics, resisting any suggestion that Yiddish had a place in the Yishuv. None of these opinions were particularly new in 1927, though their intersection at a single cultural gathering in the Yishuv was unusual.

What was new was the vigorous opposition to the conciliatory remarks voiced at the reception by Bialik, Ash, and others. Shlonsky, as we saw, had criticized Bialik in the past. Shteinman had adopted the role of the defender of Hebrew many times. But along with Barash, Lamdan, and Rabinowitz, they mixed literary, cultural, historical, and political objections in their public denunciation of the reception and Bialik's conciliatory stance on Yiddish in the diaspora. They staunchly rejected Hebrew-Yiddish bilingualism, literary or otherwise, in their efforts to bolster Hebrew and fight against Yiddish. At the reception, speakers had conceived of the relationship between Hebrew and Yiddish in spatial or familial terms, as two distinct locations that needed to be bridged or as brothers, either close or estranged. The *Ketuvim* writers countered those metaphors with their own aggressive ones, invoking a variety of metaphorical battlefields: Shlonsky's tubercular bilingual lungs, Lamdan's *yablit* (couch grass), Barash and Shteinman's talk of waging war. What had started as a polite encounter between representatives of Yiddish and Hebrew literary establishments catalyzed a change in discursive practices in the Yishuv, importing combative language politics into the literary sphere. Even in the Yishuv, the emerging center of Hebrew literature and the bastion of Zionist language politics, Yiddish was neither excluded from literary debates and texts nor relegated to the cultural margins. Literary-linguistic contact, in this case physical contact between Hebrew and Yiddish writers, situated the question of Yiddish at the epicenter of debates about Hebrew literature.

However, debates about the necessary and desirable relationship between Hebrew and Yiddish in prestate Palestine belied a reality in which some of the same writers who railed against Yiddish were still publishing in Yiddish and incorporating Yiddish in their literary work. For Shlonsky, poems like "Le-aba-ima" show the extent to which Yiddish was part of the poet's linguistic idiolect, a presence within the innovative linguistic and stylistic reservoir from which the collections *Le-aba-ima* and *Ba-galgal* were crafted. The Yiddish resonances in Shlonsky's poetry compel a reassessment of his incendiary anti-Yiddish rhetoric. Shlonsky simultaneously used Yiddish as a pretense for an attack on his literary "father figure" and a vehicle for a nostalgic return to his lyricized father and mother. In Shlonsky's own terms, the bilingual "tuberculosis" that had to be eradicated was far more intractable than it might seem, as the poet breathed a Hebrew inflected with Yiddish. For Shteinman, publishing in both Hebrew and Yiddish was ideological and pragmatic: ideological because his frequent Yiddish essays promoted Zionism and Hebrew, and thus were not threatening to the Hebrew cause; pragmatic, because such work paid the bills, in effect subsidizing his Hebrew fiction. Shteinman exhorted his readers to defend Hebrew by attacking Yiddish, but saw his own Zionist writing in Yiddish as exempt. For both writers, Yiddish was a tool—poetic or pragmatic—for them to realize their literary goals as well as a marker of the continued entanglement of Hebrew and Yiddish literary spheres.

Shteinman himself and Shlonsky's texts shifted between Hebrew and Yiddish and in the process tacitly endorsed sanctioned roles for Yiddish in service of Hebrew literary culture: bilingualism and translingualism could be deployed within a monolingual framework. Shteinman's columns in the Yiddish press maintained a traditional literary bilingualism by using Yiddish's popular reach in Eastern Europe to advocate for Hebrew, Zionism, and the Yishuv. In his Yiddish essays, Shteinman accepted the reality that he and his *Ketuvim* colleagues had protested, namely the fact that most contemporary Jewish readers in Europe read in Yiddish. The Yiddish vocabulary, rhythms, and associations that filled Shlonsky's *Le-aba-ima* also ushered Yiddish into an acceptably Hebraic context, in this case within poetry. In contrast to Shteinman, who acknowledged the contemporary relevance of Yiddish as a literary and communicative tool, Shlonsky situated Yiddish in the Eastern European Jewish past. Language and specifically literary language thus serves not only as the spark for a vicious public debate but also as a vehicle for Hebrew writers' engagement with Yiddish. Ultimately, it is Shlonsky's translingual incorporation of Yiddish within Hebrew literature that comes to replace Shteinman's differential Hebrew-Yiddish bilingualism over the coming decades.

Within a few years of the 1927 debate, both Shteinman and Shlonsky ceased writing in or with echoes of Yiddish, though both writers returned to Yiddish in different ways later in their careers.[93] Their simultaneous Yiddish practice and anti-Yiddish polemic was characteristic of the literary-linguistic transition underway in the 1920s, evident in the bilingual negotiations in *Milgroym* and *Rimon* and in the furor over bilingualism in the Yishuv. But by the 1930s, movement between the two languages became increasingly difficult, even for writers who came of age during the height of Hebrew-Yiddish literary bilingualism at the beginning of the twentieth century. Zalman Shneour and Y. D. Berkovitz, like Shteinman, had entered the literary arena when bilingual writing, and specifically self-translation, was a legitimate and pragmatic choice for a young Jewish writer in Eastern Europe. Their careers spanned drastic changes in Jewish literary life, changes that were registered in their literary-linguistic attempts to navigate the new cultural circumstances in which they found themselves in Paris, New York, and Tel Aviv.

3

The Belated Bilingualism of Zalman Shneour and Y. D. Berkovitz

A FEW MONTHS after the uproar provoked by Ash and Hirshbeyn's visit to Palestine, *Ketuvim* published an interview with Paris-based writer Zalman Shneour, part of a series of conversations with literary figures. Interviewer Moshe Ungerfeld wasted no time asking Shneour the question most Hebrew readers were wondering: "Why are you primarily publishing in Yiddish now?"[1] From the 1906 publication of his first collection of poems in Hebrew, *Shirei yeladim* (Children's Poems), until the mid-1920s, Shneour was a distinct and bold voice in Hebrew poetry, perceived as Bialik's protégé and heir-apparent. Then from the mid-1920s on, Shneour published vignettes and stories weekly in the Yiddish press. In response to Ungerfeld's question, he explained his literary-linguistic shift in pragmatic terms: "The novels that I am now publishing in America, I began to write them in Hebrew, but I stopped in the middle and wrote them in Yiddish. The reason? Simple: there is no place to publish. All of the monthlies and collections have gone under. The few that do exist have almost all ceased to pay writers. . . . Why should I write and archive it in my desk? . . . I decided, therefore, to take a break and for the past two years I have not written anything new in Hebrew."[2]

Shneour attributed his switch from Hebrew to Yiddish to his finances, blaming the paucity of publishing opportunities in Hebrew. The mid-1920s were a difficult time for Hebrew publishing, especially outside of Palestine: the venerable journal *Ha-shiloach* stopped publishing in 1926; *Ha-tsfira* (The Dawn) was in rapid decline, though it was published until 1931; and *Ha-tkufa* (The Era) was published only quarterly.[3] Even in the Yishuv, the Association of Hebrew Writers saw expanding publication opportunities as one of its priorities, founding *Ketuvim* in 1926. But with the Hebrew reading public in Palestine mired in economic depression and the economic situation for Polish Jews not much better, it was not surprising that Shneour found it difficult to publish his Hebrew poetry and prose.[4] Then again, Avraham Shlonsky managed to publish two collections of poetry in 1927 alone, suggesting that Shneour's difficulty in finding a Hebrew publisher was not solely financial. Yiddish newspapers proved far more hospitable and lucrative for Shneour, as he started publishing stories regularly in the Yiddish press.

Given the events earlier in 1927, *Ketuvim* was a strange venue for a Hebrew writer to profess his love for Yiddish. But that is precisely what Shneour proceeded to do in his interview. Throughout, he showed his estrangement from modern trends in Hebrew literature: he expressed strong reservations about the poetry of Shlonsky, Yitzhak Lamdan, and Uri Zvi Greenberg; insisted on the impossibility of poetry in the new "Sephardi" accent; and criticized "our enthusiastic Hebrews" for the tumult they caused surrounding the reception for Ash and Hirshbeyn. Shneour also affirmed his deep connection to Yiddish: "I do not want to conceal the fact that I have deep sentiments for the spoken language. I do not wish to and I could not uproot it from my heart and I feel myself as free and adept in it as in Hebrew."[5] Shneour justified his own use of Yiddish by explaining its emotional appeal and broader cultural significance as a conduit—in his words, a "paper-bridge"—from foreign cultures to Hebrew. He referred to Yiddish as "the spoken language," relegating Hebrew to its traditional role as the nonspoken language while promoting Yiddish's expressive capacities. Throughout, Shneour emphasized his own bilingualism and his literary mastery of both Hebrew and Yiddish.

On the surface, Shneour's frequent publication in Yiddish newspapers like *Der moment* (The Moment) and *Forverts* (Jewish Daily Forward) resembled Eliezer Shteinman's own essays in the Yiddish press. Yet Shneour's defense of Hebrew-Yiddish literary bilingualism provoked a short editorial comment, presumably written by *Ketuvim* editor Shteinman, printed in small type at the conclusion of the interview: "The pages of *Ketuvim* have, at different times, included opinions contradictory to those expressed here by Z. Shneour with respect to several questions, in particular the question of languages."[6] Shteinman managed to communicate his disagreement with Shneour in restrained fashion, but this editorial intervention placed Shneour and his comments outside of the Hebrew literary mainstream, or at least the mainstream as imagined by *Ketuvim*. His transformation from a heralded Hebrew poet to a popular Yiddish novelist shows the opportunities for bilingual reinvention and financial self-preservation. However, the difficulties Shneour faced in his attempts to return to Hebrew point to the limits of interwar Hebrew-Yiddish bilingualism. The literary-linguistic fluidity that had characterized early twentieth-century Eastern European Jewish culture was increasingly stymied by the geographical, ideological, and cultural distances between the emerging centers of Jewish-language literature in Palestine and the United States.

Shneour was not the only writer questioned about his linguistic allegiances in the late 1920s. Like Shneour, Yitzhak Dov Berkovitz wrote extensively in Hebrew and Yiddish from the beginning of his literary career in Eastern Europe. He, too, was interviewed for *Ketuvim* on the occasion of his visit to Palestine in early 1928, and primarily discussed Jewish culture in the United States and the poor state of American Hebrew language and literature.[7] But a far more revealing exchange appeared in the New York–based Yiddish paper *Vokh* (Week), which in late 1929 reflected on Berkovitz's recent immigration to Palestine from the United States: "[H]e traveled from here to Palestine as if one of us . . . A Yiddish writer, more Yiddish than Hebrew. And if not more—surely fifty-fifty."[8] But, the editorial bemoans, he had embraced Hebrew in Palestine and had abandoned Yiddish. Two weeks later, the paper published a rejoinder from Berkovitz, who defended his literary bilingualism: "I write Hebrew and write Yiddish and have been involved with both for already more than twenty five years. . . . For me they both come from one lively source—from the heart of our people. I know not—and do not wish to know—about the domain of political intentions or purposes: I cannot conceive of them. . . . It sounds like a strange joke when you divide my relationship to Hebrew and Yiddish into fifty and fifty. I myself have never broken this very relationship into 'fractions.' It seems to me that even with my great joy at the revival of Hebrew in the Land of Israel my relationship has always been and continues to be one hundred and one hundred."[9] Berkovitz not only denied that his relationship with Yiddish had changed but also rejected the premise that language allegiance could or should be divided. Instead, he insisted on an additive view of literary language, arguing that a writer could fully participate in more than a single literature regardless of political and ideological demands on language. For Berkovitz, Hebrew-Yiddish bilingualism was anchored in a particular time: he began writing during the early years of the twentieth century when literary bilingualism was widespread and saw no reason to change his bilingual approach. He avoided the politicization of Jewish culture, the "domain of political intentions or purposes," by speaking entirely in personal terms. Rejecting the Romantic equation of one language = one land = one people, he maintained that the two Jewish languages would continue to transcend linguistic and political divisions.

Both Berkovitz and Shneour, two writers who had launched their literary careers during the heyday of Hebrew-Yiddish literary bilingualism, found themselves in literary environments increasingly hostile to their efforts to traverse boundaries between Yiddish and Hebrew. Though the interwar period was characterized by extensive geographical mobility within an expanding Jewish world—Shneour lived in Paris, published in Poland and New York, and traveled often to Palestine and the United States; Berkovitz had accompanied his father-in-law Sholem Aleykhem all over Europe before World War I and then spent fifteen years in the United States before moving to Palestine in 1928—Hebrew and Yiddish literary establishments placed distinct limits on the linguistic and ideological fluidity that had once characterized Eastern European Jewish literature. Shneour and Berkovitz could simply be regarded as literary relics of an earlier time who stubbornly clung to outdated literary-linguistic practices. But as they translated their texts between Yiddish and Hebrew, their work registers both lingering literary bilingualism and alternative translingual approaches that defied Hebrew and Yiddish monolingualism.

In *Milgroym* and *Rimon*, literary-linguistic contact on the pages of the bilingual periodical sought to harness the Jewish languages of Eastern Europe together to promote a new approach to Jewish art. In the Yishuv, physical contact between writers reignited the Language War and its ferocious rhetoric. The self-translations of Shneour and Berkovitz shift the locus of contact inward, highlighting the intersections between Hebrew and Yiddish inside of texts, between texts, and between literary cultures. Shneour, often thought of as a Hebrew-turned-Yiddish writer, pursued self-translation throughout the 1930s in hopes of replicating his Yiddish commercial success in Hebrew. His self-translated novels looked backward into Jewish history, representing a past world and its literary-linguistic dynamics. But the Hebrew version of *Shklover yidn* (Shklov Jews), his breakthrough Yiddish novel, flopped with Hebrew audiences in the Yishuv. Berkovitz, by contrast, focused on contemporary linguistic dynamics in his reliably bilingual texts. Esteemed for his Hebrew translations of Sholem Aleykhem, it was in fact his own self-translations of stories like "Ha-nahag"/"Der shofer" (The Driver) that portray a new literary-linguistic climate in which Hebrew-Yiddish bilingualism was being replaced by other kinds of linguistic contact. Despite many differences in their self-translations, Shneour and Berkovitz's work demonstrates the changing politics and poetics of bilingual writing and the growing strength of Hebrew-Yiddish translingualism.

Changing Literary-Linguistic Dynamics

Modern literary self-translation has often been seen as a novelty: by some, as a path of reconciliation from *Muttersprache* to a second language; by others, as a peculiarly Beckettian bilingual synthesis; and by others, as one of the cultural implications of colonialism.[10] But for Eastern European Jewish writers at the turn of the twentieth century, self-translation was a logical extension of well-established literary bilingualism. As Jan Walsh Hokenson and Marcella Munson point out, self-translation was a common practice in early modern Europe among writers who translated between the learned language of Latin and vernacular tongues.[11] Eastern European Jewish society maintained distinctive internal and external bilingualism long after European vernaculars replaced Latin as languages of intellectual discourse, which facilitated Jewish self-translation as a common practice into the twentieth century. Since most educated Eastern European Jewish writers in the late nineteenth century had grown up speaking Yiddish and were intensively schooled in Hebrew texts, many found it natural to try writing and translating in Hebrew and Yiddish, not to mention Russian and Polish.

There were practical and ideological incentives for Eastern European Jewish writers to produce texts in both Hebrew and Yiddish. During a period of financial crisis before and after the 1905 Russian Revolution, writing in Yiddish became an appealing and sensible step for a generation of young Hebrew writers.[12] In his memoirs, published in both Yiddish and Hebrew, Berkovitz recalled that Sholem Aleykhem would gently suggest from time to time that it was not wise for a "young Jewish writer to close himself off in the narrow corner of Hebrew literature, whose readers were a handful of *maskilim* [proponents of the Jewish Enlightenment] and Hebrew teachers, and even this handful is dwindling from year to year."[13] Eager to demonstrate his professional independence from his famous father-in-law, Berkovitz instead couched the language issue in terms of social responsibility; as an aspiring realist writer "who seeks his path in describing the life of his people," he asked himself how he could ignore Yiddish, "the natural language, living on the lips and in the hearts of the majority of the house of Israel."[14] He explained that he and his fellow writers concluded that bilingualism was the only sensible strategy. Together with a group of young writers living in Vilna—Z. Shneour, Z. Y. Anokhi, Perets Hirshbeyn, and Y. Bershadsky—Berkovitz decided "that it was incumbent upon us to write in Yiddish *too*. Bershadsky, a practical dreamer, proposed an ambitious, unique plan-of-action: to make ourselves into a single association, so as to translate our work from Hebrew into Yiddish."[15] Self-translation between Hebrew and Yiddish became a defining feature of this group of young Jewish writers. They saw no need to write new texts for their Yiddish audience but were content to translate their existing work. Striking in this retrospective account is the writers' confidence not only that they could produce worthy literary texts in Yiddish but also that self-translation would be a worthwhile endeavor, both ideologically and financially.

Berkovitz's turn to self-translation followed the precedent set by S. Y. Abramovitsh's extensive Hebrew-Yiddish self-translations. By 1905 Abramovitsh was busy polishing parallel versions of his collected works, attributed to his literary persona, Mendele Mokher Sfarim (or, in Yiddish pronunciation, Mendele Moykher Sforim). The "Mendele model," as Dan Miron terms it, is predicated on what initially seems to be a paradox: Yiddish and Hebrew versions of the text were supposed to be at once parallel (substantially similar if not identical in plot and characters) and original (the creative work of a single writer).[16] A related element of Abramovitsh's writing that was adopted by many early twentieth-century writers was a more or less continuous oscillation between languages within a single cultural space, what Miron calls "integral bilingualism."[17] Unlike émigré writers like Joseph Conrad and Vladimir Nabokov, who abandoned their native languages in favor of new literary languages, Abramovitsh wrote in both Hebrew and Yiddish throughout his long career. With Abramovitsh as their paragon, early twentieth-century Hebrew-Yiddish writers like Berkovitz and Shneour approached self-translation as an exercise in literary reinvention: finding the linguistic and stylistic resources to render a Hebrew text in Yiddish, or vice versa.

Of course, not everyone agreed with Abramovitsh's systematic self-translation. Writer Micha Yosef Berdichevsky objected to the widespread practice of self-translation and argued that Hebrew and Yiddish each had their own distinct "worlds" that should not be conflated. Buoyed with a Romantic belief in the spirit of languages, Berdichevsky insisted that language was a critical dimension of a given work's poetics that could not be translated.[18] Therefore each language in a shared cultural space should be allotted specific literary tasks, an arrangement that Miron calls "differential bilingualism."[19] Berdichevsky's objections to the work of early twentieth-century bilingual writers like H. D. Nomberg, Sholem Ash, and Avrom Reyzen—a telling set of examples, as all three shifted more or less decisively to Yiddish within years of his essay—was that it was impossible to know whether their texts were written originally in Hebrew or Yiddish. As a result, Berdichevsky lamented, "language, the foundation of all literature, becomes among us merely a tool, unimportant."[20] Berdichevsky was not against writing in multiple languages, as he himself wrote extensively in Hebrew, Yiddish, and German, but he rejected self-translation as authentic literary expression.[21] He believed that the integrity of a literary work depended on its creation in a single language. Several years later, Shteinman expressed similar sentiments in his argument for the creation of a separate association for Hebrew writers, arguing that bilingual writers were fundamentally torn and thus unable to create worthwhile literature in either language. Despite these objections, there were many Jewish writers who not only wrote in more than one language but also embraced self-translation during the early decades of the twentieth century.

Underlying the different approaches to Jewish self-translation were complex and changing power dynamics. Some bilingual writers, Rainier Grutman points out, publish in languages of equal prestige that contribute to a sense of self-translational symmetry. Samuel Beckett, for example, wrote extensively in English and French. Others do not have the luxury of voluntary bilingualism in metropolitan languages.[22] For the many bilingual writers who move between minor and major languages, "self-translation is not just a matter of personal choice but always part of an historical pattern, a collective venture fraught with systemic difficulties."[23] These difficulties, Grutman continues, stem from the "very real socially rooted power differential between the languages self-translators have at their disposal," what Uriel Weinreich calls "dominance configuration" on a local level, as well as "the unequal weight languages carry within the global economy of languages."[24] In the case of early twentieth-century Hebrew-Yiddish self-translation, both Jewish languages had relatively little cachet on the global market, at least as modern literary languages. On a local level, however, there existed a deeply rooted power differential between Hebrew and Yiddish that had been established over several centuries of Jewish life in Eastern Europe. The entrenched hierarchal relationship between the two languages dictated asymmetric translational dynamics: a writer's decision to translate a Hebrew text into Yiddish was understood as what Grutman calls "downhill" self-translation, from a more dominant or prestigious language to a lesser one of the Jewish masses; the decision to translate from Yiddish into Hebrew was "uphill," not because it was necessarily more difficult but because it was perceived as more prestigious and culturally valuable.

Yet that localized power differential was in flux during the early decades of the twentieth century, evident in the differences between Berkovitz's enthusiastic embrace of bilingualism in 1905 and his defensive comments in 1929. Both Yiddish and Hebrew writers rebelled against the literary-linguistic roles prescribed by traditional bilingualism and sought to promote self-sufficient monolingual literary cultures. With changes in Jewish cultural geography, what had been a localized Jewish-language literature was fragmented across multiple locations: the power dynamics in New York, with a vibrant Yiddish literary scene and strong Yiddish press, looked very different from those in Tel Aviv, where the ideological imperatives to use Hebrew were enforced by groups like the Brigade of Defenders of the Language. For bilingual writers, self-translation became "uphill" both ways as each language asserted its own strength within a given locale. The decision to translate their own works from Hebrew to Yiddish that had seemed perfectly reasonable in 1905 was fraught with geographical and ideological difficulties by the 1930s. In contrast to the common self-translation scenarios Grutman lists—writers from languages of lesser diffusion who rewrite their texts in major languages; colonial and postcolonial writers who move between native and colonial tongues; immigrant writers who write in native and adopted languages—the Hebrew-Yiddish case provides an instance of dynamic asymmetry in which the power relations between the languages shift dramatically from place to place (Eastern Europe, United States, Palestine) and over a relatively short period of time (within the span of a writer's professional career).

By the late 1920s, Shneour and Berkovitz were among the few writers of this literary generation to maintain their literary bilingualism. They were the only members of the group of young Hebrew writers who, according to Berkovitz, embraced Hebrew-Yiddish bilingualism in 1905 and had continued to publish extensively in both languages. Bershadsky had limited success with a handful of Yiddish and Russian short stories and died soon after; Hirshbeyn started writing naturalist dramas in Yiddish in 1906 and never returned to Hebrew; and even Anokhi, who wrote Hebrew poetry and Yiddish prose until World War I, spent the interwar years primarily translating his earlier Yiddish stories into Hebrew.[25] Financial motivations for bilingual writing remained compelling into the interwar period, apparent in Shneour's interview and in Shteinman's continued publishing in *Der moment.* But the ideological climate surrounding bilingual writing had been transformed in the intervening decades. The idealistic desire to address the Jewish masses and the intelligentsia that Berkovitz described in 1905 could no longer traverse the literary-linguistic battle lines that had been drawn in places like *Ketuvim* only a few months earlier. When Shneour professed his love for Yiddish in an interview in Hebrew, he found himself tarred by *Ketuvim* editors for being on the "wrong side" of the language debate. When Berkovitz participated in Hebrew periodicals in Palestine, the editors of *Vokh* lamented his abandonment of Yiddish. Even though both writers sought to maintain earlier literary-linguistic practices, their bilingual writing encountered increasing resistance.

The changing nature of Hebrew-Yiddish self-translation in the late 1920s and early 1930s makes self-translated texts a rich site for literary-linguistic contact. Menakhem Perry argues that a writer's translation of his/her own work allows what would otherwise be called "bad" translations: "Since the writer himself is the translator, he can allow himself bold shifts from the source text which, had it been done by another translator, probably would not have passed as an adequate translation. Such bold shifts, if they are systematic, serve as powerful indicators of the activities of norms."[26] In other words, Perry sees self-translation as a spur to literary innovation and a means for analyzing a single literary tradition, in this case, Hebrew rather than Yiddish. But self-translations can also spotlight translingual negotiations. Hokenson and Munson, making the case for a distinct history and theory of literary self-translation, privilege self-translation in a different manner: "The bilingual text, from its two sides, directly opens out on that space, the interliminal region between languages, disclosing residues of the social and intellectual history that both systems now exhibit, in virtual overlap and intersection, through bilinguality. The single voice of standard second-hand translation silences that space. Intercultural self-translation constructs it stereoscopically as a unique reading field."[27] By emphasizing continuities rather than differences, Hokenson and Munson argue that self-translated texts reveal a shared intercultural space in which aspects of both linguistic systems, their cultures, and their histories coexist. Self-translation, in this reading, facilitates a unique stereoscopic perspective on translingual contact and its literary and cultural implications.[28] In the work of Shneour and Berkovitz, self-translation reveals not only the continued contact between Hebrew and Yiddish but also transitional literary-linguistic dynamics in these Jewish-language literatures.

Zalman Shneour and Pragmatic Bilingualism

By the time his interview appeared on the pages of *Ketuvim*, Zalman Shneour had experienced both literary acclaim and indifference. At a young age, Shneour vaulted to prominence as a Hebrew poet in the cultural centers of Jewish Eastern Europe. In a 1907 essay, Bialik heralded Shneour as one of the new poets "who have recently blessed our young literature": "Here is Shneour—a young 'Samson,' who overnight grew all seven of his tresses. A lion cub with family marks of 'the highest order.'"[29] Bialik singled out Shneour's poetic boldness and fierceness in the company of the elegant and gentle Ya'akov Kahan and the high-flying Ya'akov Shteinberg. But twenty years later, feeling abandoned by the Hebrew literary establishment in Palestine,

Shneour devoted his literary efforts to Yiddish prose, becoming a fixture in New York's daily *Forverts.* This transition from Hebrew poet to Yiddish writer, however, was punctuated by periodic efforts to engage in both Hebrew and Yiddish literary arenas via self-translation.

A variety of factors contributed to Shneour's estrangement from Hebrew poetry and his decision to devote his efforts to Yiddish prose. First of all, Shneour's poetry was at odds with the literary styles and themes that dominated Hebrew writing after World War I. Throughout his poems, he privileged the individual voice rather than the collective spirit that animated the Labor poetry of the early 1920s. Shneour's best-known long poems are bold, vivid, and often verbose texts laden with stylistic flourishes that contrast with the experimentation and neologisms of the expressionist language of poets like Shlonsky and Greenberg.[30] His ideas and his landscapes are inspired by European poetic trends but were often perceived as old-fashioned, relying on prewar romantic views of the mountains and idealized urban scenes rather than a grittier, darker interwar perspective—on Nietzschean rebellion rather than later expressionist subjectivities and sensations. Y. H. Brenner was one of Shneour's harshest critics; he conceded Shneour's poetic talent but rejected the patently Nietzschean elements of his writing.[31] Other critics targeted his verbosity, unbridled rhetoric, high sense of self, and intellectualism.[32] Second, Shneour was notoriously difficult, bitterly squabbling with prominent cultural figures like his employer, Hebrew publisher A. Y. Stybel, and his fellow Jewish writer in France, Sholem Ash.[33] Most often cited by critics, however, was Shneour's distance from Palestine. Yeshurun Keshet faulted Hebrew readers for not sufficiently appreciating Shneour's work, but added that Shneour's isolation, specifically his decisions to continue living in Paris and not to write about the land of Israel, did not endear him to his Hebrew readership.[34] His detachment from the Zionist project, Dan Miron argues, contributed to the presiding sense that Shneour was overblown and irrelevant for contemporary Hebrew poetry.[35] At the same time, Shneour declined to ally himself with the small but active American Hebrew literary scene, which tended to be more conservative stylistically and ideologically.[36] By the early 1920s, the chasm between Shneour, in Berlin but soon to settle in Paris, and the emerging center of Hebrew poetry in the Yishuv was evident; Shneour was disconnected from key stylistic and ideological developments in Hebrew literature.

Discussions of Shneour's shift from Hebrew to Yiddish often overlook the fact that Shneour had published in Yiddish well before the late 1920s. For example, his first significant collection of Hebrew poetry, *Im shki'at ha-chama* (With the Setting Sun, 1907), was quickly followed by the Yiddish *Gezamlte shriftn* (Collected Writings, 1909). The prolific poet found the time to produce an impressive amount of prose in both languages along with several self-translations, most notably the Yiddish novella *A toyt* (A Death, 1910) and its Hebrew counterpart *Min ha-chayim ve-ha-mavet* (From Life and Death, 1910).[37] Despite these examples of integral literary bilingualism, Shneour tended toward a differential approach to writing, assigning different roles to each of the literary languages in which he wrote. As one of the few critics to broach Shneour's bilingualism, Miron insists that he functioned, at least in literary terms, as two separate people: the "Hebrew Shneour," celebrated then essentially abandoned by readers and the Hebrew canon; and the "Yiddish Shneour," who chronicled the disappearing world of the Eastern European shtetl for an interwar Yiddish reading public.[38] But within a few years of his turn to Yiddish prose, Shneour blurred this distinction between his Hebrew and Yiddish writing by translating his own work between the two languages in response to the changing geography and dynamics of the interwar Jewish literary landscape.

This transition from differential to integral bilingualism, or in other words, toward more frequent self-translation, can be seen in one of Shneour's best-known Hebrew long poems, "Vilna." Vilna (Vilnius) had long been a center of Jewish culture, renowned for its large Jewish population; its religious life, with prominent figures like the eighteenth-century Vilna Gaon; and its vibrant intellectual life as a center of the Haskalah (Jewish Enlightenment), Jewish journalism, and Jewish politics in the nineteenth and early twentieth centuries. Regardless of Lithuanian, Russian, or Polish rule, Vilna was regarded as the capital of the substantial population of Lithuanian Jewry, the "Jerusalem" of Lithuania.[39] Shneour was one of the first poets to celebrate Vilna in verse, but far from the last; a remarkable number of poets, particularly Yiddish poets, wrote about Vilna during the interwar period.[40] First published in Berkovitz's New York Hebrew journal *Miklat* in 1919, Shneour's long poem travels through the landscape and history of this beloved "Jerusalem of Lithuania," evoking both place—the remnants of its ancient palace, the Strashun Library, the Vilija River, the cathedral—and people, such as the Hebrew poet Micha Yosef Lebenson, the Vilna Gaon, Graf Potocki, Chmielnitzki, and Napoleon, among others.[41] Less known is Shneour's self-translation of the poem into Yiddish, dated 1929 by the poet and first published in 1935.[42] Though there are many similarities between the Hebrew text and its Yiddish translation, Shneour's self-translation highlights the differences between writing in Hebrew in 1917 and in Yiddish in 1929.

Praised as the first long poem of its kind in Hebrew, "Vilna" views the city, its Jewish inhabitants, and its esteemed history with great affection and a bit of sarcasm.[43] Like much of Shneour's Hebrew verse, it is ambitious in scope, encompassing Jewish life in Vilna through the ages. Its language is rich in imagery and allusions, and toward the end of its six sections it embraces a prophetic poetic mode. Drawing on the Bible's feminization of Jerusalem in Lamentations, the poem opens with a grandmotherly Vilna, whose body and clothing, her grey hair and apron, are metaphorically mapped onto the silver roof and embroidered ark curtain of Vilna's Alte Shul, the old synagogue. But this nostalgic view of the city is shattered by the poem's conclusion, an abrupt shift from past idyll to present-tense destruction. In its sixth and final section, the poem returns to the initial evocation of the city-as-grandmother, who now finds herself in reduced circumstances: "How I pity you, elder-mother, downtrodden, unhappy, storm-tossed one! . . . You shared the glory of Jerusalem and so shall you share her fate."[44] Marked "Berlin 1917" at its conclusion, the long poem brings the trope of the city-as-woman to quasi-biblical fruition. The destruction of this Lithuanian Jerusalem is suffused with biblical allusions to the destruction of Jerusalem in Lamentations and the biblical prophets. For example, Vilna is no longer the "great" figure of the opening lines, but "unhappy and storm-tossed," using the words of Isaiah's prophecy (54:11), which promises the woman-as-nation that she will be rebuilt by God. Like the children of Jerusalem in Lamentations (2:12), Vilna's children suffer, "who would believe that we would see your hungry orphans swooning," as their grandmother can only watch, helpless.

Though the pitiful state of the city and its Jewish inhabitants is a result of modern war, the poem looks to the past to find concluding consolation and hope:

נַחֲמוּ, נַחֲמוּ עַמִּי, וְאַתְּ, עִיר וָאֵם, הִנָּחֲמִי!
שִׂימִי שָׁבִיס חָדָשׁ עַל רֹאשֵׁךְ, חִגְרִי סִנָרֵךְ הַמְדֻנָּג,
זֶה לְבוּשׁ אֵשֶׁת חָיִל . . .[45]

> Take comfort, take comfort my people, and you, city and mother, take comfort!
> Place a new coif on your head, tie the waxed apron,
> This is the clothing of a woman of valor . . .

The poem's lyric speaker assumes the role of the prophet consoling the people, providing comfort in the words of Isaiah (40:1–2) and encouragement for the grandmother-as-city to resume her pious role.[46] This postwar revival is envisioned by Shenour in 1917 as the restoration of the past order, with its modestly dressed grandmotherly icon, the traditional regional delicacies, the reopening of the synagogues, and restoration of their ritual objects. Despite the revolutionary winds of the time, Shneour's poem can only conceive of "rejoicing of the new dawn" (l. 307) within a thoroughly traditional context, the morning prayer voiced by long-bearded men and bewigged women in the old synagogue rather than the dawning of a new revolutionary age. Shneour's Vilna is to remain the bastion of Jewish tradition in Eastern Europe. Despite its flirtation with familiar themes of modernist estrangement and the desire to be a citizen of the broader world, Shneour's text comes full circle, seeking renewal in the very traditional spaces that Bialik's poetic speaker had abandoned with great fanfare two decades earlier.

At first, Shneour's Yiddish version of "Vilne" appears to be a straightforward translation of the Hebrew poem. As in the Hebrew text, it begins in dactylic hexameter and then switches to amphibracs in the third line. This Yiddish grandmother resembles her Hebrew counterpart quite closely: the same gray head beloved by grandchildren, the worn embroidered apron compared to the ark curtain, the same images domesticating the synagogue and its ritual objects. She, too, takes care of her inhabitants:

מיט פֿורימדיקע טייגלעך — באַרימט,
מיט פּסחדיקע מאָנעלעך, איינגעמאַכץ,
פֿאַרזיסט האָסטו זייערע צרות;
פֿאַרוויגט מיט דער הויכער מליצה
פֿון דײַנע לאַנגבערדיקע שרײַבער.[47]

With Purim pastries—famous,
With Passover poppy cakes and preserves,
You have sweetened their troubles;
Lulled them with the flowery language
Of your longbearded writers.

Like her Hebrew precursor, the Yiddish grandmother helps make life's burdens more palatable in a world defined by its Jewish sites and customs, here the holiday sweets of Purim and Passover. In a similarly maternal role, she lulls her grandchildren to sleep with the "flowery language," the Hebraic word *melitse*, of her many writers. The city, in both versions of the poem, is simultaneously the addressee of this poetic work and the beneficiary of generations of Jewish writers, both Hebrew and Yiddish. The nearly identical themes, imagery, and meter indicate a very close relationship between the text's two linguistic versions. As in Hebrew, the Yiddish text maintains the overall tendency to evoke urban space and then focus on the people who occupy that space, moving from the city-as-grandmother to her daughters and upstanding citizens, from wandering the city streets to the elderly residents living in fear of the cross, from nearby village Trocki to the Karaite community.

Yet it is the poem's abrupt conclusion that is most jarring to a reader familiar with the Hebrew "Vilna." In "Vilne," the Yiddish lines are far longer than their more concise Hebrew equivalents, so it makes sense that Shneour divided and rearranged the forty-six lines of the first Hebrew section into four shorter sections.[48] More significant, however, is that Shneour's Yiddish version excludes the last three sections of the Hebrew long poem and, as a result, omits the speaker's ambivalence about the city and its anti-Semitic history, his desire to flee to the West, and the destruction that World War I wreaked on Vilna. Thus the Hebrew poetic journey from the past glories to the present devastation is rewritten into an innocuous Yiddish poetic reminiscence of a city with a rich Jewish past. The Hebrew "Vilna" dwells in the moment of its creation in 1917, vividly describing the effects of war. The Yiddish "Vilne," however, is nothing more than a poetic tour of the famed city. Though the poem's representation of wartime was timely at its first publication in 1919, perhaps by 1929 interwar nostalgia trumped postwar trauma.

Despite the close textual resemblance between "Vilna" and "Vilne," Shneour was reluctant to describe this and other Yiddish versions of poems first published in Hebrew as "translations." In the retrospective collection *Fertsik yor lider un poemen* (Forty Years of Poems and Long Poems), Shneour was careful to distinguish between his poems in each language: "This collection of more than forty years of poems and long poems is not to be confused with my six volumes of Hebrew poems. In other words: these are original rhythmic works, written in Yiddish from 1903 to 1944, which appear for the first time in book form. . . . Only a small part of the poems . . . with which Hebrew readers are less familiar are included in the Yiddish collection, so thoroughly revised by the writer, that calling them 'translations' (from my own Hebrew work) would not be correct."[49] With texts spanning the breadth of his literary career, Shneour was adamant that his Yiddish poems should not be confused with his Hebrew work, nor considered derivatives or translations. Yet he does not clearly differentiate between original work and translation. Presumably, a lightly revised self-translation would in fact be a translation, but these "thoroughly revised" texts merit the status of originals. Despite the obvious thematic and poetic intersections between "Vilna" and "Vilne," he insists that they are distinct, original texts.

However, there are compelling reasons to compare Shneour's long poem in Hebrew and Yiddish. Together, the two texts highlight the challenges of translation between the two languages. Shneour's "Vilne" transposes the bold imagery and strong poetic voice that he had crafted in his Hebrew long poem into Yiddish. The density of his poetic language is achieved differently in Yiddish, as the lines in "Vilne" are necessarily wordier than those in "Vilna" and change the pacing of the text. But perhaps the trickiest problem Shneour faced as translator of his own text was what to do with the many allusions to the biblical prophets. In the Hebrew poem's second stanza, for example, the poetic persona's memories of the city of his youth are couched in the words from Jeremiah (2:2), as God's address to the Children of Israel, "I accounted to your favor the devotion of your youth," becomes the persona's ode to Vilna, "I accounted to your favor your devotion in my youth, the love for your Jewish daughters."[50] Shneour's persona stands in for God in a series of recollections of the city and its greatest institutions and eminent Jewish residents. In Yiddish, which cannot use the precise words of Jeremiah, the allusion is diluted to a general reflection on the city, "I still remember your favor and the love / of your hot-eyed daughters."[51] Without the biblical overtones, the emphasis shifts here from the God-like persona to a lyrical remembrance of youthful flirtations. Though the Yiddish text explicitly invokes Ezekiel's vision of the dry bones a few lines later and shares many other bold images, the muted prophetic speech and the removal of the concluding sections tempers the language and tone of the self-translation. The aggressive Hebrew that typifies so many of Shneour's poems is crafted into softer, more nostalgic Yiddish verse.

Reading the long poems together also underscores the challenges of self-translation. Self-translation, as Hokenson and Munson argue, can stereoscopically and stereophonically construct the intersecting space between the two languages at a particular historical moment. Shneour's Hebrew poem explores the glorious past and post–World War I reality of this Lithuanian Jerusalem, affectionately anthropomorphized as a kindly grandmother. In Hebrew, Uri Zvi Greenberg's "Kfitsat ha-derekh" (The Shortcut, 1924) similarly addresses Vilna, but instead of dwelling in past glories it imagines a grand project to magically relocate Lithuania's Jerusalem to Palestine in lurching expressionist lines.[52] While Shneour's melodic stanzas seek to reinstate the honor and pride of this venerable Jewish center, Greenberg's disjointed verses look for an alternative geography and future. In Yiddish, too, Shneour's "Vilne" departs from contemporaneous works like Moyshe Kulbak's "Vilne" (1926). Romantic in tone, Kulbak's poem lovingly addresses a greying and decaying city, but with a sharp undertone that acknowledges both an imperfect past and a changing present. As Avraham Novershtern demonstrates, Kulbak's text praises and mourns the city as it fiercely critiques it.[53] It was Kulbak's "Vilne" rather than Shneour's "Vilne" that became the canonical representation of the city within Yiddish culture, notable for its intricate poetic structure, deft imagery, and deep ambivalence about the city. By contrast, Shneour's Yiddish text offers a polished, superficial view of this Jewish historical and cultural center. In this case, reading bilingually highlights the extent to which Shneour's poetry departed from contemporary trends in Hebrew and Yiddish, as both literatures valued more complex, ambivalent representations that combined the vaunted past of the city with its vexed present and future.

If Shneour's self-translation of "Vilna"/"Vilne" was one attempt to render his Hebrew poetry in Yiddish, the Hebrew versions of his Yiddish Shklov narratives represented a far more ambitious effort to translate his newfound Yiddish success to Hebrew. *Shklover yidn* (Shklov Jews) was the first in what proved to be several immensely popular serialized Yiddish novels, including the five-volume epic of the Jewish teamster *Noyekh pandre* (Noah Pandre, published in book form, 1938–1939) and the historical novel *Keyser un rebe* (Emperor and Rebbe, 1944–1952), which chronicled the rise of Lubavitch Hasidism and

Napoleon. Soon after meeting with *Forverts* editor Abraham Cahan in Paris in 1927, Shneour began publishing weekly vignettes that detailed the life of a middle-class Jewish family in Shklov in *Forverts* and in Warsaw's *Der moment*.[54] These portraits of shtetl life captivated Yiddish readers nostalgic for the old country, receptive to precisely the kind of narrative that the narrator offers his readers in the opening chapter of *Shklover yidn*: "I decided to erect a gravestone [*matseyve*] for what once was and has passed."[55] Though Shneour was hailed as a modern-day Sholem Aleykhem for his comic depictions of shtetl life, his prose, as Dan Miron argues, is not simply nostalgic or derivative. "Outwardly static and replete with descriptive ethnographic detail, it seethes within with the bitter alienation of a boyhood in a restrictive society, with rebellious critique of the Jewish traditional family, with vicissitudes of a difficult puberty, and with a welter of negative emotions and childish libido gone wild."[56] This thematic and emotional complexity surfaces in both Yiddish and Hebrew versions of the text.

Shneour's Shklov looks quite similar in Yiddish and Hebrew. The series' second installment, for example, demonstrates both the critical edge that runs throughout these stories as well as the overall translational fidelity between Yiddish and Hebrew versions. The two versions of the narrative have different titles: the straightforward Yiddish "Men leyent tsaytungen" (Reading Newspapers); and the more oblique Hebrew "Keitsad korim" (How Does One Read), which alludes to the rabbinic query, "how does one dance before a bride."[57] The colloquial nature of one and the allusive gesture of the other are good previews of texts that follow, both of which satirize Jewish newspaper-readers. Shneour's Yiddish narrator begins,

> אַמאָל, אין די ״גוטע יאָרען,״ העט-העט אַ יאָר דרײַסיק צוריק, האָט נאָך שקלאָוו ניט געוווסט פֿון צײַטונגען. דער איין-איינציגער עקזעמפּליאַר ״המליץ,״ וואָס פֿלעגט זיך באַקומען בײַ דעם אַפּטייקער, איז געווען דער מקור פֿון אַלע נײַעס. ווילענדיק ניט ווילענדיק פֿלעגן שקלאָווער יידן טרינקען פֿונעם דאָזיגען פֿאַדעכטיגען קוואַל. אַז ס׳איז ניטאָ קיין אתרוג, בענשט מען מיט אַ בולבע.[58]

Once in the "good old days," oh thirty years ago or so, Shklov still knew nothing of newspapers. The one and only copy, *Ha-melits*,

> which was received by the apothecary, was the source of all news. Willingly or unwillingly, Shklov Jews used to drink from the very same suspicious source. When there is no *esrog*, one makes the blessing on a potato.

From its opening words, the narrative rejoices in the "good old days," before the press made inroads into Jewish life in Shklov. While the narrator is not explicitly identified, his colloquial Yiddish and "suspicions" about the maskilic paper *Ha-melits* (1860–1904), the first Hebrew-language weekly in tsarist Russia, establish his traditionalist stance. The translation achieves much the same tone in Hebrew:

> לפנים "כשהיו השנים כתיקונן," כלומר לפני ארבעים שנה בערך, לא ידעה עוד שקלוב מה טעמם של עיתונים. הטופס היחידי של "המליץ," עליו השלום, היה מתקבל בבית הרוקח ושמש מקור לכל החדשות. וברצונם או שלא ברצונם היו יהודי-שקלוב שותים מתוך עציץ זה, החשוד באפיקורסות. זהו שאומרים: "כשאין אתרוג מברכין על הבולבוס."[59]

> Before, "when the years were as they should be," that is to say about forty years ago, Shklov still didn't know about newspapers. A single copy of *Ha-melits*, may it rest in peace, was received at the apothecary, and was the source of all news. Willingly or unwillingly, the Jews of Shklov would drink from this little plant, suspected of heresy. As they say, "When there is no *etrog*, one blesses on a potato."

The Hebrew text is significantly more formal than its Yiddish counterpart, as for example the concise *gute yorn* (good old days) is replaced by the repurposed rabbinic *ke-she-hayu ha-shanim ke-tekunam* (when the years were as they should be),[60] but the overall effect is similar. Shneour's Hebrew narrator sets up the comic exposition of "Jewish news" that follows (highlights include the Prince of Wales' hankering for gefilte fish and Tolstoy's imminent conversion to Judaism) by striving for a colloquial effect in Hebrew: inserting the exclamation *alav ha-shalom* (may it rest in peace) after mentioning the newspaper *Ha-melits*, and importing the Yiddish phrase *az s'iz nito ken esrog, bensht men mit a bulbe*, "when there's no citron [ritual fruit for the holiday of Sukkot], one blesses on a potato." In this Hebrew passage, a combination of Hebrew stock phrases and calques from Yiddish gives the narrator a chatty, comfortable tone similar to the Yiddish.

Several paragraphs later, however, the narrative shifts into a mock-epic mode that delights in the formality of Hebrew prose. Shneour's Yiddish is more than adequate in previewing the shift in style and mentality through the use of dramatic repetition: "There arose a man, a hero, with one hand in the forsaken shtetl, a former cobbler who had lost his cobbler's last when he lost his hand."[61] But in Hebrew, we can see glimpses of the historical strata of Hebrew language:

> ויקם איש-חיל בעירה הנדחת, גדם מידו הימנית, סנדלר לשעבר, שהזניח את מרצעו לאחר שאבד את ידו. עמד והושיט את זרועו השמאלית, שנשארה לו לפליטה, קרע חלון לאירופה ונתן לזרם המרשרש של עתונים לשלוח מעיניו גם לשקלוב.[62]

> And there arose a man of valor in a forsaken town, a man with an amputated right hand, a former cobbler, who neglected his awl after he lost his hand. He stood and put forth his left hand, that which remained, and broke a window through to Europe, and allowed a rushing stream of newspapers to trickle into Shklov.

The narrator musters a pastiche of biblical Hebrew to introduce the unlikely hero, a one-armed cobbler who turns to selling Russian newspapers to make ends meet. This *ish chayil* (man of valor) is first cast in the mold of the soldiers and leaders from Samuel and Kings and makes good use of his own "remainder," an arm that stands in for the loyal remnants of the Jewish people alluded to throughout the prophetic books of the Bible.[63] The left-handed hero is then elevated to quasi-divine status in a comic comparison to both the God of Exodus, who redeems the Jewish people "with an outstretched hand,"[64] and Peter the Great, the late seventeenth- and early eighteenth-century tsar who ruthlessly Westernized Russia, including establishing St. Petersburg as a "window to the West."[65] Here, the agents of change are the Russian-language newspapers, a cheap luxury that our brave hero supplies to Shklov's middle class. Both Yiddish and Hebrew texts share the mock-epic tone, though it is achieved more effectively, in this case, in Hebrew. Each of the languages excels at different narrative moments, though they share a single premise and, ultimately, stylistic sensibility.

The Shklov story also thematizes language in the "good old days" of Jewish Eastern European life in both versions of the self-translated text. Newspapers were one of the main vehicles of modernization in Ashkenazi Jewish society, expressing changes in Jewish life in the Russian Empire in the 1860s and mediating between Jewish readers and the government.[66] Shneour's narrator sketches three distinct periods in the history of Jewish newspaper-reading: first, the Hebrew weekly *Hamelits* (The Advocate, Odesssa/St. Petersburg, 1860–1904, with interruptions), which passed through many Shklovian hands; soon after, the "necessity" of reading Yiddish papers, which the story references in passing; and finally, the prestige of receiving the Russian newspaper.

The narrative, however, mercilessly if comically critiques Shklovian reading habits, identifying the newspaper's primary function as a desirable status symbol rather than a source of information. Motte, the aforementioned one-armed deliveryman, relieved his customers of the work of reading the papers he brings them every day. As the Yiddish narrator describes: "Ever since Motte had been selling newspapers, two dozen Russian words had crept into his head, and he used them, when necessary and when unnecessary. With *gavrit on* he meant to say *govorit on* [says he] like a genuine Russian, with a goyish click. . . . But who this is, who 'says' and who is the 'he,' one cannot figure out. . . . 'In Riga, *gavrit on*,' Motte the newspaper-carrier scares her [Aunt Feige] further and gesticulates with his stump of an arm. 'In Riga they'll come out on *devyatnatsete avgust* [19th of August] with red *simfonyes* [banners], the *tsitchilisten* [Socialists] will. It's *yezheli, gavrit on* [if, says he], if they go out they'll be ground to dust and smoke.'"[67] Motte's jumbled and mispronounced Russian phrases, transliterated in both Yiddish and Hebrew versions, digest the news for his customer, Aunt Feige, who has neither the motivation nor the Russian-language skills to read the paper herself. Of course, Aunt Feige has little interest in the *tsitchilist* troublemakers, but she's suitably impressed by Motte's flawed but authoritative Russian. Shneour's text incorporates bits of Russian to lend the narrative multilingual flavor and comic flair. However, that textual translingualism does not extend to the representation of Yiddish in the Hebrew text. Though the characters presumably are speaking in Yiddish, the Hebrew version is resolutely Hebraic, as we saw above, either calquing expressions or finding suitable Hebrew equivalents.

Both versions of Shneour's text hearken back to a time in which Yiddish, Hebrew, and Russian coexisted harmoniously, at least in the narrative's imagination. In this episode and throughout the Shklov stories, language is primarily a vehicle for expression, not a point of contention or even innovation. Thus the narratives could be rendered in Yiddish and Hebrew in much the same form. In the opening passage of the story above, for example, the Hebrew newspaper *Ha-melits* is still a shared reference point for both versions of the text, just as the Yiddish proverb ("when there is no citron, one blesses on a potato") is conveyed in both languages, expressing the presiding "take what you can get" mentality. The narrative also mimics the symbiotic relationship between Hebrew and Yiddish here; Hebrew maintains its status as the language of the foundational text, in this case the first modern newspaper; and Yiddish takes its place as the vernacular, regardless of the language of the overall text. Shneour's prose is chiefly retrospective, set in the "good old days" that allow it to sidestep contemporary literary-linguistic controversies. That is not to say that language is insignificant in the Shklov narrative, but even in a story about newspapers in different languages, the linguistic hierarchy that emerges is secondary to the broader comic critique of middle-class reading habits. Taking cues from Sholem Aleykhem but with a sharper critical edge, Shneour's Shklov stories submerge issues of language and ideology within plot and characterization.

But that critical edge and the Shklov stories overall did not translate well into Hebrew literary culture in the 1930s. The Shklov narratives were first published in Hebrew in the London-based *Tekufoteinu* (Our Era, 1933) and a few years later were serialized in Palestine in the daily paper *Davar* (1936–1937). In a short statement in the paper in late 1935, *Davar*'s editors lamented that the Hebrew reading public had been deprived of this fine writer's recent work: "Z. Shneour was exiled from the Hebrew table and the prose works that he has dedicated himself to in recent years have been published almost entirely in Yiddish, on the pages of Jewish newspapers across the diaspora."[68] Implicit in this statement is an assumption that Hebrew readers were not familiar with the Yiddish Shneour, imagining little communication between Hebrew writing in Palestine and Yiddish writing in the diaspora. Furthering the case that Shneour's prose should be published in Hebrew in Palestine is Shneour himself, who is depicted as a writer eager to reenter the Hebrew literary universe: "In his letter to *Davar* the poet writes: 'For ten years without pause I gave all my strength to Yiddish. During this time I published around 16 large volumes, whose creative beginnings were *Hebrew*, but I did not have a place to publish them. That's a fact!' The editors of *Davar* see self-evident value such that they have taken on [this project] and have not recoiled from these efforts and now have the opportunity to distribute this work and to bring Z. Shneour back to Hebrew literature and the Hebrew reader. From now on Z. Shneour's prose writing will be published *as they were adapted anew and written by the author in Hebrew*, on a regular basis in the pages of *Davar*."[69] Both Shneour and *Davar*'s editors emphasize the pedigree of Shneour's Hebrew works, the writer suggesting Hebrew foundations for his Yiddish works, and the editors stressing the originality of these self-translations. These words, printed in bold font, demonstrate a resistance to translation: Shneour is not translating his own work into Hebrew, but being returned to Hebrew literature, a literary return to Zion. As in Shneour's introduction to his collected Yiddish poetry, *Davar* assures its readers that they will be reading the author's adaptations of the text, written in—not translated into—Hebrew.[70]

This insistence on adapting rather than translating represents a striking convergence of critical views on translation and language ideology. For Shneour and his editors, the process of "adapting anew" from Yiddish to Hebrew confers the rewritten text with the status of an original so as to avoid the impression that his texts are dependent on or derivative of their Yiddish predecessors. *Davar* clearly articulates the editors' desire to claim Shneour the prose writer for Hebrew literature. In order to do so, his works had to be sufficiently Hebraic, necessitating this process of being "adapted anew" and "written" rather than translated or even rewritten.[71] Since the late eighteenth century, Lawrence Venuti argues, Western culture has valorized fluency in translation, to produce "an effect of transparency, whereby the translated text is taken to represent the foreign author's personality or intention or the essential meaning of his text."[72] As a result, the translator becomes invisible: "the more 'successful' the translation, the more invisible the translator, and the more visible the author or meaning of the original text."[73] In Shneour's case, it is the visibility of the translator, and specifically the purported correspondence between author and translator, that allows his translation to become invisible. Thanks to self-translation, the translated text can replace the original, particularly when the original is ideologically problematic. Both Shneour and *Davar*'s editors make the case for self-translation as a kind of original writing, whether in Yiddish or Hebrew, rather than translation.

Yet it is difficult to sever the translation from the translated text. First of all, the similarities between Hebrew and Yiddish texts are indisputable, evident to anyone who might be reading in Yiddish and Hebrew. Second, the translations "Vilne" and *Anshei Shklov* encountered difficulties in their respective literary environments, Yiddish poetry and Hebrew prose. As Venuti writes, "the transformative process of translation not only involves a change in semiotic and internal context, but occurs within a context which must be construed as social and external."[74] In contrast to the literary-linguistic fluidity at the beginning of the century, it was difficult for the Hebrew poet Shneour to make much of an impact in Yiddish poetry in the 1920s and 1930s with verse fundamentally Hebraic in form and tone, if not language. It was not just Kulbak who was writing very different poetry in Yiddish at the time; Dovid Hofshteyn, Perets Markish, Moyshe Leyb Halperin, Yankev Glatshteyn, and A. Leyeles were among many Yiddish poets who were crafting innovative, modernist Yiddish poetry. Similarly, it was difficult for the Yiddish novelist Shneour to succeed in Palestine, where the largest audience of Hebrew readers lived, with a serialized novel that resonated with Yiddish, not Hebrew literary trends. Hebrew prose in the 1930s was strongly oriented toward Palestine, from Natan Bistritski's expressionist narratives of collective life to Aharon Reuveni's unstintingly realist evocations of Palestine. There were exceptions: S. Y. Agnon was publishing Hebrew prose set in Eastern Europe, permeated with psychological ambivalence; David Fogel crafted modernist European novels in his minimalist Hebrew. But Shneour's Yiddish prose resembled the ambitious historical novels of Yoysef Opatoshu and the realist panoramas of Sholem Ash far more than anything in Hebrew literature. Like Opatoshu and Ash, Shneour's work satisfied demand for historical or rural idylls among American Jewish readers anxious about radical changes in interwar life.[75] It was far less satisfying for readers living in a self-consciously Zionist society still trying to sever its connections to the diasporic past. Despite Shenour's best efforts, he could not bridge the growing distance between Hebrew and Yiddish audiences.

As a result, Shneour's *Anshei Shklov* was met with indifference rather than the hoped-for acclaim. When Shneour visited Palestine in early 1936, just as *Davar* was publishing his *Shklov* stories, writers in Tel Aviv welcomed him at a public reception. Unlike the reception for Ash and Hirshbeyn nine years earlier, Shneour's appearance caused little controversy and merited only a brief summary in the local papers. But the writer's ambivalent status in the Yishuv was apparent from Shaul Tchernikhovsky's opening comments, as he conceded that "Shneour is distant from us," but insisted that this reception in his honor would not address those concerns.[76] A few years later, critic Natan Grinblat complained that Shneour's *Noyekh Pandre* had been translated into nine different languages, but not into Hebrew. In his words, this "positive Jewish novel, juicy and folksy, a novel that has won over hundreds and thousands of readers in all nine languages into which it has been translated—why should it not be in the original language of creation of its artist?"[77] Grinblat again claims Shneour as a Hebrew writer, finding a different kind of Hebrew "origin" to compensate for his Yiddish texts by asserting that Hebrew was the writer's "original language of creation."[78] But there was little interest in the Yishuv in "rescuing" this Hebrew-turned-Yiddish writer, beyond his supporters at *Davar* and his long-time advocate Yosef Klausner.[79] The ability to produce literary texts in both Yiddish and Hebrew did not guarantee success in the separate literary markets, a fact that had been taken for granted only a few decades earlier.

Y. D. Berkovitz, Self-Translator Par Excellence

On the surface, Yitzhak Dov Berkovitz's literary career followed a trajectory similar to that of Shneour. From the very beginning of the twentieth century, Berkovitz published consistently in Hebrew and Yiddish; he wrote and published virtually all of his short stories and novels in both languages. Like Shneour, he was heralded as one of the best Hebrew writers of his generation, only to find himself on the margins of both Hebrew and Yiddish literary canons within a few decades. But in contrast to Shneour, Berkovitz was increasingly perceived as a Hebrew writer rather than a bilingual one. As we saw in *Vokh*, Berkovitz's insistence that he could continue to be a committed Yiddish writer living in Palestine was met with suspicion in the United States. At the same time, Berkovitz never quite achieved literary recognition in Palestine, despite the Zionist tenor of his Hebrew texts. If Shneour's *Anshei Shklov* revisited an Eastern European past and its linguistic arrangements, Berkovitz's texts from the late 1920s and early 1930s highlighted the linguistic diversity of the Yishuv—in both Hebrew and Yiddish.

Berkovitz burst onto the literary scene in 1903 as the winner of daily newspaper *Ha-tsofe*'s inaugural prize for the best Hebrew short story "from the life of our people." Berkovitz's "Moshkele chazir" (Moshkele the Pig) was praised by judges Y. L. Peretz, E. L. Levinsky, and Yosef Klausner as far superior to the other submissions, a story "new and original in our literature."[80] The judges commented on the psychological skill of the characterizations and the convincing nature of the plot, which traces the life of a Jewish man who converted to Christianity after a difficult childhood, only to find himself drawn back to the study house on Yom Kippur Eve. The "convincing nature" of his characters and plots, along with his deft command of descriptive language, are central aspects of the realism that defines Berkovitz's early short stories. Though his earliest stories appeared in Hebrew, by 1906 he was publishing in both Hebrew and Yiddish, culminating in the near-simultaneous release of his Hebrew collection *Sipurim* (Stories, 1910) and his Yiddish collection *Gezamlte shriftn* (Collected Works, 1910). These collections are both marked by their literary realism and their themes of alienation and uprootedness, and share eleven stories that appear in substantially similar versions in Hebrew and Yiddish.[81] Thus from the early years of his literary career, Berkovitz wrote and published extensively in both languages.

Berkovitz, unlike Shneour, did not significantly change the bilingual habits he established at the beginning of his writing career. From the very beginning, he typically published the same stories in Yiddish and Hebrew versions within a few years of each other. One particularly interesting example of Berkovitz's penchant for self-translation is the early story "Be-yad ha-lashon" (The Tongue's Power)[82] and its Yiddish counterpart "On loshn" (Without a Tongue), which thematize language and the difficulties of communication and provide insight into Berkovitz's bilingual method.[83] First appearing in the Hebrew newspaper *Ha-tsofe* in 1904, the story follows a hapless young tailor's attempt to deliver a school uniform to a wealthy Eastern European Jewish family. In his nervousness, Pesach-Zalman, renamed Bentzi in later Yiddish and Hebrew versions, initiates conversation in Russian though his Russian skills are rudimentary at best. His struggles to express himself are registered by both Hebrew and Yiddish texts in transliterated Russian, from an opening *Izdrostvo* (Hello) to pitiful bleats of *ni-tschi-vo* (no matter) as his verbal abilities rapidly disappear under stress. The earliest version of the text does not translate the Russian phrases; all subsequent versions gloss Pesach-Zalman/Bentzi's attempts to speak Russian, no longer assuming their Hebrew or Yiddish audiences will understand the original. Though Bentzi's halting Russian is transliterated into Hebrew characters, the fluent Russian speech of the *madamikhe* (madam) and her son is rendered in polished Hebrew or Yiddish in the respective texts. Thus both Eastern

European Jewish languages assert their credentials as modern literary languages in Berkovitz's story by "speaking" for Russian. At the same time, both versions of the story depict the thoroughly multilingual environment of the shtetl and the issues of class and socioeconomic status intertwined with language choice, not unlike Shneour's Motte the newspaper carrier. But Berkovitz's Bentzi finds himself in a much harsher linguistic predicament than Shneour's Motte, suffering from his inability to shift between languages rather than benefiting from an ability to embellish his Yiddish with Russian. Representing the protagonist's muteness in the face of a non-Jewish language, the stories enact the tense power asymmetries of language by using their respective linguistic resources to convey the social dynamics of this scenario.

The narrative and linguistic dynamics of "Be-yad ha-lashon"/"On loshn" are characteristic of Berkovitz's early works. Bentzi, like so many of Berkovitz's protagonists, is at odds with his environment, expressed most vividly through his simultaneous desire and inability to speak Russian.[84] Within this brief narrative, Berkovitz deftly sketches the socioeconomic disparities between his characters and captures the deep sense of discomfort his protagonist feels upon entering this world of wealthy Russified Jews, the woman presiding over the polished samovar and her loutish gymnasium-educated son. The focus on inequalities in Eastern European Jewish society and the unmooring of the protagonist become hallmarks of Berkovitz's short stories from before World War I, the majority of which were published in both Hebrew and Yiddish. Thematically and linguistically, Berkovitz's texts were embedded within the Eastern European Jewish literary environment in which dual writing and publishing seemed so normal.

However, the circumstances in which Berkovitz pursued his literary bilingualism changed dramatically after he emigrated from Russia following the 1905 Revolution and the ensuing pogroms. Berkovitz spent several years traveling throughout Europe and lived in New York for more than a decade (1914–1928) before moving to Palestine in 1928. He continued to publish the same stories in Yiddish and Hebrew versions, typically within a few years of each other. But by the late 1920s, a clear geographic distinction emerged between

Berkovitz's Hebrew texts, published in *Moznayim*, *Ha'arets*, and *Davar* in Palestine, and his Yiddish ones, published in *Forverts*, *Der tog*, and *Di tsukunft* in New York. If a key aspect of S. Y. Abramovitsh's self-translations was the knowledge that all of his Hebrew readers could read his work in Yiddish (and most of them did, at least before they were translated in Hebrew), then a defining feature of Berkovitz's later self-translations was the absence of those assumptions. By the late 1920s, Berkovitz's texts continued to depict the translingualism of Jewish life even as they reached two substantially separate audiences in Palestine and the United States.

Berkovitz's stories "Ha-nahag" (The Driver, *Moznayim*, 1929) and "Der shofer" (The Driver, *Der tog,* 1929) provide vivid representations of the literary-linguistic dynamics of time. In contrast to Shneour's bygone days in Shklov, Berkovitz's narratives take place in the Yishuv, marked as contemporary by the cars on the roads, Jewish tourists from the United States and Czechoslovakia (formed as an independent country in 1918), and the use of spoken Hebrew. The Hebrew and Yiddish stories chronicle a day trip from Jerusalem to the Dead Sea, as a loquacious driver transports American and Czechoslovakian Jewish tourists through the Judean desert. The Eastern European snow of Berkovitz's early stories has been replaced by what the driver sees as "blazing snow," the sand of the "desolate wilderness, bleached as far as the eye can see." Still, the driver is quite similar to his Eastern European literary precursors, a man haunted by his past and alienated from the collective Zionist enterprise.[85] He is immensely proud of his firsthand knowledge of the land and represses, to the best of his ability, his diasporic life and its traumas. But he cannot embrace the pioneer collective and flees his collective settlement in the Galilee. In one of many long-winded monologues, he confesses, in the Hebrew version: "Six months I worked alongside them with a shovel and plow, and in the seventh month I up and fled from them to the four winds. I could not stand the immense silence, the silences of the surrounding hills . . . my soul longed for the distances, to be carried from one end of the land to the other, to be shot from the slingshot between great pangs for Ukrainian fields, perish the thought, and my love blazing like fire for the desolation of the amazing land of my fathers."[86] The driver's alienation puts him in good company in early twentieth-century Jewish literature, alongside *talush* (uprooted) figures like Berdichevsky's Michael, Nomberg's Fliglman, Bergelson's Yoysef Shur, Brenner's Yechezkel Chefetz, and, of course, Berkovitz's own Dr. Vinik, featured in the story "Talush" (Uprooted).[87] In both versions of the "The Driver," however, Berkovitz adds a key linguistic component to his interwar *talush.*

At the core of the narrative is a peculiar linguistic situation: the driver, his passengers, and the text skip from language to language, mixing Hebrew, English, Yiddish, Russian, and German. From the very beginning, both versions of the story pay close attention to speech and the language in which it is spoken. In Berkovitz's Hebrew version:

,אתה הוא הַמִּיסְטֶר, הרוצה לנסוע לים-המלח? — פנה אלי באנגלית נלעגת בהטעימו כל מלה להברותיה.

כן, אני הוא המיסטר — אמרתי.

ואני הנהג. — התיצב לפני מתוך קידה מגוחכת מעשה שחקן, ומיד הוסיף ביהודית: — אבל עליך לדעת למפרע, מיסטר, כי לאנגלית אינני מומחה רב. אם תרצה לשוחח עמי בדרך, תצטרך לדבר אלי יהודית פשוטה.

מוטב — אמרתי — בשעת בדחק נדבר יהודית פשוטה.

הלא מלשון הקודש, כדרך הטבע, שמר אלהים את נפשך באמריקה?[88]

"You are the *mister* who wants to travel to the Dead Sea?" he turned to me in ridiculous English, stressing each word's syllables.

"Yes, I am the *mister*," I said.

"And I am the driver." He stood before me, bowed absurdly, like an actor, and immediately added in Yiddish: "However it is upon you to know in advance, *mister*, that in English I am no great expert. If you should wish to converse with me on the journey, you must speak simple Yiddish to me."

"Fine," I said. "At the hour of need we will speak simple Yiddish."

"And from the holy tongue, naturally, God has guarded your soul in America?"

The Hebrew narrative captures the translingual conversation, which switches from the driver's broken English to his comfortable Yiddish, the common language between two early twentieth-century Ashkenazi Jews. The languages are descriptively rather than linguistically marked in the text, except for the use of the transliterated English word "mister," brimming with its American capitalism and ostentation. This "mister" signals an ironic linguistic moment as the narrator's first English statement, *ani hu ha-mister* (I am the *mister*) echoes the syntax of the Yiddish *dos bin ikh der mister* (that's me, the mister). But for the most part, Berkovitz's Hebrew text follows established *nusakh* conventions for Hebrew dialogue, integrating few of the literary features (sentence structure, calques, rhythms) that would suggest Yiddish speech.[89] "However it is upon you to know in advance," the driver says in fine rabbinic Hebrew, "that in English I am no great expert." Our Hebrew-speaking narrator responds in an equally polished rabbinic Hebrew purporting to be simple Yiddish, "At the hour of need. . . ." Berkovitz's characters shift from language to language, but his text is firmly Hebraic.

Not surprisingly, Berkovitz's Yiddish version of the story renders these lines in far more colloquial fashion:

> - איר זענט דאָס דער מיסטער, וואס וויל פֿאָרען צום ים-המלח?
> האָט ער גלייך אָנגעהויבען אויף א שלעכטען ענגליש, קוועטשענדיק יעדע זילב באַזונדער.
>
> יאָ, דאָס בין איך דער מיסטער — האָב איך געזאָגט.
>
> און איך בין דער שאָפֿער! — האָט ער זיך פֿאָרגעשטעלט פֿאַר מיר, זיך קאָמיש פֿאַרנייגט, מעשה אַקטיאָר, און באַלד איברגעגאַנגען אויף יידיש: איך מוז אייך אָבער פֿרייער זאָגען, מיסטער, אַז מיט ענגליש בין איך ניט אַזאַ נאָענטער מחותן, ווי איר מיינט. אויב איר וועט חשק האָבען צו שמועסן אין וועג, וועט איר נעבאָך מוזען רעדען מיט מיר פּראָסט יידיש.
>
> גוט — זאָג איך — פֿאַר נויט וועלען מיר רעדען פּראָסט יידיש.
>
> וואָרעם פֿון לשון-קודש, כדרך הטבע, האָט אייך גאָט מסתמא אויסגעהיט אין אמעריקע?[90]

"You're the *mister* who wants to travel to the Dead Sea?" He immediately started off in poor English, stressing [*kvetshendik*] each and every syllable.

> "Yes, that's me, the *mister*," I answered.
>
> "And I am the driver!" He introduced himself to me, comically bowed like an actor, and soon continued in Yiddish: "But first I've gotta tell you, *mister*, that with English I am not such a close cousin, as they say. If you want to have a conversation on the way, you will, poor thing [*nebekh*], have to speak to me in simple Yiddish."
>
> "Good," said I, "If necessary we will speak simple Yiddish."
>
> "Since from *loshn koydesh*, naturally, God has probably protected you in America."

The driver's Yiddish provides quite a contrast to the language of his Hebrew-speaking twin: straightforward and down-to-earth, his words are punctuated with attitude (stressing each and every syllable), an idiom (*bin ikh nit aza noenter mekhusn*, I am not such a close cousin) and a characteristically Yiddish interjection (*nebekh*, poor thing). At this point in the narrative, there is no suggestion that the narrator in fact does know Hebrew; that revelation comes later, once it becomes clear that he understands the driver's soliloquies.

From the beginning of the story, even mutually agreed-upon "simple Yiddish" is not as simple as it might appear, particularly in the driver's barbed question about whether or not the narrator speaks Hebrew. The Hebrew and Yiddish versions of the story converge on the term *lashon kodesh/loshn koydesh*, the holy tongue. Originally a Hebrew phrase, *lashon kodesh* had long been used in Yiddish to refer to Hebrew, particularly in its premodern religious context.[91] However the phrase only appears once in the Yiddish story, which otherwise uses the word *hebreish* to refer to Hebrew language and speech. In contrast to the historical resonance of the Hebraic *loshn koydesh*, the Germanic component *hebreish* stresses the modern manifestation of the language, and in this context, the language of the Zionist pioneer. It makes sense that the driver chooses *loshn koydesh* in his sarcastic comment to the narrator, assuming—incorrectly, as it turns out—that his American passenger couldn't possibly know the traditional *loshn koydesh* much less modern *hebreish*. The Hebrew version, or more accurately, the Hebrew representation of the driver's Yiddish comments about Hebrew, gestures toward Yiddish sentence structure, foregrounding the Yiddish-inflected *lashon ha-kodesh* in the first clause and giving the entire statement a peculiarly Yiddish interrogative tone. This represents a subtle integration of Yiddish into the Hebrew text, on the model of Itamar Even-Zohar's claim that modern Hebrew was inclined to borrow elements from Yiddish that were not readily recognizable as Yiddish.[92] The brief Yiddish exchange about *loshn koydesh* and the narrator's decision to conceal his knowledge of Hebrew are critical to the development of the narrative. The passenger's profession of ignorance of the holy tongue also suggests a differentiation being made between the older linguistic paradigm and the new Zionist linguistic framework; the narrator may not speak *loshn koydesh*, but that is not to say he does not speak modern Hebrew, the *hebreish* or *ivrit* of the Yiddish and Hebrew versions. Language, the stories emphasize, is not necessarily what it appears to be.

In these passages and throughout the story, Hebrew-Yiddish bilingualism is situated within a broader multilingual context, as the characters skip from language to language. After the narrator agrees to let the driver pick up another passenger, the driver muses aloud to himself in Hebrew and then switches to German to converse with Edna, a Czechoslovakian young woman who joins the group. Edna herself speaks German with the driver then switches to a flawless English to address her fellow passenger. Deeply frustrated that Edna declines the opportunity to sit beside him, the driver exclaims in Russian: "*Heyda! Propadai moya telyega, visye tchertire kolyesa!*" (Go to hell, my cart, with all four of your wheels!) The phrase, transliterated in both versions of the story but only glossed in the Hebrew text, alludes to Chekhov's *The Cherry Orchard* as it incorportes a fifth language into the narrative.[93] With the exception of the driver's interjection in Russian, the profusion of languages is marked in both Hebrew and Yiddish texts primarily in descriptive fashion, the narrator keeping track of the language being spoken at any given moment. Moments of linguistic crossover do exist, as for example the narrator invites Edna to sit beside him with a polite *Bitte* (please) in his English speech as recorded in the Yiddish text, and the driver's Yiddish and Hebrew are sprinkled with English words ("mister," "missus," "shop," "dollar," "capitalist," "opera"). Much like Shneour's Shklov, Jewish translingualism is represented within the language of the text, whether the Hebrew of "Ha-nahag" or the Yiddish of "Der shofer." On this point, Berkovitz and Shneour pursue a very different approach from writers like Brenner, who stressed the foreignness of languages such as Russian, German, and English within his Hebrew text by representing them in their original orthography or setting them apart in quotation marks.[94] Like Shneour, Berkovitz's texts are firmly monolingual even as they represent the constant translingual movement between these different languages.

Berkovitz also departs from Brenner by foregrounding dialogue between characters, more like the Yiddish prose of writers like Shneour and Opatoshu than the Hebrew prose of the time. In the Hebrew version of the text, the decision to focus on spoken language is a bold one in the late 1920s. Presenting natural, convincing Hebrew speech and dialogue was the most daunting challenge faced by late-nineteenth- and early twentieth-century Hebrew writers. Early twentieth-century Hebrew prose was filled with attempts to shift away from the *nusakh* style and its stilted dialogue, whether through psycho-narration or interior and narrated monologues that tended to avoid reported speech. But they were still plagued by the inadequacies of Hebrew speech, as Gershon Shaked writes: "Hebrew still suffered from the appearance of having been translated, as if the written language were only a representation of some other, oral language."[95] Berkovitz's "The Driver" upends this statement by accentuating the artificiality of the protagonist's speech both in Hebrew and in Yiddish. The driver is characterized, first and foremost, by his Hebrew speech, unlike the tortured silence and fragmented inner language of his fictional contemporaries in Hebrew and the natural speech of his Yiddish counterparts.

Berkovitz not only uses stilted Hebrew speech but amplifies its allusive density to represent the title character in seriocomic fashion. In Hebrew, the driver's reported speech is often a pastiche of biblical phrases adapted to fit his relatively mundane concerns, namely his personal history and his infatuation with Edna. For example, after she chooses to sit in the back of the car rather than up front with the driver, the driver bewails his fate in his deep baritone: "Edna, you ingrate! Behold: I accounted to your favor the devotion of your youth, how you followed me from the valley, and I came to your aunt's house to take you with me to the Dead Sea, for our last parting voyage. And you are suddenly done with me and you choose to sit and to seek warmth next to the American capital, next to a sack full of dollars. . . . Do not imagine that you, Edna, will escape from me on the pretext of dust. It is not the dust of the roads, but rather the dust of gold, American gold, that has distanced you from me."[96] The driver articulates his intense jealousy in a Hebrew monologue clothed in biblical allusions, elevating his complaints to comic proportions. Beginning with the phrase *kfuyat-tova* (ingrate), which the Talmud uses to describe Moses's rebuke of the children of Israel (B. Avodah Zarah 5a), the driver fires off a pastiche of biblical phrases of loyalty and betrayal, each adapted to his situation: God's praise of the children Israel's devotion from Jeremiah 2:2 ("I accounted to your favor the devotion of your youth"), featuring the driver in God's role and Edna as Israel, and replacing the prophecy's wilderness with the pioneering settlements of the Jezreel Valley; playing on the different meanings of *dodati*, both the more literal "aunt" and the beloved of Song of Songs; and finally, Mordekhai's injunction to Esther, "Do not imagine that you, of all the Jews, will escape with your life" (Esther 4:13), elevating Edna's choice of seats in the car to a momentous decision. Far from attempting naturalistic Hebrew speech, Berkovitz's driver lofts into verbal flights of fancy, flaunting his allusive prowess in comic fashion, much like Shneour's Hebrew narrator in the Shklov story. The driver's soliloquies are reminiscent of Berkovitz's translations of Sholem Aleykhem's Yiddish prose into Hebrew, particularly Tevye's corrupted biblical allusions and malapropisms. Here, however, Hebrew becomes the "original" mode of discourse rather than a translation.

The Hebrew story's emphasis on quoted speech creates a dilemma for the Yiddish version of the story. The narrative relies on the driver's verbal outpouring in Hebrew, or, in the words of the narrator, the "strange confession of a strange man."[97] By necessity, the Yiddish text jettisons many of the stylistic flourishes of its Hebrew counterpart. The driver's wounded outburst after Edna chooses to sit behind him loses much of its allusive richness. "Edna, see here, how ungrateful you are to me! I have remembered your youthful graces, your faithfulness following me from the valley."[98] Echoes of Jeremiah's well-known lines are still present, but the driver's words are simplified in Yiddish. A few lines later, the melodramatic comparison with Esther is also rendered in far simpler terms: "Don't think, Edna, that you will get away with the excuse that you were bothered by the dusty road."[99] Again, the vernacular strength of Yiddish, its capacity for natural, juicy conversation, is lost in the driver's formal speech. In a story built around the ironic contrast of speech and silence, the driver's soliloquies lose their piquancy in Yiddish. Berkovitz's self-translation tries to approximate the Hebrew, but its depiction of Hebrew speech eviscerates the liveliness of Yiddish speech. Although not all of Berkovitz's later Yiddish texts run into this problem, this narrative does suffer from, as Shaked wrote about early twentieth-century Hebrew dialogue, "the appearance of being translated."[100]

Ironically, "The Driver" places the Yiddish text in the linguistic position that Hebrew had long occupied: seeking a way to represent foreign speech with all of its idiosyncrasies. In Berkovitz's early story "Be-yad ha-lashon," the Hebrew version had to convey the tension and nuances between spoken Yiddish and spoken Russian, something more easily accomplished in the Yiddish version, which could comically represent the same differences within its own idioms. "Der shofer," however, had to find a way to capture the comically elevated Hebrew in Yiddish. This is an essential difference between Berkovitz's writing in 1904 and 1929, as the first text was set in an Eastern European context in which Yiddish was at the center of daily discourse and the second was set in a Palestinian context that promoted a newly vernacular Hebrew. Berkovitz's tendency to focus on contemporary settings, writing about Eastern Europe, the United States, and Palestine in turn, means that his texts foreground contemporary literary-linguistic dynamics that are elided in Shneour's depiction of a remembered Eastern European shtetl.

With its shifts from language to language, the narrative makes two main claims about language. First, it portrays the proliferation of languages in the Yishuv. Unlike Shneour's clear differentiation between Russian, Hebrew, and Yiddish in Shklov, Berkovitz represents what seems to be a linguistic free-for-all, with his characters constantly moving between Hebrew, Yiddish, English, German, and Russian in both versions of this bilingual text. At the same time, the story also plays with notions of comprehensibility. The driver assumes that his American and Czech passengers cannot understand his Hebrew, thus he draws on his knowledge of English, Yiddish, and German to communicate across this microcosm of the Jewish diaspora. But the crux of the story is that both of his listeners do understand him, as the driver learns in a wry concluding twist. A week after the day trip, the narrator bumps into the driver strolling along the beach in Tel Aviv after having dropped off Edna at the Jaffa port. Astonished to learn that the narrator had understood his Hebrew "chatter," the driver is initially flustered by the idea that Edna, too, had understood him. But he recovers quickly from his surprise to conclude the story on a hopeful note; the driver says "but . . . but . . . perhaps she too understood? If they understand Hebrew in America, perhaps they understand it too in Prague?"[101] Though the driver had confessed his past trauma and present infatuation only when he believed his Hebrew was incomprehensible to his listeners, he is heartened by the prospect that he was in fact heard and understood. Modern Hebrew is vindicated as a new lingua franca among young Zionist men and women across the Jewish diaspora, rendering unnecessary, at least in retrospect, the linguistic switching that occurred throughout the narrative. To extend the story's logic, the characters' translingual movement from language to language yields to a triumphant Hebrew. Whether or not Hebrew is the actual language of the text, Hebrew serves as what Harshav calls the "base language" of the world depicted in the text, a crucial component in establishing a new Hebrew culture.[102]

Yet this literary representation of Hebrew's triumph is complicated by the story's bilingualism. "Ha-nahag" was published in the inaugural issue of *Moznayim* (Scales), a journal established in 1929 by the Association of Hebrew Writers in Palestine to replace the unruly *Ketuvim*. Berkovitz, a founding coeditor of the journal, introduced the mission of this new periodical with gusto: "Our Hebrew literature . . . has deviated in recent years from its straight path, paved by its many faithful and their followers. With the great revolution that occurred in the public life of the land of Israel because of the disintegration of Eastern Europe's major [Jewish] population, our literature has undergone not a spiritual revolution, carrying upon its wings the seeds of future renewal, but a disturbance of order and confusion of ideas. . . . *Moznayim* is the first effort to purify the literary environment from these bad influences."[103] Writing as a spokesperson for Hebrew literature in the Yishuv, Berkovitz embraces a model of engaged literature to combat the "bad influences" that have come with the disintegration of Eastern European Jewish culture. Representing Eastern Europe as the source of both a modern Hebrew literary tradition and dangerous contemporary trends, *Moznayim* stresses the centrality of Palestine to Hebrew literature. Though this introductory manifesto concludes with an invitation to writers in Palestine and in the diaspora, it is focused first and foremost on setting Hebrew literature in Palestine on the correct ideological and literary path. As part of this first issue, Berkovitz's story "Ha-nahag" presumably works toward *Moznayim*'s goal "to repair the damaged wholeness" by communicating the Association's aesthetic and didactic goals. Despite the protagonist's ambivalence about a Zionist reality—after all, he flees the socialist collective in search of solitude and is haunted by his diasporic past—"Ha-nahag" celebrates the emergence of Hebrew as the new Jewish lingua franca, a literary message that resonates in "the natural habitat of Hebrew creation and its great hopes for the future."[104]

In the New York Yiddish daily *Der tog* (The Day), however, Berkovitz's "Der shofer" has different resonance. *Der tog*'s independent and nonpartisan nature contrasted with the political affiliations of other Yiddish papers, like the democratic socialist *Forverts* in which Shneour published his Yiddish prose. On the pages of *Der tog*, Yiddish replaces Hebrew as the language of the narrative, conveying the driver's elevated Hebrew speech and directly representing the spoken exchanges between the driver and his passenger. Since much of the conversation takes place in Yiddish, Yiddish is entirely plausible as the language of the text. So while the story maintains the same concluding linguistic twist, it emphasizes the translingualism of the text and its characters, skipping between Hebrew, Yiddish, English, German, and Russian. Hebrew turns out to be a language that all of the story's characters share, but Hebrew is still theoretical rather than real in the logic and language of the Yiddish text. Reading bilingually balances the Hebrew text's case for monolingualism with the Yiddish's amplification of the translingual dynamics within the text. In this sense, the two versions of Berkovitz's "The Driver" can be read together as a modern drama of language-crossing, with the different languages represented within the text trumped by a mutual comprehensibility—that of the characters, who ultimately do understand each other, and that of the reader, who is presented with a text that is simultaneously monolingual (when reading either the Hebrew or the Yiddish text) and translingual (the narrative itself).

The contemporary literary-linguistic dynamics at the heart of "Ha-nahag" and "Der shofer" are present in many of Berkovitz's texts from the 1930s. The Hebrew and Yiddish versions of the novel *Menakhem-Mendl in the Land of Israel*, for example, further emphasize the writer's own bilingualism as they blur lines between original and translated texts. Menakhem-Mendl was one of Sholem Aleykhem's most famous characters, who first appeared in an 1887 feuilleton and later starred in an extended series of epistolary exchanges between a peripatetic speculator and his long-suffering wife, Shayna-Sheyndl.[105] Berkovitz's later novel, first serialized in *Forverts* (1933–1934) and soon after in *Ha'aretz* (1934–1935), opens with Sholem Aleykhem's luckless Menakhem-Mendl on a ship headed for Palestine. In the prefaces to the Yiddish and Hebrew editions, both dated 1934, Berkovitz explains that he had come across numerous real-life Menakhem-Mendls in the new generation living in the Land of Israel and hoped that his fictional protagonist could help expose the base selfishness, corruption, and immorality of these types.

Berkovitz, however, was careful to differentiate his Menakhem-Mendl from his literary predecessor: "I take for the needs of my work solely the symbolic kernel of Menakhem-Mendl, his last metamorphosis . . . wandering in our midst, excited and acting according to the conditions of our lives in the Land. Given his new situation and given the nature of things surrounding him, he is different from the first in his moods, in his ways of expression, and sometimes even in his achievements. I left only characteristic external signs in him, like the connections to his family, the set phrasing in which he begins and ends his letters, and so on and so forth. To clarify: I took the symbol of Menakhem-Mendl as a literary tool and I invested it with new content for the needs of the place and the time."[106] Berkovitz viewed Sholem Aleykhem's character as a symbol that could be reimagined and rewritten into a new place and a new time, in this case the Jewish community in Palestine. The "original" Menakhem-Mendl is still recognizable—the entire novel relies on the characters' and reader's familiarity with Sholem Aleykhem's Menakhem-Mendl—but has been changed to suit the needs of this new text and new time. An experienced translator, Berkovitz seems less concerned about the originality of the literary text than its specific elements and circumstances, evident both in his reflections on the previous manifestations of Menakhem-Mendl and his two linguistic versions of the text. While the novel is substantially similar in Yiddish and Hebrew, there are small but significant differences between the two prefaces. In Hebrew, Berkovitz firmly situated his novel in the Yishuv and from a Zionist perspective: he uses Menakhem-Mendl as a representative of the ills of the Jewish diaspora and emphasizes that Palestine will be Menakhem-Mendl's permanent home, as he is now "wandering in our midst, excited and acting according to the conditions of our lives in the Land."[107] The Yiddish preface traces Menakhem-Mendl to Palestine, but it omits references to the diaspora and the third-person-plural Zionist voice prevalent in the Hebrew. The prefaces address distinct audiences, divided not only by language but also by presumed geography and ideology.

In *Menakhem-Mendl in the Land of Israel*, Berkovitz the translator intersects with Berkovitz the bilingual Hebrew-Yiddish writer. Intimately familiar with Sholem Aleykhem's work and the creator of Sholem Alyekhem's Hebrew voice, Berkovitz was well suited to reinvent Menakhem-Mendl for the 1930s. His justification for appropriating Sholem Aleykhem's character, however, not only illuminates his approach to writing but also offers a striking analogy to his self-translations. In contrast to Shneour's insistence on the authenticity of his Yiddish "Vilne" and Hebrew *Anshei Shklov*, Berkovitz represents even original writing as a kind of rewriting. Sholem Aleykhem may have created Menakhem-Mendl, but that in no way limited Berkovitz's transposition of that character, first into his Hebrew translation of Sholem Aleykhem's text and later into his own novel.[108]

In an effort to invest translation and other forms of what he calls "literary manipulation" with greater credibility and prestige, translation studies critic André Lefevere argued that rewriting should be seen as a major mode of literary production. Translators, editors, critics, and literary historians, he claims, "adapt, manipulate the originals they work with to some extent, usually to make them fit in with the dominant, or one of the dominant ideological and poetological currents of their time."[109] Berkovitz, however, took rewriting a step further in *Menakhem-Mendl*, creating a new literary text in Yiddish and Hebrew using pieces of texts that he himself had translated into Hebrew. That same process of investing literary frameworks with different content "for the needs of the place and the time" resonates with Berkovitz's self-translations of texts like "The Driver," as he created two related but distinct literary versions of the text. While Shneour demonstrated his anxieties about translation, Berkovitz placed the challenges of translation, of adapting "kernels" to different linguistic, literary, and ideological contexts, at the center of his literary texts. Language is only one of several elements that are in flux in *Menakhem-Mendl*. But like so many of Berkovitz's works, this novel constantly traverses linguistic boundaries, bringing into contact Sholem Aleykhem's Yiddish prose, Berkovitz's Hebrew translation, and Berkovitz's Hebrew and Yiddish versions of the text. While this linguistic tangle deserves further elucidation, it reveals the extent to which bilingualism, translingualism, and translation were key components of Berkovitz's representation of contemporary Jewish life well into the 1930s. As a realist writer, Berkovitz not only wrote bilingually but also developed his own mimetic translingualism to try to register the linguistic currents of the time that were so often elided within Yiddish and Hebrew literary texts.

Lingering Bilingualism?

In 1936, critic Shmuel Niger castigated the American Yiddish literary establishment for neglecting to mark Berkovitz's fiftieth birthday: "Is this really only a Hebrew *simkhe* [celebration]? Berkovitz is a Yiddish-Hebrew writer—to Hebrew literature he has given Sholem Aleykhem, to Yiddish—himself. . . . Is the situation such that Hebrew and Yiddish writers cannot sit around one table? Is the situation really that sad?"[110] In both Hebrew and Yiddish literatures, writers' jubilees were important moments of celebration and, at times, introspection. For example, Shaul Tchernikhovsky, writing in *Rimon*, and Avraham Shlonsky, writing in *Hedim*, participated in two of many Hebrew literary paeans to Ch. N. Bialik on the occasion of his fiftieth birthday in 1923. Yiddish newspapers also feted the poet, with *Haynt* devoting three full pages, including the banner headline and front page, to this "holiday for the Jewish people."[111] Though Berkovitz never reached Bialik's legendary status in either language, Niger saw the marginalization of Berkovitz in Yiddish as a disturbing development. He did not want to believe that Hebrew and Yiddish literatures could no longer "share" a single writer by the mid-1930s. But Berkovitz's and Shneour's texts demonstrate the difficulties of crossing these literary-linguistic boundaries, much less convening a table full of Hebrew and Yiddish writers.

A prolific critic and a strong proponent of Jewish literary bilingualism, Niger recognized the changes underway in Jewish-language literature. Yet he insisted that Jewish bilingualism was still relevant. A few years later, in the book *Di tsveyshprakhikayt fun undzer literatur*

(Bilingualism in Our Literature, 1941), he conceded that writers had been more likely to "live and breathe" the two languages before World War I than after, and also more likely to do so in Eastern Europe than in the United States.[112] But he argued that changing times necessitated concomitant changes in the conception of bilingualism rather than a rejection of bilingualism. Writers like Ash, Nomberg, Hirshbeyn, Fichman, Berkovitz, and Shneour, Niger wrote, were welcome guests in both Hebrew and Yiddish presses and literatures, just like the older generation of Abramovitsh, Peretz, Frishman, and Berdichevsky had been. He continued: "These writers (and many others not mentioned here) were bilingual not only in the sense that they wrote in both Jewish languages, but in a more profound and internal sense as well. The heritage of both linguistic spheres can be felt in *everything* that they composed: everything—be it written in Hebrew or in Yiddish. Their Yiddish had within it something of Hebrew, and not just something linguistic; their Hebrew had certain elements from the Yiddish, and (again) not just elements from the Yiddish language."[113] Niger contends that Jewish literary bilingualism went beyond the language of a given text to what he referred to as "internal bilingualism." This is not what Grutman calls "heretolingualism," the presence of other languages within a text in a given language, because Niger stressed that the "something" of Hebrew or Yiddish was not necessarily linguistic in nature.[114] Nor is it strictly bilingualism, if bilingualism is understood as the alternate use of or competence in two or more languages.[115] Looking more closely at his examples of bilingual writers, only Berkovitz and Shneour had published in both Hebrew and Yiddish within a decade of the book's publication. Arguing that Hebrew and Yiddish maintained a special cultural relationship, Niger redefines traditional bilingualism as literary translingualism, the incorporation of elements of another language into a text in a variety of linguistic and nonlinguistic manners. The Jewish-language texts of certain writers, Niger argued, were inherently translingual because they shared a single "heritage." Thus for Niger, translingualism had less to do with the individual writer than the dynamics of the Jewish literary-linguistic system, which he traced from ancient times to the twentieth century. He expressed confidence that the Jewish languages would continue to "run a joint household" and to "cook one dish, although in two separate pots," provided that the artificial obstacles erected against Hebrew in the Soviet Union and Yiddish in Palestine did not interfere. [116]

Niger's comments about Jewish bilingualism resonate with later critical assessments of literary bilingualism. In her book *Alien Tongues*, Elizabeth Beaujour writes that "bilingual or polyglot writers perform an essential service to the vaster readership of monolinguals when they allow the pressure of their polyglotism to infuse, but not overwhelm, the 'national' languages in which they write."[117] Focusing on the first generation of modern Russian émigré writers, Beaujour's analysis demarcates a writer's native first language from a second acquired language. Her assumptions of linguistic priority and the national nature of these languages are complicated by the Hebrew-Yiddish case: partisans of Hebrew and Yiddish had nationalist aspirations but no national status; and it was not necessarily clear which language was primary for many early twentieth-century Jewish writers. At the same time, Beaujour calls attention to the ways in which bilingual writers can integrate "the pressure of polyglotism" into their texts. Like Niger, Beaujour avoids defining precisely what the pressure of polyglotism might be, but she includes both awareness of language-crossing and actual instances of language-crossing within the literary text. It is Beaujour's pressure of polyglotism, Niger's internal bilingualism, or what this book terms "literary translingualism" that differentiates between the bilingual writing of Shneour and Berkovitz.

For Shneour, bilingualism proved to be a pragmatic strategy for literary survival in a hostile cultural environment. Shneour did little to endear himself to publishers and writers, either personally or ideologically. Living in Paris, he interacted long-distance with colleagues in New York, Tel Aviv, and Warsaw and thus avoided most of the stylistic and ideological battles that punctuated literary life in these centers of interwar Jewish literature. Given the battle lines drawn between the Yishuv and the diaspora in partisan periodicals like *Ketuvim*, Shneour's decision to stay in Paris was perceived by many in Palestine as his selection of Yiddish over Hebrew, diaspora over Zionist return. Shneour's penchant for keeping his Hebrew and Yiddish work separate, both in his inclination toward differential bilingualism and his insistence on the originality of his self-translated texts, reinforces the separation between Hebrew and Yiddish literatures. He was not seeking to bridge the literatures, but rather to market his own "original" work within each literary marketplace. His self-translations yield a distinct Hebrew "Vilna" and a Yiddish "Vilne" as well as a Yiddish Shklov and a Hebrew Shklov. In the Shklov narratives, the representation of a linguistically stratified Eastern European Jewish society mines multilingualism for its comedy, but ultimately relies on the literary-linguistic strengths of each language in, for example, the Hebrew mock-epic style and Yiddish conversation. Hebrew-Yiddish bilingualism thus becomes one of many elements that typified Jewish life in the shtetl and is thus memorialized rather than enacted in the narrative. Ultimately, Shneour's literary work and his literary bilingualism were perceived, particularly in Hebrew, as old-fashioned and out of step with the literature of its time.

Berkovitz, however, seems to have been the more successful bilingual writer into the 1930s, and certainly the more emphatically bilingual of the two. Publishing weekly in New York and Tel Aviv, Berkovitz did not need to be reintroduced to Hebrew writers, nor did he blame the literary establishment for his disappointments. His literary work was rigorously bilingual, published in dual linguistic versions from the very beginning of the century until the late 1930s. Language-saturated texts like "Be-yad ha-lashon"/"On loshn" and "Ha-nahag"/"Der shofer" emphasize the linguistic fluidity of contemporary Jewish life in both Yiddish and Hebrew versions and implicitly insist that contemporary literature reflect that reality. They represent a rare convergence of what could be called "old" and "new" bilingualisms, in Niger's terms, Beaujour's pressure of polyglotism or, in other words, the textual coexistence of literary bilingualism and translingualism. Critical to Berkovitz's interwar texts are precisely the extra-literary dimensions absent in Shneour's work: both "The Driver" and *Menakhem-Mendl* are set in Palestine and enlist translingual dynamics in service of Zionist ideology, one putting diasporic languages within a Hebraic framework and the other recruiting a Yiddish fictional icon to the Zionist cause. While Shneour's *Shklov* stories position Hebrew-Yiddish bilingualism in the past, Berkovitz's texts bilingually represent a translingual interwar Jewish reality.

Despite his efforts to navigate contemporary literary dynamics, Berkovitz, too, became increasingly distant from Yiddish and Hebrew literatures. After his wife's death in 1938, Berkovitz essentially stopped writing new works, revising his earlier work and continuing his translations of Sholem Aleykhem.[118] Shneour kept churning out historical novels in Yiddish, although he tried his luck again at Hebrew poetry in 1950 with *Luchot genuzim* (Hidden Tablets), poems that evoke ancient Canaan.[119] Neither Berkovitz nor Shneour were in the ideological or literary vanguard of Hebrew or Yiddish; if anything, their bilingualism represented a stylistic conservatism, in which both writers continued producing texts substantially similar in style and sensibility to those they had published in the early years of the twentieth century. But their different approaches to bilingual writing register the radical changes that occurred in Hebrew and Yiddish literature and rendered the most promising writers at the turn of the century virtually irrelevant thirty years later.

By the 1930s, it was clear that Hebrew-Yiddish self-translation was less sustainable with the growing distances between Hebrew and Yiddish audiences and literatures. Writers like Aharon Zeitlin and Gabriel Preil continued to translate their own literary works between the languages, but they were exceptions even among the many writers fluent in Yiddish and Hebrew. Berkovitz's dual roles as a prolific self-translator and acclaimed translator anticipate the extent to which different forms of literary translingualism, and specifically translation between Hebrew and Yiddish, came to replace bilingual writing by the early 1940s. Jewish literary bilingualism had not disappeared; Berkovitz, Shneour, Zeitlin, Preil, and others continued to move between the two languages in various ways. But with the end of the interwar period, many Hebrew and Yiddish writers were further removed than they ever had been from Eastern European Jewish life and the heyday of literary bilingualism. More and more translators stepped in to fill the linguistic and cultural void by providing Hebrew readers with glimpses of Yiddish life and culture and Yiddish readers with glimpses of Hebrew life and culture.

4

Bound Up in the Bond of Hebrew Literature

Translating Yiddish in the 1940s

IN LATE 1925, Yiddish journalist and writer Rokhl Feygenberg (later, Rachel Feygenberg-Imri) accused the Hebrew literary establishment of discriminating against Yiddish. Hebrew writers, she argued in an article published in *Davar*, were quick to translate even mediocre European novels like Arthur Schnitzler's *Fraulein Else* but were reluctant to translate Yiddish literature. Though the majority of Jews spoke Yiddish as their living language, she continued, the Yiddish writer was a despised stepchild in the institutions of Hebrew culture, and Yiddish literature was scorned by Hebrew publishing houses. As a result, Jewish youth in Palestine were completely estranged from Yiddish writing and Jewish life. Arguing that Hebrew literature, its writers, and its readers needed to pay attention to Yiddish literature, Feygenberg concluded: "Oh, we've had enough of the great, strange world. The time has come for us to recognize ourselves a bit. Perhaps then we will succeed in creating our own bookshelves and we will not have to exaggerate the value of others."[1]

Feygenberg's call for increased translation from Yiddish into Hebrew was countered a few days later by a withering response from none other than Avraham Shlonsky. Responding on the pages of *Davar*, Shlonsky let loose his rhetorical fury: "It is ridiculous (and it would even be insulting if it was not so ridiculous) that R. F., without a sense of place, could publish on the pages of a Hebrew newspaper such scornful statements and contempt for the Hebrew language, literature, writers, and presses."[2] Rejecting Feygenberg's attempt to intervene in Hebrew literature, Shlonsky insisted that there was no reason to translate from Yiddish to Hebrew: "Since the majority of the nation (in the diaspora) speaks Yiddish (and, I will add—let our Yiddishists take some pleasure in this fact) and does not know Hebrew (in the diaspora) indeed it is an obligation, to the contrary, to worry about translating Hebrew works into Yiddish! We the Hebraists do not dandify our boorishness and many still know Yiddish, even in the Land of Israel, so for the time being we can read the books in the original."[3] Shlonsky argued that it was more valuable to translate Hebrew literature into Yiddish for the Yiddish-speaking majority in the diaspora. Writing in late 1925, Shlonsky pointed out that there were enough Yiddish-speaking Hebraists that translating Yiddish literature into Hebrew was unnecessary. At the same time, he used his parenthetical comments to differentiate between the linguistic situation in the diaspora (Yiddish) and in the land of Israel (Hebrew). As a prelude to his offensive against Ash and Hirshbeyn in 1927, Shlonsky categorically rejected Feygenberg's desire to establish a Yiddish presence—via translation—within Hebrew literature.

This public skirmish between Feygenberg and Shlonsky encapsulates the literary-linguistic climate of the 1920s: deeply ideological cultural discourse; competition between Palestine and the diaspora; and the ongoing bilingualism of many writers and readers. Although Feygenberg and Shlonsky disagreed about the need for Hebrew translations from Yiddish, both envisioned futures in which translation played an important role. Feygenberg imagined a future in which "our" bookshelves would be well stocked with Hebrew texts, both original works and translations from Yiddish.[4] Shlonsky, too, saw the ultimate destination of a smaller subset of Yiddish literature in Hebrew translation: "As the number of readers able to read the works in the original shrinks—the need to translate these works into Hebrew will increase. And this will happen. What was most important in our temporary languages was rescued, and when necessary, bound up in the bond of life of Hebrew literature. That which is significant in Yiddish will be as well. History has time."[5] Unlike Feygenberg, Shlonsky was in no rush to translate Yiddish into Hebrew, but he was confident that it would eventually happen to the best of Yiddish literature. Equating Yiddish with other "temporary" Jewish languages that had come and gone, he used a phrase familiar from the Jewish funeral liturgy, *li-tsror bi-tsror ha-chayim* (to be bound up in the bond of life), to pronounce the inevitable death of Yiddish and to commit Hebrew to perpetuating its memory "when necessary."

Neither Shlonsky nor Feygenberg could have imagined that within fifteen years the circumstances surrounding Hebrew-Yiddish translation would change dramatically. By the 1940s, the pace of translation from Yiddish to Hebrew had accelerated, but not for reasons that Feygenberg or Shlonsky could have foreseen in 1925. The number of translations from Yiddish to Hebrew slowly but steadily increased over the course of the 1930s, matched by an equally slow increase in translations from Hebrew to Yiddish, particularly in the United States.[6] But reports of the Nazi genocide in Europe spurred a precipitous rise in Hebrew translation from Yiddish in the 1940s. History, as it turned out, did not have the time Shlonsky had expected.

In the early 1940s, Feygenberg and Shlonsky as well as several other writers in the United States and Palestine embarked on projects to translate Yiddish literature into Hebrew. These projects highlight major changes in the Jewish literary-linguistic landscape that had occurred during the interwar years. The ideological terms of debate had shifted away from Czernowitz-inspired scuffles over "*the* Jewish language" and, as we saw in the 1927 Yiddish Affair in Palestine, toward the fate of Jewish culture in the diaspora. Palestine and the United States were well on their way to replacing the shared Hebrew-Yiddish cultural centers of Eastern Europe. Individual and literary bilingualism were far less common. Shlonsky's assertion in 1925 that most Hebrew writers could read Yiddish texts was no longer a safe assumption by the 1940s, particularly among younger writers. Likewise, fewer and fewer Yiddish readers had access to Hebrew literature unless it was translated. Translation became an increasingly important way of sustaining literary contact between the two languages. Hebrew texts were translated into Yiddish, but it is the dramatic rise in the number of Yiddish texts translated into Hebrew in the late 1930s and early 1940s that calls attention to a significant shift in Jewish translingual practice. From the end of the nineteenth century, Hebrew and Yiddish writers had turned to literary translation to help develop their own modern literatures. But the changing relationship between the two languages during the interwar period culminated with a shift away from Hebrew translation and Yiddish translation as strategies for building modern literary cultures and toward Yiddish-Hebrew translation as a method for preserving Eastern European Jewish culture.

This chapter compares two Yiddish-to-Hebrew translation projects, Feygenberg's Ha-me'asef (Collector) Press in Palestine and the anthology *Achisefer* (Brothers of the Book), edited by Sh. Niger and Menachem Ribalow, in New York City. Translation brings Hebrew and Yiddish texts, writers, and readers into contact, but each of these translation projects conceived of the purpose of translingual contact in surprisingly different ways. In Ha-me'asef books, translation was intended to usher Yiddish into a Hebraic framework. In *Achisefer*, translation sought to sustain cultural bilingualism in the face of waning individual and literary bilingualism. These texts acknowledged radical changes underway in the ideological and geographical configurations of modern Jewish culture. Their translations and the commentary surrounding those translations demonstrate the extent to which Hebrew-Yiddish bilingualism was increasingly a legacy of a shared Eastern European past rather than a reality. But with immense anxiety about the fate of European Jewry in the early 1940s, the relationship between Hebrew and Yiddish became one aspect of this shared legacy that could be revisited. In Palestine and in New York, literary translation was enlisted to fill the void left by the destruction of Eastern European Jewish life and culture.

Translating between Hebrew and Yiddish

Translation, Lawrence Venuti writes, "is the forcible replacement of the linguistic and cultural differences of the foreign text with a text that is intelligible to the translating-language reader."[7] While not all scholars of translation agree with Venuti about the violence with which translation is imposed on a text, most are concerned with both the linguistic and the cultural differences at play in translation. Rainier Grutman, for example, insists that literary translation is a sociocultural rather than a purely linguistic phenomenon, calling attention to the inequality of the literatures brought into contact through translation.[8] Systems-based approaches, like Gideon Toury's descriptive translation studies, similarly define translation as an activity "which inevitably involves at least two languages and two cultural traditions."[9] These and other approaches assume that discrepancies necessarily exist between source language and target language and between source culture and target culture, to use Toury's terminology.

Hebrew-Yiddish translation shows that translation is translingual, but it is not inevitably transcultural. Jewish literary bilingualism challenges assumptions that all languages are affiliated with distinct, nonoverlapping cultures, much less national cultures. Nineteenth-century Hebrew writers translated everything from idioms to full texts from Yiddish to help develop Hebrew literature, what Ken Frieden has called "innovation by translation."[10] This took place in an environment in which Hebrew readers were a subset of the Yiddish reading public; well into the twentieth century, most European Hebrew readers would have been able to read the source text in Yiddish. Menakhem Perry notes that Abramovitsh's self-translations were not intended to provide a reader with a text that he could not otherwise read but rather to provide a reader with new versions of texts he had already read.[11] This fundamentally changes the act of translation, emphasizing the translingual rather than transcultural dimensions of a given text's passage from one language to the next. In the first decades of the twentieth century, Hebrew and Yiddish boasted distinct literatures, but the intercultural dimension of translations between the two languages was still marginal.

While most Hebrew translations from Yiddish were not strictly necessary, the reverse was not always the case; Hebrew texts were not comprehensible to many Yiddish readers, particularly women. In the traditional Jewish communities of Eastern Europe, young boys learned at least rudimentary Hebrew in *heder*, schools for children in Eastern European Jewish communities, to read the Bible and recite prayers. Girls, however, were typically taught to read in Yiddish or local languages like Russian or Polish.[12] Yiddish literature has a long history of translations and quasi-translations intended to give non-Hebrew readers access to, or at least glimpses of, religious texts in the Holy Tongue. Perhaps best known is the *Tsenerene*, a seventeenth-century version of the Bible in Yiddish that was more a compilation of traditional commentaries on weekly Torah readings than a Bible translation.[13] However, the intracultural nature of these translations and rewritings fundamentally shaped translational norms. To borrow Venuti's phrase, translations between Hebrew and Yiddish were often more creative replacements of the linguistic differences in a shared cultural text than "forcible replacements." Venuti locates the violence of translation in "the reconstitution of the foreign text in accordance with values, beliefs, and representations that preexist it in the translating language and culture."[14] But that is precisely what is unusual about Hebrew-Yiddish translation, at least before World War I; both "foreign" and "familiar" texts largely shared values, beliefs, and representations, though they were expressed in different linguistic manners for overlapping audiences. The intracultural nature of nineteenth- and early twentieth-century translation between Yiddish and Hebrew, however, did not eliminate the complex power dynamics between the two languages, as we saw in the cases of Shneour and Berkovitz. But it is the transition from intracultural translation to intercultural translation that defines the latter half of the interwar period.

From the very end of the nineteenth century, both Hebrew and Yiddish writers embraced translation as an essential way to establish modern literatures. Itamar Even-Zohar writes that "translated literature simply fulfills the need of a younger literature to put into use its newly founded (or renovated) tongue for as many literary types as possible in order to make it serviceable as a literary language and useful for its emerging public."[15] Both Yiddish and Hebrew were, in Even-Zohar's terms, "weak" literatures, or following Pascale Casanova, "dominated" languages, with respect to English, Russian, German, and other European languages and their literatures.[16] As Kenneth Moss points out, the commitment to the translation of canonical Western literary texts traversed Jewish linguistic and ideological fault-lines, uniting Zionist Hebraists like Joseph Klausner, Hebraist aesthete David Frishman, and radical Yiddishist Moyshe Litvakov.[17] Eliezer Shteinman, for example, praised the Stybel publishing house in 1919 for paying no attention to political divisions in their efforts to bring "everything, everything to us: from the first fruits of realism, from the flowers of Romanticism, and from the grapes of modernism, original and translated."[18] Writers in both literatures saw translation as a critical means of literary innovation, a way of establishing universal modern literatures on par with their European counterparts. As a result, translation from European languages into Yiddish and Hebrew was first and foremost propelled by the needs of the translating culture, with an emphasis on making foreign texts of high canonical status intelligible to the Hebrew or Yiddish reader.

The importance placed on translation into Yiddish and Hebrew, however, did not extend to translation between Hebrew and Yiddish. After the peak of self-translations at the beginning of the twentieth century, there was surprisingly little translation between the two Jewish languages. Chayim Nachman Bialik called for Hebrew translations of worthy Jewish texts written in other languages, including the "Jewish jargons," part of his emphasis on *kinus* (gathering), the creation of a national canon of Jewish texts to serve as the foundation for modern Jewish culture.[19] But major proponents of translation like Frishman and Litvakov rejected this focus on Jewish texts, arguing instead that their respective literary languages needed to free themselves from a stifling tradition and create universal literatures by translating canonical European literary texts.[20] For writers trying to reorient their respective literatures toward universal—or really, European—models, translation between Hebrew and Yiddish was perceived as unnecessary if not counterproductive. Well into the interwar period, there were surprisingly few books of Yiddish literature published in Hebrew translation; translations of European literary texts were still valued far more than translations between Yiddish and Hebrew. There were also complicated power asymmetries at work in Jewish-language translation. While Yiddish and Hebrew occupied similarly "weak" positions vis-à-vis most European languages, the power dynamic shifted radically in translations between the two languages. Hebrew possessed the prestige and deep literary and linguistic reservoir of the Jewish textual tradition but for decades lacked a reliable readership, particularly in Europe. Yiddish had a much larger potential readership, though it lacked the stature of Hebrew. Hebrew was often assumed to be the dominant language, but Hebrew debates about translation reveal major anxieties about Yiddish.

A few weeks after the public exchange between Feygenberg and Shlonsky in *Davar*, A. Y. Stybel, the patron and guiding force of the Stybel Press, refuted Feygenberg's accusation that his press disdained Yiddish. In an article titled "A Comment for Miss Feygenberg" he wrote: "I, for example, would never become angry at a Hebrew editor, even the editor of *Ha-tkufa*, if he were to give space to a Yiddish author or authoress . . . provided that the Yiddish creative work has not already been published or that it was translated by the writer. But with all my strength, I would oppose, for example, giving space in *Ha-tkufa* for a literary work translated from Yiddish since I fear for the Hebrew reader and the existence of *Ha-tkufa*. The majority of Hebrew readers understand Yiddish and, those for whom literature is dear, read that which is created in Yiddish just like that which is created in Hebrew."[21] Stybel denied Feygenberg's accusation that his press would not publish Yiddish on principle. Rather, he insisted that translated Yiddish works were welcome within his Hebrew publications as long as they appeared as "original" works: either not previously published in Yiddish, or the writer's own translation. Like *Davar*'s insistence that Shneour's *Anshei Shklov* (People of Shklov) was an original text and not a translation, Stybel sees self-translations as more authentic than other translations. His conditions, which were not applied to any other languages, resulted in few Hebrew translations of Yiddish literature.

As we saw in the cases of Shneour and Berkovitz, fewer and fewer writers were able or willing to translate their own literary texts, and few unpublished and thus unproven Yiddish works were likely to be chosen for Hebrew translation. Stybel Press's publication list shows the tiny percentage of translations from Yiddish: between 1918 and 1939, fewer than ten of the press's 186 Hebrew translations were from Yiddish.[22] Stybel's small percentage of Hebrew translations from Yiddish was typical of the publishing industry more broadly; Zohar Shavit counts 110 translated works published in Hebrew between 1918 and 1928, but only 12 were in Yiddish.[23] Interestingly enough, only a few years after Stybel's condescending response to Feygenberg, his press published her novel *Le-shnatayim* (For Two Years). The novel fulfilled both of Stybel's conditions: it was translated by the author from Yiddish into Hebrew and it was published first in Hebrew (1929) and later in Yiddish (1932). But it was more than issues of authenticity that kept the press from publishing translations from Yiddish. Stybel perceived Yiddish, even translations from Yiddish, as dangerous to Hebrew literature and its institutions. He knew that his readers could read Yiddish, but he wanted them to choose Hebrew instead. What incentive would they have to pick up a copy of *Ha-tkufa* if it featured translations from Yiddish that they could read in the original? Stybel essentially rejects the bilingual writing and reading that had once defined Eastern European Jewish literature.

Stybel was not the only one to worry about the threat posed by Yiddish translation, or translation more generally, to Hebrew literature. Before 1920, Shavit argues, "the emphasis lay at this time not only, or not primarily, on Hebrew literature but on literature *in Hebrew*."[24] By the mid-1920s, with Hebrew literature on firmer footing, Hebrew writers were more ambivalent about translated literature and questioned its effects on Hebrew writing. In Asher Barash's words, "The great translation enterprise established in the land of Israel and abroad seems to cast a shadow over original Hebrew prose, and to reduce it to a mere fraction."[25] Despite these concerns, publishing houses like the Berlin-based Stybel continued to publish a significant number of translations throughout the early 1930s. As their publication dwindled in the mid-1930s, new presses like Am Oved, Sifriyat Po'alim,

Schocken, and N. Twersky continued to present the Hebrew reading public with translations through the 1940s.

This transition from European-based presses to a new generation of presses in Palestine coincided with the acceleration of translation from Yiddish into Hebrew. From the late 1930s through the 1940s, there was a veritable explosion of Yiddish literary works published in Hebrew. Not surprisingly, novels that were popular among Yiddish readers were more likely to be translated into Hebrew: Sholem Ash and Yoysef Opatoshu were the best-represented Yiddish writers in Hebrew translation.[26] Other Yiddish writers translated into Hebrew included Perets Markish, H. Leyvik, Itzik Manger, Y. Y. Singer, Dovid Bergelson, and Moyshe Kulbak. Despite their public debate about translation in 1925, both Feygenberg and Shlonsky played key roles as editors and translators in promoting Hebrew translations from Yiddish.

Why did translation from Yiddish become increasingly acceptable within the sphere of Hebrew literature? The obvious answer is that World War II and the Shoah, the Nazi genocide of European Jewry, transformed Jewish life and culture in ways previously unimaginable and shook both Hebrew and Yiddish literatures to their very foundations. In Palestine and in the United States, the "old" Eastern European centers had been reliable guardians of traditional life and culture. The self-consciously "new" literary endeavors in the New World and the New Hebrew were predicated upon the existence of the "old," even when they rejected that world. As Anita Norich writes: "In the 1930s and '40s, Yiddish writers were increasingly united not only by an intimate relationship to a threatened and finally obliterated East European world and by their own acute consciousness of that relationship, but also by their revived memory of that world."[27] Norich focuses on American Yiddish writers, but her comments resonate for Hebrew writers and particularly the cultural agents involved in Hebrew translations from Yiddish: translators, editors, and publishers. The overwhelming majority of these individuals had extensive Eastern European connections even if they had rejected European Jewish life. Like their American Yiddish colleagues, they were acutely aware of the devastation in Eastern Europe. By the early 1940s, Feygenberg and Shlonsky as well as many other writers and translators were seeking to revive or enshrine Yiddish literature within a Hebraic framework.

However, the war is not the sole reason for this sea change within Hebrew literature and the corresponding change in the relationship between Hebrew and Yiddish cultural spheres. The shift from Eastern Europe to the United States and Palestine, from intracultural to intercultural translation and from Hebrew-Yiddish bilingualism to other forms of Hebrew-Yiddish translingualism, was well underway in the 1930s. Even before the Shoah, it was clear to Jewish writers and Jewish publishers that the Jewish-language reading public had divided to an unprecedented degree. Translation became a key strategy in reconfiguring the relationship between Hebrew and Yiddish and sustaining contact between the two languages as the centers of Hebrew and Yiddish literature shifted to Palestine and the United States, respectively. If the internal bilingualism of Jewish Eastern Europe had been the primary rationale against Yiddish-Hebrew translation, the decline of that bilingualism spurred translation between the two languages.

Yiddish as Steppingstone: Rachel Feygenberg's Ha-me'asef Translations

Given her comments in *Davar*, it is not surprising that Rachel Feygenberg proposed an ambitious project to translate Yiddish literature into Hebrew. Yiddish-turned-Hebrew writer Feygenberg (1885–1972) was one of the first female Yiddish journalists and, in Melekh Ravitch's estimation, a combative personality who fought her way into male-dominated Yiddish newspapers and always kept fighting.[28] Born in a small town in White Russia, Feygenberg started publishing fiction and essays in the Yiddish press at an early age, from short stories featuring female protagonists to essays about Ukrainian pogroms.[29] She immigrated to Palestine in 1925, but spent several years in Warsaw and Paris before settling permanently in Palestine in 1933.[30] Feygenberg published three novels in Hebrew, including two self-translations of her Yiddish novels, but she never received much attention from

Hebrew critics or writers. For decades she worked tirelessly to promote the development of Hebrew literature as a writer and editor, arguing that Yiddish literature needed to be translated into Hebrew to support Zionism and Hebrew monolingualism.

Feygenberg first announced plans to publish a series of translations from Yiddish literature in Hebrew newspapers in late 1943: "Under the name 'Ha-me'asef' a new national publishing house is being organized in Jerusalem, with the goals of publishing in Hebrew the best and most acclaimed literature written in Yiddish and bringing the Jews of the diaspora closer to Hebrew culture. The press will also rescue any book written in a foreign language whose contents are taken from the life of Jews, if it is worthy from an artistic standpoint."[31] With the name "Ha-me'asef" (The Collector), the new publishing house alluded to the first Hebrew journal, *Ha-me'asef* (Königsberg, 1784–1832), as it cast itself as a storehouse for Yiddish and other Jewish literatures. Though a number of illustrious Yishuv figures lent their names to the editorial board, including scholar and ideologue Yosef Klausner, historian Bentzion Dinaburg (Dinur), journalist David Zakai, and writer and educator Rachel Yanait (Ben Zvi), the driving figure behind Ha-me'asef was Feygenberg. The press's goal of bringing "the Jews of the diaspora closer to Hebrew culture" at first sounds like Shlonsky's 1925 argument for translating Hebrew literature into Yiddish. But in 1943, this statement took on a far more ambiguous cast. Was the purpose of these Yiddish-to-Hebrew translations to encourage diaspora readers to improve their Hebrew by reading familiar Yiddish texts in Hebrew translation? Or were they intended to bring diasporic Jews as subjects into the sphere of Hebrew culture through translation? Feygenberg made clear in the announcement that her focus was the first of those options, further explaining the press's goals in explicitly pedagogical terms. "The press's goal is to educate new Hebrew readers in the Yishuv and in the diaspora, and so the press's leadership will endeavor to make reading easier for the Hebrew reader."[32] Yet it is in fact the second option, translation as a means of cultural preservation, that became increasingly significant in the three translations published by Ha-me'asef between 1945 and 1947.

Feygenberg had long advocated for the cultural significance of translation. From her first foray into the Hebrew press, Feygenberg challenged the presiding wisdom that translation from European languages into Hebrew was an essential step in cultivating modern Hebrew literature. In contrast to Shneour and Berkovitz, she also rejected Eastern European Jewish bilingualism as a sustainable model for modern literary production. Rather, she emphasized the importance of unidirectional translation from Yiddish to Hebrew to realize literary and ideological goals. In the 1936 book *Di velt vil, mir zoln zayn yidn* (The World Wants Us to Be Jews), Feygenberg surveyed the state of Yiddish culture worldwide.[33] She argued that Yiddish had been declining ever since Eastern European Jews had been permitted to assimilate into Russian and Polish societies. "Isn't it clear," she asked rhetorically, "that in our time it is impossible to have extra-territorial languages and cultures?"[34] The futures of Yiddish and Hebrew, Feygenberg continued, were rooted in two different territories, the land of Israel and the Soviet Union. Those who wished to continue to write in Yiddish, Feygenberg argued, should follow Moyshe Kulbak and Dovid Bergelson and move to the Soviet Union. Those who chose Hebrew, like Feygenberg herself, should live in Palestine.[35] Feygenberg rejected bilingualism as a valid literary path, but she accepted the geographical division of Jewish languages that the *Ketuvim* writers had challenged nearly a decade earlier.

Given her strong convictions about Hebrew in Palestine, Feygenberg's translation project must be understood in the context of her allegiance to Zionism, initially mainstream Labor Zionism but later tending toward Revisionism. Her approach to language was thoroughly nationalist in its faith both in a single national language and culture and the centrality of literature in nation-building. At the same time, Feygenberg described a sociolinguistic reality in Palestine that belied efforts of groups like the Brigade of Defenders of the Language to prohibit Yiddish and instill Hebrew as the language of daily life in Palestine. She insisted that "Jews in the Land of Israel don't want to speak Hebrew."[36] Many immigrants had great reverence for Hebrew, but they found it difficult to learn and they could get around easily enough without it. For Feygenberg, the key was not to ignore Yiddish in the Yishuv, but rather to harness it within a Hebraic framework. Feygenberg staunchly believed that Jewish bilingualism, in which Yiddish and Hebrew were seen as legitimate Jewish languages, should yield to a cultivated translingualism in which Yiddish was gradually ushered into and ultimately replaced by Hebrew.

Ever the pragmatist, Feygenberg set forth a concrete program for incorporating Yiddish into Hebrew culture: Hebrew lectures about Yiddish literature, a monthly Hebrew journal for Yiddish literature, and, most of all, a press to publish Yiddish books in Hebrew translations, with vowels to facilitate easier reading.[37] She insisted, particularly in her Hebrew essays on the subject, that translation from Yiddish would benefit Hebrew literature in terms reminiscent of earlier twentieth-century arguments on behalf of translation: "The integration of Yiddish literature into Hebrew will also bring great benefit to living, spoken Hebrew, expand its present boundaries, add living blood to its frozen body, liberate it from its allusive classicism and do away with its theological rust."[38] But this translation, according to Feygenberg, had to be done in organized fashion, "collected and nurtured from a unified idea and a unified approach . . . to coordinate, translate, and publish worthy Yiddish literature in Hebrew."[39] Worthwhile Yiddish literature in translation was to become a vehicle of literary innovation and cultural assimilation.

While Feygenberg clearly envisioned what would become Hame'asef Press in the mid-1930s, it took years before she was able to establish the press. The public announcement of the press in *Ha-boker* spurred many would-be translators to offer their services.[40] Yet Feygenberg found it difficult to find literary institutions willing to support the translation initiative. In 1936 Feygenberg contacted Hebrew publisher Salman Schocken, who encouraged her efforts but declined to help. "I read with great interest your plan to publish Yiddish writers in Hebrew . . . I have absolutely no doubt that the majority of ideas that found expression in your letter as well as the fundamental explanations of your proposal are just and deserve special cultivation."[41] However Schocken concluded by stating that he did not know his press's current plans and could not commit to the project. Several years later, desperately trying to pay the bills and sustain the publishing project, Feygenberg received a similarly polite rejection from David Hanegbi, longtime editor at Sifriyat Po'alim: "Today we discussed your proposal but to my regret, we cannot help due to constraints on our press. . . . Believe us, we are greatly sorrowed that we are not able to extend you substantial help for this responsible and great work you have taken upon yourself."[42] Later in life, Feygenberg bitterly reflected on the financial struggle to realize the translation project and accused various Hebrew cultural figures of being anti-Yiddish.[43] Without the support of the literary establishment, Feygenberg turned to a public financing plan as an alternative, seeking to sell shares in the press to offset publication costs. Remarkably, she managed to cobble together enough of these individual donors and small grants that—in combination with her own savings—allowed her to print Hebrew translations of Yiddish writers Y. Y. Singer, Dovid Bergelson, and Moyshe Kulbak.

The first book published by Ha-me'asef was Shimshon Meltzer's translation of Y. Y. Singer's Yiddish prose, titled *Mi-shnei evrei ha-visla* (From Both Sides of the Visla, 1945). The volume features an assortment of psychologically probing short stories written in the 1920s by Singer, an acclaimed writer and journalist and the older brother of Yiddish writer and Nobel laureate Isaac Bashevis Singer, as well as Feygenberg's substantial introduction to Singer's work. Meltzer, who published poetry in Yiddish and Hebrew and translated many texts from Yiddish, largely followed Feygenberg's prescription that Ha-me'asef translations should be "in a language clear and understandable for all and with full vocalization."[44] From its title page, the text is provided with vowels, a feature typically reserved for printing poetry and books for young children. But the stories themselves usher the reader into Singer's realistic depictions of Jewish life in Poland.

The story "Tefila" (Prayer), a translation of Singer's "Davnen" (Praying), exemplifies both thematic features of Singer's short stories and defining aspects of Meltzer's translation. It follows the difficult life of Shimke, an orphan abused by the uncle who took him in after his mother's death. Soon after his uncle informs him that he will be staying behind to guard the orchards instead of joining the rest of the family in town for the High Holidays, Shimke catches sight of his cousin Khaye as he walks past the kitchen.

> נעבן אַ קליין טישל האָט אַ יונגער מיידלשער קאָפּ אין רונדע אַקסלען געזינקען, אַ פּאָר ווײַסע פֿולע הענטלעך האָבן בײַ לאַנגע רויטע און בלויע פּעדים געצויגן . . . ער האט לאַנג זײַן שוואַרצן בליק אויף דער בלענדנדיקער ווײַסקייט געהאַלטן און אַן אומרויקייט האָט זיך אונטער דער ברוסט זײַנער געהויבן.
>
> זי איז אַזוי ווײַס — האָט אים געאָרט און ער איז אַזוי שוואַרץ, אַזוי פּאַרמיסטיקט, אַז ער זאָל זי כאָטש מיט זײַנע אויגן נישט אײַנריכטן.[45]

> Near a small table a young girl's head is sunk on round shoulders, a pair of white, full little hands pulled on long blue and red ribbons [on braids]. . . . For a long time his black gaze stayed fixed on the blinding whiteness and a restlessness rose in his chest.
>
> She is so white—it troubled him, and he is so black, so filthy that he should not soil her with his eyes.

This passage foregrounds color—the pure, "white" Khaye, and the downtrodden "black" Shimke—and uses Yiddish syntax to emphasize the contrasts between the characters. The long, descriptive sentences at the beginning of the passage detail Khaye's body parts as they become visible to her cousin, postponing the second part of the Yiddish verbal phrase until the very end of these lengthy clauses. In the second sentence quoted above, the contrast is sharpened by bracketing "his dark gaze on her blinding whiteness" between the pronoun and auxiliary verb (*er hot*) and the past participle (*gehaltn*). The Hebrew translation, without two-part verbs, has to achieve this effect in a different manner:

> ליד שלחן קטן ראה ראש צעיר של נערה שקוע בין כתפים עגלות, וזוג ידים קטנות, צחורות ומלאות, שמשכו בחוטים ארכים, אדומים וכחולים. . . . הוא הצמיד זמן רב את מבטו השחור אל הלבנוניות המסנורת, ואי-מנוחה צמחה ועלתה בחלל חזהו.
>
> היא לבנה כל כך — הרגיז אותו הדבר — והוא הריהו כה שחור, מלכלך, חשש שמא ילכלך אותה חלילה במבט עיניו בלבד.[46]

> Next to a small table he saw the young head of a girl sunk between round shoulders, and a pair of small hands, white and full, that pulled on long ribbons, red and blue . . . he fixed for a long time his black gaze on the blinding whiteness, and uneasiness sprouted and rose in the space of his chest.
>
> She is so white—this irritated him—and he, he is so black, dirty, afraid lest he dirty her, God forbid, solely with the gaze of his eyes.

The Hebrew version hews close to the Yiddish, creating a similar visual confrontation between black and white. But there are subtle points at which the translation draws on conventions of Hebrew prose. The first sentence adds an additional verb, "he saw," that frames the entire scene in Shimke's gaze. In the Yiddish, the indeterminacy of the subject position invites the readers to peep with Shimke, involving them in the deliberate way in which parts of Khaye come into view, one by one. In subsequent sentences, this penchant to add verbs to better reflect Hebrew's verbal system continues to tweak the scene: instead of a restlessness *zikh geboybn* (born) in Shimke's breast, it "spouted and rose in the space of his chest," a classic *nusakh* pairing of verbs; in the last sentence, it is not just that Shimke "should not soil her" but that he is "afraid that he will dirty her, God forbid," adding not only another verb (fear) but also a characteristically Hebraic exclamation, *chalilah* (God forbid). The Hebrew version more explicitly frames the scene within Shimke's view, and it enlists Hebrew linguistic registers to elevate the scene and bring it closer to early twentieth-century Hebrew prose. In contrast to the Yiddish repetition of the word "white" (*vayse*, *vayskayt*, *vays*), the Hebrew text features several different words for white (*tsechorot*, *livnoniyut*, *levana*), losing the stark white-black opposition here and throughout the story. The Hebrew version of Singer's story follows the Yiddish plot and syntax, but still cultivates what we could call an updated *nusakh* Hebrew prose, or what Nitsa Ben Ari, focusing on later translations into Hebrew, calls *tirgumit*, a stylized Hebrew specific to translations.[47] This Hebrew stylization shapes the text to suit literary Hebrew linguistic conventions and lends it a subtle old-fashioned tone, one more akin to

Berkovitz's prose than the modernist prose of the 1920s and 1930s or the early novels of the Statehood Generation that started to appear in the 1940s. Yiddish prose in translation becomes part of the Hebrew literary past, not its stylistic present.

Like Meltzer's translation, Feygenberg's introductory comments also situate Singer's stories in the past. In the first translation and in subsequent books in the series, she emphasized the same goals evident in the *Ha-boker* announcement and in her 1936 essays: these translations were intended to "redeem" the best of Yiddish literature; to educate the Hebrew readership about contemporary Jewish life in the diaspora; and to promote Hebrew literacy via a clearly written and vocalized text, all of which were realized to varying degrees in the Singer translation. Feygenberg also tried to make Singer's stories, as well as the work of Dovid Bergelson and Moyshe Kulbak in Ha-me'asef's second and third volumes, respectively, geographically representative of Jewish Eastern European life. In the preface to the Kulbak translation, *Chevle ge'ulah* (Redemption Pangs, 1947), Feygenberg wrote: "The writers of these three books—Y. Y. Singer, D. Bergelson, and M. Kulbak—show the Hebrew reader the character of Jews in Poland, Ukraine, and Lithuania from the eve of the destruction. In these works are reflected the faces of the generation and trends of the time, and within them there is an artistic expression of the sharp negation [*shlilah*] of materialism and assimilation that ruled over the life of the Jewish public, depleted individuals, and Jewish society, and positioned them without power and salvation in the days of distress."[48] Feygenberg framed these works in geographic and chronological terms to convey the prevalence of social and cultural decline in Eastern Europe in the years before World War II. While she acknowledged that they were literary representations, she wielded them as didactic weapons. Yiddish literature was intended not just to lend a glimpse of Eastern European Jewish life, but to prove the corruption and decline of each of its population centers. Feygenberg, unlike many of her contemporaries in Palestine, did not fault the passivity of diasporic Jews when confronted by the Nazis but rather their social and cultural disintegration caused by modern materialism and assimilation. One of the fundamental components of Zionist ideology was the negation of the diaspora, which argued that there could be no Jewish future, and certainly no Jewish nation, outside of the Land of Israel. Using the Hebrew term *shlilah,* negation, Feygenberg updated negative stereotypes about diasporic Jews, no longer targeting their landlessness, alienation from nature, and religious superstition, but instead condemning their lack of Jewish identity and assimilation.[49] Literary translation in Ha-me'asef is marshaled in service of Feygenberg's deeply ideological view of Jewish culture.

Yet the translated texts challenge Feygenberg's argument, sharing profound ambivalence with regard to place and providing a variety of social critiques. Singer's stories may have been set in Poland, but the majority of them are far more interested in probing their characters' psychology than in depicting the place in which they lived. Anita Norich writes that Singer's short stories lack "a material sense of place, even when his characters are men who cultivate the land. The Polish countryside and the Catskills are largely indistinguishable from each other."[50] Bergelson's early novellas, translated in Ha-me'asef's *Dimdumim* (Twilight, 1946), highlighted the static nature of the shtetl in "Arum vokzal" (At the Station) and the tensions of modernity in "Yoysef Shur" without any particular focus on assimilation or Ukraine. Kulbak's experimental "Meshiekh ben Efrayim" (Messiah, Son of Ephraim) and the drama "Yankev Frank" (Jacob Frank) take the reader on surreal messianic journeys set in the past, not in contemporary Lithuania. These Yiddish texts in translation reveal the tensions that existed within Ha-me'asef's goals of preserving the paragons of modern Yiddish literature and providing readers with accurate and accessible representations of Eastern European Jewish life. Worthy literary texts were not necessarily the most effective ethnographic or didactic tools.

While the literary texts and Feygenberg's project had predated the war, the translations were affected by historical circumstances. The Jewish community in Palestine knew about Nazi plans for mass extermination of Jews by late 1942 but, according to Dina Porat, the full extent of the Shoah was understood only in March 1945.[51] Several months before Ha-me'asef's first book appeared in print, for example, a week of mourning was proclaimed in Palestine, accompanied by demands to save European survivors.[52] No translation project from Yiddish published in the Yishuv could ignore the Shoah, even if it had been conceived years earlier. According to Feygenberg, Singer's stories and the other translations from Yiddish were intended to acquaint the Hebrew reader with diasporic life, specifically with diasporic life in the "decades before Hitler's ascent to power."[53] This is critical, she argued, because those who immigrated to Palestine thirty or forty years ago had a sentimental view of the victims rather than a clear understanding of the decline and collapse of diasporic Jewish life. Never one to shy away from controversy, Feygenberg articulated her views in the collective Zionist voice: "We, the builders of the homeland and designers of new Jewish education here in the land of Israel must . . . revise the term that has been sanctified by the people, '*Kiddush ha-shem*' [martyrdom]. Instead of sanctifying the [holy] name in death, even the death of heroes, it is better to sanctify it in the name of life. It is incumbent upon us to learn anew the *torah* of life. We will learn in essence how we should live. From diaspora Jews devoured by assimilation we should not learn what to do, but there is much we can learn from them about what we must not do."[54] Feygenberg saw translations from Yiddish as part of the debate about memory and commemoration in the Yishuv, which began even before the war was over.[55] Feygenberg, however, distanced herself from the sanctification of Shoah victims and set aside the heroism of those who resisted. Instead, she stressed that Eastern European life should be a lesson in how to live, not how to die. She was not particularly interested in celebrating Eastern European Jewish life but rather in contextualizing representations of that life as a cautionary lesson on Jewish life in the diaspora. She encouraged her readers not merely to sympathize with Singer's downtrodden Shimke or admire the ways in which Singer's prose sketches the inner world of an abused but besotted teenager but to understand Shimke and his fellow characters as symbols of the breakdown of diaspora life. Similarly, her comments encourage readers to focus on how Kulbak's Reb Benye and his eclectic followers in "Meshiekh ben Efrayim" offer a harsh indictment of the poverty, ignorance, and suffering of Eastern European Jewish life. Rather than framing these translations as memorials to the dead, Feygenberg foregrounded Eastern European Jewish life, with all of its problems, over its death.

Feygenberg's Hebrew readers did not necessarily follow her injunction to prevent postwar sympathies from obscuring the problems of prewar Jewish life in the diaspora. Critic Natan Grinblat (later, Goren), reviewing *Mi-shnei evrei ha-visla* in *Davar*, heaped praise on Singer, Meltzer, and Feygenberg for their roles in producing the text. Writing at the end of 1945, Grinblat regarded the translation first and foremost as a product of the postwar moment: "The literary undertaking of Ha-me'asef . . . is a good deed at the right time [*mitzvah she-ha-zman garma*], as Yiddish literature, which absorbed the whispers of Israelite life, its radiance and shadows from the struggles of rebirth to the humility of decline, was utterly destroyed in the days of mass murder, Yiddish and the majority of its writers . . . it is upon us to incorporate them into the space of our literature, the eternal literature of Israel."[56] Grinblat saw translation from Yiddish as a historical obligation, or, in rabbinic terms, the timely fulfillment of a divine commandment. While Feygenberg had stressed Singer's portrayal of the decline of diasporic life even before its destruction, Grinblat shifted his focus to the need to memorialize that which the Shoah annihilated. He overlooked the sharp, didactic edge of Feygenberg's critique of Holocaust martyrdom and represented Ha-me'asef's translation project as literary martyrdom, with the Hebrew language paying homage to and preserving Yiddish literature and its writers.

Who was the target audience of these translations, whether they were understood as cautionary lessons about the life of Eastern European Jewry or as memorials to Holocaust victims? Ha-me'asef was billed as a "public" press rather than a commercial one. It sought to usher new readers into Hebrew by using the familiarity and appeal of Yiddish culture as a conduit to Hebrew culture. Since the majority of these intended readers would have known Yiddish, they represented a 1940s version of the classic audience for Hebrew translations from

Yiddish: bilingual readers who were willing to read translations even though they had access to the original texts. Unlike Abramovitsh, Feygenberg did not envision these translations as aesthetic challenges in which the Hebrew versions might complement the Yiddish text. Rather, Feygenberg used translation as a path to monolingualism, a necessary translingual step on the road to Hebrew acculturation.

At the same time, Feygenberg inscribed a different kind of intended reader in her introductory comments. In the preface to Singer's *Mishnei evrei ha-visla*, she emphasized a second didactic project, seeking to educate her readers about Jewish life in the diaspora, and specifically the precipitous decline of that Jewish diaspora. She assumed that these readers had no contact with Eastern European Jewish life, were not familiar with twentieth-century Yiddish literature, and could not or would nor read in Yiddish. Feygenberg rarely concretized this intended reader, but in her preface she referred to older readers who had immigrated to Palestine thirty or forty years earlier and held outdated ideas about the diaspora and to younger readers who apparently had no exposure to Yiddish in the Yishuv.[57] These implied readers reflect a major change in Jewish-language culture. In the 1920s, Shlonsky and Stybel had assumed that Hebrew readers would naturally be able to read in Yiddish if they chose. By the 1940s, however, Feygenberg believed that there was a substantial audience of Hebrew readers who had no independent access to this material. Thus her translation project was not just interlinguistic, but also intertextual and intersemiotic, to use Lawrence Venuti's terms.[58] Feygenberg's introductions sought to provide an ideological overlay for these intended readers' encounter with Jewish diasporic culture. The translations that followed aimed to promote translingualism by creating knowledge of and appreciation for Yiddish culture within a Zionist framework.

Their effect on the intended readers was blunted, however, by the simple fact that Ha-me'asef's translations seemed to have trouble finding any *real* readers. Feygenberg's proclamation of the press's success in the third volume of translations was followed by the announcement that the press would take a two-year hiatus from publishing to better establish itself in "spiritual and material terms."[59] Though she elaborated ambitious future publishing plans, Ha-me'asef would never resume publishing. In fact, the three extant volumes were published at immense personal cost to Feygenberg. As she later wrote, "The three books that I published cost me in blood. I stole bread from my own mouth and paid the debts of Ha-me'asef."[60] In a 1957 letter to the editor printed in *Davar*, she resorted to the rhetoric of martyrdom that she had avoided in Ha-me'asef translations when she asked the Israeli public to "help save the books of Dovid Bergelson and Moyshe Kulbak, the martyrs killed in the USSR" by buying some of the 1,000 remaining copies of the original 5,000 Ha-me'asef books at the low price of 1 lira per book.[61]

Feygenberg's translation project may have struggled to find readers, but it marks a transitional intersection of Hebrew and Yiddish literatures. In its original conception in the 1930s, Feygenberg's plan to inscribe Yiddish literature within Hebrew culture enlisted translation in the service of monolingualism. By encouraging Yiddish readers to read familiar literary works in Hebrew translation, Feygenberg's project invoked translation as a means of culture building, much like the Hebrew translations from European languages that she criticized in 1925. But by the time the project came to fruition, translation from Yiddish had become a mode of cultural preservation. Feygenberg tried to show the cultural bankruptcy that she believed permeated Eastern European Jewish culture even before World War II, seeing the Shoah as a consequence rather than a precipitating factor, but those distinctions were overwhelmed by the magnitude of the destruction. By 1945, critics like Grinblat firmly situated Feygenberg's desire to create a space for Yiddish literature within Hebrew culture as a memorial project rather than an ideological one. What had started out as a deliberate attempt to usher Yiddish into the Hebrew sphere became one of many attempts to "rescue" Yiddish literature.

Achisefer and American Cultural Bilingualism

In September 1943, just a few months before Rachel Feygenberg announced Ha-me'asef, the American Hebrew newspaper *Ha-do'ar* advertised the publication of the Hebrew anthology *Achisefer*. While

Ha-me'asef's translations did not appear in print until 1945, *Achisefer* appeared immediately afterward, a hefty 583-page volume of essays and translations published by the Louis LaMed Foundation for the Advancement of Hebrew and Yiddish Literature. Editors Shmuel Niger and Menachem Ribalow, two of the most prominent American literary critics in Yiddish and Hebrew, respectively, identified three aims of the collection, namely: "(1) to research the problem of bilingualism in the history of Israel and its literature, (2) to inform the Hebrew reader about the situation and accomplishments of our literature in both languages in America, (3) to give the Hebrew reader translations of the wonders of Yiddish poetry, old and new."[62] In contrast to Feygenberg's attempt to promote Hebrew culture, Niger and Ribalow envisioned their anthology as a means for revitalizing Hebrew-Yiddish literary bilingualism. By educating readers about Jewish bilingualism and providing them with translations, this project endeavored to prove that bilingualism was still relevant, at the very least in the United States. In *Achisefer*, contemporary Jewish bilingualism no longer relied on linguistic practice but instead was redefined as cultural awareness. Even as the anthology sought to promote Hebrew-Yiddish unity, epitomized by the meaning of its title, "brothers of the book," it in fact ushered Yiddish into a thoroughly Hebraic framework.

Achisefer was part of the Louis LaMed Foundation's efforts to promote Hebrew-Yiddish bilingualism in the United States.[63] The anthology's preface explains: "Once not too long ago, bilingual writers were ubiquitous in our lives. But in the last decades it has become a rare occurrence, especially among the literature-bearers of the young generation, even more so in our literature in America. More and more we meet Jewish artists-of-the-pen who have no share or stake in our national literary heritage, and therefore are ripped and detached from the language of the nation and its literary treasures. This cultural one-sidedness has spread and continues to spread among Jewish readers."[64] Bemoaning the decline of literary bilingualism, the foundation sought to "to stitch together the rift between our Hebrew and Yiddish literatures."[65] As much as foundation chair Niger wanted to remedy the growing "cultural one-sidedness," the answer in 1943 was not to promote individual literary bilingualism. Much as Niger had argued in *Di tsveyshprakhikeyt fun undzer literature* (Bilingualism of Our Literature, 1941), also published by the Louis LaMed Foundation, the historical climate necessitated a new approach to bilingualism that relied on cultural rather than linguistic knowledge. The LaMed Foundation supported projects that were intended to reconnect readers and writers to Jewish "literary treasures" and give them a share "in our national literary heritage": awarding yearly prizes for the best literary works in Hebrew and Yiddish;[66] publishing books relating to Jewish bilingualism;[67] providing American periodicals with updates about Hebrew and Yiddish literature; and publishing *Achisefer*, the first of two planned collections introducing Hebrew readers to Yiddish literature and Yiddish readers to Hebrew literature.

Based on these programs, the Foundation promoted cultural rather than individual bilingualism; efforts were not directed at teaching Hebrew or Yiddish or encouraging writers to attempt self-translation, but rather in cultivating familiarity between readers of each language and the literature they did not necessarily read. Thanks to the Louis LaMed Foundation, American Yiddish readers could be apprised of developments in Hebrew literature and culture, but in the comfort of the Yiddish journal *Zukunft* (Future); the reverse was true for Hebrew readers, who could find updates relating to Yiddish literature and culture in *Ha-do'ar*. What Niger and the Foundation understood to be cultural bilingualism relied on translingual rather than bilingual practice, that is to say, the inscription of another Jewish language within a given literary-linguistic sphere. While Rachel Feygenberg had advocated for a unidirectional Jewish translingualism in which Yiddish was imported into Hebrew, this American project cultivated a bidirectional translingualism by carving out space within Hebrew and Yiddish literatures for the recognition and appreciation of the other literature. Perhaps the most important means of fostering this translingualism was through translation.

Surprisingly, neither the publisher's statement nor the short preface from the editors discussed Yiddish or Hebrew literature outside of the United States. American Yiddish culture was still closely tied to

Europe throughout the interwar period, as American Yiddish writers were published in Warsaw and reviewed in Kiev, Odessa, and Moscow, and American Yiddish papers reported on political, social, and cultural news from Jewish Eastern Europe.[68] Yet *Achisefer* gives the impression of a self-sufficient American Jewish culture, with few glimpses of the immense fear and soul-searching pervading American Jewish culture at the time. In November 1942, nearly a year before the publication of *Achisefer*, Rabbi Stephen S. Wise, chairman of the World Jewish Congress, had announced that two million Jews in occupied Europe had been slain in an "extermination campaign."[69] Deborah Lipstadt argues that news of massacres of Eastern European Jews was relatively common on the pages of American newspapers, though not necessarily foregrounded.[70] Yiddish readers, Anita Norich writes, "inhabited a cultural world in which journals and critics, poets and short story writers placed themselves in explicit relationships to the unfolding events of the war. . . . Virtually every writers' conference convened, every new Yiddish publication, every literary symposium in Yiddish—and there were a surprisingly large number of each—was prefaced with a discussion of what it meant to enter into a creative enterprise at this historic moment of war and catastrophe."[71] Yet *Achisefer* made no reference to the war in its introductory comments.

Niger and his fellow editors were certainly aware of the events unfolding in Europe. In a May 1940 letter, Niger responded to LaMed's proposal for a creating a new foundation: "Your letter which I received today delighted me greatly. The news reaching us from all over the world has been gloomy and distressing, and suddenly a ray out of the future appears. The least flare in the darkness drives the gloom away. Particularly when that which you propose to do is no trivial matter. It will enhance our efforts and uplift our spirits. Moreover, it is important right now. We feel so dejected, that we have lost faith even in relief. So we must come out and declare: the world is not coming to an end. In spite of Hitler and the peril of Hitler, we will begin to build for tomorrow."[72] While the anthology could certainly be viewed as one attempt to begin building for the future, it is perplexing that Niger and Ribalow did not mention the war in their introductory comments. In essays later in the volume, both briefly referenced the uncertain future of European Jewish culture: Ribalow situated his literary survey of American Hebrew literature in the context of a "period of ruin and destruction" between the two world wars, raising the unanswerable question, "and who knows what will be the strength and what will be the image of that very great Jewish population of Poland after the war";[73] Niger concluded his discussion of American Yiddish literature with a vague reflection on the uncertainties regarding Jewish life "across the ocean."[74] The war seeped into the anthology in other ways, particularly in the literary section. By focusing entirely on the American Jewish cultural sphere, *Achisefer* depicted a Hebrew-Yiddish bilingualism that saw itself as independent of global Jewish culture and barely registered the contemporary crisis in European Jewish life.

Looking more closely at the massive anthology, *Achisefer* is divided into three main sections, all in Hebrew: academic essays relating the history of Jewish bilingualism; critical surveys of American Hebrew and Yiddish literature; and translations from Yiddish prose and poetry. The first set of essays focus on issues such as translation in biblical and post-biblical times, multilingualism in the Mishnaic period, and Hebrew's historical interactions with Aramaic, Arabic, and Yiddish. Together, they stress that translation and multilingualism had always benefited the Hebrew language. While Pinchas Churgin was ostensibly writing about the Second Temple Period, his comment that "the appearance of translations did not narrow the place of Hebrew language and did not darken its light in life" resonated within *Achisefer*'s broad support of bilingualism.[75] Similarly, when Aharon Zeitlin claimed that "Mendele the creator and Mendele the translator—one and the same," he was arguing not only that S. Y. Abramovitsh's literary innovations relied on translation but also that Yiddish was not a threat for the development of Hebrew literature.[76] Editor Sh. Niger's imprint is visible in this section, even if he did not contribute an essay. In his book *Di tsveysh-prakhikeyt fun undzer literatur* (1941), Niger emphasized the long history of Jewish bilingualism and argued, "We must at least remember and mention to others that the program of linguistic exclusivity, the doctrine of only Hebrew or exclusively Yiddish, has no roots in the evolution of Jewish literary life, and that historically we have been and remain one people with two languages, a people with a bilingual literature."[77] While *Achisefer*, like Niger's book, stressed the bilingual roots of Jewish culture, from its opening essay it privileged Hebrew.

After several critical essays on the state of American Yiddish and Hebrew literature, the anthology provided four short stories, mixing Hebrew and translated Yiddish stories, and a larger selection of poetry translated from Yiddish.[78] As with any anthology, the selection of texts suggests a great deal about both editorial logic and the publication circumstances. *Achisefer* shows a strong preference for contemporary American Yiddish poets, representing twenty-three of the thirty-two included poets.[79] A short editoral note, however, cautions readers not to make too much of the selection due to editorial challenges; apparently not all of the requested translations were completed and not all of the completed translations were deemed worthy of publication. More revealing, however, were the criteria the editors listed for translations: "Of course, we chose only the good ones, those faithful to the source that provided the reader with the essence of the poet and the quality of the translated poems."[80] Niger and Ribalow listed two criteria for good translations: fidelity to the source text and poetic quality. Given the anthology's intentions to bridge the divide between Yiddish and Hebrew culture, it makes sense that the translations were assessed with respect to both source and target cultures. Yet the desire to stay true to the Yiddish poet and the need to produce a high-quality Hebrew poem were not necessarily easy to balance in a single poem.

Achisefer's large poetry section relied upon several translators, leading to translations that demonstrate a variety of approaches and varying degrees of success. One of the most revealing translations is Aharon Zeitlin's Hebrew version of Yankev Glatshteyn's poem "A gute nakht velt" (Good Night, World). Glatshteyn (1896–1971) was one of the most outspoken American Yiddish poets of his time, a cofounder of the Introspectivist movement and a proponent of Yiddish modernism.[81] Zeitlin (1898–1973) was no slouch himself, a bilingual Hebrew-Yiddish writer who published an impressive number of poems, short stories, and essays in both languages.[82] In a 1940 Yiddish essay about Hebrew-Yiddish bilingualism, Zeitlin argues that translation between the languages was necessary to strengthen bilingual Hebrew-Yiddish culture, which was being threatened by individuals with their own political agendas.[83] With his translation of Glatshteyn's "A gute nakht velt," Zeitlin took on a well-known poem that "became a touchstone for Yiddish intellectuals in America faced with increasingly frightening news from Europe and seeking new ways to understand their own relationship to modernity."[84] His translation, however, not only embellished the poem's raw language but also stripped it of its Yiddishness. Glatshteyn's opening lines read:

אַ גוטע נאַכט, ברייטע וועלט.
גרויסע, שטינקענדיקע וועלט.
נישט דו, נאָר איך פֿאַרהאַק דעם טויער.
מיט דעם לאַנגן כאַלאַט,
מיט דער פֿײַערדיקער, געלער לאַט,
מיט דעם שטאָלצן טראָט,
אויף מײַן אייגענעם געבאָט —
גיי איך צוריק אין געטאָ.[85]

Good night, wide world.
Big, stinking world.
Not you, but I, slam the gate.
In my long robe,
With my flaming, yellow patch,
With my proud gait,
At my own command—
I return to the ghetto.[86]

Published immediately after Germany's annexation of Austria in March 1938, Glatshteyn's poem is shocking in its bitterness and crudeness. These opening lines echo the poetic speaker's act of slamming the gate on Western culture and its promise of Enlightenment, with repeated words and phrases in lines that virtually all end with the strong alveolar stop of the repeated "t" (*tes*) and include many of these harsh "t"s in the opening lines. Zeitlin's translation of those same lines reads:

לֵיל מְנוּחָה, תֵּבֵל רַבָּה.
תֵּבֵל נִבְאָשָׁה, בַּת־גֹּעַל.
לֹא אַתְּ — אֲנִי הוּא הַנּוֹעֵל
בִּסְעָרָה הַשַּׁעַר.
בִּגְאוֹן־צַעַד,
בְּאַבְנֵטִי הָאָרֹךְ, בְּמַטְלִית צְהֻבָּה יוֹקֵדָה
עַל פִּי צִוּוּי אָנֹכִי בִּלְבַד —
אָשׁוּב אֵרֵדָה
אֶל הַגֵּטוֹ.[87]

Restful night, great world.
Odious universe, revolting one.
Not you—I am the one who locks
In a storm the gate.
Stepping proud,
In my long girdle, blazing yellow patch
At my command alone—
I will return, I will descend
To the ghetto.

From the first line, the Hebrew version's elevated language contrasts with the baseness of the Yiddish, both in the mundane adjectives "wide" and "big" (*breyte*, *groyse*) and in the stunning coarseness of "stinking" (*shtinkendike*). Rather than echoing the familiar "good night" greeting with a similarly familiar Hebrew salutation like *laila tov*, the poem opens with the formal line *leil menucha, tevel raba* (restful night, great world), the internal rhyme anticipating the translation's attention to rhyme and the word choices indicating the generally high register of the Hebrew poem. In choosing the biblical *tevel*, world or universe, rather than the more commonly used *olam*, the translator keeps the grammatical feminine gender but loses the shock value of Glatshteyn's flat *velt*. The Yiddish "good night, wide world" takes a familiar, colloquial salutation but directs it at an unanticipated recipient, the whole wide world. The Hebrew, however, sounds like poetry from the very beginning, with its decorous "Restful night, great universe," replacing the strong "t"s with a cascade of lateral "l"s. Even its second line softens the Yiddish coarse condemnation of the "big, stinking world" by again choosing refined biblical words that knit together the lines through rhyme. This world is "odious" (*niv'asha*), which echoes the previous line's *menucha* (restful) and *raba* (great), and "revolting one" (*bat go'el*), which maintains the meter and rhymes with the subsequent *no'el* (locks). Glatshteyn's opening lines are harsh and raw, a pounding indictment of a stinking world. Zeitlin's translation adds a poetic layer that softens the effect, even as it locks the gate instead of slamming it and makes explicit a "descent" rather than just a return to the ghetto.

While the Hebrew version of the poem tends to add words and exclamation points to heighten the poem's outrage, its omissions are equally important. In *Achisefer*, the first four lines of the second stanza are omitted, leaving out the Yiddish denunciation of enemies present and past: "Piggish German, hostile Polack, / Sly Amalek, land of guzzling and gorging. / Flabby democracy, with your cold / Compresses of sympathy."[88] Joseph Leftwich, the first of many English translators of the poem, also left out these lines and the rest of the second stanza, perhaps to avoid "the problem of naming the enemies of the Jews and itemizing the Jewish signs to which the speaker returns."[89] But unlike English translators, Zeitlin does not have to take into account non-Jewish readers of his translation. By omitting the aggressors, the translation reads as a broader indictment of European culture rather than an explicit response to Nazism.

Another omission in the translation is small but significant. When Glatshteyn's poem dramatizes, in the second half of the second stanza, the return "to my kerosene . . . to my crooked alleys, hunchbacked street-lamp,"[90] the physical return is accompanied by a textual return to the once abandoned pages of the Bible and rabbinic texts: "My stray pages, my Twenty-Four-Books, / My Talmud, to the puzzling / Questions, to the bright Hebrew-Yiddish, / To Law."[91] Glatshteyn uses the "insider" terms for these traditional texts: *svarbe*, a Yiddish contraction of the Hebrew *esrim ve-arba*, the twenty-four books of the Bible; and *ivri-taytsh*, literally "Hebrew-Yiddish," the traditional Yiddish translation of the Hebrew Bible. The Hebrew poem, however, shifts the focus to a different set of canonical religious texts, first to the six orders of Mishnah, instead of the *svarba*, likely because of the better rhyming prospects of *shisha sedarim* (six volumes of the Mishnah); then, after a quick reference to the Talmud, straight "To the depths of knowledge, to the good law-of-the-fathers, / to justice and duty."[92] The translation ends up focusing on rabbinic texts at the expense of the Bible and the Yiddish textual tradition.

A closer look at the poem shows a similar phenomenon in the translation of the adjective *yiddish,* which can mean Jewish or Yiddish. Glatshteyn's poem uses the phrase *yiddish lebn*, Jewish life, three times over the course of the poem. Zeitlin's translation consistently substitutes the nationally inflected *yisra'el*, Israel, in the first two instances (*chayei-yisra'el*; *darkei-yisra'el*), but chooses the explicitly national *chayei-ami,* life of my people, in the third. The last example, in the penultimate line, marks a major departure from the Yiddish. Glatshteyn's poem concludes:

כ'קוש דיך, פֿאַרקאָלטנט ייִדיש לעבן.
ס'וויינט אין מיר די פֿרייד פֿון קומען.[93]

I kiss you, tangled Jewish life.
It cries in me, the joy of coming.[94]

In Hebrew:

נוֹשֵׁק אֲנִי אֶתְכֶם, חַיֵּי-עַמִּי הַנֶּאֱלָחִים.
בּוֹכָה בִּי שִׂמְחַת הַשִּׁיבָה.[95]

I kiss you, despicable lives of my people
It cries in me, the joy of return.

The Yiddish "tangled Jewish life" becomes "despicable lives of my people," deflecting attention from the complexity of Jewish attempts to navigate past and present worlds to the travails of the present.

Rather than embracing these ambivalences, the Hebrew speaker takes pity on his downtrodden compatriots. And perhaps most significantly, the Hebrew poem closes on a different note with the choice of "retuning" (*shiva*) rather than the Yiddish "coming" (*kumen*). Though the poem slammed the gate at the very beginning, the shift from the wide world to the crooked alleys is still in process. Anita Norich suggests that the poem ends with a gerund "as if to underscore the uncompleted nature of the movement, the slippage between noun and verb, naming and doing, thing and act. Even at this very end, he still cannot fully embrace the goal toward which he has been moving, stopping short of naming the return to which he now lays claim."[96] On this key point of returning, the Hebrew poem is less fraught; the speaker is returning to the life not only of the Jewish people but also specifically of *his* people. Thus the Hebrew poem ends on a more conclusive return than its Yiddish counterpart, which is frozen in the process of coming.

Any translation will differ from a previous version of the same text. The overall Hebraizing effect of this translation, not unlike Meltzer's translation of Singer's short story, prioritizes Hebrew's linguistic and ideological needs over loyalty to the source language and original text. As Gideon Toury argues, the limited literary and vernacular resources in Hebrew meant that translation into Hebrew typically posited "acceptability as a major constraint on literary translation, to the almost complete forfeiture of translation adequacy; a kind of Hebraic *belle infidèle*, if you wish."[97] Much as *Achisefer*'s editors might have sought translations that balanced fidelity and acceptability, Zeitlin's translation systematically erased traces of Yiddish, replaced traditional Yiddish texts with Hebrew holy books, and placed Jewish life in a national rather than religious framework. At the same time, Zeitlin's translation of Glatshteyn's poem represents distinct conditions of translation that, in Lydia Liu's terms, ensued from interlingual contacts between languages at this specific historical moment. In the poem's last line, the Hebrew word *shiva* (returning) is ideologically loaded with the Zionist *shivat tsiyon*, the return to Zion. Historically, the term refers to the first Jewish return from exile in Babylonia, as chronicled in the Book of Ezra, but was extended into modern Zionist thought as the longing to return to the biblical land of Israel. The poem's bitter return to the ghetto is thus rewritten linguistically and ideologically as a return "home." Home to the ghetto? To the Jewish people? To the Land of Israel? In translation, Glatshteyn's bitter denunciation of a world hostile to Jews suggests a Zionist return as an answer to the European threat that had only become more menacing between the Yiddish poem's initial publication in 1938 and the translation's publication in 1943.

The perceived quality, or lack thereof, of the anthology's translations was frequently addressed in reviews of the collection. In the Yishuv, what little attention Feygenberg's Ha-me'asef attracted came primarily from Hebrew literary critics. In the United States, however, *Achisefer* was reviewed in both the Yiddish monthly *Tsukunft* (edited by Niger) and the Hebrew weekly *Ha-do'ar* (edited by Ribalow).[98] Kadya Molodovsky, one of the Yiddish poets included in *Achisefer*, reflected at length on the goals of the anthology. Poetry, she conceded, is difficult to translate and inevitably carries the stamp of the poet and the translator. "It is necessary that between the two partners [poet and translator] of a translated poem souls should draw close, a spiritual closeness."[99] Writing in Yiddish, Molodovsky understood translation not strictly in terms of fidelity, but rather intimacy between poet and translator. That intimacy, which Molodovsky proposed first in the Hebrew phrase *hitkarvut ha-nefesh*, the souls drawing close, and then glossed with the Yiddish *gemit-noentkayt*, a spiritual closeness, is predicated on the "spirit" rather than the "body" of poetry. Using Molodovsky's distinction, *Achisefer*'s translations are on the whole far more concerned with the poetic "bodies," the formal and lexical-semantic features of a given poem, rather than the "spirit," the intertextual and intersemiotic aspects of a specific text. In the case of Glatshteyn's poem, the largely intact poetic body had been infused with a very different poetic spirit.

Molodovsky expressed her reservations about the anthology's translations and questioned the anthology's goal of nurturing Jewish cultural bilingualism: "Is *Achisefer* really put together so as to influence a rapprochement between both literatures? Making whole the rift?"[100] A rapprochement, she argued, had to be reciprocal, not unidirectional like *Achisefer*: "I rejoice with the revival of Hebrew in the Land of Israel, like the entire Palestinian Yishuv, but we must not associate this revival with the idea that Hebrew should swallow up Yiddish like the Egyptian cows in Pharaoh's dream. Ways of bringing Yiddish and Hebrew closer must be found, here and in the Land of Israel and everywhere there are Jews."[101] Invoking Pharaoh's dream in which seven thin cows ate seven fat cows (Genesis 41:1–4), Molodovsky warned that Hebrew's revival must not be at Yiddish's expense. Molodovsky was optimistic about the possibilities of Hebrew-Yiddish reconciliation, but did not see translation, and specifically *Achisefer*'s translations, as an appropriate way of pursing such reconciliation. Translation had the potential to create a "spiritual closeness," but that intimacy was lost in *Achisefer*.

Yankev Glatshteyn voiced his objections to *Achisefer* and its translations in a far more dramatic fashion. Glatsheyn had already established his wariness with regard to literary translation, verging on hostility.[102] But Glatshteyn's Yiddish poem "Reading *Achisefer*" goes beyond resistance to translation by offering a poetic indictment of the anthology's goals and translations.[103] The poem, published in the Yiddish journal *Svive* a few months after *Achisefer* appeared, opens with a nightmarish scene filled with ingenious sound-play in which the lyric speaker finds himself besieged by menacing and fantastic creatures with sheets of paper in their mouths: *vild iz mir un vald iz mir . . . in vildn vald aleyn* (wild am I and in wood am I . . . in wild wood alone).[104] Invoking the historical and psychological associations of Yiddish with women, the lyric speaker implores his grandmother, his aunt, and his mother to help defend him, each one armed with her Yiddish holy text of choice: the grandmother's *korbn minkhe*, a women's prayer book in Yiddish; the aunt's *Tsenerene*, a Yiddish collection of Bible stories; and the mother's *taytsh-chumesh*, a Yiddish Bible translation.[105] This is precisely the *taytsh-khumesh* that Zeitlin erased from his translation of "A gute nakht velt." The lyric speaker is clearly under siege, but at this point in the poem, we still know nothing about the threat, only that he feels his sole defense comes from the Yiddish textual tradition—his foremothers and their religious texts.

That threat appears soon enough, in the unlikely form of seventeen shepherds taking an afternoon nap. The lyric persona is greeted by one of the shepherds, who opens an eye and addresses him in a strange mixture of Hebrew and Yiddish. While the shepherds are never named over the course of the poem, the lines contribute revealing bits and pieces: "we are the wholesalers" interested perpetually in buying and selling, emphasizing their capitalism; for every Sabbath "we slaughter a turkey," suggesting that they are Americans; and, most importantly, the shepherd's warning against speaking Yiddish: "Shh, do not wake up the crew / they speak only Hebrew, / and should they hear a word in Yiddish, / they will become quite skittish."[106] The brilliant rhyme between *hebreish* (Hebrew) with *nerveish* (nervous), here rendered with the rhyme Yiddish/skittish, crafts a verbal portrait of neurotic American Hebraists in the guise of classic literary shepherds. Who are these seventeen Hebraists masquerading as shepherds, guiding a mixed flock of cows and sheep? It seems far from accidental that *Achisefer*'s table of contents lists ten essayists and eight translators, including Aharon Zeitlin twice as both an essayist and translator, for a total of seventeen contributors. And it seems likely that the lyric persona's interlocutor is none other than the most Yiddishly inclined of the *Achisefer* crew, Shmuel Niger himself.

When asked if he is a friend or foe, Glatshteyn's poetic persona does not hesitate to identify himself:

כ'בין אַ יידישער שרײַבער,
דער סאַמע, סאַמע לעצטער.
כ'קום אַצינדערט צו אײַך,
אינגאַנצן אַן איבערגעזעצטער.[107]

I am a Yiddish writer,
The very, very last.
I come now to you,
Entirely in translation.

Suddenly, the lyric speaker's instinctive turn to his female precursors for protection makes more sense. The Yiddish writer is represented as an endangered species facing extinction, threatened by fierce creatures hungry to "translate" him. After the loquacious shepherd has the chance to tell his allusion-laden tale, the shepherds' plan is finally revealed:

הײַנט נאָך חצות,
אויב ס׳וועטער וועט נישט שטערן,
ווע׳מיר צו קבורה פֿירן ייִדיש,
בײַם שײַן פֿון אַ לאַמטערן.
ס׳איז סך־הכל, אַרונטער פֿון מאַרק,
נפטר, הלך לעולמו,
ס׳איז די אונטערשטע שורה —
הײַנט בײַנאַכט פֿירן מיר, מערצישעם,
ייִדיש צו קבורה.[108]

Tonight after midnight,
If the weather does not impede,
We'll bring Yiddish to its grave,
By the light of a lantern.
It is, after all, down in the market,
Passed, gone to its world,
The bottom line—
Tonight we will bring, G'dwilling,
Yiddish to its grave.

According to the shepherd, Yiddish will be buried under the cover of night. If Yiddish is truly dead in commercial terms ("in the market") and in physical terms (with the Hebraic euphemism *halakh le-olamo*, lit., went to his world, i.e., the next world) as the shepherd claims, then this act could be considered a tribute, bringing Yiddish to its final resting place. But the stealthy nature of the plan, the fact that this burial can only be carried out in the dark of night, points to nefarious motives on the part of these volunteer gravediggers. The poem vividly depicts what Venuti calls the violence of intercultural translation, "the forcible replacement of the linguistic and cultural differences of the foreign text with a text that is intelligible to the translating-language reader."[109]

Glatshteyn concludes, however, not with Yiddish's death, but with the poet's afterlife. Suddenly, the poetic persona finds himself cavorting in a pastoral landscape, full of green grass and babbling brooks: "I have cast off from me / entire packs with their yokes / I clamber between mountains and valleys / my soul sings in me with joy."[110] What accounts for this transformation? Glatshteyn's lyric persona explains, "A dear hand has translated me." So while the lyric voice rejoices—ironically—in the freedom of having been translated, he is reminded of the cost of this freedom at the very end of the poem. Every once and a while, a horrible voice calls out: "singer, your path is easy for you, / because you are eternal and dead—you have lost your body."[111] Translation is the death of the Yiddish poem and the poet. Poet and language here are intimately linked, such that the death of a language is necessarily the death of the poet. If *Achisefer*'s contributors envisioned translation as salvation, sustaining literary bilingualism and ensuring Yiddish's posterity, Glatshteyn's poem counters that translation is akin to murder, and that *Achisefer* is a conspiracy to bury Yiddish alive.

For all its insistence on bilingualism, *Achisefer* is a monolingual text. Niger, in an interview published in *Davar* several years after the anthology's publication, recounted how he was accused of both "selling Yiddish" and "betraying Hebrew." In response, he insisted "it is not the vessel that is essential, but its content, and the content is one, even if it is created in two languages."[112] But in reading *Achisefer*, the vessel is immensely important. Written entirely in Hebrew and addressing "the Hebrew reader," the anthology situates itself within Hebrew literature. Linguistically, it is difficult to find traces of Yiddish in the Hebrew translations of Zeitlin and the other translators. Conceptually, Hebrew is presented as *the* language of Jewish life and literature while Yiddish is represented as one of a changing cast of Jewish languages. As Molodovsky pointed out, the anthology's attempt to bring the two languages into productive contact occurred primarily through mediocre translations. As Glatshteyn sardonically argued, *Achisefer* may have claimed bilingual intentions, but it buried the very Yiddishness of the texts it translated into Hebrew. Had *Achisefer* intermingled Hebrew and Yiddish poems on similar themes, or presented two comparable sections of Hebrew and Yiddish poetry, or even provided Yiddish and Hebrew versions of each poem, it might have presented itself as a bilingual text. Instead, it packaged thoroughly Hebraic versions of Yiddish poetry for an audience it imagined had no access to that poetry.

The question of audience is a particularly difficult one with respect to *Achisefer*. Alan Mintz argues that American Hebraists were marginal within American Jewish culture: "Hebraists were in fact a drop in the Yiddishist bucket. There were millions of Jewish immigrants to America for whom Yiddish was their first language and the primary medium for fulfilling their cultural needs. But there were virtually none when it came to Hebrew. . . . Never did they have anything resembling the mass audience potentially available to their counterparts through the Yiddish press."[113] Thus the potential audience for *Achisefer* in the United States was extremely small. Since American Hebrew writers could read Yiddish, the anthology's goals of educating readers about American literature and providing them with Hebrew translations of Yiddish poetry must have been conceived with Hebrew readers in the Yishuv in mind. But *Achisefer* was essentially ignored in Palestine, mentioned only in a few booksellers' advertisements in the Palestinian Hebrew press. While the rising number of translations demonstrates growing interest in Yiddish literature in the Yishuv, *Achisefer*'s emphasis on cultural bilingualism was alien to Zionist cultural sensibilities. In 1943, it was easier to bridge the Hebrew-Yiddish linguistic divide than the geographical distance between the two literatures.

The Louis LaMed Foundation had initially conceived of *Achisefer* as the first installment of a two-volume series that would translate Yiddish into Hebrew and Hebrew into Yiddish. Though a Yiddish version of *Achisefer* never appeared in print, Niger and the Foundation published a very different anthology in Yiddish a few years after *Achisefer*. In 1948, the Louis LaMed Foundation released *Kiddush ha-shem* (Martyrdom), the first Holocaust anthology to appear in Yiddish. Niger's introduction highlights the differences between producing a Hebrew anthology in 1943 and a Yiddish anthology in 1948: "The idea of publishing a book about *kiddush ha-shem* [martyrdom] arose a few years ago at the Louis LaMed Fund for our literature in both languages. World War II was in the very middle of the burning; between us and those tortured, dark camps was a wall of clouds of smoke and fiery flames . . . what we know now about those very darkest of all dark decrees, about the very *khurbn* [Holocaust] . . . we still did not yet know."[114] This postwar Yiddish anthology foregrounds precisely the reaction to the Shoah that is missing in the wartime Hebrew *Achisefer*. For Niger, the best literary response to cultural or existential threats seems to have been the anthology. Like *Achisefer*, *Kiddush ha-shem* mixes genres, combining personal testimony, poetry, essays, and historical texts. A replacement of sorts for the never-realized Yiddish *Achisefer*, this anthology registers less the desire to preserve evident in *Achisefer*'s Hebrew translations than the need to testify, to protest, and to mourn in Yiddish. Thus within just a few years, the American attempt to promote Jewish cultural bilingualism in *Achisefer* was replaced by efforts to craft a collective response to catastrophe in Yiddish.

From Building to Preserving

Ha-me'asef Press and *Achisefer* both used translation to foster their editors' visions for the future of Jewish-language literature. Situated within a Zionist ideological framework, Ha-me'asef translations ushered worthy Yiddish texts into Hebrew for their own preservation and to educate Hebrew readers. Translation, as Feygenberg argued in 1936, was a necessary step in the promotion of Hebrew monolingualism because it could help Yiddish speakers transition to their new Hebrew reality in Palestine. *Achisefer*, by contrast, saw Hebrew-Yiddish bilingualism and not Hebrew monolingualism as its goal. Conceived as part of a larger Yiddish-Hebrew/Hebrew-Yiddish translation project, *Achisefer* asserted that providing Hebrew translations of Yiddish literature could help sustain bilingualism as a cultural phenomenon at a time when literary bilingualism was no longer practical. Bilingualism, in the anthology's logic, becomes a mode of cultural awareness in which both Hebrew and Yiddish would accord a special status to the other Jewish literature.

Notwithstanding their different agendas, both translation projects placed Yiddish within thoroughly Hebraic frameworks. As a result, they each shared a vision for Hebrew-Yiddish contact that became dominant in Hebrew discourse: Hebrew as the repository of Yiddish literature. In his 1925 exchange with Feygenberg, Shlonsky had insisted that the best of Yiddish literature would be rescued by Hebrew when necessary, anticipating the conceptual shift that occurred in the early 1940s. Based on his 1925 comments, few would have expected Shlonsky himself to be extensively involved in efforts to translate Yiddish poetry and prose into Hebrew. But historical circumstances provoked major changes in literary practice: starting in 1939, Shlonsky produced Hebrew translations of Yiddish literature at a speedy pace.[115] In addition to translating from Yiddish, Shlonsky was an editor at Sifriyat Poʻalim, a press that published an impressive number of translations from Yiddish from the late 1930s, many part of "Doron," the literary series that Shlonsky edited. Affiliated with the socialist Zionist party Ha-shomer ha-tsaʻir, Sifriyat Poʻalim was particularly attuned to the situation in Eastern Europe because of the party's strong roots in Poland.[116]

One Sifriyat Poʻalim book, the anthology *Bein saʻar le-saʻar* (From One Storm to the Next), demonstrates the extent to which literary preservation became a dominant mode of translingual contact. Edited by Dov Ber Malkin and published in 1943, the anthology features sixteen short stories translated from Yiddish into Hebrew by Malkin and five other credited translators. Malkin (1901–1966) was a journalist, critic, and translator who immigrated to Palestine in 1934 and was active in Yiddish and Hebrew circles. Far less ambitious in its literary aspirations than Feygenberg's Ha-me'asef, and far more modest in scale than *Achisefer*, Malkin's *Bein saʻar le-saʻar* shared the other projects' goal of acquainting a Hebrew readership with Yiddish literature but did so explicitly in the shadow of the Shoah. The stories are organized geographically, but the strongest common denominator linking the stories is anti-Semitic violence and the suffering it causes in the lives of Jewish characters across the Jewish diaspora. From Yona Rozenfeld's evocation of the terror of a Ukranian pogram to Dovid Bergelson's revenge-obsessed Jewish refugee in Berlin to Yoysef Opatoshu's sketch of anti-Semitic hooligans on an American train, the collective portrait of Yiddish life that emerges in *Bein saʿar le-saʿar* is one of Jews living at the whims of their non-Jewish neighbors, some good, some bad, and some indifferent.

While Feygenberg grafted the reality of the war onto her interwar program for Yiddish literature and *Achisefer*'s editors sought to transcend contemporary events in promoting Jewish bilingualism, Malkin had no compunction about the centrality of the Shoah. The war, and specifically the Nazi genocide of European Jewry, was the precipitating force behind this literary collection. Malkin wrote in the introduction: "It had never been like this. Not wartime distress, but a decree of destruction. . . . With every step closer grows the horror in the question: What still remains of Israel's diaspora in Europe?" [117] Malkin's dramatic words are the most explicit references to the Shoah in any of the translation projects, and they provide the rationale for the project. He continued a few lines later: "Therefore: . . . comes the mighty and compelling desire to return and to see the Jewish diaspora up close in the short-long period of time between one storm and the next."[118] The anthology presents a glimpse of interwar Jewish life through Yiddish literature to fill the uncertainty of 1943. Literary translation tries to make sense of contemporary events and to assuage the anxiety of the present, substituting Yiddish texts for the Yiddish speakers who could not be reached in Nazi-occupied Europe. Malkin concluded his introduction with the statement: "Is not from there—precisely from there—the news of the storm can be heard? We did not pay attention and the world did not listen. . . . And when we and the world were forced to listen and pay attention and even to see, that storm was already raging at full strength."[119] Malkin backshadows, to use Michael André Bernstein's term, Yiddish literary texts in the context of national soul-searching; translation becomes a way of expressing not "they should have known" but rather "we should have known."[120] Yiddish short stories are not treated as literary representations but as ethnographic documents, forecasts of the "raging storm." Feygenberg similarly emphasized Yiddish literature's ability to educate Hebrew readers about the Jewish diaspora, but she was invested in Yiddish as an artistic pursuit as well as a didactic tool. Malkin instrumentalized literature in *Bein sa'ar le-sa'ar*, giving the barest of attention to literary trends in his introduction and eliding issues of language and translation altogether. In contrast to Ha-me'asef and *Achisefer*, Malkin's anthology uses Yiddish literature as a way of glimpsing the Jewish life that was being destroyed. Translation takes on, in Jeffrey Shandler's words, "a very different and more urgent symbolic worth," enlisted first and foremost to document and thus preserve Yiddish life.[121]

Translation from Yiddish into Hebrew in the early 1940s reflects the transition underway in the relationship between the two Jewish-language literatures. In *Achisefer* and Ha-me'asef translations, elements of traditional Hebrew-Yiddish bilingualism are still visible: *Achisefer*'s insistence on continued Jewish literary bilingualism; Feygenberg's assumption that readers would use Hebrew translations of familiar Yiddish texts to facilitate their integration into Hebrew culture. At the same time, these texts as well as Malkin's *Bein sa'ar le-sa'ar* also show the increasing power of a Jewish translingualism that sought to preserve Yiddish and provide a glimpse of prewar Eastern European Jewish life within Hebrew. The object of their preservation was not so much Yiddish as a language, but Yiddish literature as an artistic achievement (Ha-me'asef, *Achisefer*) and Yiddish literature as an ethnographic source (Ha-me'asef, *Bein sa'ar le-sa'ar*). Neither Feygenberg's vision for translation paving the way to Hebrew monolingualism nor *Achisefer*'s vision for translation that cultivated cultural bilingualism was realized. Instead, as bilingualism retreated as an active force in Jewish-language literature, it was replaced by different forms of translingualism. Yiddish literature was ushered into Hebrew culture in these three anthologies for what was understood to be its own good and for the good of Hebrew readers.

Perhaps it is the bilingual Hebrew-Yiddish critic Dov Sadan who best encapsulates the shift that undergirded Hebrew translations of Yiddish literature in the 1940s. Sadan's career spanned the changing dynamics of modern Hebrew and Yiddish literature, from his early days advocating for Hebrew literature in *Davar* in the 1930s to his prominent role as the first Chair of Yiddish Studies at the Hebrew University in 1951. He mediated between Hebrew and Yiddish for decades, translating Yiddish poetry and prose into Hebrew, writing critical essays in both languages, and providing Yiddish writers with Hebrew commentary on their work.[122] In 1941, Sadan wrote an afterword to Shlonsky's translation of Itzik Manger's creative history of Yiddish literature, published in Hebrew as *Dmuyot krovot* (Close Figures). While Shlonsky's translation systematically Hebraized Manger's Yiddish text, Sadan incorporated Manger and Yiddish literature into Hebrew culture. His afterword concludes: "[T]he book is now given in the language of the Bible, and Itzik moves from the language of the time to the language of eternity [*me-sfat ha-zman le-sfat ha-netsach*], realizing the biblical promise 'through Isaac shall your seed be acclaimed.'"[123] Alluding to God's promise to Abraham in Genesis, when Abraham is instructed to send away Ishmael in favor of Isaac, Sadan linked the newly Hebraic Itzik Manger to the biblical Isaac and banished Yiddish along with Ishmael. Like the other Hebrew translation projects in this chapter, he claimed Yiddish literature in its Hebrew guise for posterity.

Yet Sadan's representation of an eternal Hebrew and a transitory Yiddish is only one side of the complex story of Hebrew-Yiddish contact. As Hebrew translators and critics continued their efforts to preserve a Yiddish past within Hebrew culture, many Yiddish writers were preoccupied with envisioning the future of Yiddish in the years after World War II and the establishment of the State of Israel in 1948. They debated the place of Yiddish in American society and in Israeli society and sought to negotiate the relationship between Yiddish writers and readers in the diaspora and the new Hebrew-speaking state.[124] In a 1950 symposium in New York, for example,

Yiddish poet Arn Glantz-Leyeles demanded that Israel recognize the national importance of Yiddish culture and incorporate it as a living cultural force into the state's intellectual life.[125] He did not object to Hebrew translations of Yiddish literature, but rather to the heavy ideological hand evident in these translations. Dovid Pinski went a step further in another American Yiddish debate about the future of Yiddish. Recognizing that Israel would never be a Yiddish-speaking country, he proposed a familiar—if unlikely—solution. "The remedy is bilingualism. Yiddishism and Hebrew in the diaspora, Hebraism and Yiddish in the Land of Israel."[126] World War II and the Holocaust profoundly ruptured Jewish life, obliterating the Eastern European Jewish culture that had cultivated traditional Hebrew-Yiddish bilingualism and undergirded the transition to modern translingualism. But as in the years after World War I, the new postwar reality provoked major shifts in Hebrew-Yiddish contact, not an end to the ever-evolving relationship.

Postscript

IN 1986, half a century after the fierce interwar debates about the future of Hebrew-Yiddish bilingualism, Israeli poet Avot Yeshurun wrote a poem that engages familiar questions about language and bilingualism.

„דּוּ-לְשׁוֹנִיּוּת חַיֶּבֶת גַּם הַיּוֹם
לִהְיוֹת אַקְטֻאָל". כָּךְ פָּסַק עוֹרֵךְ
„יידיש-וועלט" הַיּוֹשֵׁב בְּיִשְׂרָאֵל
וְכָךְ עוֹזֵר לְעִנְיְנֵי לָשׁוֹן הַיּוֹשֵׁב בְּעִתּוֹן.

אֵם אַחַת הָיְתָה לָעָם.
לָשׁוֹן אַחַת הָיְתָה לָאֵם.
לִהְיוֹת יֹדֵעַ כָּל אָדָם: זֶה פְּלָנִים לֹא אֲוָזִים"
וְשָׂפָה מֵעַצְמָם אֹחֲזִים." (מִיקוֹלַי רֶאִי).

הַאִם נֵלֵךְ מִמָּקוֹם לְמָקוֹם לְבַקֵּשׁ מִלָּה?
שָׂפָה אַחַת מְדַבֶּרֶת אֵלַי.
שָׂפָה אַחַת מְדַבֶּרֶת אֵלֶיהָ.
שֳׁבִי נַפְשִׁי מִן הַיֵּאוּשׁ וּמִן הַיִּידִישׁ.[1]

"Bilingualism must, even today,
be a reality." So ruled the editor of
Yiddish-velt sitting in Israel
and so the language assistant, sitting at the paper.

One mother had the nation.
One tongue was that mother's.

"Among other nations let it always be known
That the Poles are not geese, have a tongue of their own."
(Mikołaj Rej).

Shall we go from place to place to request a word?
One language speaks to me.
One language speaks to her.
Return, my soul, from despair and from Yiddish.

The poem's opening lines quote Itzhak Korn, the president of the World Council for Yiddish and Jewish Culture and the driving force behind the council's monthly Yiddish paper, *Yiddish-velt* (Yiddish World). Korn published an essay titled "Tsvey shprakhikayt darf oykh haynt zayn aktuel" (Bilingualism Must Even Today Be a Reality) on the front page of the March 1986 issue of *Yiddish-velt.* In the article he acknowledges that bilingualism is disappearing, but argues that it must be preserved so as not to lose a significant part of Jewish history and culture. He tasks his readers with a *goyrldike shlikhus*, a fateful mission, to cultivate a new generation of Yiddish speakers in Israel and the diaspora, stressing Yiddish's moral right to be respected by Hebrew culture in Israel and the need for Yiddish speakers to support Zionism and Israel.[2] Avot Yeshurun's poem, however, complicates the bilingualism Korn celebrates and the monolingualism he criticizes. In lines that move between Hebrew and Yiddish, the poem questions such grand statements about language.

Examining many declarations about language and bilingualism, this book has focused on similar attempts to will literary and linguistic realities into being via the power of the printed word. Yeshurun's poetic commentary exposes the limits of such exhortations: Can bilingualism be realized simply because a late twentieth-century Yiddish periodical in Israel said so? Was bilingualism, even decades earlier, a formidable force in Jewish-language literature because people like Y. D. Berkovitz, Shmuel Niger, and Dov Sadan claimed it was? While recognizing the limits of such speech acts, this book contends that bilingualism and its lingering traces were central elements in the development of twentieth-century Yiddish and Hebrew cultures.

Writing in Yiddish in a periodical on the margins of Israeli culture, *Yiddish-velt*'s editor may not have been able to singlehandedly revive bilingualism. Yiddish, as we saw in the 1940s translation projects, had been circumscribed within Hebrew culture in specific, nonthreatening ways. Korn's World Council for Yiddish and Jewish Culture, established with support from the Israeli Ministry of Education in the early 1970s, represents a later iteration of literary-linguistic contact, one of many attempts to situate Yiddish within Israel. But it is Yeshurun himself who provides glimpses of Yiddish within this and other Hebrew poems, practicing translingualism even as he sardonically questions Korn's call for bilingualism.

The untitled poem is presented in Yeshurun's idiosyncratic Hebrew, filled with nonstandard spelling, quotations, and Yiddish. Many of Yeshurun's poems mix Yiddish as well as Arabic and Polish words into Hebrew lines. In "Safa telavivrit" (Tel Aviv Hebrew), another poem Yeshurun wrote in 1986, archaic biblical Hebrew diction brackets Yiddish and Hebrew phrases in a single line.[3]

אֹדְכֶם אוּנְדזֶער לָשׁוֹן יִידִישׁ. לָשׁוֹן שֶׁלָּנֵ. יִידִישׁ לֻשְׁן. אוּנְדזֶער יִידִישׁ לֻשְׁן, אֹדֵכִי.[4]

> I shall thank ye *undzer* Yiddish language. Our language. *Yidish lushn. Undzer yidish lushn*, I shall thank thee.

The high register of the archaic Hebrew *odkhem* (I shall thank ye) and *odekhi* (I shall thank thee) contrasts with the creeping inclusion of Yiddish: first just the pronoun *undzer* (our), then the nominal phrase *yidish lushn* (Yiddish language), and finally the full possessive phrase *undzer yidish lushn* (our Yiddish language). Rendered in Yeshurun's Polish Yiddish pronunciation (*lushn* rather than *loshn*) but with Hebrew vowels, this line exemplifies Yeshurun's style of splicing Yiddish within his Hebrew poetic language. Meir Wieseltier compares Yeshurun's use of Yiddish to that of other nineteenth- and early twentieth-century writers. For decades, he explains, Hebrew literature was the trapeze act and Yiddish was its safety net, present but virtually invisible in the work of poets like Bialik and Uri Zvi Greenberg. By contrast, "here Yiddish is invited to come in and be seen in public. It is no longer a safety net, but an inseparable part of the content."[5] In the poem on bilingualism, however, Yiddish surfaces in a variety of less obvious but still significant linguistic and literary manners. The opening quote imports the overly formal diction of this editorial comment into a poem with a touch of Yiddish. Insisting that bilingualism must be *aktuel* (a reality), Yeshurun chooses the Yiddish adverbial version of the Latin *actualis* that Korn uses in his Yiddish title rather than the Hebrew adjectival *aktuali*. Yiddish becomes even more palpable in the third line, when the journal's title is provided in its Yiddish spelling and not in vocalized Hebrew.[6] Despite widespread efforts in Israel to consign Yiddish to the Jewish past, the poem's first stanza demonstrates ways in which Yiddish continued to exist within Israeli literature.

In subsequent stanzas, the poem contrasts Korn's call for bilingualism with an apparent emphasis on monolingualism. It reinforces the power of the mother tongue as the language of the nation, quoting the famous verses of Polish poet Mikołaj Rej (1505–1569), the first to write exclusively in Polish rather than Latin: "Among other nations, let it always be known / That the Poles are not geese, they have a language of their own."[7] The inclusion of this poetic proclamation of national monolingualism suggests that the Jews underwent a similar transition from premodern multilingualism to modern monolingualism in order to become a nation. But in contrast to Rej's famous Polish lines, Yeshurun writes about the mother tongue but not in the mother tongue. In the Ashkenazi Jewish context, the language of the mother, the *mameloshn*, was Yiddish and not Hebrew. Thus the poem seems to endorse monolingualism but in fact enacts Jewish bilingualism by using Hebrew to describe Yiddish as literally the tongue of the nation's mother. The stylized syntax and sonic resonance of the first two lines of the second stanza, "One mother had the nation. / One tongue was that mother's," stress the disjunction between that mother's tongue (Yiddish) and the national tongue (Hebrew), between the near-homonyms *em* (mother) and *am* (nation), and not their organic relationship.

By the third stanza, the power of Yiddish that lurks within Yeshurun's Hebrew becomes explicit. The poetic speaker and his soul are devoted not to the Hebrew of the poem but to the Yiddish of its last line, expressed in the language of Psalm 116: "Return, O my soul, to your rest, for the Lord has been good to you. You have delivered me from death, my eyes from tears, my feet from stumbling. I shall walk before the Lord in the lands of the living."[8] While the psalmist recognizes God's deliverance from death, Yeshurun's poetic speaker asks for deliverance from despair and from Yiddish, the two words linked by the sound play *ye-ush* and *yi-dish*. Unlike the psalm, in which the speaker is restored to the "lands of the living," the poem is ominously silent, concluding with the plea and not its fulfillment. The poetic speaker's soul is still bound up with Yiddish even though Yiddish is linked explicitly to despair and allusively to death. Thus we are left with a poem that "speaks" Hebrew as Yiddish "speaks" to its poetic speaker. In contrast to Korn's call for bilingualism, Yeshurun's poem is in fact a "real" (*aktuel*) expression of the legacy of bilingualism: Hebrew poetry that speaks Yiddish.

This poem is one of many lingering literary intersections between Hebrew and Yiddish, written by a poet who reliably transgressed linguistic, aesthetic, and political boundaries. Avot Yeshurun (1904–1992), the adopted name of Yechiel Perlmutter, was a formidable figure on the margins of Israeli poetry, one who resisted Zionism's break with the past, the obliviousness to the Arab presence, and the rejection of bilingualism and Yiddish.[9] The Hebrew of his poems is "brutally broken up, fragmented, deformed, and mangled" by other languages like Yiddish, Arabic, and Polish.[10] But he was not a bilingual poet in the strict sense of the term; he published in Hebrew, not in Yiddish. He is, however, an extreme example of a translingual poet. Not unlike Shlonsky's poetic collection *Le-aba-ima* and Berkovitz's story "Ha-nahag," Yeshurun's poetry integrates Yiddish within a fundamentally Hebraic text. In Lilach Lachman's words, "The 'lost' mother tongue is therefore not altogether lost: animated as an 'inset language' . . . it can be combined with a new language, condensed, disseminated, covered up, transported."[11] As such, his work is part of a broad spectrum of translingual writing that defined and, in different ways, continues to define modern Hebrew and Yiddish literatures.

Unlike writers moving between Yiddish and Hebrew fifty years earlier, however, Yeshurun's poem does not offer a vision for the future of Hebrew-Yiddish bilingualism. As central as Yiddish is to Yeshurun's poems, it is firmly rooted in the past, in the destroyed world of his mother and the Polish town of Krastnystaw.

Yeshurun's translingual poetics can be seen as a later manifestation of the literary-linguistic contact that recurs in the texts and between writers examined in this book. In contrast to literary histories that located an irreconcilable split between Yiddish and Hebrew in the years surrounding World War I, this book has traced the continuing contact between the two Jewish languages as they, their writers, and their readers left the bilingual cultural centers of Eastern European Jewish society. Historical ruptures like World War I and World War II did not sever relations between Hebrew and Yiddish but rather triggered profound changes in literary-linguistic practice. In speeches, essays, and literary texts, Jewish writers defied the ideological imperatives of monolingualism. These literary encounters reverberated across the expanding map of twentieth-century Jewish life. Intersections between the languages catalyzed debates over the nature of Jewish culture, the relationship between Palestine and the diaspora, the future of bilingual writers, and Hebrew's responsibility for Yiddish culture. Hebrew and Yiddish were neither a single literature nor were they two entirely separate literatures. Rather, their intersections underscore the dynamic range of literary-linguistic contact that emerged with the breakdown of traditional Jewish bilingualism.

Collectively, these episodes of Hebrew-Yiddish contact offer two distinct visions for translingual literary cultures. The first conceives of a transnational, translingual modern culture that resists both territorialization and monolingualism. Rachel Wischnitzer Bernstein sought to promote a unified concept of Jewish art that transcended the particularities of language in *Milgroym* and *Rimon*. The decision to publish simultaneously in Yiddish and Hebrew targeted a geographically dispersed and ideologically diverse readership and contended that a single cultural program could traverse national and linguistic boundaries. *Achisefer* also turned to literature as a means of crossing even more formidable boundaries in the 1940s, particularly in its original conception as a two-volume bilingual translation project. While *Milgroym* and *Rimon* used literature in both languages to counterbalance a transcendent Jewish visual art, *Achisefer* turned to literature, and specifically literature in translation, to anchor American cultural bilingualism. Perhaps more surprisingly, Zalman Shneour's efforts to translate his own work between Yiddish and Hebrew also participated in a transnational, translingual cultural vision because he tried to sustain early twentieth-century bilingualism rather than adapt to changing times. From his isolated vantage point in Paris, Shneour sought refuge in the Eastern European past and its historical bilingualism as he tried to move between contemporary Hebrew and Yiddish. Each of these examples demonstrates the desire to craft nonnational alternatives to cultural monolingualism and the immense difficulty in doing so. Yet the work of these writers resonates with postwar efforts to shape autonomist and diasporic Jewish-language cultures and, later, linguistically and culturally hybrid texts.

At the same time, a second vision for Hebrew-Yiddish contact emerged, one that carved out space for linguistic multiplicity within a national literary culture. The dramatic rhetoric of the language debates in the Yishuv obscured the ways in which Yiddish continued to play significant roles in Hebrew literature and its texts. Shlonsky infused his Hebrew poetry with Yiddish words and rhythms, communicating nostalgia for an Eastern European childhood through language. Berkovitz incorporated the wildly multilingual reality of the Yishuv within a firmly Zionist ideological framework. Both Feygenberg's Ha-me'asef Press and Malkin's anthology ushered Yiddish into Hebrew via ideologically freighted translations. The ways in which Yiddish was incorporated into Hebrew culture suggest that translingualism does not necessarily resist national culture but can be mobilized in support of it. More specifically, these examples enlisted Yiddish in support of Hebrew culture even as they defied Zionism's monolingual imperative. By establishing acceptable precedents, these writers laid the foundations for a different kind of postwar Jewish translingualism, one that sanctioned Yiddish within Hebrew literature, paradoxically serving and resisting the national language. As a result, they act as literary precursors to more sophisticated efforts not only to assimilate but also to mobilize Yiddish within Israeli culture. If interwar national translingualism was marked by its ideological conformity, postwar translingualism has gradually given way to nuanced and linguistically complex texts such as Ya'akov Shabtai's *Past Continuous* (1977), David Grossman's *See Under: Love* (1986), Yoel Hoffman's *Book of Yosef* (1988), and Matan Hermoni's *Hebrew Publishing Company* (2011).[12]

These dual cultural visions are a fitting conclusion for a narrative that has revolved around binaries. Starting with the two salons on Ceglana Street in Warsaw as sites of an originary fiction for Hebrew-Yiddish bilingualism, I have examined twin periodicals, charismatic duos, and paired projects, all the while emphasizing the crossovers, links, attractions, and repulsions that complicate these binaries. My hope is that this duality contributes to what Jordan Finkin has aptly called "cultural binocularism": when the close analysis of literary texts and their sociocultural and discursive conditions allows parallel literary images to resolve into a larger cultural vision.[13]

I see Avot Yeshurun's poem as one such stereoscopic image that comes into sharper focus thanks to earlier instances of Hebrew-Yiddish literary-linguistic contact. On the one hand, the poem resists the dominance of monolingualism by emphasizing the historical and emotional power of Yiddish and infusing its Hebrew lines with Yiddish. One the other, it inscribes itself within Hebrew literature by its choice of language and by situating Yiddish in the past. Yeshurun's poem is incomprehensible without the dual reference points of Hebrew-Yiddish bilingualism and Hebrew monolingualism. As a result, it not only crosses clearly demarcated linguistic boundaries but also flaunts its linguistic transgressions. It achieves the translingual effect that Niger sought when he insisted on the relevance of contemporary Jewish bilingualism, but does so from inside of Hebrew literature, a radical form of translingual poetics shared with writers like Shlonsky and Berkovitz. Literary translingualism in this poem and beyond can exist both alongside and inside of seemingly monolingual national literatures.

In European languages like English, German, and French, the notion of monolingualism displaced multilingual life and literature over the course of the eighteenth century.[14] As Yasemin Yildiz argues, "the appearance of the monolingual paradigm substantially changes the meaning and resonance of multilingual practices."[15] Consequently, "recognizing the monolingual paradigm and its workings can be a step towards denaturalizing monolingualism as an unquestioned norm and standard according to which other linguistic configurations and practices are measured."[16] This book has shown the ways in which the ascendance of a comparable monolingual paradigm in Hebrew and Yiddish literatures altered the practice and resonance of Jewish multilingualism, specifically Hebrew-Yiddish bilingualism. But the belated emergence of Jewish monolingualism at the beginning of the twentieth century and the long history of Jewish multilingualism intensified literary-linguistic negotiations in both Yiddish and Hebrew. This accelerated process of linguistic change, combined with the disruptions of early twentieth-century Jewish life, means that the Jewish monolingual paradigm has always been incomplete. Even in Israel, loyal proponents of Hebrew contended with the reality of Yiddish-speaking—and Arabic- and Russian-speaking—residents, immigrants, and visitors. Some bilingual writers chose a single literary language; others continued to write in both languages; and still others shifted their attentions to languages like Arabic, English, Polish, and Russian. Yiddish and Hebrew writers have perpetually debated the shifting and often porous boundaries between their respective literatures.

Given these and many other intersections between the two languages, Yeshurun's poetry does not represent the reemergence of Jewish multilingualism, but rather the persistence of bilingual and translingual practices in Hebrew and Yiddish literatures. These forms of literary contact not only show the multiple, and at times contradictory, attachments to language lurking within monolingualism but also highlight the range of experimentation and innovation within modern Jewish-language literatures.

Notes

◆

Bibliography

◆

Index

Notes

Introduction

1. The quotation in the opening epigraph is from Stephen Greenblatt, "Racial Memory and Literary History," *PMLA* 116 (2001): 62.

2. Zalman Shneour, *David Frishman va-acherim* (Tel Aviv: Dvir, 1959), 69–70. All translations from Hebrew and Yiddish throughout the book are mine unless noted.

3. Ibid., 70.

4. Peretz and Klausner were not the only ones to host literary gatherings in Warsaw. David Frishman, who maintained a long-standing feud with Peretz, hosted Hebrew writers in his Warsaw home, while Hillel Zeitlin also welcomed young Hebrew and Yiddish writers from his arrival in Warsaw in 1906 until his death in 1942. Natan Cohen, *Sefer, sofer ve-iton: merkaz ha-tarbut ha-yehudit be-varsha, 1918–1942* (Jerusalem: Hotsa'at sefarim al shem Magnes, ha-universitah ha-ivrit, 2003), 12.

5. Yitzhak Dov Berkovitz, *Kitvei Y. D. Berkovitz*, 2 vols. (Tel Aviv: Dvir, 1959), 2:21. Other writers who recalled Ceglana Street fondly include Sholem Ash, "Mayn ershte bakantshaft mit peretsn," *Di tsukunft*, no. 20 (1915): 458–63; H. D. Nomberg, *Gezamlte verk*, 9 vols. (Warsaw: Farlag kultur-lige, 1930), 8:32–35; Der Nister, *Dertseylungen un eseyen* (New York: Ikuf, 1957), 286–89.

6. Shneour, *David Frishman va-acherim*, 74.

7. Max Weinreich, *History of the Yiddish Language* (Chicago: University of Chicago Press, 1980), 256, 270.

8. Jean Baumgarten and Jerold C. Frakes, *Introduction to Old Yiddish Literature* (Oxford and New York: Oxford University Press, 2005), 26–37; Jerold C. Frakes, *Early Yiddish Texts, 1100–1750* (Oxford: Oxford University Press, 2004).

9. Benjamin Harshav, *The Polyphony of Jewish Culture* (Stanford, CA: Stanford University Press, 2007), 4.

10. See, e.g., Leonard Forster, *The Poet's Tongues: Multilingualism in Literature* (London: Cambridge University Press, 1970); Elizabeth Klosty Beaujour, *Alien Tongues: Bilingual Russian Writers of the "First" Emigration* (Ithaca: Cornell

University Press, 1989), 263; Hana Voisine-Jechova, "Peut-on choisir sa langue?," *Revue de littérature comparée*, no. 69 (1995): 5–11.

11. Though male writers dominate literary histories of early twentieth-century Hebrew and Yiddish literature, women writers also moved between the many languages of Jewish Eastern Europe, including Devorah Baron (Yiddish-Hebrew), Dvoyre Fogel (Yiddish-German-Polish), Rachel Feygenberg (Yiddish-Hebrew), and Leah Goldberg (Russian-Hebrew).

12. Shneour, *David Frishman va-acherim*, 70.

13. Ibid., 70.

14. Joshua A. Fishman, "Attracting a Following to High-Culture Functions for a Language of Everyday Life: The Role of the Tshernovits Language Conference in the 'Rise of Yiddish,'" in *Never Say Die!: A Thousand Years of Yiddish in Jewish Life and Letters* (The Hague: Mouton, 1981), 374.

15. Ibid., 382–86.

16. Nakhmen Mayzel, for example, argued that Czernowitz should be seen as "the first mobilization" of Yiddish, quoted in ibid., 387. More recent accounts of the conference have similarly emphasized the symbolic significance of Czernowitz. Robert D. King, "The Czernowitz Conference in Retrospect," in *Politics of Yiddish: Studies in Language, Literature, and Society*, ed. Dov-Ber Kerler (Walnut Creek, CA: Altamira Press, 1998), 48; Emanuel S. Goldsmith, *Architects of Yiddishism at the Beginning of the Twentieth Century: A Study in Jewish Cultural History* (Rutherford, NJ: Fairleigh Dickinson University Press, 1976); Keith Weiser and Joshua A. Fogel, *Czernowitz at 100: The First Yiddish Language Conference in Historical Perspective* (Lanham, MD: Lexington Books, 2010).

17. Dan Miron, *From Continuity to Contiguity* (Stanford, CA: Stanford University Press, 2010), 134–35.

18. Ibid., 135.

19. After World War I, Vilna, Warsaw, Cracow, and Lvov were in the Second Polish Republic; Kiev and Odessa were in the new Soviet Union; and Czernowitz was in Romania. Weinreich, *History of the Yiddish Language*, 297–98.

20. Tlomackie 13, which opened its doors in 1918, became "the dominant cultural institutions for Jews living in Warsaw between the world wars." Ruth R. Wisse, *The Modern Jewish Canon* (New York: Free Press, 2000), 135. Hebrew organizational efforts were far more limited in scope, as the Association of Hebrew Writers and Journalists in Poland was not created until 1929, and its address changed several times during the 1930s. See Cohen, *Sefer, sofer ve-iton*, 142–46.

21. George Steiner, *Extraterritorial* (New York: Atheneum, 1971), viii.

22. Itamar Even-Zohar, *Polysystem Studies* (Durham, NC: Duke University Press, 1990), 83. Later in the same collection of essays, Even-Zohar suggests that the polysystem disintegrated only in the years after World War I. Ibid., 101.

23. Even-Zohar, *Polysystem Studies*, 126.

24. Miron, *From Continuity to Contiguity*, 39–40.

25. Chana Kronfeld, "The Joint Literary History of Hebrew and Yiddish," in *Where and What Are Jewish Languages*, ed. Joshua Miller and Anita Norich (Ann Arbor: Frankel Institute, University of Michigan, (forthcoming), 16. On Potash, see Yael Chaver, *What Must Be Forgotten: The Survival of Yiddish in Zionist Palestine* (Syracuse: Syracuse University Press, 2004), 166–205. On Fogel, see the special issue of *Prooftexts* 13, no. 1 (1993).

26. Naomi Seidman, *A Marriage Made in Heaven: The Sexual Politics of Hebrew and Yiddish* (Berkeley: University of California Press, 1997), 6.

27. Ibid., 131.

28. Allison Schachter, *Diasporic Modernisms: Hebrew and Yiddish Literature in the Twentieth Century* (New York: Oxford University Press, 2011), 7.

29. Hebrew-Yiddish literary contact predates the Haskalah, but since this study focuses on modern Hebrew-Yiddish literary bilingualism, the Haskalah represents the beginning of concerted, self-conscious efforts to develop each Ashkenazi Jewish language as a modern literary language. For more on earlier Hebrew-Yiddish bilingualism, see Baumgarten and Frakes, *Introduction to Old Yiddish Literature*, 72–81. For more on Levinson and Perl, see Jeremy Dauber, *Antonio's Devils* (Stanford, CA: Stanford University Press, 2004), 209–51.

30. Israel Bartal, "From Traditional Bilingualism to National Monolingualism," in *Hebrew in Ashkenaz*, ed. Lewis Glinert (Oxford: Oxford University Press, 1993), 144–46.

31. Miron, *From Continuity to Contiguity*, 423; Yael S. Feldman, *Modernism and Cultural Transfer: Gabriel Preil and the Tradition of Jewish Literary Bilingualism* (Cincinnati: Hebrew Union College Press, 1986), 15–17; Ken Frieden, "Innovation by Translation: Yiddish and Hasidic Hebrew in Literary History," in *Arguing the Modern Jewish Canon*, ed. Justin Cammy and Ruth Wisse (Cambridge, MA: Harvard University Press, 2008), 417–25.

32. Bal Makhshoves, "Tsvey shprakhn—eyneyntsike literature," in *Never Say Die!: A Thousand Years of Yiddish in Jewish Life and Letters*, ed. Joshua A. Fishman (The Hague: Mouton, 1981), 465.

33. Ibid., 466.

34. Reine Meylaerts defines heterolingualism as "the use of foreign languages or social, regional and historical language varieties *in* literary texts." Reine Meylaerts, "Heterolingualism in/and Translation," *Target* 18, no. 1 (2006): 4. See Rainier Grutman, "Refraction and Recognition: Literary Multilingualism in Translation," *Target* 18, no. 1 (2006): 18–20.

35. I base this definition on transnationalism as defined by Ian Tyrrell, as concerned with "the movement of people, ideas, technologies and institutions across

national boundaries." Ian Tyrell, "What Is Transnational History?," 2007, http://iantyrrell.wordpress.com/what-is-transnational-history/. Similarly, Steven Vertovec argues that despite many different understandings of the term "transnationalism," "most social scientists working the field may agree that 'transnationalism' broadly refers to multiple ties and interactions linking people or institutions across the borders of nation-states." Steven Vertovec, "Conceiving and Researching Transnationalism," *Ethnic and Racial Studies* 22, no. 2 (1999): 447.

36. Steven G. Kellman, *The Translingual Imagination* (Lincoln: University of Nebraska Press, 2000), ix.

37. While my choice of "translingualism" resonates with recent critical elaborations of the term by scholars like Kellman, Suresh Canagarajah, and Lydia Liu, it was provoked by the overuse of the term "bilingualism": Max Weinreich discusses internal and external bilingualism, Niger differentiates a different kind of internal bilingualism in the 1940s, while Harshav uses both multilingualism and polylingualism. Weinreich, *History of the Yiddish Language*; Shmuel Niger, *Di tsveyshprakhikeyt fun undzer literatur* (Detroit: Louis LaMed Foundation for the Advancement of Hebrew and Yiddish Literature, 1941), 156; Harshav, *The Polyphony of Jewish Culture*, 35–40; Benjamin Harshav, *The Meaning of Yiddish* (Berkeley: University of California Press, 1990), 8–9, 24–25.

38. Bilingualism, in Uriel Weinreich's definition, is "the practice of alternately using two languages." Uriel Weinreich, *Languages in Contact* (The Hague and Paris: Mouton, 1968), 1. Hamers and Blanc add a social dimension to the term, understanding bilingualism as "the state of a linguistic community in which two languages are in contact with the result that two codes can be used in the same interaction and that a number of individuals are bilingual." Josiane F. Hamers and Michel Blanc, *Bilinguality and Bilingualism* (Cambridge: Cambridge University Press, 1989), 6. These and other definitions of bilingualism stress the independent nature of each the languages.

39. Aihwa Ong, *Flexible Citizenship: The Cultural Logics of Transnationality* (Durham: Duke University Press, 1999), 4.

40. Yasemin Yildiz, *Beyond the Mother Tongue* (New York: Fordham University Press, 2012), 6–9; A. Suresh Canagarajah, *Translingual Practice: Global Englishes and Cosmopolitan Relations* (Milton Park: Routledge, 2013), 20. For more on Jewish national movements and the question of language, see Bartal, "From Traditional Bilingualism to National Monolingualism," 141–50.

41. See discussions of premodern and early modern bilingualism in Jan Hokenson and Marcella Munson, *The Bilingual Text: History and Theory of Literary Self-Translation* (Manchester, UK: St. Jerome, 2007).

42. Bartal, "From Traditional Bilingualism to National Monolingualism," 147.

43. Kronfeld, "The Joint Literary History of Hebrew and Yiddish," 9.

44. Ibid., 10.

45. Weinreich, *History of the Yiddish Language*, 298. Weinreich attributes the state of disequilibrium to the effects of westernization and the impact of external languages rather than the splitting of the two Jewish languages. In fact, he insists that both Hebrew and Yiddish were strengthened after Czernowitz. While I agree with Weinreich's view that Hebrew and Yiddish writers were still reconfiguring the relationship between the languages, I see these efforts as more ambivalent than Weinreich.

46. Ronald Kim, "Uriel Weinreich and the Birth of Modern Contact Linguistics," *Languages in Contact* 4 (2011): 101–3. Weinreich rarely refers to Yiddish in his elaboration of languages in contact, drawing instead on a wide range of global linguistic encounters, with particular focus on Swiss linguistic contact. It is not until his conclusion that he identifies Yiddish as a particularly interesting case of multiple language contacts, notable for its "structural variety of outside influences in different socio-cultural settings." He also identifies countries like India and Israel as promising sites for future investigation. Weinreich, *Languages in Contact*, 114.

47. Donald Winford, *An Introduction to Contact Linguistics* (Malden, MA: Blackwell, 2003), 10; René Appel and Pieter Muysken, *Language Contact and Bilingualism* (London: E. Arnold, 1987).

48. Weinreich, *History of the Yiddish Language*, 29–34; Dovid Katz, "Hebrew, Aramaic and the Rise of Yiddish," in *Readings in the Sociology of Jewish Languages*, ed. Joshua A. Fishman (Leiden: Brill, 1985), 98–100.

49. Ghil'ad Zuckermann, "A New Vision for Israeli Hebrew," *Journal of Modern Jewish Studies* 5, no. 1 (March 2006): 58–59. See also Uzzi Ornan's argument against Zuckermann, Uzzi Ornan, *Be-reshit haya ha-safa* (Jerusalem: Ha-akademiyah le-lashon ha-ivrit, 2013), 2–3.

50. Weinreich, *Languages in Contact*, 4. Weinreich examines linguistic elements of contact such as phonic, grammatical, and lexical interference; contact in terms of the bilingual individual, incorporating psychology into linguistics; and, finally, the sociocultural setting of language contact within bilingual groups and communities. This approach is evident in his father Max Weinreich's authoritative *History of the Yiddish Language*, published in Yiddish in 1973.

51. Lydia He Liu, *Translingual Practice: Literature, National Culture, and Translated Modernity—China, 1900–1937* (Stanford, CA: Stanford University Press, 1995), 26.

52. Ibid.

53. Liu uses the terms "host" and "guest" to replace more commonly used source and target languages in translation theory as a way to emphasize the host language and to set aside concepts of priority that are often associated with "source." Ibid., 27.

54. Ibid.

55. Even-Zohar, *Polysystem Studies*; Pascale Casanova, *The World Republic of Letters* (Cambridge, MA: Harvard University Press, 2004); André Lefevere, *Translation, Rewriting, and the Manipulation of Literary Fame* (London and New York: Routledge, 1992); Lawrence Venuti, *The Translator's Invisibility: A History of Translation* (London and New York: Routledge, 1995).

56. David N. Myers, "'Distant Relatives Happening onto the Same Inn': The Meeting of East and West as Literary Theme and Cultural Ideal," *Jewish Social Studies* 1, no. 2 (1995): 75.

57. "Te'udat ha-shiloach," *Ha-shiloach* 1, no. 1 (1896): 1.

58. Myers, "'Distant Relatives Happening onto the Same Inn,'" 76.

59. The years immediately after the Bolshevik revolution in particular saw a plethora of single-volume or short-lived literary journals in Hebrew and Yiddish, among them *Olameinu* (Odessa/Moscow 1917), *Kolot* (Warsaw, 1923), *Ringen* (Warsaw, 1921–1922), and *Di khalyastre* (Warsaw 1922, Paris 1924).

60. Sarah Abrevaya Stein, *Making Jews Modern: The Yiddish and Ladino Press in the Russian and Ottoman Empires* (Bloomington: Indiana University Press, 2004), 16.

61. Sean Latham and Robert Scholes, "The Rise of Periodical Studies," *PMLA* 121, no. 2 (2006): 517–18.

1. "Only a World War Could Bring Us Such Elegance"

1. Eric D. Weitz, *Weimar Germany: Promise and Tragedy* (Princeton: Princeton University Press, 2013), 11.

2. Peter Gay, *Weimar Culture* (New York: Harper & Row, 1968), xiv.

3. Franz Rosenzweig, *Zweistromland* (Berlin: Philo Verlag, 1926). See also Paul R. Mendes-Flohr, *German Jews* (New Haven: Yale University Press, 1999), 23–24.

4. See Michael Brenner, *The Renaissance of Jewish Culture in Weimar Germany* (New Haven: Yale University Press, 1998). Even Henry Wasserman, who challenges the existence of such a renaissance, concedes that a Jewish subculture existed in Weimar. Henry Wasserman, "How to Invent a Cultural Renaissance in Weimar Germany," *Katharsis* 2 (2004): 85.

5. I follow Shachar Pinsker in referring to Berlin as an enclave rather than a center of Jewish modernism, recognizing both the significance of Berlin to early interwar Jewish culture and the relatively short duration of its cultural hospitality. See Shachar Pinsker, "Deciphering the Hieroglyphics of the Metropolis: Literary Topographies of Berlin in Hebrew and Yiddish Modernism," in *Yiddish in Weimar Berlin*, ed. Gennady Estraikh and Mikhail Krutikov (Oxford: Legenda, 2010), 28–29; Shachar Pinsker, "Spaces of Hebrew and Yiddish Modernism—The Urban Cafes of Berlin," in *Transit und Transformation*, ed. Verena Dohrn and Gertrud Pickhan (Göttingen: Wallstein, 2010), 58–59.

6. Leo Fuks and Renata Fuks, "Yiddish Publishing Activities in the Weimar Republic, 1920–1933," *The Leo Baeck Institute Yearbook* 33, no. 1 (1988): 421. Since the majority of Hebrew and Yiddish readers—and thus the prospective buyers—lived outside of Germany, these presses had access to a steady flow of American, British, and other capital. New Yiddish and Hebrew publishing houses sprouted overnight to take advantage of the favorable economic conditions, and several existing publishers relocated their operations to Berlin during the early 1920s.

7. Mark Wischnitzer and Rachel Wischnitzer Bernstein were the founders and driving forces of the Rimon Publishing Company. Wischnitzer Bernstein, the magazines' art editor and a frequent contributor of essays about Jewish art, was born in Minsk, studied art at the Universities of Heidelberg and Munich, and was one of the first women to receive an architect's diploma at the École Spéciale d'Architecture in Paris. After taking refuge in New York during World War II, she studied and taught art history for decades. See Bezalel Narkiss, "Rachel Wischnitzer, Doyenne of Historians of Jewish Art," in *From Dura to Rembrandt*, ed. Rachel Wischnitzer (Milwaukee: Aldrich, 1990), 9–25. Mark Wischnitzer, her husband, did not publish in the magazines but was their editor-in-chief. A historian by training, specializing in Jewish and Russian history, Wischnitzer was the general secretary of the Hilfsverein der Deutschen Juden from 1921 to 1937. "Dr. Mark Wischnitzer, Jewish Historian, Dies," *Jewish Telegraphic Agency Archive*, October 15, 1955, http://www.jta.org/1955/10/18/archive/dr-mark-wischnitzer-jewish-historian-dies-was-73.

8. Rachel Wischnitzer, "From My Archives," *Journal of Jewish Art* 6 (1979): 6.

9. Bezalel Narkiss claims that Paenson withdrew his support after the second issue. Narkiss, "Rachel Wischnitzer, Doyenne of Historians of Jewish Art," 18. There are clear cost-cutting measures taken in the fifth and sixth issues of both magazines, including scaled-down covers featuring far smaller pen-and-ink sketches, fewer illustrations, and fewer pages.

10. Wischnitzer, "From My Archives," 6.

11. Francesco Melfi, examining the semiotics of this publishing project, argues that *Rimon* and *Milgroym* comprise a single magazine. Francesco Melfi, "A Rhetoric of Image and Word: The Magazine Milgroym/Rimon, 1922–1924 and The Jewish Search for Inclusivity" (PhD diss., Jewish Theological Seminary, 1996), 6–7. I analyze them as distinct but closely related periodicals because of the changes in content, language, and formatting necessitated by the separate belletristic sections. Also, I refer to these as magazines rather than journals following the texts' own English translations, which reflects the editors' desire to circulate *Milgroym* and *Rimon* beyond the small, elite journal-reading audience.

12. Susanne Marten-Finnis and Igor Dukhan, "Dream and Experiment," *East European Jewish Affairs* 35, no. 2 (2005): 226–31. See also Susanne Marten-Finnis,

"'A Beautiful Lie'—Zhar-Ptitsa (The Firebird)—Sustaining Journalistic Activity and Showcasing Russia in 1920s Berlin," in *The Russian Jewish Diaspora and European Culture, 1917–1937*, ed. Jörg Schulte, Olga Tabachnikova, and Peter Wagstaff (Leiden: Brill, 2012), 301–26.

13. Fuks and Fuks, "Yiddish Publishing Activities in the Weimar Republic, 1920–1933," 424.

14. Brenner, *Renaissance of Jewish Culture in Weimar Germany*, 185–211; Gennady Estraikh and Mikhail Krutikov, eds., *Yiddish in Weimar Berlin* (Oxford: Legenda, 2010), xii–xiii, 15; Zohar Shavit, "On the Hebrew Cultural Center in Berlin in the Twenties," *Gutenberg-Jahrbukh* 68 (1993): 371.

15. Joseph Sherman and Gennady Estraikh, eds., *David Bergelson: From Modernism to Socialist Realism* (London: Modern Humanities Research Association and Maney Publishing, 2007), 29; Pinsker, "Deciphering the Hieroglyphics of the Metropolis," 28–29.

16. Brenner, *Renaissance of Jewish Culture in Weimar Germany*, 201–2.

17. In his highly critical review of *Milgroym* for the Soviet Yiddish journal *Shtrom*, artist Yoysef Tshaykov parenthetically acknowledges it has a Hebrew counterpart. Yoysef Tshaykov, "Milgroym," *Shtrom* 3 (1922): 78–79. Ya'akov Kopelevitz does not mention *Milgroym* at all in his review of *Rimon*. Ya'akov Kopelevitz, "Ha-Rimon," *Ha-shiloach* 41 (1924): 357–66. Most modern scholars have followed suit. Delphine Bechtel, for example, comments that "the editors of *Milgroym* were torn between their desire to create international bridges between Yiddish, European and German Jewish cultures." Delphine Bechtel, "Babylon or Jerusalem: Berlin as Center of Jewish Modernism in the 1920s," in *Insiders and Outsiders: Jewish and Gentile Culture in Germany and Austria*, ed. Dagmar C. G. Lorenz and Gabriele Weinberger (Detroit: Wayne State University Press, 1994), 117. Though she notes that *Milgroym* had a Hebrew counterpart, her analysis focuses on the magazine solely within the sphere of Yiddish culture. Arthur Tilo Alt refers to the Hebrew connection with the simple sentence, "A Hebrew edition of *Milgroym* appeared under the name *Rimon*." Arthur Tilo Alt, "The Berlin Milgroym Group and Modernism," *Yiddish* 6, no. 1 (1985): 35. Less has been written about *Rimon*, but Israeli art scholar Gidon Ofrat's article on the significance of *Rimon* for the development of modernist art in the Yishuv makes no mention of *Milgroym*: Gideon Ofrat, *Al ha-arets: ha-omanut ha-eretsyisra'elit* (Tel Aviv: Y. Golan, 1993), 1015–24.

18. Menuha Gilboa profiles both *Rimon* and *Milgroym*, primarily surveying the highlights of the six issues. Menuha Gilboa, "Rimon = Milgroym," *Kesher* 10 (1993): 102–5. David Myers also discusses the bilingual nature of the magazines in the context of Jewish East-West encounters in Germany: Myers, "'Distant Relatives Happening onto the Same Inn,'" 91. Francesco Melfi's dissertation analyzes the magazines in depth, considering them as a single publication; see Melfi, "A Rhetoric

of Image and Word." Also, see Shachar Pinsker's brief discussion of the two magazines: Shachar Pinsker, *Literary Passports: The Making of Modernist Hebrew Fiction in Europe* (Stanford, CA: Stanford University Press, 2011), 117–18.

19. Harshav, *The Polyphony of Jewish Culture*, 25.

20. Ibid., 25–26.

21. E. L. [El Lissitzky], "Vegn der mohilever shul," *Milgroym*, no. 3 (1923): 9; E. L. [El Lissitzky], "Beit knesset be-mohilev," *Rimon*, no. 3 (1923): 10.

22. Bal Makhshoves, "Tsvey shprakhn—eyneyntsike literature"; Niger, *Di tsveyshprakhikeyt fun undzer literatur*, 112, 156; Dan Miron, *Harpayah le-tsorekh negi'ah* (Tel Aviv: Am oved, 2005), 149–50; Miron, *From Continuity to Contiguity*, 282; Yosef Klausner, *Historiya shel ha-sifrut ha-ivrit ha-chadasha* (Jerusalem: Hotsa'at-sefarim ahi'asaf, 1955).

23. Brenner, *Renaissance of Jewish Culture in Weimar Germany*, 182.

24. Alan Mintz, "The Many Rather Than the One: On the Critical Study of Jewish Periodicals," *Prooftexts* 15, no. 1 (1995): 2.

25. I would like to thank Michelle Brenner, Marc Michael Epstein, and Beth Merfish for their comments on these cover images.

26. See the Jewish National and University Library's digital version, *Machzor Worms* (Israel National and University Library, n.d.), http://www.jnul.huji.ac.il/dl/mss/worms/; Thomas C. Hubka, *Resplendent Synagogue: Architecture and Worship in an Eighteenth-Century Polish Community* (Hanover, NH: Brandeis University Press, 2003), 97–98. See also Marc Michael Epstein's discussion of Jewish animal iconography in Marc Michael Epstein, *Dreams of Subversion in Medieval Jewish Art and Literature* (University Park: Pennsylvania State University Press, 1997).

27. For more about these artists, see Seth L. Wolitz, "The Jewish National Art Renaissance in Russia," in *Tradition and Revolution: The Jewish Renaissance in Russian Avant-Garde Art, 1912–1928*, ed. Ruth Apter-Gabriel (Jerusalem: Israel Museum, 1987), 29–31.

28. Most differences between the introductory statements in Hebrew and Yiddish are minor, but an interesting one is the word used for "Jewish art": in Hebrew, *omanut yisra'elit* (Israelite art) and in Yiddish *yidishe kunst* (Jewish art).

29. "[Preface]," *Rimon* 1 (1922): unpaginated. This statement is provided in Hebrew and Yiddish in all issues of *Rimon* and *Milgroym*, in German (*Rimon* 1) and in English (*Milgroym* 1–6; *Rimon* 2–6).

30. Marek Bartelik, *Early Polish Modern Art: Unity in Multiplicity* (Manchester, UK: Manchester University Press, 2005), 93–96; Seth L. Wolitz, "Between Folk and Freedom: The Failure of the Yiddish Modernist Movement in Poland," *Yiddish* 8, no. 1 (1991): 28–32.

31. See Seth Wolitz, "Chagall's Last Soviet Performance: The Graphics for 'Troyer,' 1922," *Jewish Art* 21–22 (1995): 95–115.

32. The first two issues foregrounded expressionism, featuring the linoleum cuts of Marek Shvarts (Szwarc) alongside the poetry and prose of Greenberg, Melekh Ravich, and Perets Markish. The final issue, however, limited its literary contributors as it expanded its artistic participants to enlist not only the expressionist Shvarts but also abstract constructivists Henryk Berlewi and Yoysef Tshaykov, as well as graphic artist Y. B. Ryback, on behalf of Greenberg's Zionism. See Avidov Lipsker, "The Albatrosses of Young Yiddish Poetry: An Idea and Its Visual Realization in Uri Zvi Greenberg's *Albatros*," *Prooftexts* 15, no. 1 (1995): 100–101; Shalom Lindenbaum, *Shirat Uri Tsvi Grinberg: ha-ivrit ve-ha-yidit* (Tel-Aviv: Hadar, 1984), 160–64.

33. Stephen J. Lee, *The Weimar Republic* (London and New York: Routledge, 1998), 148. Peter Gay articulates the same sentiment is a slightly different manner, writing that expressionists were "in general revolutionary without being political or, at least, without being programmatic." Gay, *Weimar Culture*, 105.

34. Rachel Wichnitzer Bernstein, "Eine Selbst-Anzeige," *Soncino-Blatter* 1 (1925–1926): 95–96.

35. Kenneth B. Moss, *Jewish Renaissance in the Russian Revolution* (Cambridge, MA: Harvard University Press, 2009), 30.

36. Wischnitzer, "From My Archives," 7.

37. Ibid.

38. Ironically, most of the canonical writers that Wischnitzer Bernstein mentions by name (Bergelson, Agnon, Bialik) wrote in Hebrew and Yiddish at various points in their careers. Yet none of them were publishing in both languages on a regular basis by the 1920s.

39. Marten-Finnis and Dukhan, "Dream and Experiment," 237.

40. When referring to essays that appeared in both *Milgroym* and *Rimon*, the Hebrew title or phrase will be listed first, then the Yiddish, and finally the English translation.

41. Rachel Wischnitzer Bernstein, "Di naye kunst un mir," *Milgroym*, no. 1 (1922): 2; Rachel Wischnitzer Bernstein, "Ha-omanut ha-chadasha va-anachnu," *Rimon*, no. 1 (1922): 2. This quotation is translated from Yiddish but the translations are very similar, since both Hebrew and Yiddish were translated from German. *Rimon* credits the translation to editor Krupnik; *Milgroym* does not credit a translator.

42. Douglas Kellner provides a strongly historicized rethinking of expressionism that focuses on the nature of expressionist rebellions of subjectivity, modernity, and capitalism. Douglas Kellner, "Expressionism and Rebellion," in *Passion and Rebellion: The Expressionist Heritage* (New York: Columbia University Press, 1988). It is worth noting German Expressionism came under attack after World War I, though expressionist tendencies appear in Weimar German literature and film.

Wischnitzer Bernstein's embrace of expressionism in *Milgroym* and *Rimon* reflects a belated Jewish version of those earlier trends.

43. Wischnitzer Bernstein, "Ha-omanut ha-chadasha va-anachnu," 4. *Milgroym*'s version of the same essay is substantially similar. Here is the same passage, translated from Yiddish: "Once again, for the first time in a long time, they feel their connection to the past—to the Jewish past. And painfully sweet, with all the excitement of despair they feel the cooperation of the present. Are we not one people through all the persecutions, and thus all of our fate is closely bound up together? Since they feel this way, their creations are so important for contemporary art and carry within them such a strong, personal accent. Because most of all, our torn and anguished generation is searching for expression. It [the generation] froths with restrained suffering, for himself and others the Jew now battles." Wischnitzer Bernstein, "Di naye kunst un mir," 4–5.

44. There are significant differences between Buber's approach to rejuvenating Jewish creativity and Wischnitzer Bernstein's praise of modernist trends in Jewish artists' work, yet both hoped to find the expression of Jewish spirit in Jewish art. See Martin Buber, "Jüdische Renaissance," *Ost und West* 1, no. 1 (1901): 7–10; Asher D. Biemann, "Aesthetic Education in Martin Buber: Jewish Renaissance and the Artist," in *New Perspectives on Martin Buber*, ed. Michael Zank (Tübingen: Mohr Siebeck, 2006), 87–88.

45. Moss, *Jewish Renaissance in the Russian Revolution*, 108.

46. For more on Bergelson's years in Berlin, see Sherman and Estraikh, *David Bergelson*, 29–34; Schachter, *Diasporic Modernisms*, 84–120.

47. See Sherman and Estraikh, *David Bergelson*; G. Estraikh, Kerstin Hoge, and Mikhail Krutikov, *Uncovering the Hidden: The Works and Life of Der Nister* (London: Legenda, 2014).

48. Dovid Bergelson, "Der gesheener afbrokh," *Milgroym* 1, no. 1 (1922): 42.

49. While Bergelson's conception of modern poetry is markedly revolutionary in contrast to Wischnitzer Bernstein's approach to Jewish art, it was strongly critiqued by Marxists such as Moyshe Litvakov and Perets Markish for its Western aestheticism and ongoing links to Jewish culture. Perets Markish, "Biznes," *Khalyastre* 1, no. 1 (1922): 62–64; Moyshe Litvakov, "Yerushe un hegemonye," in *In umru*, vol. 2 (Moscow: Farlag shul un bukh, 1926). The implicit debate between Wischnitzer Bernstein and Bergelson in *Milgroym* is particularly striking in view of the 1919 debate between Bergelson and Litvakov about the future of Yiddish literature; Seth Wolitz, "The Kiev-Grupe (1918–1920) Debate: The Function of Literature," *Studies in American Jewish Literature* 4, no. 2 (1978): 97–106.

50. Dovid Hofshteyn, "Dos lid fun mayn glaykhgilt," *Milgroym*, no. 1 (1922): 44.

51. Moyshe Kulbak, "In a vald a yadlavn," *Milgroym*, no. 1 (1922): 20.

52. Kopelevitz, "Ha-Rimon," 357–58.

53. On *Eygns,* see Wolitz, "Kiev-Grupe (1918–1920) Debate," 97–101; David Shneer, *Yiddish and the Creation of Soviet Jewish Culture, 1918–1930* (Cambridge: Cambridge University Press, 2004), 136–39.

54. See Hannan Hever, *Paytanim u-viryonim: tsmichat ha-shir ha-politi ha-ivri be-erets-yisra'el* (Jerusalem: Mosad Bialik, 1994); Pinsker, *Literary Passports.*

55. Barash signed this review as B. Feliks. Asher Barash [B. Feliks], "Rimon," *Hedim*, no. 4 (1923): 63.

56. Ibid.

57. Tshaykov, "Milgroym," 78–79.

58. Ibid., 79.

59. Markish, "Biznes," 63; Melekh Ravitch, "Di dezertern fun dem yiddishn emes," *Di vog* 1, no. 2 (1922): 40.

60. Ravitch, "Di dezertern fun dem yiddishn emes," 40.

61. Dovid Bergelson and Der Nister, "[Letter to the Editor]," *Shtrom*, no. 3 (1922): 83.

62. Melekh Ravitch, *Di vog* 1, no. 2 (1922): 90.

63. Bechtel, "Babylon or Jerusalem," 118.

64. Years before assuming the literary editorship of *Rimon* and *Milgroym*, Kleinman discussed the "language question" in a Yiddish pamphlet (1909) and a lengthy Hebrew article in *Ha-shiloach* (1908), later republished in book form. Both articles, written in response to the Czernowitz conference, assert the bilingualism of European Jewish life, emphasizing the significance of Yiddish in the diaspora and insisting on Hebrew as the Jewish national language. Moshe Kleinman, *Leshonoteinu* (Odessa: Achiasaf, 1908), 385; Moshe Kleinman, *Undzer natsional-shprakh* (Odessa: Tsiyonistishe kopike-bibliyotek, 1909).

65. The fact that Bialik's sole contribution to *Rimon* and *Milgroym* appeared in the first issue edited by Kleinman is not coincidental. Kleinman was a part of Bialik's Odessa circle, and precipitously left Odessa with him in 1921, a story that he recounted in detail; Moshe Kleinman, "Be-tokh ha-se'ara," *Ha-shiloach* 52 (1924): 367–73; 466–71; 516–28.

66. Chayim Nachman Bialik, "Ha-kadosh Yisrael Vakser z"l," *Rimon*, no. 3 (1923): 33–34; Chayim Nachman Bialik, "Ha-kadosh Yisroel Vakser z"l," *Milgroym*, no. 3 (1923): 33–35.

67. Yisrael Vakser, "In zibn tog arum," *Milgroym*, no. 3 (1923): 35–37; Yisrael Vakser, "Le-shivat ha-yamim," *Rimon*, no. 3 (1923): 37–38; Yisrael Vakser, "Di letste trer," *Milgroym*, no. 3 (1923): 37–39; Yisrael Vakser, "Ha-dim'ah ha-achronah," *Rimon*, no. 3 (1923): 35–36.

68. Several of Vakser's stories were published in *Tsukunft* and *Frayhayt* in the early 1920s, along with those in *Milgroym* and *Rimon*. The Yiddish Culture League

in Bessarabia also issued a slim collection of his children's stories in 1923. Yisrael Vakser, *Mayselekh far kinder* (Bessarabia: Yiddishe kultur-lige, 1923). But Bialik's hopes for a full-fledged collection do not seem to have been realized.

69. Both Bialik and Sh. Niger emphasize that Vakser was murdered, seeing his tragic death as an integral part of his literary significance. See Shmuel Niger, *Yiddishe shrayber in Sovyet-Rusland* (New York: Sh. Niger bukh-komitet baym alveltlekhn yidishn kultur-kongres, 1958), 31–40.

70. On Stencl, see Siegbert Salomon Prawer, *A. N. Stencl: Poet of Whitechapel* (Oxford: Oxford Centre for Postgraduate Hebrew Studies, 1984); Heather Valencia, *Else Lasker-Schüler und Abraham Nochem Stenzel: Eine Unbekannte Freundschaft* (Frankfurt am Main: Campus, 1995).

71. Avrum Nokhum Stencl, "Vider un vider," *Milgroym*, no. 6 (1924): 35; SOAS Library, PP MS 44 Abraham Nahum Stencl.

72. Chana Kronfeld, *On the Margins of Modernism: Decentering Literary Dynamics* (Berkeley: University of California Press, 1996), 210–11; Jordan D. Finkin, "Constellating Hebrew and Yiddish Avant-Gardes," *Journal of Modern Jewish Studies* 8, no. 1 (2009): 4, 12.

73. Benjamin Harshav et al., *A shpigl af a shteyn* (Tel-Aviv: Farlag di goldene keyt, 1964), 375.

74. Bergelson, "Der gesheener afbrokh," 41.

75. See Matthew Hoffman, *From Rebel to Rabbi: Reclaiming Jesus and the Making of Modern Jewish Culture* (Stanford, CA: Stanford University Press, 2007); Lindenbaum, *Shirat Uri Tsvi Grinberg*, 118–35.

76. Stencl, "Vider un vider," 35.

77. Ibid.

78. A modified version of the poem, "Ba-ma'arav," was included in Greenberg's first collection published in prestate Palestine; Uri Zvi Greenberg, *Eima gedola veyareach* (Jerusalem: Beit ha-sefarim ha-le'umi veha-universita'i bi-rushalayim, 1983), 33–37. For other readings of Greenberg's poem see Hannan Hever, Mordekhai Nadav, and Uri Zvi Greenberg, *Uri Tsvi Grinberg bi-melot lo shemonim* (Jerusalem: Beit ha-sefarim, 1977), 55–56; Tamar Wolf-Monzon, *Le-nogah nekudat hapele* (Haifa: Hotsa'at ha-sefarim shel universitat Haifa, 2005), 122–31; Dan Miron, *Akdamut le-atsag* (Yerushalayim: Mosad Bialik, 2002), 62–63.

79. In fact, Greenberg ended up in Berlin because of *Albatros*; the journal's second issue fell afoul of the Polish government's cultural commissar, Greenberg was charged with blasphemy, and further publication of *Albatros* was prohibited. Wolf-Monzon, *Le-nogah nekudat ha-pele*, 21.

80. Ibid., 28–33.

81. See Greenberg's long poem "In malkhus fun tseylem" (In the Kingdom of the Cross) in *Albatros*, nos. 3–4 (1923). One of the only reviews of this issue of

Albatros appeared in *Milgroym*, as editor Moshe Kleiman commented on Greenberg's "wholly new Yiddish tone, an entirely new sort of attention to Yiddish fate and its condition among the peoples of Europe." Moshe Kleinman, "Kunst un literatur kronik," *Milgroym*, no. 5 (1923): 40. Kleinman gently expressed his reservations about "futurism" but praised Greenberg's "emotional-expression" (*gefil-oysdrukn*) and its powerful effects on the reader.

82. Lipsker, "Albatrosses of Young Yiddish Poetry," 90.

83. Spengler's monumental two-volume work foresees the protracted deterioration of Western culture, a gloomy prophecy that resonated in interwar Germany. Both *Rimon* and *Milgroym* published reviews of Spengler's revised 1922 edition: Oswald Spengler, *Der Untergang des Abendlandes* (Munich: Beck, 1922).

84. Uri Zvi Greenberg, "Al derakhim ba-ma'arav," *Rimon*, no. 6 (1924): 20.

85. Lindenbaum, *Shirat Uri Tsvi Grinberg*, 118–19.

86. Ibid., 148.

87. Hoffman, *From Rebel to Rabbi*, 158.

88. B. Gittin 39a.

89. Greenberg, "Al derakhim ba-ma'arav," 19.

90. Ibid., 20.

91. Ibid., 21.

92. Chayim Nachman Bialik, *Kol kitvei Ch. N. Bialik* (Tel Aviv: Dvir, 1938), 31–32.

93. See Ariel Hirschfeld, *Kinor arukh: lashon ha-regesh be-shirat Ch. N. Bialik* (Tel Aviv: Am oved, 2011), 158–60; Hillel Barzel, *Shirat ha-techiyah: Chayim Nachman Bialik* (Tel-Aviv: Sifriyat po'alim, 1990), 203–5.

94. Greenberg, "Al derakhim ba-ma'arav," 21.

95. Harshav, *Polyphony of Jewish Culture*, 25.

96. Alt, "The Berlin Milgroym Group and Modernism," 43. Along similar lines, Bechtel writes that "The story of *Milgroym* . . . only tells of the failed attempt of the exiled Yiddish writers to create a new branch of Yiddish culture." Delphine Bechtel, "1922 *Milgroym*, a Yiddish Magazine of Arts and Letters, Is Founded in Berlin by Mark Wischnitzer," in *Yale Companion to Jewish Writing and Thought in German Culture, 1096–1996*, ed. Sander L. Gilman and Jack Zipes (New Haven: Yale University Press, 1997), 424.

97. Gershon Shaked, "'Ve-halevai nitnah ha-yekholet le-hamshikh,'" *Tarbits* 51, no. 3 (1982): 487n41. Zohar Shavit focuses on the Hebrew cultural center in Berlin in greater detail, but she argues that Berlin was at best an ambiguous center given that it was the product of immigrants with essentially no local readership or standing and thus "served as a platform for the beginning of Hebrew culture (the Haskalah) as well as for its defeat." Shavit, "On the Hebrew Cultural Center in Berlin in the Twenties," 380.

2. Breathing Hebrew with Both Lungs

1. Ash (1880–1957) had lived in the United States since 1914, but traveled throughout Europe and Palestine during the interwar years. See Nanette Stahl, *Sholem Asch Reconsidered* (New Haven, CT: Beinecke Rare Book and Manuscript Library, 2004), 3–34; Joseph Sherman, "Sholem Asch," *The YIVO Encyclopedia of Jews in Eastern Europe*, accessed December 28, 2014, http://www.yivoencyclopedia.org/article.aspx/Asch_Sholem. Hirshbeyn (1880–1948) also traveled extensively, sending accounts of his experiences in exotic locations to the Yiddish press. See Joel Berkowitz, "Hirshbeyn, Perets," *The YIVO Encyclopedia of Jews in Eastern Europe*, accessed December 29, 2014, http://www.yivoencyclopedia.org/article.aspx/Hirshbeyn_Perets. Shumiatsher (1899–1985), overlooked in virtually all press accounts of the reception, traveled with Hirshbeyn and published modernist poetry in journals like Greenberg's *Albatros*. See Faith Jones, "Esther Shumiatcher-Hirschbein," *Jewish Women's Archive Encyclopedia*, accessed December 29, 2014, http://jwa.org/encyclopedia/article/shumiatcher-hirschbein-esther .

2. "Kabbalat panim le-Ash u-le-Hirshbeyn," *Davar*, May 4, 1927, 1. *Davar*'s two-part article on the gathering is the most detailed, so I draw primarily from its report. All quotations from the reception are from newspaper reports, and there are difference between articles.

3. Ibid.

4. "Ne'umei Bialik, Ash ve-Hirshbeyn," *Davar*, May 5, 1927, 3.

5. "Ash ve-Hirshbeyn be-mesibat ha-sofrim," *Ha'aretz*, May 4, 1927, 1. This version is identical to the version of the speech included in Chayim Nachman Bialik, *Devarim she-be-al peh* (Tel Aviv: Dvir, 1935), 2:211–13. Bialik complained that his remarks at the reception were taken out of context, which is evident in the different newspaper reports of his speech. *Ha'aretz*'s version of the metaphor is far more concrete and physical, stressing the shared environment of this "married couple." *Ha'aretz* also adds, parenthetically, that Sholem Ash stood up and shook Bialik's hand mid-speech, calling out "wonderful" after this statement. *Davar*'s version, however, is more explicitly national: "A match made in the heavens, that will never be divided, even for a moment, that will not separate in the elevated life of the nation, and will nourish one from the other." "Ne'umei Bialik, Ash ve-Hirshbeyn," 3.

6. Ya'akov Shavit, "Ma'amadah shel ha-tarbut be-tahalikh yetsiratah shel chevrah le'umit be-erets yisra'el—emdot yesod u-musagei yesod," in *Toldot ha-yishuv ha-yehudi be-erets yisra'el me-az ha-aliyah ha-rishonah*, ed. Moshe Lisak, vol. 3 (Jerusalem: Mosad Bialik, 1999), 10–11.

7. Cited in Zohar Shavit, "Mavo le-beniyatah shel tarbut ivrit be-erets yisra'el," in *Toldot ha-yishuv ha-yehudi be-erets yisra'el me-az ha-aliyah ha-rishonah*, ed. Moshe Lisak, vol. 3 (Jerusalem: Mosad Bialik, 1999), 6.

8. Chaver, *What Must Be Forgotten*, 34.

9. Arye Leyb Pilowsky, "Yidish ve-sifrutah be-erets yisra'el, 1907–1948" (PhD diss., Hebrew University, Jerusalem, 1980), 113–14. Pilowsky's extensive work on the controversy and his bibliography have been invaluable to my analysis of this episode.

10. Zohar Shavit, *Ha-chayim ha-sifrutiyim be-erets yisra'el, 1910–1933* (Tel Aviv: Ha-kibbutz ha-me'uchad, 1982), 176–77.

11. Seidman, *A Marriage Made in Heaven*, 127.

12. Ibid., 131.

13. Malcolm Bradbury and James Walter McFarlane, *Modernism: 1890–1930* (New York: Penguin, 1976), 96–103. Jessica Berman also calls attention to a transnational modernism that existed outside of the European cultural centers. Jessica Berman, *Modernist Commitments: Ethics, Politics, and Transnational Modernism* (New York: Columbia University Press, 2011).

14. Daniel Soyer, "Back to the Future: American Jews Visit the Soviet Union in the 1920s and 1930s," *Jewish Social Studies* 6, no. 3 (2000): 127–28. See also Michael David-Fox, *Showcasing the Great Experiment: Cultural Diplomacy and Western Visitors to the Soviet Union, 1921–1941* (Oxford: Oxford University Press, 2011).

15. Soyer, "Back to the Future," 149.

16. Ibid., 146–47; Albert Waldinger, "Abraham Cahan and Palestine," *Jewish Social Studies* 39, nos. 1/2 (1977): 75. See also Abraham Cahan, *Palestine: a bazukh in yor 1925 un in 1926* (New York: Forverts, 1934).

17. Liu, *Translingual Practice*, 46.

18. See, for example, Ash's book about Palestine, Hirshbeyn's newspaper articles about his trip to Palestine, and Bialik's speeches from his 1926 trip to London and the United States. Sholem Ash, *Erets yisroel* (New York: Forverts, 1918); Perets Hirshbeyn, "Nisht far keyn zilber-shtiker vet ir oysgeleyzt veren," *Der moment*, September 2, 1927, 6; Bialik, *Devarim she-be-al peh*, 64–105.

19. Benjamin Harshav, *Language in Time of Revolution* (Berkeley: University of California Press, 1993), 31–32.

20. "Kabbalat panim le-Ash u-le-Hirshbeyn," 1.

21. Ibid.

22. "Ne'umei Bialik, Ash ve-Hirshbeyn," 3. *Ha'aretz*'s account renders the last line of the quote differently and made note of the audience response: "Yet at the very hour Yiddish stood to sever herself from Hebrew, she ceased to be ours (applause and calls from the audience: she was transformed into 'Orpah'!)." "Ash ve-Hirshbeyn be-mesibat ha-sofrim," 1.

23. "Ne'umei Bialik, Ash ve-Hirshbeyn," 3.

24. "Be-erets yisra'el," *Ha-tsfira*, May 13, 1927, 3. *Ha-tsfira*'s account of the reception was notably shorter than those of *Davar* and *Ha'aretz*, focusing primarily on Bialik's speech

25. "Ne'umei Bialik, Ash ve-Hirshbeyn," 3.

26. Ibid. Note that this quotation, as well as those from Hirshbeyn's speech, are taken from *Davar*'s account of the event, thus the Yiddish speeches were summarized and recounted in Hebrew.

27. "Ash ve-Hirshbeyn be-mesibat ha-sofrim," 1.

28. S. Pietrushka, "Vos men hert un men zet in erets yisroel," *Haynt*, May 20, 1927, 9.

29. Moshe Glikson, "Al 'ha-inyan,'" *Ha'aretz*, May 17, 1927, 2.

30. Y. L. Wohlmann, "Vos ikh her un zeh in erets yisroel," *Der moment*, May 20, 1927, 3. Wohlmann adds that such translation was not carried out, highlighting the fact that most Hebrew-speakers could still understand Yiddish.

31. Arye Leyb Pilowsky, *Tsvishn yo un neyn: Yidish un Yidish-literatur in Erets-Yisroel, 1907–1948* (Tel Aviv: Veltrat far Yidish un Yidisher kultur, 1986), 198–200. See also Shimon A. Shur, *Gdud meginei ha-safa* (Haifa: Haifa University, 2000).

32. "Asefah pumbit be-Tel Aviv al kavod ha-safa," *Davar*, May 15, 1927, 1. The article reports that the large and enthusiastic crowd was urged by Chayim Bograshov, a prominent teacher at the prestigious Herzliya Hebrew Gymnasium and inspiration to the Brigade faithful, to zealously protect the Hebrew language. With indignation mounting, *Davar* editor Berl Katznelson and poet Uri Zvi Greenberg intervened to call for cultural unity and to stop verbal attacks on Bialik.

33. Glikson, "Al 'ha-inyan,'" 2; Pietrushka, "Vos men hert un men zet in erets yisroel," 9; A. Z. Ben Yishai, "Milchamah be-tachanot-ruach," *Davar*, May 17, 1927, 3; Y. Ch Ravnitsky, "Al 'milchemet mitzvah,'" *Ha'aretz*, May 18, 1927.

34. Asher Barash, "Acharei ha-mesiba," *Ketuvim*, nos. 34–35 (1927): 1.

35. Eliezer Shteinman, "Kol korei le-yehudei polin," *Ketuvim*, no. 13 (August 13, 1926): 1; Ben Zion Dinaburg, "Ha-ivrit be-rusya," *Ketuvim*, no. 33 (1927): 2.

36. Ya'akov Rabinowitz, "Devarim gluyim," *Ketuvim*, nos. 34–35 (1927): 2.

37. Yitzhak Lamdan, "Kalpei gilui ha-tishtush be-tocheinu," *Ketuvim*, nos. 34–35 (1927): 1.

38. It is clear that the Soviet crackdown on Hebrew was a raw topic in the Yishuv. At the Tel Aviv rally protesting Bialik's metaphor, Berl Katznelson took to the podium to try to calm the crowd and redirect their indignation to a more suitable target than Bialik. He warned them not to follow the path of the *Evseksiia* in the Soviet Union. "Asefah pumbit be-Tel Aviv al kavod ha-safa," 1.

39. Avraham Shlonsky, "Al 'ha-shalom,'" *Ketuvim*, nos. 34–35 (1927): 1.

40. Avraham Grossman, *Chakhamei ashkenaz ha-rishonim* (Jerusalem: Magnes Press, Hebrew University, 2001), 134.

41. A. Sh [Shlonsky], "Chatoteret olam," *Hedim* 1, no. 4 (1922): 60.

42. Shavit, *Ha-chayim ha-sifrutiyim*, 145–50; Avraham Hagorni-Green, *Shlonsky be-avotot Bialik* (Tel Aviv: Or am, 1987), 5–6.

43. Shlonsky, "Al 'ha-shalom,'" 1.

44. Ibid.

45. Lamdan, "Kalpei gilui ha-tishtush be-tocheinu," 1.

46. Eliezer Shteinman, "Milu'im," *Ketuvim*, nos. 34–35 (1927): 2.

47. Ya'akov Fichman, "Kalpei ha-mafginim," *Ketuvim*, no. 36 (1927): 1.

48. Glikson, "Al 'ha-inyan,'" 2.

49. Pietrushka, "Vos men hert un men zet in erets yisroel," 9; Wohlmann, "Vos ikh her un zeh in erets yisroel," 3; "Der tuml arum dem kabalas-ponim fun Sholem Ash un Perets Hirshbeyn," *Literarishe bleter*, June 3, 1927, 423.

50. Wohlmann, "Vos ikh her un zeh in erets yisroel," 3.

51. Perets Hirshbeyn, "Undzer tseshpoltene tsung," *Literarishe bleter* 51, no. 4 (December 23, 1927): 1002–4. Soon after Hirshbeyn's essay appeared in Warsaw, *Ketuvim* printed out-of-context quotations, in Hebrew translation, such as: "Millions of our people will come [to Palestine] . . . and Yiddish will also be the national language in the Land of Israel" to prove that the Association of Hebrew Writers had underestimated the threat posed by Hirshbeyn's comments. "Hed ha-'shalom,'" *Ketuvim*, no. 64 (1927): 4.

52. Yosef Klausner, "Bi-sha'at cherum," *Ketuvim*, no. 37 (May 25, 1927): 1. Apparently Shteinman and Shlonsky asked Klausner to lend his prestige to the debate. Pilowsky, "Yidish ve-sifrutah be-Erets Yisra'el, 1907–1948," 111–12.

53. Sholem Ash, "Mikhtav predah," *Ketuvim*, no. 37 (May 25, 1927): 1.

54. More than a decade earlier, in 1911, Bialik compared the relationship between Hebrew and a different vernacular, Aramaic, to the biblical Naomi and Ruth. Writing in response to the Czernowitz Conference, his description of a Jewish vernacular dedicated to serving her "mistress" that ultimately enriched the national tongue offers a distinctly Hebraist vision for relations between Jewish languages. Bialik, *Kol kitvei Ch. N. Bialik*, 198. In 1930, Bialik also reiterated the eternal nature of Hebrew and the temporary status of Yiddish. Bialik, *Devarim she-be-al peh*, 2:155–56.

55. Shlonsky, "Al 'ha-shalom,'" 1.

56. Lamdan, "Kalpei gilui ha-tishtush be-tocheinu," 1.

57. Klausner, "Bi-sha'at cherum," 1.

58. Avigdor Ha-me'iri, "Be-urvat ha-pegasusim," *Ha-machar* 2 (1927): 15–16.

59. This was not the first time that Shteinman's ongoing publication in Yiddish had been challenged; several months earlier, Uri Zvi Greenberg had mocked Shteinman for not practicing what he preached: fighting for Hebrew but continuing to publish regularly in the Polish press. Ha-me'iri, aware of the earlier exchange, points out that Greenberg, favorably disposed toward Yiddish, had not published in the language since his arrival in Palestine in 1923, while the anti-Yiddish Shteinman

continued to support himself by publishing in Yiddish. Uri Zvi Greenberg, "Bemots'ei ha-shtikah," *Davar*, September 3, 1926; Hagit Halperin, *Ha-ma'estro: chayav vi-yetsirato shel Avraham Shlonsky* (Tel Aviv: Sifriyat po'alim, 2011), 300.

60. Natan Cohen, "Der Moment," *Historical Jewish Press*, accessed December 29, 2014, http://web.nli.org.il/sites/JPress/English/Pages/DahrMamanet.aspx.

61. Eliezer Shteinman, *Mi-dor el dor* (Tel Aviv: Neuman, 1950).

62. Several of these writers would cease bilingual writing, most notably Uri Zvi Greenberg, who renounced Yiddish upon his immigration to Palestine in 1923 (though by the 1930s he was publishing political and ideological texts in Yiddish and would later return to poetry). Still, Shteinman was in good company as a Hebrew-Yiddish bilingual writing in the early 1920s.

63. Eliezer Shteinman, *Esther Chayot* (Warsaw: A. Y. Stybel, 1923), 10.

64. Gershon Shaked, *Ha-siporet ha-ivrit, 1880–1980* (Jerusalem: Keter, 1977), 3:27; Hagit Halperin, "Torat ha-alilah shel E. Shtaynman u-mimushah be-sipurav," *Moznayim* 43, no. 1 (1976): 22–24.

65. Yisrael Zmora, "Birkat ha-shefa," *Moznayim* 14, no. 3 (1962): 185–86.

66. Eliezer Shteinman, "Ha-lashon al ha-ovnayim," *Ketuvim*, no. 7 (1933): 16–17.

67. Eliezer Shteinman, "Tvusat ha-sipur," *Moznayim* 4, no. 5 (1936): 467.

68. Eliezer Shteinman, *Duda'im* (Tel Aviv: Ketuvim, 1931), 3–4.

69. Halperin, "Torat ha-alilah shel E. Shtaynman u-mimushah be-sipurav," 24–25; Shaked, *Ha-siporet ha-ivrit, 1880–1980*, 3:27.

70. Eliezer Shteinman, *Ukraine veynt* (Warsaw: Farlag alt-yung, 1923), 7.

71. Eliezer Shteinman, "Der goyrl fun a literat," *Der moment*, September 26, 1924, 6; Eliezer Shteinman, "Vegn iberike yudn," *Der moment*, July 22, 1927, 7; Eliezer Shteinman, "Vegn film bikhlal un vegn yishn film," *Der moment*, October 28, 1927, 5.

72. Shaked, *Ha-siporet ha-ivrit, 1880–1980*, 3:30–31.

73. Eliezer Shteinman, *Tsu mentsh un folk* (Warsaw: Derakhim, 1922), iii.

74. Ibid., 56–64.

75. Eliezer Shteinman, "Machshavot bi-zmanan," *Kolot* 1, no. 1 (1923): 31.

76. Eliezer Shteinman, *Sefer ha-ma'amarim* (Warsaw: Derakhim, 1923), 140.

77. Miron, *From Continuity to Contiguity* , 301–2. See also Micha Yosef Berdichevsky, "Bi-dvar lashon ve-sefer," in *Kitvei M. Y. Berdichevsky*, vol. 2 (Tel Aviv: Dvir, 1960).

78. See Halperin, *Ha-ma'estro*, 127–60.

79. Avraham Shlonsky, "Le-yovel Bialik," *Hedim* 1 (1923): 8–9.

80. The implication here is that "I ate meat" so I cannot have any dumplings. Jewish dietary laws prohibit eating milk after eating meat, so this phrase expresses

the speaker's frustration with the unattainable, at least unattainable within a traditional religious context.

81. See Finkin, "Constellating Hebrew and Yiddish Avant-Gardes," 3; Avraham Hagorni-Green, "Gishot yesod u-foetika mutsheret," in *Sefer Shlonsky,* ed. Yisrael Levine (Merhavya: Sifriyat po'alim, 1981), 118–19.

82. Like many of his contemporaries, Shlonsky often published poems in literary journals and newspapers and later in his own collections. "Halbishini" first appeared as the concluding section of the poem "Amal," published in A. Tsiporni, A. Z. Rabinovitsh, and D. Shimonovitsh, eds., *Sefer ha-shana shel erets-yisra'el 1924–1925* (Tel Aviv: Hotsa'at agudat ha-sofrim ha-ivrim, 1926), 253–56.

83. Avraham Shlonsky, *Le-aba-ima* (Tel Aviv: Ketuvim, 1927), 42–43; Avraham Shlonsky, *Ba-galgal* (Tel Aviv: Davar, 1926), 98–99. Among the many readings of this poem, see Leah Goldberg, "Al arba'a shirim shel A. Shlonsky," *Moznayim* 38 (1974): 275–87; Dan Laor, "Shirei 'Gilboa' veha-etos shel ha-aliya ha-shlishit," *Moznayim* 42 (1979): 134–40; Hever, *Paytanim u-viryonim*, 38–40; Finkin, "Constellating Hebrew and Yiddish Avant-Gardes," 9–12; Ari Ofengenden, *Ha-he'eder be-shirato u-va-haguto shel Avraham Shlonsky* (Jerusalem: Hotsa'at sefarim Magnes, ha-universita ha-ivrit, 2010), 31–32.

84. Goldberg, "Al arba'a shirim shel A. Shlonsky," 276.

85. Shlonsky, *Ba-galgal*, 103–5.

86. Song of Songs 8:8.

87. Halperin, *Ha-ma'estro*, 308–9.

88. I am grateful to Chana Kronfeld for this and many other observations relating to Shlonsky's poetry.

89. Shlonsky, *Le-aba-ima*, 33.

90. Finkin, "Constellating Hebrew and Yiddish Avant-Gardes," 12.

91. Shlonsky, *Le-aba-ima*, 30.

92. Leah Hovev, "Motivim le'umiyim ve-historiyim be-shnei shirei eres," in *Be-mish'olei ever yehudi*, ed. Zion Ukshi, Sigalit Rozmarin, and Yisrael Rosenson (Jerusalem: Hotsa'at mikhlelet efrata, 2006), 534. Shlonsky incorporated many motifs from Yiddish folksongs into his poetry and encouraged the creation of new Hebrew folksongs and lullabies. See Moshe Gefen, *Mi-tachat la-arisa omedet gdiya* (Tel Aviv: Hotsa'at ha-kibbutz ha-artsi ha-shomer ha-tsa'ir, 1986), 61–68; Hagit Halperin, Galiyah Sagiv, and Abraham Shlonsky, *Me-agvaniya ad simfonya* (Tel Aviv: Universitat Tel-Aviv: Sifriyat po'alim, 1997), 11–12.

93. Shteinman resumed publishing in the Yiddish press in Israel and the United States in the late 1950s. Many of his essays were collected in Eliezer Shteinman, *Intim mit der velt* (Tel Aviv: Ha-menorah, 1971). Shlonsky, as we will see in chapter 4, translated from Yiddish to Hebrew starting in the late 1930s. See also Hagorni-Green, *Shlonsky be-avotot Bialik*, 51–52.

3. The Belated Bilingualism of Zalman Shneour and Y. D. Berkovitz

1. Moshe Ungerfeld, "Sicha im Z. Shneour," *Ketuvim*, no. 55 (1927): 2.

2. Ibid.

3. See Shavit, *Ha-chayim ha-sifrutiyim be-erets yisra'el, 1910–1933*, 108–9; Shmuel Werses, "Kitvei-et ivriyim le-sifrut be-Polin ben shtei milchamot olam," in *Ben shtei milchamot olam* (Jerusalem: Magnes Press, Hebrew University, 1997), 96–127.

4. See "Report to His Britannic Majesty's Government to the Council of the League of Nations on the Administration of Palestine and Trans-Jordan," *UNISPAL Documents Collection*, 1927, http://unispal.un.org/UNISPAL.NSF/0/D0523C86855FAA6E052565E700693905; E. Garrison Walters, *The Other Europe: Eastern Europe to 1945* (Syracuse, NY: Syracuse University Press, 1987), 173–81.

5. Ungerfeld, "Sicha im Z. Shneour," 2.

6. Ibid.

7. Y. Karnieli, "Sicha im Y. D. Berkovitz," *Ketuvim*, nos. 28–29 (1928): 2.

8. *Vokh*, November 29, 1929, 2.

9. Yitzhak Dov Berkovitz, "A briv tsu der 'Vokh,'" *Vokh* 13 (December 13, 1929): 19.

10. Beaujour, *Alien Tongues*, 51–53; Brian T. Fitch, *Beckett and Babel*, series 57 (Toronto: University of Toronto Press, 1988), 123; Susanne Klinger, "Translated Otherness, Self-Translated In-Betweenness," in *Self-Translation: Brokering Originality in Hybrid Culture*, ed. Anthony Cordingley (London: Bloomsbury Academic, 2013), 113–26.

11. Hokenson and Munson, *Bilingual Text*, 1, 19–20.

12. For example, David Frishman bemoaned the poor state of Hebrew literature in 1901, writing that "we have no writers, we have no subscribers, we have no book buyers" in an editorial piece in the final issue of his short-lived journal *Ha-dor*. Dan Miron, *Bodedim be-mo'adam* (Tel Aviv: Am oved, 1987), 23.

13. Berkovitz, *Kitvei Y. D. Berkovitz* 2:117.

14. Ibid.

15. Ibid., 2:117–18. Yona Altschuler points to a partial Yiddish translation of the Hebrew story "Malkot" with Berkovitz's note "Ekaterinoslav," suggesting that he had started working on the Yiddish version as early as 1904. Yitzhak Dov Berkovitz, *Yiddishe dertseylungen 1906–1924*, ed. Yona Altschuler (Jerusalem: Ha-universitah ha-ivrit, ha-chug le-Yiddish: Hotsa'at sefarim Magnes, 2003), xi.

16. Miron, *From Continuity to Contiguity*, 423.

17. Ibid., 287.

18. Berdichevsky, "Bi-dvar lashon ve-sefer,", 184. Though Berdichevsky uses the word "shira" here, in the broader context of his discussion of literary bilingualism and Abramovitsh's prose, it seems more akin to "poetics" than "poetry."

19. Miron, *From Continuity to Contiguity*, 283.

20. Berdichevsky, "Bi-dvar lashon ve-sefer," 184.

21. Shmuel Werses, *Mi-lashon el lashon* (Jerusalem: Hotsa'at sefarim a. sh. Y. L. Magnes, ha-universitah ha-ivrit, 1996), 59–60.

22. Rainier Grutman, "Beckett and Beyond: Putting Self-Translation in Perspective," *OLI Orbis Litterarum* 68, no. 3 (2013): 196–97.

23. Ibid., 198.

24. Ibid., 198–99. See also Uriel Weinreich, *Languages in Contact* 79–80; A. de Swaan, *Words of the World: The Global Language System* (Cambridge, MA: Polity, 2001).

25. Avner Holtzman, "Aronsohn, Zalman Yitshak," *The YIVO Encyclopedia of Jews in Eastern Europe*, accessed December 31, 2014, http://www.yivoencyclopedia.org/article.aspx/Aronsohn_Zalman_Yitshak; Avner Holtzman, "Bershadsky, Yesh'ayahu," *The YIVO Encyclopedia of Jews in Eastern Europe*, accessed December 31, 2014, http://www.yivoencyclopedia.org/article.aspx/Bershadsky_Yeshayahu; Joel Berkowitz, "Hirshbeyn, Perets," *The YIVO Encyclopedia of Jews in Eastern Europe*, accessed December 29, 2014, http://www.yivoencyclopedia.org/article.aspx/Hirshbeyn_Perets.

26. Menakhem Perry, "Thematic and Structural Shifts in Autotranslations by Bilingual Hebrew-Yiddish Writers: The Case of Mendele Mokher Sforim," *Poetics Today* 2, no. 4 (1981): 181. Perry is drawing on Gideon Toury, *Normot shel tirgum veha-tirgum ha-sifruti le-ivrit ba-shanim 1930–1945* (Tel Aviv: Porter Institute of Poetics and Semiotics, University of Tel Aviv, 1977). Perry uses the term "autotranslation," but I prefer "self-translation," to stress the personal dimension of this translation process.

27. Hokenson and Munson, *Bilingual Text*, 12.

28. See, e.g., Jordan Finkin's analysis of Peretz's self-translations, in Jordan D. Finkin, *A Rhetorical Conversation: Jewish Discourse in Modern Yiddish Literature* (University Park: Pennsylvania State University Press, 2010), 109–46.

29. Bialik, *Kol kitvei Ch. N. Bialik*, 230.

30. For a detailed chronological overview of Shneour's Hebrew poetry, see Hillel Barzel, *Shirat ha-techiyah: omanei ha-zhanr* (Tel Aviv: Sifriyat po'alim, 1997), 57–215.

31. Ibid., 706.

32. Ibid., 706–8; Zalman Shneour, *Anshei Shklov* (Tel Aviv: Dvir, 1999), 321; Eisig Silberschlag, *From Renaissance to Renaissance* (New York: Ktav, 1973), 196–208.

33. Moshe Dluznovsky, "Shalom Ash ve-Zalman Shneour: pegisha be-ruach nizemet u-ve-ruach tova," *Moznayim* 42, no. 4 (1976): 273–77.

34. Yeshurun Keshet, *Havdalot* (Tel Aviv: Agudat ha-sofrim ha-ivrim, 1962), 81–82.

35. Shneour, *Anshei Shklov*, 324.

36. For an analysis of American Hebrew literature as a peripheral Hebrew literary center, see Alan Mintz, *Sanctuary in the Wilderness: A Critical Introduction to American Hebrew Poetry* (Stanford, CA: Stanford University Press, 2011).

37. Zalman Shneour, *A toyt* (Warsaw: Ha-shachar, 1910); Zalman Shneour, *Min ha-chayim ve-ha-mavet* (Warsaw: Tushiya, 1910), 11–92.

38. Shneour, *Anshei Shklov*, 337. Avraham Shaanan puts it even more bluntly, writing that Shneour "did not see the contradiction between the greatness of the poetic, which he reached in a few of his works, and the vulgarity and primitiveness of some of his novels, especially the Yiddish novels." Avraham Shaanan, *Ha-sifrut ha-ivrit ha-chadasha le-zerameha*, vol. 4 (Tel Aviv: Masada, 1967), 17.

39. See Leyzer Ran, *Vilna, Jerusalem of Lithuania* (Oxford: Oxford Centre for Postgraduate Hebrew Studies, 1987).

40. See Yefim Yeshurin, ed., *Vilne: a zamelbukh gevidmet der shtot vilne* (New York: Vilner brentsh 367 Arbeter ring, 1935).

41. Zalman Shneour, "Vilna," *Miklat* 1, no. 1 (1919): 1–14.

42. The Yiddish version first appeared as Zalman Shneour, "Af'n shlosbarg," in *Vilne*, ed. Yefim Yeshurin (New York: Vilner Branch 367—Workmen's Circle, 1935), 781–83. A longer version titled "Vilne" appeared in Zalman Shneour, *Fertsik yor lider un poemen, 1903–1944* (New York: Yiddishn natsionaln arbeter-farband, 1945), 77–85.

43. D. A. Friedman sees "Vilna" as an altogether new genre in Hebrew poetry, "the portrait of a city." D. A. Friedman, "Vilna; Ba-meitsar," *Ein ha-kore* 1–3 (1923): 170. Similarly, Klausner heralds Shneour as the Hebrew poet of the city, in contrast to Bialik (poet of the shtetl) and Tchernikhovsky (poet of the village), part of his efforts to defend Shneour's elite status in Hebrew poetry. Yosef Klausner, *Z. Shneour: ha-meshorer ve-ha-mesaper* (Tel Aviv: Yavneh, 1947), 5–7.

44. Zalman Shneour, *Chezyonot: shirim u-fo'emot 1912–1921* (Berlin: Ha-sefer, 1923), 280.

45. Ibid., 281.

46. This is not the only time that Shneour turned to the prophetic mode in his poetry. See Chone Shmeruk and Yisrael Bartal, *Ha-keri'ah la-navi: mechkerei historyah ve-sifrut* (Jerusalem: Ha-universitah ha-ivrit bi-yerushalayim, 1999).

47. Shneour, *Fertsik yor lider un poemen, 1903–1944*, 77.

48. Yiddish sections 1–4 comprise the first Hebrew segment, the introduction to the grandmotherly Vilna, her daughters and the upper class; sections 5–7 jump to the third Hebrew segment, a journey into Vilna's winding alleys and childhood memories; and concluding sections 8–12 cover the second Hebrew segment, surveying Gediminas Hill and its surroundings.

49. Shneour, *Fertsik yor lider un poemen, 1903–1944*, unpaginated preface.

50. Shneour, *Chezyonot*, 268–69.

51. Shneour, *Fertsik yor lider un poemen, 1903–1944*, 78.

52. Greenberg, *Eima gedola ve-yareach* (Jerusalem: Beit ha-sefarim ha-le'umi veha-universita'i bi-rushalayim, 1983), 63.

53. Avraham Novershtern, "Shir hallel shir kina," in *Me-vilna le-yerushalayim*, ed. David Asaf (Jerusalem: Hotsa'at sefarim al shem Magnes, 2002), 494–96.

54. Ellen Kellman provides a detailed narrative of how Shneour came to publish the Shklov stories, initially titled *Shklov far der revolutsye*, in *Forverts*. Ellen Kellman, "The Newspaper Novel in the Jewish Daily Forward (1900–1940)" (PhD diss., Columbia University, 2000), 312–14.

55. This comment comes from the introduction added to the book *Shklover yidn*. Zalman Shneour, *Shklover yidn* (Vilna: Farlag B. Kletskin, 1929), 12.

56. Dan Miron, "Shneour, Zalman," *YIVO Encyclopedia of Jews in Eastern Europe*, n.d., http://www.yivoencyclopedia.org/article.aspx/Shneour_Zalman.

57. B. Ketubot 16b.

58. Shneour, *Shklover yidn*, 13.

59. Zalman Shneour, "Anshei Shklov," *Tekufotenu* 1 (1933): 372.

60. See, e.g., B. Shekalim 3b.

61. Shneour, *Shklover yidn*, 14.

62. Shneour, "Anshei Shklov," 372.

63. Both "*ish chayil*" and "remainder" (*pleta*) are frequently used in the Bible, and thus lend this passage its biblical tone. But they also contribute to the elevation of this hero, as demonstrated in I Samuel 31:12; Isaiah 37:32; Joel 3:5; Isaiah 4:2.

64. "*Bi-zro'ah netuyah*" becomes a rallying cry for God's power and redemption, and is repeated many times in the Hebrew Bible, including Exodus 6:6; Deuteronomy 4:34, 7:19; Jeremiah 21:5.

65. James Cracraft, *The Revolution of Peter the Great* (Cambridge, MA: Harvard University Press, 2003), 155.

66. Israel Bartal, *The Jews of Eastern Europe, 1772–1881* (Philadelphia: University of Pennsylvania Press, 2011), 107–10.

67. Shneour, *Shklover yidn*, 18–19. The Hebrew versions (1933 and 1958) gloss the Russian words, see Shneour, "Anshei Shklov," 374–75.

68. "Z. Shneour yishtatef be-kvi'ut be-'Davar,'" *Davar*, November 14, 1935, 10.

69. Ibid. Emphasis in the original.

70. Several individuals have suggested that Shneour did not actually translate *Shklov* into Hebrew, but employed a ghost translator. Though the absence of drafts of a Hebrew translation in Shneour's archive may be suggestive, I have not found conclusive proof either way. For my purposes, the fact that Shneour was publicly represented as a self-translator is as important as the actual translation. Thanks to Avraham Novershtern and Lilach Netanel for their thoughts on this point.

71. Awarding Shneour the 1945 Louis LaMed Prize for Hebrew literature in the United States, Sh. Niger made a similar claim, insisting that Shneour had not translated *Shklover yidn* from Yiddish but had written *Anshei Shklov* as a new work in Hebrew. Niger's concern was not erasing the Yiddish version, but claiming Shneour's accomplishment for American Hebrew literature. Shmuel Niger, "Sifrut ivrit ve-yidish be-arhab," *Mishmar*, January 24, 1946, 4.

72. Lawrence Venuti, "The Translator's Invisibility," *Criticism* 28, no. 2 (1986): 187.

73. Ibid., 179.

74. Ibid., 184–85.

75. Joseph Sherman, "Sholem Asch," *The YIVO Encyclopedia of Jews in Eastern Europe*, accessed December 28, 2014, http://www.yivoencyclopedia.org/article.aspx/Asch_Sholem.

76. "Z. Shneour be-mechitsat ha-sofrim ha-ivrim," *Davar*, March 23, 1934, 7.

77. Natan Grinblat, "Psukim," *Davar*, August 24, 1938, 4.

78. Ibid.

79. Klausner lauded Shneour's Hebrew poetry from early in his career, evident in Klausner, *Z. Shneour: ha-meshorer ve-ha-mesaper*, 84.

80. G. Kressel, "Shtei te'udot," *Moznayim* 25 (1967): 20–21.

81. Yona Altschuler compares the Hebrew and Yiddish versions of Berkovitz's early stories in great detail. Berkovitz, *Yiddishe dertseylungen 1906–1924*, xviii.

82. A more literal translation of the title would be "In the hands of the tongue," a phrase taken from Proverbs 18:21. Here, I follow Robert Alter's translation for a more idiomatic English translation of the verse, "Death and life are in the tongue's power," in Robert Alter, trans., *The Wisdom Books* (W. W. Norton, 2011), 272.

83. Yitzhak Dov Berkovitz, "Be-yad ha-lashon," *Ha-tsofe*, September 6, 1904; Yitzhak Dov Berkovitz, "On loshn," *Der fraynd*, August 20, 1908. Both stories were included in Berkovitz's 1910 collections of stories: Yitzhak Dov Berkovitz, *Sipurim* (Cracow: Yosef Fisher Press, 1910); Yitzhak Dov Berkovitz, *Gezamelte shriftn* (Warsaw: Ha-shachar, 1910). Avner Holtzman also analyzes the representation of multilingualism in the Hebrew version of the text in Avner Holtzman, "Ha-lashon ke-khli, ke-etgar ve-ke-nose," *Am va-sefer* 1 (1991): 97–102.

84. Dov Sadan highlights this estrangement as one of the recurring features of Berkovitz's prose. Dov Sadan, "Ha-merchak ha-nora," in *Y. D. Berkovitz, mivchar ma'amarim al yetsirato*, ed. Avraham Holtz (Tel Aviv: Am oved, 1966), 69.

85. Yitzhak Dov Berkovitz, "Ha-nahag," *Moznayim* 1, no. 1 (1929): 7.

86. Ibid.

87. See Micha Yosef Berdichevsky, "Machanayim," in *Sipurim* (Tel Aviv: Dvir, 1980), 9–53; H. D. Nomberg, "Fliglman," in *Shriften* (Warsaw: Farlag bikher far ale, 1908), 1:67–88; Dovid Bergelson, "Yoysef Shor," in *Geklibene verk fun Dovid*

Bergelson, vol. 3 (Vilna: B. Kletskin, 1929), 61–126; Yosef Hayim Brenner, *Shkhol ve-khishalon* (Tel Aviv: Am oved, 1972); Berkovitz, "Talush," in *Kitvei Y. D. Berkovitz*, vol. 1, 37–45. For criticism on the *talush* figure, see Marcus Moseley, *Being for Myself Alone: Origins of Jewish Autobiography* (Stanford, CA: Stanford University Press, 2006), 463; Nurith Govrin, *Alienation and Regeneration* (Tel Aviv: MOD Books, 1989), 24; Sheila E. Jelen, *Intimations of Difference: Dvora Baron in the Modern Hebrew Renaissance* (Syracuse: Syracuse University Press, 2007), 13–24.

88. Berkovitz, "Ha-nahag," 6.

89. Bialik anointed S. Y. Abramovitsh as "the creator of *nusakh*" because of his stylistic innovations in Hebrew prose, including a switch to rabbinic Hebrew and a radically new approach to allusions to Hebrew biblical and postbiblical texts. By the late 1920s, however, an increasing number of Hebrew writers were rejecting *nusakh* prose and seeking alternatives. See Bialik, *Kol kitvei Ch. N. Bialik*, 240–41; Robert Alter, *The Invention of Hebrew Prose* (Seattle: University of Washington Press, 1988), 30–38; Shaked, *Ha-siporet ha-ivrit, 1880–1980*, 1: 83–89.

90. Yitzhak Dov Berkovitz, "Der shofer," *Der tog*, May 1, 1929, 3.

91. See Neil G. Jacobs, *Yiddish: A Linguistic Introduction* (Cambridge: Cambridge University Press, 2005), 7; Finkin, *A Rhetorical Conversation*, 151–52.

92. Even-Zohar, *Polysystem Studies*, 126.

93. Thanks to Vitaly Bergelson for his help with the Russian. The Russian phrase is translated as "confound it all" in Anton Chekhov, *The Cherry Orchard* (New York: Scribner's, 1917), 9. See Helena Rimon, "Transformation of Solitudes: Chekhovian Plots in the Prose of Y. D. Berkowitz," in *Around the Point*, ed. Hillel Weiss, Roman Katsman, and Ber Kotlerman (New Castle: Cambridge Scholars, 2014), 70–98.

94. Yael Chaver, *What Must Be Forgotten: The Survival of Yiddish in Zionist Palestine* (Syracuse: Syracuse University Press, 2004), xx.

95. Gershon Shaked, *Modern Hebrew Fiction* (Bloomington: Indiana University Press, 2000), 103.

96. Berkovitz, "Ha-nahag," 6.

97. Ibid., 7.

98. Berkovitz, "Der shofer," 3.

99. Ibid.

100. Shaked, *Modern Hebrew Fiction*, 103.

101. Berkovitz, "Ha-nahag," 9; Berkovitz, "Der shofer," 3.

102. Harshav, *Language in Time of Revolution*, 89–92.

103. Yitzhak Dov Berkovitz, "Moznayim," *Moznayim* 1, no. 1 (1929): 1.

104. Ibid.

105. See Avraham Novershtern, "Menakhem Mendl le-Shalom Aleikhem: Ben toldot ha-tekst le-mivneh ha-yetsirah," *Tarbits* 54, no. 1 (1984): 105–46.

106. Berkovitz, *Kitvei Y. D. Berkovitz*, 215. In Yiddish, Berkovitz is far more concise on this point, writing simply: "I take here only Menakhem-Mendl as a fully-formed symbolic figure, as a literary instrument for a contemporary problem." Yitzhak Dov Berkovitz, *Menakhem-Mendl in Erets Yisroel* (Tel Aviv: Beyt Sholem Aleykhem, 1973), 9.

107. Berkovitz, *Kitvei Y. D. Berkovitz*, 215.

108. Sholem Aleykhem's *Menakhem-Mendl* was first published in Hebrew translation in Sholem Aleykhem, *Kitvei Shalom Alekhem*, trans. Yitzhak Dov Berkovitz, vol. 3 (Warsaw: Ha-shachar, 1911). It was later expanded and revised by Berkovitz in Sholem Aleykhem, *Kitvei Shalom Alekhem*, trans. Yitzhak Dov Berkovitz (Tel Aviv: Dvir, 1939).

109. Lefevere, *Translation, Rewriting, and the Manipulation of Literary Fame*, 8.

110. Shmuel Niger, "Geleynt un geshribn," *Der tog*, February 2, 1936, 6.

111. A. Einhorn, "Der yontif fun yidishn geyst. Khayim Nakhmen Byalik's 50 yoriker yubileum," *Haynt*, January 14, 1923, 1–3.

112. Writing in 1941 in the United States, Niger overlooks other contemporary forms of bilingualism like Yiddish-English bilingualism. Shmuel Niger, *Bilingualism in the History of Jewish Literature* (Lanham, MD: University Press of America, 1990), 56.

113. Emphasis in original. Niger, *Di tsveyshprakhikeyt fun undzer literatur*, 112. English translation from Niger, *Bilingualism in the History of Jewish Literature*, 94.

114. Grutman, "Refraction and Recognition," 18–19.

115. Weinreich, *Languages in Contact*, 1.

116. Niger, *Di tsveyshprakhikeyt fun undzer literatur*, 113.

117. Beaujour, *Alien Tongues*, 263.

118. Berkovitz, *Yiddishe dertseylungen 1906–1924*, xxx–xxxii. Toward the end of his life, Berkovitz devoted himself to his literary autobiography, published in Hebrew as *Pirkei yaldut* (*Moznayim,* 1963–1965) and in Yiddish as *Kinder-yorn* (*Di goldene keyt*, 1964–1967).

119. Zalman Shneour, *Luchot genuzim* (Tel Aviv: Am oved, 1952).

4. Bound Up in the Bond of Hebrew Literature

1. Rachel Feygenberg, "Maskilim," *Davar*, November 4, 1925, 2.

2. Avraham Shlonsky, "To'anot," *Davar*, November 13, 1925, 2.

3. Ibid.

4. Feygenberg, "Maskilim," 2.

5. Shlonsky, "To'anot," 3. Shlonsky's view of the future of Yiddish was quite similar to Bialik's vision of *kinus*, the gathering of multilingual Jewish culture and its translation into Hebrew, articulated in "Ha-sefer ha-ivri," Bialik, *Kol kitvei Ch. N. Bialik*, 194–201.

6. Earlier translations tended to be in periodicals, making them difficult to quantify. Gideon Toury, working with a limited corpus, sees only a slight rise in the percentage of translations from 1928–1929 to 1930–1945 (from 9 percent to 10 percent). However, his statistics would not account for differences between the 1930s and early 1940s because they are grouped as a single category. Toury, *Normot shel tirgum ve-ha-tirgum ha-sifruti le-ivrit ba-shanim 1930–1945*, 115–17.

7. Venuti, *The Translator's Invisibility*, 14.

8. Grutman, "Refraction and Recognition," 25.

9. Gideon Toury, "Norms in Translation," in *The Translation Studies Reader*, ed. Lawrence Venuti (London and New York: Routledge, 2012), 200.

10. Frieden, "Innovation by Translation,", 422–23.

11. Perry, "Thematic and Structural Shifts in Autotranslations by Bilingual Hebrew-Yiddish Writers,"183. Perry also argues that although the two literatures shared writers and readers, Hebrew and Yiddish were separate and competing literary systems. The proximity of Hebrew and Yiddish texts, writers, and readers shows that the boundaries between the two literatures were, at the very least, far more porous than Perry suggests.

12. Iris Parush argues that in nineteenth-century Eastern European Jewish society, traditional education institutions took steps "to create deliberate ignorance of the Hebrew language and to prevent most of the men who studied in its settings from gaining the literacy skills necessary for reading modern Hebrew literature . . . the absence of Hebrew instruction for both sexes sealed off, for most men and virtually all women, any avenues to modern Hebrew literature." Iris Parush, *Reading Jewish Women: Marginality and Modernization in Nineteenth-Century Eastern European Jewish Society* (Waltham, MA: Brandeis University Press, 2004), 5.

13. See Finkin, *A Rhetorical Conversation*, 82–85; Yaakov ben Yitzchak Ashkenazi, *Tsenerene* (Buenos Aires: Yosef Lifshits-fond fun der literatur-gezelshaft baym yivo, 1973).

14. Venuti, *Translator's Invisibility*, 14.

15. Even-Zohar, *Polysystem Studies*, 47.

16. Ibid.; Casanova, *The World Republic of Letters*, 9–10. Grutman compares Even-Zohar and Casanova, emphasizing that both share the conviction that translation is inherently assymetrical, but that Even-Zohar focuses on *items* (texts, genres, writing styles, conventions) while Casanova focuses on *people*, the agents and power-brokers of literary exchange. Grutman, "Refraction and Recognition," 24–25.

17. Kenneth B. Moss, "Not the Dybbuk but Don Quixote: Translation, Deparochialization, and Nationalism in Jewish Culture, 1917–1919," in *Culture Front: Representing Jews in Eastern Europe*, ed. Benjamin Nathans and Gabriella Safran (Philadelphia: University of Pennsylvania Press, 2007), 212, 216. Concerted efforts to provide Jewish Eastern European readers with translations from European

literature began with Ben-Avigdor's Tushiya publishing house (1896) and continued at a rapid pace at presses like Stybel, Moriah, and Omanut (Hebrew) and Kiever Farlag, Kultur-Lige, and Folks-Farlag (Yiddish).

18. Eliezer Shteinman, "Hotsa'at Stybel," in *Erets* (Odessa: Dos naye leben, 1919), 30.

19. Bialik, *Kol kitvei Ch. N. Bialik*, 198–99.

20. Moss, *Jewish Renaissance in the Russian Revolution*, 109–15.

21. A. Y. Stybel, "He'ara le-marat Rachel Feygenberg," *Davar*, January 1, 1926, 3.

22. See the appendix in Dania Amichay-Michlin, *Ahavat Ish: Avraham Yosef Shtybel* (Jerusalem: Mosad Bialik, 2000), 445–54.

23. Zohar Shavit, "The Status of Translated Literature in the Creation of Hebrew Literature in Pre-State Israel (the Yishuv Period)," *Meta: Translators' Journal* 41, no. 1 (1998): 51.

24. Emphasis in the original. Ibid., 47.

25. Quoted in ibid., 49.

26. At least fourteen separate books written by Ash appeared between 1926 and 1939, most of them translated by Y. L. Baruch and published by Dvir. Six of Opatoshu's novels appeared in Hebrew between 1943 and 1947.

27. Anita Norich, *Discovering Exile* (Stanford, CA: Stanford University Press, 2007), 7.

28. Melekh Ravitch, *Mayn leksikon*, vol. 1 (Montreal: Komitet in Montreal, 1945), 1:194. Rachel Auerbach describes Feygenberg's penchant for writing scathing essays and letters as part of her overall fond portrait of Feygenberg, characterizing her as the "angry aunt at a *heymishe* [traditional] wedding." Rachel Auerbach, "Rokhl Feygenberg," *Di goldene keyt* 17 (1953): 214–15. In response, Feygenberg wrote a furious twenty-two-page letter to Auerbach in which she gives her perspective on her own life history. Rachel Feygenberg, "A brif [Letter to Rachel Auerbach]," undated, 602/ כ36112-א, Gnazim Institute.

29. See Auerbach, "Rokhl Feygenberg"; Sheva Zucker, "Rokhl Faygnberg (Imri)," *Jewish Women: A Comprehensive Historical Encyclopedia*, accessed November 26, 2014, http://jwa.org/encyclopedia/article/faygnberg-imri-rokhl.

30. Feygenberg claims that she learned Hebrew as a child but essentially retaught herself the language by translating her own Yiddish writing in Hebrew. Rachel Feygenberg-Imri, *Yiddish ve-sofreha* (Tel Aviv: Zeman, 1967), 3–5.

31. "Ha-me'asef," *Ha-boker*, December 10, 1943, 4.

32. Ibid.

33. The essays were published with the bitter prefacing statement, "Seven articles, four of which no Yiddish or Hebrew newspaper in the world would publish." Rachel Feygenberg, *Di velt vil, mir zoln zayn yidn* (Warsaw: Farn folk, 1936), title page.

34. Ibid., 61.

35. Ibid., 63.

36. Ibid., 47.

37. Ibid., 70.

38. Rachel Feygenberg, *Bi-mevukhat ha-yamim* (Tel Aviv: Zman, 1938), 126–27.

39. Rachel Feygenberg-Imri, *Mi-ven gidre ha-til: tsror mikhtavim al pig'e ha-zman* (Jerusalem: La-am, 1947), 86. Writing in 1947 Feygenberg argued that Ha-me'asef should coordinate translation efforts so that individual presses would not pursue their own (poor) translations from Yiddish.

40. Feygenberg's archives in *Gnazim* include several letters from would-be translators offering their services. See, e.g., Rachel Feygenberg, "Letter to Chaver M. Shalgi," undated, 602/46259-א, Gnazim Institute; Menakhem Mavshan, "Letter to Rachel Feygenberg," 1944, 602, Gnazim Institute.

41. Shlomo Z. Schocken, "Letter to Rachel Feygenberg," October 21, 1936, 602/45559-א, Gnazim Institute.

42. David Hanegbi, "Letter to Rachel Feygenberg," February 27, 1927, 60245457-א, Gnazim Institute.

43. Feygenberg, "A brif [Letter to Rachel Auerbach]."

44. Y. Y. Singer, *Mi-shnei evrei ha-visla* (Jerusalem: Ha-me'asef, 1945), 7. Though correspondence between Feygenberg and Meltzer reveals that the two argued over style and timely payment, Meltzer shared Feygenberg's conviction that Hebrew translations from Yiddish were essential, later quoted as saying, "The victory of Hebrew over Yiddish was decisive, and for Sabras to appreciate the Yiddish literary treasures a Hebrew translation was necessary." "Renowned Poet Shimshon Meltzer to be Commemorated on Tuesday," *Jerusalem Post*, May 18, 2009, http://www.jpost.com/Israel/Renowned-poet-Shimshon-Meltzer-to-be-commemorated-on-Tuesday.

45. Y. Y. Singer, *Perl un andere dertseylungen* (Warsaw: Farlag kultur lige, 1922), 198.

46. Singer, *Mi-shnei evrei ha-visla*, 23.

47. Nitsa Ben Ari, "Tirgumit o ivrit shel tirgumim," in *Aderet le-vinyamin*, ed. Ziva Ben-Porat, vol. 1 (Tel Aviv: Ha-kibbutz ha-me'uchad, 1999), 294–300.

48. Moyshe Kulbak, *Chevle ge'ulah* (Jerusalem: Ha-me'asef, 1947), iii.

49. Eliezer Shweid calls attention to different formulations of the rejection of Jewish life in the diaspora, see Eliezer Schweid, "The Rejection of the Diaspora in Zionist Thought: Two Approaches," *Studies in Zionism* 5, no. 1 (1984): 43–70.

50. Anita Norich, "Israel Joshua Singer," *YIVO Encyclopedia of Jews in Eastern Europe*, accessed February 6, 2015, http://www.yivoencyclopedia.org/article.aspx/Singer_Israel_Joshua.

51. Dina Porat, *Israeli Society, the Holocaust and Its Survivors* (London: Vallentine Mitchell, 2008), 253.

52. Ibid., 274.

53. Singer, *Mi-shnei evrei ha-visla*, 5.

54. Ibid., 7.

55. Roni Stauber, *The Holocaust in Israeli Public Debate in the 1950s* (London and Portland, OR: Vallentine Mitchell, 2007), 20–22; Tom Segev, *The Seventh Million* (New York: Hill and Wang, 1993), 104, 427–33.

56. Natan Grinblat, "Ha-me'asef ve-sifro ha-rishon," *Davar*, December 28, 1945, 4.

57. Singer, *Mi-shnei evrei ha-visla*, 5.

58. Lawrence Venuti, "Translation, Intertextuality, Interpretation" (Ohio State University, Columbus OH, October 11, 2013).

59. Kulbak, *Chevle ge'ulah*, iii.

60. Rachel Feygenberg, "Letter to Histadrut Secretary A. Becker," June 25, 1961, 602/46446-א, Gnazim Institute.

61. Rachel Feygenberg, "Mikhtav la-maʿarekhet," *Davar*, July 22, 1957, 2.

62. Shmuel Niger and Menachem Ribalow, eds., *Achisefer* (New York: Louis LaMed Foundation for the Advancement of Hebrew and Yiddish literature, 1943), ii. Menachem Ribalow (1895–1953) was the longtime editor and columnist at the American weekly Hebrew paper, *Ha-do'ar*, and proponent of Hebrew culture in the United States. Shmuel Niger (pseudonym of Shmuel Tsharni, 1883–1955) was an active literary figure in Hebrew, Russian, and Yiddish in Eastern Europe before immigrating to the United States in 1919. In New York, he was a prolific Yiddish literary critic, writing extensively in the Yiddish press.

63. Born in Ukraine, Louis LaMed (1898–1979) settled in Detroit in 1921 and dedicated profits from his furniture companies to creating a foundation for Jewish culture. He recruited Niger to chair the foundation. See Jay Rosenshine, "Louis LaMed, Jewish Culture His Hobby," *Michigan Jewish History* 3, no. 3 (1963): 18–20.

64. Niger and Ribalow, *Achisefer*, ii.

65. Ibid., i.

66. The Louis LaMed Foundation prizes were awarded annually from 1940 to the 1960s to a stellar list of American Yiddish writers and lesser-known list of American Hebrew writers, including Yoysef Opatoshu (1943), Isaac Bashevis Singer (1950), Itzik Manger (1952), Arn Glantz Leyeles, Aharon Zeitlin, and Rokhl Korn (1957) in Yiddish; and Eisig Silverschlag (1942), H. Seckler (1943), Menachem Ribalow (1950), Reuben Wallenrod (1952), as well as Zalman Shneour (1944) for *Anshei Shklov*, in Hebrew.

67. The Foundation tried to establish a series at Israeli publishing house Dvir for the publication of Hebrew translations of Yiddish literature, resulting in

the publication of Hebrew translations of I. B. Singer's *Ha-satan be-goray* (Satan in Goray) in 1953 and Glatshteyn's *U-ve-hagi'a yash* (When Yash Comes) in 1957. Rosenshine, "Louis LaMed, Jewish Culture His Hobby," 21.

68. Ruth Wisse, "Language as Fate," *Studies in Contemporary Jewry* 12 (1996): 139.

69. Deborah E. Lipstadt, *Beyond Belief: The American Press and the Coming of the Holocaust, 1933–1945* (New York: Free Press, 1986), 180–81. Yet many Americans found such news hard to believe. See Henry L. Feingold, *Bearing Witness: How America and Its Jews Responded to the Holocaust* (Syracuse: Syracuse University Press, 1995), 173–74, 271–73.

70. Lipstadt, *Beyond Belief*, 151–54.

71. Norich, *Discovering Exile*, 23.

72. Quoted in Rosenshine, "Louis LaMed, Jewish Culture His Hobby," 19–20.

73. Menachem Ribalow, "Ha-sifrut ha-ivrit ba-amerika," in *Achisefer*, ed. Shmuel Niger and Menachem Ribalow (New York: Louis LaMed Foundation for the Advancement of Hebrew and Yiddish Literature, 1943), 94.

74. Shmuel Niger, "Ha-sifrut ha-yidit ba-amerika," in *Achisefer*, ed. Shmuel Niger and Menachem Ribalow (New York: Louis LaMed Foundation for the Advancement of Hebrew and Yiddish Literature, 1943), 215.

75. Pinchas Churgin, "Reshit ha-targumim," in *Achisefer*, ed. Shmuel Niger and Menachem Ribalow (New York: Louis LaMed Foundation for the Advancement of Hebrew and Yiddish Literature, 1943), 22.

76. Aharon Zeitlin, "Mendele ha-mekarev," in *Achisefer*, ed. Shmuel Niger and Menachem Ribalow (New York: Louis LaMed Foundation for the Advancement of Hebrew and Yiddish Literature, 1943), 80.

77. Niger, *Bilingualism in the History of Jewish Literature*, 112.

78. *Achisefer*'s short story section includes Sholem Ash's story "Yitgadal ve-yitkadash," a brutal narrative set in Nazi-occupied Prague. Sholem Ash, "Yitgadal ve-yitkadash," in *Achisefer*, ed. Shmuel Niger and Menachem Ribalow (New York: Louis LaMed Foundation for the Advancement of Hebrew and Yiddish Literature, 1943), 305–15.

79. A twenty-fourth poet, Itzik Manger, would settle in New York after the war. All but seven of the poets were still alive when the volume was published in 1943.

80. Niger and Ribalow, *Achisefer*, ii.

81. See Janet Hadda, *Yankev Glatshteyn* (Boston: Twayne, 1980).

82. See Yechiel Szeintuch and Carrie Friedman-Cohen, *Be-reshut ha-rabim u-ve-reshut ha-yechid: Aharon Zeitlin ve-sifrut Yiddish* (Jerusalem: Magnes Press, Hebrew University, 2000).

83. Aharon Zeitlin, "Dernenterung un noentkeyt tsvishn yidish un hebreish," in *Literarishe un filosofishe eseyen* (New York: Altveltlekhn yiddishn kultur-kongres, 1980), 203.

84. Norich, *Discovering Exile*, 42.

85. Yankev Glatshteyn, "A gute nakht velt," *Inzikh* 3, no. 8 (1938): 1.

86. Benjamin Harshav and Barbara Harshav, *American Yiddish Poetry* (Berkeley: University of California Press, 1986), 305.

87. Yankev Glatshteyn, "Leil menucha, tevel . . . ," in *Achisefer*, ed. Shmuel Niger and Menachem Ribalow, trans. Aharon Zeitlin (New York: Louis LaMed Foundation for the Advancement of Hebrew and Yiddish Literature, 1943), 557.

88. Harshav and Harshav, *American Yiddish Poetry*, 305.

89. Norich, *Discovering Exile*, 51. See also Norich's analysis of several English translations of this poem: Anita Norich, *Writing in Tongues: Translating Yiddish in the Twentieth Century* (Seattle: University of Washington Press, 2013), 66–96.

90. Harshav and Harshav, *American Yiddish Poetry*, 305.

91. Ibid., 307.

92. Glatshteyn, "Leil menucha, tevel . . . ," 557.

93. Glatshteyn, "A gute nakht velt," 1.

94. Harshav and Harshav, *American Yiddish Poetry*, 307.

95. Glatshteyn, "Leil menucha, tevel . . . ," 558.

96. Norich, *Discovering Exile*, 59.

97. Gideon Toury, *Descriptive Translation Studies and Beyond* (Amsterdam and Philadelphia: J. Benjamins, 1995), 131.

98. *Achisefer* received glowing reviews in "Achisefer," *Ha-do'ar* 23, no. 5 (1943): 70; Y. K. Miklishanski, "Brider-bukh," *Tsukunft* 49, no. 8 (1944): 514–19. But it was only mentioned in passing in the Hebrew press in Palestine in articles like Yosef Vilfland, "Letter from New York," *Al ha-mishmar*, December 9, 1943, 2.

99. Kadya Molodovsky, "Akhisefer," *Svive* 6 (1943): 68.

100. Ibid., 62.

101. Ibid., 63–64.

102. Even before the war, Glatshteyn saw the desire to be translated into Hebrew or any other "minor" language as a betrayal of Yiddish. See Wisse, "Language as Fate," 142.

103. I want to thank Avraham Novershtern for suggesting this poem.

104. Yankev Glatshteyn, "Leyendik dem 'Akhisefer,'" *Svive* 7 (1944): 25.

105. See Chava Weissler, "For Women and Men Who Are Like Women: The Construction of Gender in Yiddish Devotional Literature," *Journal of Feminist Studies and Religion* 5, no. 2 (1989): 9; Sh. Niger, "Yiddish Literature and the Female Reader," in *Studies in the History of Yiddish Literature*, ed. H. Leyvik (New York:

Sh. Niger bukh komitet, 1959), 35–108; Seidman, *A Marriage Made in Heaven*, 1–5, 15–22.

106. Glatshteyn, "Leyendik dem 'Akhisefer,'" 26.

107. Ibid.

108. Ibid., 28.

109. Venuti, *Translator's Invisibility*, 14.

110. Glatshteyn, "Leyendik dem 'Akhisefer,'" 29.

111. Ibid.

112. Yitzhak Ivri, "Sicha im Shmuel Niger," *Davar*, September 30, 1953, 4.

113. Mintz, *Sanctuary in the Wilderness*, 24.

114. Shmuel Niger, *Kiddush ha-shem* (New York: Louis LaMed Foundation, Cyco, 1946), 7. See David Roskies, "The Holocaust According to Its Anthologists," in *The Anthology in Jewish Literature*, ed. David Stern (New York: Oxford University Press, 2004), 338–39.

115. Shlonsky's translations included Arye Shamri, *36 shirim al Leyzer Tsipres*, trans. Avraham Shlonsky (Merhavya: Hotsa'at ha-kibbutz ha-artsi ha-shomer ha-tsa'ir, 1939); Itzik Manger, *Dmuyot krovot*, trans. Avraham Shlonsky (Mechavya: Hotsa'at ha-kibbutz ha-artsi ha-shomer ha-tsa'ir, 1941); H. Leyvik, *Balada al beit-cholim be-denver*, trans. Avraham Shlonsky (Merhavya: Ha-kibbutz ha-artsi ha-shomer ha-tsa'ir, 1942).

116. Yosef Shamir, ed., *Ha-shomer tsa'ir be-folin 1913–1950* (Tel Aviv: Sifriyat po'alim, 1991), 103–16; Natan Shacham and Natan Yonatan, eds., *Sifriyat po'alim 50 shana* (Tel Aviv: Hotsa'at ha-kibbutz ha-artsi ha-shomer ha-tsa'ir, 1989), 16.

117. Dov Ber Malkin, ed., *Bein sa'ar le-sa'ar* (Tel Aviv: Sifriyat po'alim, 1943), xv.

118. Ibid.

119. Ibid., xvi.

120. Bernstein argues against backshadowing, a "retroactive foreshadowing in which the shared knowledge of the outcome of a series of events . . . is used to judge participants in those events *as though they too should have known what was to come.*" In particular, Bernstein faults readings that blame victims for not having correctly interpreted the signals and escaped in time, retrospectively faulting their blindness. Michael André Bernstein, *Foregone Conclusions: Against Apocalyptic History* (Berkeley: University of California Press, 1994), 16, 30–31.

121. Shandler focuses on wartime and postwar translations from Yiddish into English, but his analysis resonates for Yiddish-to-Hebrew translations. Jeffrey Shandler, *Adventures in Yiddishland* (Berkeley: University of California Press, 2006), 104–5.

122. Sadan published many Hebrew translations of Yiddish literature, including poems by Kadya Molodovsky in *Achisefer* and Opatoshu's novel *Yom be-regenspurk*

(1943), published by Sifriyat Po'alim's *Doron* series, edited by Shlonsky. See Shmuel Werses, "Sugiyat yidish be-masekhet Dov Sadan," *Sadan* 1 (1994): 9–10.

123. Manger, *Dmuyot krovot*, 153. See Sadan's later reflection on this conclusion, where he explains that he never hesitated to voice his own opinions in his criticism: Dov Sadan, *Avne bedek* (Tel Aviv: Ha-kibbutz ha-me'uchad, 1962), 178–79. As Shmuel Werses notes, Sadan adopts Bialik's distinction between Yiddish as the "language of the time" and Hebrew as the "language of eternity," subsuming Yiddish within the eternal Hebrew tradition. Werses, "Sugiyat yidish be-masekhet Dov Sadan," 16.

124. See Melekh Ravitch, "Eyn literatur, tsvey leshoynes," in *Mayn leksikon*, vol. 3 (Montreal: Jewish Book Center, 1958), 449–53; Rachel Rojanski, "The Final Chapter in the Struggle for Cultural Autonomy," *Journal of Modern Jewish Studies* 6, no. 2 (2007): 185–204; Schachter, *Diasporic Modernisms*, 152–83; "Tsu di hebreishe shrayber: vos is ayer meynung vegn yidish in yisroyel?," *Heymish* 5, nos. 48–49 (1960): 3–6.

125. Arn Glantz-Leyeles, "Medinas Yisroel," *Di tsukunft* (1951): 62.

126. Dovid Pinski, "Undzer tsvey shprakhikayt—di leyzung," *Di tsukunft* (1949): 8.

Postscript

1. Avot Yeshurun, *Kol shirav* (Tel Aviv: Ha-kibbutz ha-me'uchad, 1995), 4:73. Thanks to Jordan Finkin for his help with the English translation.

2. Itzhak Korn, "Tsveysphrakhikeyt darf oykh haynt zayn aktuel," *Yiddish-velt* 2, no. 26 (March 1986): 2.

3. The poem's title "Safa telavivrit" is essentially untranslatable, a portmanteau that combines the city Tel Aviv with *ivrit*, Hebrew language, and invokes Tel Aviv Hebrew as the dominant idiom of Hebrew culture.

4. Yeshurun, *Kol shirav*, 4:72. See also Yochai Oppenheimer, "Ir tlat-erkit," *Chadarim* 8 (1989): 21–38.

5. Meir Wieseltier, "Dibur al Avot," in *Eikh nikra Avot Yeshurun*, ed. Lilach Lachman (Tel Aviv: Ha-kibbutz ha-me'uchad, 2011), 208.

6. In his late poetry, Yeshurun frequently omitted the letter "vav" and relied instead on vowels, keeping the reader off-balance with his nonstandard spelling. The stylized concision of Yeshurun's Hebrew prose contrasts with the Yiddish spelling of *Yiddish-velt*, with its full complement of vowels.

7. Czesław Miłosz, *The History of Polish Literature* (New York: Macmillan, 1969), 436; Mikulás Teich and Roy Porter, *The National Question in Europe in Historical Context* (Cambridge: Cambridge University Press, 1993), 293.

8. Psalm 116:7–9. I have adapted the JPS translation, *JPS Hebrew-English Tanakh* (Philadelphia: Jewish Publication Society, 1999), 1559. The Hebrew poet

Yehuda Halevi also titled a poem "Shuvi nafshi la-menuchaykhi," in which he plays with the same archaic suffixes.

9. Michael Gluzman, *The Politics of Canonicity: Lines of Resistance in Modernist Hebrew Poetry* (Stanford, CA: Stanford University Press, 2003), 142–43. Also see the many essays on Yeshurun's work in Lilach Lachman, *Eikh nikra Avot Yeshurun* (Tel Aviv: Ha-kibbutz ha-me'uchad, 2011).

10. Ilan Gur-Ze'ev, *Diasporic Philosophy and Counter-Education* (Rotterdam: Sense Publishers, 2010), 255.

11. Lilach Lachman, "'I Manured the Land with My Mother's Letters': Avot Yeshurun and the Question of Avant-Garde," *Poetics Today* 21, no. 1 (2000): 84.

12. For scholarly analysis of this phenomenon, see Maya Barzilai, "Translation on the Margins: Hebrew-German-Yiddish Multilingualism in Avraham Ben Yitzhak and Yoel Hoffman," *Journal of Jewish Identities* 7, no. 1 (2014): 109–28; Yael Chaver, "The End of 'Language Wanderings'? Yiddish in David Grossman's Ayen Erekh: Ahava and Aharon Megged's Foiglman," *Journal of Jewish Identities* 7, no. 1 (2014): 143–62; Shachar Pinsker, "The Language That Was Lost on the Roads: Discovering Hebrew through Yiddish in Aharon Appelfeld's Fiction," *Journal of Jewish Identities* 7, no. 1 (2014): 129–41; Dror Burstein, "Hebrew Publishing Company me'et Matan Hermoni—kokhav be-shmei manhattan," *Ha'aretz*, March 9, 2011.

13. Jordan D. Finkin, "What Does It Mean to Write a Modern Jewish Sonnet? Some Challenges of Yiddish and Hebrew," *Journal of Jewish Identities* 7, no. 1 (2014): 80.

14. Yildiz, *Beyond the Mother Tongue*, 6; Hokenson and Munson, *The Bilingual Text*, 136–43; Daniel Baggioni, *Langues et Nations en Europe* (Paris: Payot & Rivages, 1997).

15. Yildiz, *Beyond the Mother Tongue*, 4.

16. Ibid., 205–6.

Bibliography

"Achisefer." *Ha-do'ar* 23, no. 5 (1943): 70.

Aleykhem, Sholem. *Kitvei Shalom Aleikhem.* Trans. Yitzhak Dov Berkovitz. Vol. 3. Warsaw: Ha-shachar, 1911.

———. *Kitvei Shalom Aleikhem.* Trans. Yitzhak Dov Berkovitz. Tel Aviv: Dvir, 1939.

Alt, Arthur Tilo. "The Berlin Milgroym Group and Modernism." *Yiddish* 6, no. 1 (1985): 33–44.

Alter, Robert. *The Invention of Hebrew Prose.* Seattle: University of Washington Press, 1988.

Alter, Robert, trans. *The Wisdom Books.* New York: W. W. Norton, 2011.

Amichay-Michlin, Dania. *Ahavat Ish: Avraham Yosef Shtybel.* Jerusalem: Mosad Bialik, 2000.

Appel, René, and Pieter Muysken. *Language Contact and Bilingualism.* London: E. Arnold, 1987.

Ari, Nitsa Ben. "Tirgumit o ivrit shel tirgumim." In *Aderet le-vinyamin*, ed. Ziva Ben-Porat, 1:292–304. Tel Aviv: Ha-kibbutz ha-me'uchad, 1999.

"Asefah pumbit be-Tel Aviv al kavod ha-safa." *Davar*, May 15, 1927.

Ash, Sholem. *Erets yisroel.* New York: Forverts, 1918.

———. "Mayn ershte bakantshaft mit peretsn." *Di tsukunft*, no. 20 (1915).

———. "Mikhtav predah." *Ketuvim*, no. 37 (May 25, 1927): 1.

———. "Yitgadal ve-yitkadash." In *Achisefer*, ed. Shmuel Niger and Menachem Ribalow, 305–15. New York: Louis LaMed Foundation for the Advancement of Hebrew and Yiddish literature, 1943.

"Ash ve-Hirshbeyn be-mesibat ha-sofrim." *Ha'aretz*, May 4, 1927.

Ashkenazi, Yaakov ben Yitzchak. *Tsenerene.* Buenos Aires: Yosef Lifshits-fond fun der literatur-gezelshaft baym yivo, 1973.

Auerbach, Rachel. "Rokhl Feygenberg." *Di goldene keyt* 17 (1953).

Baggioni, Daniel. *Langues et Nations en Europe.* Paris: Payot & Rivages, 1997.

Barash, Asher. "Acharei ha-mesiba." *Ketuvim*, nos. 34–35 (1927): 1.

Barash [B. Feliks], Asher. "Rimon." *Hedim*, no. 4 (1923): 62–64.

Bartal, Israel. "From Traditional Bilingualism to National Monolingualism." In *Hebrew in Ashkenaz*, ed. Lewis Glinert, 141–50. Oxford: Oxford University Press, 1993.

———. *The Jews of Eastern Europe, 1772–1881.* Philadelphia: University of Pennsylvania Press, 2011.

Bartelik, Marek. *Early Polish Modern Art: Unity in Multiplicity.* Manchester, UK: Manchester University Press, 2005.

Barzel, Hillel. *Shirat ha-techiyah: Chayim Nachman Bialik.* Tel Aviv: Sifriyat po'alim, 1990.

———. *Shirat ha-techiyah: omanei ha-zhanr.* Tel Aviv: Sifriyat po'alim, 1997.

Barzilai, Maya. "Translation on the Margins: Hebrew-German-Yiddish Multilingualism in Avraham Ben Yitzhak and Yoel Hoffman." *Journal of Jewish Identities* 7, no. 1 (2014): 109–28.

Baumgarten, Jean, and Jerold C. Frakes. *Introduction to Old Yiddish Literature.* Oxford and New York: Oxford University Press, 2005.

Beaujour, Elizabeth Klosty. *Alien Tongues: Bilingual Russian Writers of the "First" Emigration.* Ithaca: Cornell University Press, 1989.

Bechtel, Delphine. "1922 *Milgroym*, a Yiddish Magazine of Arts and Letters, Is Founded in Berlin by Mark Wischnitzer." In *Yale Companion to Jewish Writing and Thought in German Culture, 1096–1996*, ed. Sander L. Gilman and Jack Zipes, 420–26. New Haven: Yale University Press, 1997.

———. "Babylon or Jerusalem: Berlin as Center of Jewish Modernism in the 1920s." In *Insiders and Outsiders: Jewish and Gentile Culture in German and Austria*, ed. Dagmar C. G. Lorenz and Gabriele Weinberger, 116–23. Detroit: Wayne State University Press, 1994.

"Be-erets yisra'el." *Ha-tsfira*, May 13, 1927.

Berdichevsky, Micha Yosef. "Bi-dvar lashon ve-sefer." In *Kitvei M. Y. Berdichevsky*, vol. 2. Tel Aviv: Dvir, 1960.

———. "Machanayim." In *Sipurim*, 9–53. Tel Aviv: Dvir, 1980.

Bergelson, Dovid. "Der gesheener afbrokh." *Milgroym* 1, no. 1 (1922): 41–43.

———. "Yoysef Shor." In *Geklibene verk fun Dovid Bergelson*, 3:61–126. Vilna: B. Kletskin, 1929.

Bergelson, Dovid, and Der Nister. "[Letter to the Editor]." *Shtrom*, no. 3 (1922): 83.

Berkovitz, Yitzhak Dov. "A briv tsu der 'Vokh.'" *Vokh* 13 (December 13, 1929): 19.

———. "Be-yad ha-lashon." *Ha-tsofe*, September 6, 1904.

———. "Der shofer." *Der tog*, May 1, 1929.

———. *Gezamelte shriftn*. Warsaw: Ha-shachar, 1910.

———. "Ha-nahag." *Moznayim* 1, no. 1 (1929): 5–9.

———. *Kitvei Y. D. Berkovitz*. Tel Aviv: Dvir, 1959.

———. *Menakhem-Mendl in Erets Yisroel*. Tel Aviv: Beyt Sholem Aleykhem, 1973.

———. "Moznayim." *Moznayim* 1, no. 1 (1929): 1.

———. "On loshn." *Der fraynd*, August 20, 1908.

———. *Sipurim*. Cracow: Yosef Fisher Press, 1910.

———. "Talush." In *Kitvei Y. D. Berkovitz*, 1:37–45. Tel Aviv: Dvir, 1959.

———. *Yiddishe dertseylungen 1906–1924*. Ed. Yona Altschuler. Jerusalem: Ha-universitah ha-ivrit, ha-chug le-Yiddish: Hotsa'at sefarim Magnes, 2003.

Berkowitz, Joel. "Hirshbeyn, Perets." *The YIVO Encyclopedia of Jews in Eastern Europe*. Accessed December 29, 2014. http://www.yivoencyclopedia.org/article.aspx/Hirshbeyn_Perets.

Berman, Jessica. *Modernist Commitments: Ethics, Politics, and Transnational Modernism*. New York: Columbia University Press, 2011.

Bernstein, Michael André. *Foregone Conclusions: Against Apocalyptic History*. Berkeley: University of California Press, 1994.

Bialik, Chayim Nachman. *Devarim she-be-al peh*. Tel Aviv: Dvir, 1935.

———. "Ha-kadosh Yisrael Vakser z"l." *Rimon*, no. 3 (1923): 33–34.

———. "Ha-kadosh Yisroel Vakser z"l." *Milgroym*, no. 3 (1923): 33–35.

———. *Kol kitvei Ch. N. Bialik*. Tel Aviv: Dvir, 1938.

Biemann, Asher D. "Aesthetic Education in Martin Buber: Jewish Renaissance and the Artist." In *New Perspectives on Martin Buber*, ed. Michael Zank, 85–110. Tübingen: Mohr Siebeck, 2006.

Bradbury, Malcolm, and James Walter McFarlane. *Modernism: 1890–1930*. New York: Penguin, 1976.

Brenner, Michael. *The Renaissance of Jewish Culture in Weimar Germany.* New Haven: Yale University Press, 1998.

Brenner, Yosef Chayim. *Shkhol ve-khishalon.* Tel Aviv: Am oved, 1972.

Buber, Martin. "Jüdische Renaissance." *Ost und West* 1, no. 1 (1901): 7–10.

Burstein, Dror. "Hebrew Publishing Company me'et Matan Hermoni—kokhav be-shmei manhattan." *Ha'aretz*, March 9, 2011.

Cahan, Abraham. *Palestine: a bazukh in yor 1925 un in 1926.* New York: Forverts, 1934.

Canagarajah, A. Suresh. *Translingual Practice: Global Englishes and Cosmopolitan Relations.* Milton Park, Abingdon, and New York: Routledge, 2013.

Casanova, Pascale. *The World Republic of Letters.* Cambridge, MA: Harvard University Press, 2004.

Chaver, Yael. "The End of 'Language Wanderings?' Yiddish in David Grossman's *Ayen Erekh: Ahava* and Aharon Megged's *Foiglman.*" *Journal of Jewish Identities* 7, no. 1 (2014): 143–62.

———. *What Must be Forgotten: The Survival of Yiddish in Zionist Palestine.* Syracuse: Syracuse University Press, 2004.

Chekhov, Anton. *The Cherry Orchard.* New York: Scribner's, 1917.

Churgin, Pinchas. "Reshit ha-targumim." In *Achisefer*, ed. Shmuel Niger and Menachem Ribalow, 13–23. New York: Louis LaMed Foundation for the Advancement of Hebrew and Yiddish Literature, 1943.

Cohen, Natan. "Der Moment." *Historical Jewish Press.* Accessed December 29, 2014. http://web.nli.org.il/sites/JPress/English/Pages/DahrMamanet.aspx.

———. *Sefer, sofer ve-iton: merkaz ha-tarbut ha-yehudit be-varsha, 1918–1942.* Jerusalem: Hotsa'at sefarim al shem Magnes, ha-universitah ha-ivrit, 2003.

Cracraft, James. *The Revolution of Peter the Great.* Cambridge, MA: Harvard University Press, 2003.

Dauber, Jeremy. *Antonio's Devils.* Stanford, CA: Stanford University Press, 2004.

David-Fox, Michael. *Showcasing the Great Experiment: Cultural Diplomacy and Western Visitors to the Soviet Union, 1921–1941.* New York: Oxford University Press, 2011.

"Der tuml arum dem kabalas-ponim fun Sholem Ash un Perets Hirshbeyn." *Literarishe bleter*, June 3, 1927.

Dinaburg, Ben Zion. "Ha-ivrit be-rusya." *Ketuvim*, no. 33 (1927): 2.

Dluznovsky, Moshe. "Shalom Ash ve-Zalman Shneour: pegisha be-ruach nizemet u-ve-ruach tova." *Moznayim* 42, no. 4 (1976): 273–77.

"Dr. Mark Wischnitzer, Jewish Historian, Dies." *Jewish Telegraphic Agency Archive*, October 15, 1955. http://www.jta.org/1955/10/18/archive/dr-mark-wischnitzer-jewish-historian-dies-was-73.

Einhorn, A. "Der yontif fun yidishn geyst. Khayim Nakhmen Byalik's 50 yoriker yubileum." *Haynt*, January 14, 1923.

E. L. [El Lissitzky]. "Beit kneset be-mohilev." *Rimon*, no. 3 (1923): 9–12.

———. "Vegn der mohilever shul." *Milgroym*, no. 3 (1923): 9–13.

Epstein, Marc Michael. *Dreams of Subversion in Medieval Jewish Art and Literature.* University Park: Pennsylvania State University Press, 1997.

Estraikh, G., Kerstin Hoge, and Mikhail Krutikov. *Uncovering the Hidden: The Works and Life of Der Nister.* London: Legenda, 2014.

Estraikh, Gennady, and Mikhail Krutikov, eds. *Yiddish in Weimar Berlin.* Oxford: Legenda, 2010.

Even-Zohar, Itamar. *Polysystem Studies.* Durham, NC: Duke University Press, 1990.

Feingold, Henry L. *Bearing Witness: How America and Its Jews Responded to the Holocaust.* Syracuse: Syracuse University Press, 1995.

Feldman, Yael S. *Modernism and Cultural Transfer: Gabriel Preil and the Tradition of Jewish Literary Bilingualism.* Cincinnati: Hebrew Union College Press, 1986.

Feygenberg, Rachel. "A brif [Letter to Rachel Auerbach]," undated. 602/כ36112-א. Gnazim Institute.

———. *Bi-mevukhat ha-yamim.* Tel Aviv: Zman, 1938.

———. *Di velt vil, mir zoln zayn yidn.* Warsaw: Farn folk, 1936.

———. "Letter to Chaver M. Shalgi," undated. 602/46259-א. Gnazim Institute.

———. "Letter to Histadrut Secretary A. Becker." June 25, 1961. 602/46446-א. Gnazim Institute.

———. "Maskilim." *Davar*, November 4, 1925.

———. "Mikhtav la-ma'arekhet." *Davar*, July 22, 1957.

Feygenberg-Imri, Rachel. *Mi-ven gidre ha-til: tsror mikhtavim al pig'ei ha-zman.* Jerusalem: La-am, 1947.

———. *Yiddish ve-sofreha.* Tel Aviv: Zeman, 1967.

Fichman, Ya'akov. "Kalpei ha-mafginim." *Ketuvim*, no. 36 (1927): 1.

Finkin, Jordan D. *A Rhetorical Conversation: Jewish Discourse in Modern Yiddish Literature*. University Park: Pennsylvania State University Press, 2010.

———. "Constellating Hebrew and Yiddish Avant-Gardes." *Journal of Modern Jewish Studies* 8, no. 1 (2009): 1–22.

———. "What Does It Mean to Write a Modern Jewish Sonnet? Some Challenges of Yiddish and Hebrew." *Journal of Jewish Identities* 7, no. 1 (2014): 79–107.

Fishman, Joshua A. "Attracting a Following to High-Culture Functions for a Language of Everyday Life: The Role of the Tshernovits Language Conference in the 'Rise of Yiddish.'" In *Never Say Die!: A Thousand Years of Yiddish in Jewish Life and Letters*, 369–94. The Hague: Mouton, 1981.

Fitch, Brian T. *Beckett and Babel*. Vol. 57. Toronto: University of Toronto Press, 1988.

Forster, Leonard. *The Poet's Tongues: Multilingualism in Literature*. London: Cambridge University Press, 1970.

Frakes, Jerold C. *Early Yiddish Texts, 1100–1750*. Oxford: Oxford University Press, 2004.

Frieden, Ken. "Innovation by Translation: Yiddish and Hasidic Hebrew in Literary History." In *Arguing the Modern Jewish Canon*, ed. Justin Cammy and Ruth Wisse, 417–25. Cambridge, MA: Harvard University Press, 2008.

Friedman, D. A. "Vilna; Ba-meitsar." *Ein ha-kore* 1–3 (1923).

Fuks, Leo, and Renate Fuks. "Yiddish Publishing Activities in the Weimar Republic, 1920–1933." *The Leo Baeck Institute Yearbook* 33, no. 1 (1988): 417–34.

Gay, Peter. *Weimar Culture*. New York: Harper & Row, 1968.

Gefen, Moshe. *Mi-tachat la-arisa omedet gdiya*. Tel Aviv: Hotsa'at ha-kibbutz ha-artsi ha-shomer ha-tsa'ir, 1986.

Gilboa, Menuha. "Rimon = Milgroym." *Kesher* 10 (1993): 102–5.

Glantz-Leyeles, Arn. "Medinas Yisroel." *Di tsukunft* (1951): 60–62.

Glatshteyn, Yankev. "A gute nakht velt." *Inzikh* 3, no. 8 (1938): 1.

———. "Leil menucha, tevel . . ." In *Achisefer*, ed. Shmuel Niger and Menachem Ribalow, trans. Aharon Zeitlin, 557–58. New York: Louis LaMed Foundation for the Advancement of Hebrew and Yiddish Literature, 1943.

———. "Leyendik dem 'Akhisefer.'" *Svive* 7 (1944): 25–29.

Glikson, Moshe. "Al 'ha-inyan.'" *Ha'aretz*, May 17, 1927.

Gluzman, Michael. *The Politics of Canonicity: Lines of Resistance in Modernist Hebrew Poetry*. Stanford, CA: Stanford University Press, 2003.

Goldberg, Leah. "Al arba'a shirim shel A. Shlonsky." *Moznayim* 38 (1974): 275–87.

Goldsmith, Emanuel S. *Architects of Yiddishism at the Beginning of the Twentieth Century: A Study in Jewish Cultural History*. Rutherford, NJ: Fairleigh Dickinson University Press, 1976.

Govrin, Nurith. *Alienation and Regeneration*. Tel Aviv: MOD Books, 1989.

Greenberg, Uri Zvi. "Al derakhim ba-ma'arav." *Rimon*, no. 6 (1924): 19–21.

———. "Be-mots'ei ha-shtikah." *Davar*, September 3, 1926.

———. *Eima gedola ve-yareach*. Jerusalem: Beit ha-sefarim ha-le'umi veha-universita'i bi-rushalayim, 1983.

Greenblatt, Stephen. "Racial Memory and Literary History." *PMLA* 116 (2001): 48–63.

Grinblat, Natan. "Ha-me'asef ve-sifro ha-rishon." *Davar*, December 28, 1945.

———. "Psukim." *Davar*, August 24, 1938.

Grossman, Avraham. *Chakhamei ashkenaz ha-rishonim*. Jerusalem: Magnes Press, Hebrew University, 2001.

Grutman, Rainier. "Beckett and Beyond: Putting Self-Translation in Perspective." *OLI Orbis Litterarum* 68, no. 3 (2013): 188–206.

———. "Refraction and Recognition: Literary Multilingualism in Translation." *Target* 18, no. 1 (2006): 17–48.

Gur-Ze'ev, Ilan. *Diasporic Philosophy and Counter-Education*. Rotterdam: Sense, 2010.

Hadda, Janet. *Yankev Glatshteyn*. Boston: Twayne, 1980.

Hagorni-Green, Avraham. "Gishot yesod u-foetika mutsheret." In *Sefer Shlonsky*, ed. Yisrael Levine. Merhavya: Sifriyat po'alim, 1981.

———. *Shlonsky be-avotot Bialik*. Tel Aviv: Or am, 1987.

Halperin, Hagit. *Ha-ma'estro: chayav vi-yetsirato shel Avraham Shlonsky*. Tel Aviv: Sifriyat po'alim, 2011.

———. "Torat ha-alilah shel E. Shtaynman u-mimushah be-sipurav." *Moznayim* 43, no. 1 (1976): 22–34.

Halperin, Hagit, Galiyah Sagiv, and Abraham Shlonsky. *Me-agvaniya ad simfonya*. Tel Aviv: Universitat Tel-Aviv: Sifriyat po'alim, 1997.

"Ha-me'asef." *Ha-boker*, December 10, 1943.

Ha-me'iri, Avigdor. "Be-urvat ha-pegasusim." *Ha-machar* 2 (1927): 15–16.

Hamers, Josiane F., and Michel Blanc. *Bilinguality and Bilingualism*. Cambridge: Cambridge University Press, 1989.

Hanegbi, David. "Letter to Rachel Feygenberg," February 27, 1927. 60245457-א. Gnazim Institute.

Harshav, Benjamin. *Language in Time of Revolution*. Berkeley: University of California Press, 1993.

———. *The Meaning of Yiddish*. Berkeley: University of California Press, 1990.

———. *The Polyphony of Jewish Culture*. Stanford, CA: Stanford University Press, 2007.

Harshav, Benjamin, and Barbara Harshav. *American Yiddish Poetry*. Berkeley: University of California Press, 1986.

Harshav, Benjamin, Chone Shmeruk, Abraham Sutzkever, and Mendel Piekarz. *A shpigl af a shteyn*. Tel Aviv: Farlag di goldene keyt, 1964.

"Hed ha- 'shalom.'" *Ketuvim*, no. 64 (1927): 4.

Hever, Hannan. *Paytanim u-viryonim: tsmichat ha-shir ha-politi ha-ivri be-erets-yisra'el*. Jerusalem: Mosad Bialik, 1994.

Hever, Hannan, Mordekhai Nadav, and Uri Zvi Greenberg. *Uri Tsvi Grinberg bi-melot lo shemonim*. Jerusalem: Beit ha-sefarim, 1977.

Hirschfeld, Ariel. *Kinor arukh: lashon ha-regesh be-shirat Ch. N. Bialik*. Tel Aviv: Am oved, 2011.

Hirshbeyn, Perets. "Nisht far keyn zilber-shtiker vet ir oysgeleyzt veren." *Der moment*, September 2, 1927.

———. "Undzer tseshpoltene tsung." *Literarishe bleter* 51, no. 4 (December 23, 1927): 1002–4.

Hoffman, Matthew. *From Rebel to Rabbi: Reclaiming Jesus and the Making of Modern Jewish Culture*. Stanford, CA: Stanford University Press, 2007.

Hofshteyn, Dovid. "Dos lid fun mayn glaykhgilt." *Milgroym*, no. 1 (1922): 44–45.

Hokenson, Jan, and Marcella Munson. *The Bilingual Text: History and Theory of Literary Self-Translation*. Manchester, UK: St. Jerome, 2007.

Holtzman, Avner. "Aronsohn, Zalman Yitshak." *The YIVO Encyclopedia of Jews in Eastern Europe*. Accessed December 31, 2014. http://www.yivoencyclopedia.org/article.aspx/Aronsohn_Zalman_Yitshak.

———. "Bershadsky, Yesh'ayahu." *The YIVO Encyclopedia of Jews in Eastern Europe.* Accessed December 31, 2014. http://www.yivoencyclopedia.org/article.aspx/Bershadsky_Yeshayahu.

———. "Ha-lashon ke-khli, ke-etgar ve-ke-nose." *Am va-sefer* 1 (1991): 97–102.

Hovev, Leah. "Motivim le'umiyim ve-historiyim be-shnei shirei eres." In *Be-mish'olei ever yehudi*, ed. Zion Ukshi, Sigalit Rozmarin, and Yisrael Rosenson, 533–41. Jerusalem: Hotsa'at mikhlelet efrata, 2006.

Hubka, Thomas C. *Resplendent Synagogue: Architecture and Worship in an Eighteenth-Century Polish Community.* Hanover, NH: Brandeis University Press, 2003.

Ivri, Yitzhak. "Sicha im Shmuel Niger." *Davar*, September 30, 1953.

Jacobs, Neil G. *Yiddish: A Linguistic Introduction.* Cambridge: Cambridge University Press, 2005.

Jelen, Sheila E. *Intimations of Difference: Dvora Baron in the Modern Hebrew Renaissance.* Syracuse: Syracuse University Press, 2007.

Jones, Faith. "Esther Shumiatcher-Hirschbein." In *Jewish Women's Archive Encyclopedia.* Accessed December 29, 2014. http://jwa.org/encyclopedia/article/shumiatcher-hirschbein-esther.

JPS Hebrew-English Tanakh. Philadelphia: Jewish Publication Society, 1999.

"Kabbalat panim le-Ash u-le-Hirshbeyn." *Davar*, May 4, 1927.

Karnieli, Y. "Sicha im Y. D. Berkovitz." *Ketuvim*, nos. 28–29 (1928): 2.

Katz, Dovid. "Hebrew, Aramaic and the Rise of Yiddish." In *Readings in the Sociology of Jewish Languages*, ed. Joshua A. Fishman, 85–103. Leiden: Brill, 1985.

Kellman, Ellen. "The Newspaper Novel in the Jewish Daily Forward (1900–1940)." PhD dissertation, Columbia University, 2000.

Kellman, Steven G. *The Translingual Imagination.* Lincoln: University of Nebraska Press, 2000.

Kellner, Douglas. "Expressionism and Rebellion." In *Passion and Rebellion: The Expressionist Heritage*, 3–39. New York: Columbia University Press, 1988.

Keshet, Yeshurun. *Havdalot.* Tel Aviv: Agudat ha-sofrim ha-ivrim, 1962.

Kim, Ronald. "Uriel Weinreich and the Birth of Modern Contact Linguistics." *Languages in Contact 4* (2011): 99–110.

King, Robert D. "The Czernowitz Conference in Retrospect." In *Politics of Yiddish: Studies in Language, Literature, and Society*, ed. Dov-Ber Kerler, 41–49. Walnut Creek, CA: Altamira, 1998.

Klausner, Yosef. "Bi-sha'at cherum." *Ketuvim*, no. 37 (May 25, 1927): 1.

———. *Historiya shel ha-sifrut ha-ivrit ha-chadasha*. Jerusalem: Hotsa'at-sefarim ahi'asaf, 1955.

———. *Z. Shneour: ha-meshorer ve-ha-mesaper*. Tel Aviv: Yavneh, 1947.

Kleinman, Moshe. "Be-tokh ha-se'ara." *Ha-shiloach* 52 (1924): 367–73; 466–71; 516–28.

———. "Kunst un literatur kronik." *Milgroym*, no. 5 (1923): 40.

———. "Leshonoteinu." *Ha-shiloach* (1909): 385.

———. *Undzer natsional-shprakh*. Odessa: Tsiyonistishe kopike-bibliyotek, 1909.

Klinger, Susanne. "Translated Otherness, Self-Translated In-betweenness." In *Self-Translation: Brokering Originality in Hybrid Culture*, ed. Anthony Cordingley, 113–26. London: Bloomsbury Academic, 2013.

Kopelevitz, Ya'akov. "Ha-Rimon." *Ha-shiloach* 41 (1924): 357–66.

Korn, Itzhak. "Tsveysphrakhikeyt darf oykh haynt zayn aktuel." *Yiddish-velt* 2, no. 26 (March 1986): 1–2.

Kressel, G. "Shtei te'udot." *Moznayim* 25 (1967): 20–24.

Kronfeld, Chana. *On the Margins of Modernism: Decentering Literary Dynamics*. Berkeley: University of California Press, 1996.

———. "The Joint Literary History of Hebrew and Yiddish." In *Where and What Are Jewish Languages*, ed, Joshua Miller and Anita Norich. Ann Arbor: Frankel Institute, University of Michigan (forthcoming).

Kulbak, Moyshe. *Chevlei ge'ulah*. Jerusalem: Ha-me'asef, 1947.

———. "In a vald a yadlavn." *Milgroym*, no. 1 (1922): 20.

Lachman, Lilach. *Eikh nikra Avot Yeshurun*. Tel Aviv: Ha-kibbutz ha-me'uchad, 2011.

———. "'I Manured the Land with My Mother's Letters": Avot Yeshurun and the Question of Avant-Garde." *Poetics Today* 21, no. 1 (2000): 61–93.

Lamdan, Yitzhak. "Kalpei gilui ha-tishtush be-tocheinu." *Ketuvim*, nos. 34–35 (1927): 1.

Laor, Dan. "Shirei 'Gilboa' ve-ha-etos shel ha-aliya ha-shlishit." *Moznayim* 42 (1979): 134–40.

Latham, Sean, and Robert Scholes. "The Rise of Periodical Studies." *PMLA* 121, no. 2 (2006): 517–31.

Lee, Stephen J. *The Weimar Republic.* London and New York: Routledge, 1998.

Lefevere, André. *Translation, Rewriting, and the Manipulation of Literary Fame.* London and New York: Routledge, 1992.

Leyvik, H. *Balada al beit-cholim be-denver.* Trans. Avraham Shlonsky. Merhavya: Ha-kibbutz ha-artsi ha-shomer ha-tsa'ir, 1942.

Lindenbaum, Shalom. *Shirat Uri Tsvi Grinberg: ha-ivrit ve-ha-yidit.* Tel Aviv: Hadar, 1984.

Lipsker, Avidov. "The Albatrosses of Young Yiddish Poetry: An Idea and Its Visual Realization in Uri Zvi Greenberg's Albatros." *Prooftexts* 15, no. 1 (1995): 89–108.

Lipstadt, Deborah E. *Beyond Belief: The American Press and the Coming of the Holocaust, 1933–1945.* New York: Free Press, 1986.

Litvakov, Moyshe. "Yerushe un hegemonye." In *In umru.* Vol. 2. Moscow: Farlag shul un bukh, 1926.

Liu, Lydia He. *Translingual Practice: Literature, National Culture, and Translated Modernity—China, 1900–1937.* Stanford, CA: Stanford University Press, 1995.

Machzor Worms. Israel National and University Library, n.d. http://www.jnul.huji.ac.il/dl/mss/worms/.

Makhshoves, Bal. "Tsvey shprakhn—eyneyntsike literature." In *Never Say Die!: A Thousand Years of Yiddish in Jewish Life and Letters*, ed. Joshua A. Fishman, 112–23. The Hague: Mouton, 1981.

Malkin, Dov Ber, ed. *Bein sa'ar le-sa'ar.* Tel Aviv: Sifriyat po'alim, 1943.

Manger, Itzik. *Dmuyot krovot.* Trans. Avraham Shlonsky. Mechavya: Hotsa'at ha-kibbutz ha-artsi ha-shomer ha-tsa'ir, 1941.

Markish, Peretz. "Biznes." *Khalyastre* 1, no. 1 (1922): 62–64.

Marten-Finnis, Susanne. "'A Beautiful Lie'—Zhar-Ptitsa (The Firebird)—Sustaining Journalistic Activity and Showcasing Russia in 1920s Berlin." In *The Russian Jewish Diaspora and European Culture, 1917–1937*, ed. Jörg Schulte, Olga Tabachnikova, and Peter Wagstaff, 301–26. Leiden: Brill, 2012.

Marten-Finnis, Susanne, and Igor Dukhan. "Dream and Experiment." *East European Jewish Affairs* 35, no. 2 (2005): 225–44.

Mavshan, Menakhem. "Letter to Rachel Feygenberg," July 2, 1944. 602. Gnazim Institute.

Melfi, Francesco. "A Rhetoric of Image and Word: The Magazine Milgroym/Rimon, 1922–1924 and the Jewish Search for Inclusivity." PhD dissertation, Jewish Theological Seminary, 1996.

Mendes-Flohr, Paul R. *German Jews.* New Haven: Yale University Press, 1999.

Meylaerts, Reine. "Heterolingualism in/and Translation." *Target* 18, no. 1 (2006): 1–16.

Miklishanski, Y. K. "Brider-bukh." *Tsukunft* 49, no. 8 (1944): 514–19.

Miłosz, Czesław. *The History of Polish Literature.* New York: Macmillan, 1969.

Mintz, Alan. *Sanctuary in the Wilderness: A Critical Introduction to American Hebrew Poetry.* Stanford, CA: Stanford University Press, 2011.

———. "The Many Rather Than the One: On the Critical Study of Jewish Periodicals." *Prooftexts* 15, no. 1 (1995): 1–4.

Miron, Dan. *Akdamut le-atsag.* Jerusalem: Mosad Bialik, 2002.

———. *Bodedim be-mo'adam.* Tel Aviv: Am oved, 1987.

———. *From Continuity to Contiguity.* Stanford, CA: Stanford University Press, 2010.

———. *Harpayah le-tsorekh negi'ah.* Tel Aviv: Am oved, 2005.

———. "Shneour, Zalman." *YIVO Encyclopedia of Jews in Eastern Europe*, n.d. http://www.yivoencyclopedia.org/article.aspx/Shneour_Zalman.

Molodovsky, Kadya. "Akhisefer." *Svive* 6 (1943): 62–68.

Moseley, Marcus. *Being for Myself Alone: Origins of Jewish Autobiography.* Stanford, CA: Stanford University Press, 2006.

Moss, Kenneth B. *Jewish Renaissance in the Russian Revolution.* Cambridge, MA: Harvard University Press, 2009.

———. "Not the Dybbuk but Don Quixote: Translation, Deparochialization, and Nationalism in Jewish Culture, 1917–1919." In *Culture Front: Representing Jews in Eastern Europe*, ed. Benjamin Nathans and Gabriella Safran, 196–240. Philadelphia: University of Pennsylvania Press, 2007.

Myers, David N. "'Distant Relatives Happening onto the Same Inn': The Meeting of East and West as Literary Theme and Cultural Ideal." *Jewish Social Studies* 1, no. 2 (1995): 75–100.

Narkiss, Bezalel. "Rachel Wischnitzer, Doyenne of Historians of Jewish Art." In *From Dura to Rembrandt*, ed. Rachel Wischnitzer, 9–25. Milwaukee: Aldrich, 1990.

"Ne'umei Bialik, Ash ve-Hirshbeyn." *Davar*, May 5, 1927.

Niger, Shmuel. *Bilingualism in the History of Jewish Literature*. Lanham, MD: University Press of America, 1990.

———. *Di tsveyshprakhikeyt fun undzer literatur*. Detroit: Louis LaMed Foundation for the Advancement of Hebrew and Yiddish Literature, 1941.

———. "Geleynt un geshribn." *Der tog*, February 2, 1936.

———. "Ha-sifrut ha-yidit ba-amerika." In *Achisefer*, ed. Shmuel Niger and Menachem Ribalow, 183–215. New York: Louis LaMed Foundation for the Advancement of Hebrew and Yiddish Literature, 1943.

———. *Kiddush ha-shem*. New York: Louis LaMed Foundation, Cyco, 1946.

———. "Sifrut ivrit ve-yidish be-arhab." *Mishmar*, January 24, 1946.

———. "Yiddish Literature and the Female Reader." In *Studies in the History of Yiddish Literature*, ed. H. Leyvik, 35–108. New York: Sh. Niger bukh komitet, 1959.

———. *Yiddishe shrayber in Sovyet-Rusland*. New York: Sh. Niger bukh-komitet baym alveltlekhn yidishn kultur-kongres, 1958.

Niger, Shmuel, and Menachem Ribalow, eds. *Achisefer*. New York: Louis LaMed Foundation for the Advancement of Hebrew and Yiddish Literature, 1943.

Nister, Der. *Dertseylungen un eseyen*. New York: Ikuf, 1957.

Nomberg, H. D. "Fliglman." In *Shriften*, 1:67–88. Warsaw: Farlag bikher far ale, 1908.

———. *Gezamlte verk*. Warsaw: Farlag kultur-lige, 1930.

Norich, Anita. *Discovering Exile*. Stanford, CA: Stanford University Press, 2007.

———. "Israel Joshua Singer." *YIVO Encyclopedia of Jews in Eastern Europe*. Accessed February 6, 2015. http://www.yivoencyclopedia.org/article.aspx/Singer_Israel_Joshua.

———. *Writing in Tongues: Translating Yiddish in the Twentieth Century*. Seattle: University of Washington Press, 2013.

Novershtern, Avraham. "Menakhem Mendl le-Shalom Aleichem: Ben toldot ha-tekst le-mivneh ha-yetsirah." *Tarbits* 54, no. 1 (1984): 105–46.

———. "Shir hallel shir kina." In *Me-vilna le-yerushalayim*, ed. David Asaf, 485–511. Jerusalem: Hotsa'at sefarim al shem Magnes, 2002.

Ofengenden, Ari. *Ha-he'eder be-shirato u-va-haguto shel Avraham Shlonsky.* Jerusalem: Hotsa'at sefarim Magnes, ha-universita ha-ivrit, 2010.

Ofrat, Gideon. *Al ha-arets: ha-omanut ha-eretsyisra'elit.* Tel Aviv: Y. Golan, 1993.

Ong, Aihwa. *Flexible Citizenship: The Cultural Logics of Transnationality.* Durham, NC: Duke University Press, 1999.

Oppenheimer, Yochai. "Ir tlat-erkit." *Chadarim* 8 (1989): 21–38.

Ornan, Uzzi. *Be-reshit haya ha-safa.* Jerusalem: Ha-akademiyah le-lashon ha-ivrit, 2013.

Parush, Iris. *Reading Jewish Women: Marginality and Modernization in Nineteenth-Century Eastern European Jewish Society.* Waltham, MA: Brandeis University Press, 2004.

Perry, Menakhem. "Thematic and Structural Shifts in Autotranslations by Bilingual Hebrew-Yiddish Writers: The Case of Mendele Mokher Sforim." *Poetics Today* 2, no. 4 (1981): 181–92.

Pietrushka, S. "Vos men hert un men zet in erets yisroel." *Haynt*, May 20, 1927.

Pilowsky, Arye Leyb. *Tsvishn yo un neyn: Yidish un Yidish-literatur in Erets-Yisroel, 1907–1948.* Tel Aviv: Veltrat far Yidish un Yidisher kultur, 1986.

———. "Yidish ve-sifrutah be-Erets Yisra'el, 1907–1948." PhD dissertation, Hebrew University, Jerusalem, 1980.

Pinsker, Shachar. "Deciphering the Hieroglyphics of the Metropolis: Literary Topographies of Berlin in Hebrew and Yiddish Modernism." In *Yiddish in Weimar Berlin*, ed. Gennady Estraikh and Mikhail Krutikov, 28–53. Oxford: Legenda, 2010.

———. *Literary Passports: The Making of Modernist Hebrew Fiction in Europe.* Stanford, CA: Stanford University Press, 2011.

———. "Spaces of Hebrew and Yiddish Modernism—The Urban Cafes of Berlin." In *Transit und Transformation*, ed. Verena Dohrn and Gertrud Pickhan, 56–75. Göttingen: Wallstein, 2010.

———. "The Language That Was Lost on the Roads: Discovering Hebrew through Yiddish in Aharon Appelfeld's Fiction." *Journal of Jewish Identities* 7, no. 1 (2014): 129–41.

Pinski, Dovid. "Undzer tsvey shprakhikayt—di leyzung." *Di tsukunft* (1949): 6–8.

Porat, Dina. *Israeli Society, the Holocaust and Its Survivors.* London: Vallentine Mitchell, 2008.

Prawer, Siegbert Salomon. *A. N. Stencl: Poet of Whitechapel.* Oxford: Oxford Centre for Postgraduate Hebrew Studies, 1984.

"[Preface]." *Rimon* 1 (1922).

Rabinowitz, Ya'akov. "Devarim gluyim." *Ketuvim*, nos. 34–35 (1927): 2.

Ran, Leyzer. *Vilna, Jerusalem of Lithuania.* Oxford: Oxford Centre for Postgraduate Hebrew Studies, 1987.

Ravitch, Melekh. "Di dezertern fun dem yiddishn emes." *Di vog* 1, no. 2 (1922): 35–43.

———. *Di vog* 1, no. 2 (1922).

———. "Eyn literatur, tsvey leshoynes." In *Mayn leksikon*, 3:449–53. Montreal: Jewish Book Center, 1958.

———. *Mayn leksikon.* Vol. 1. Montreal: Komitet in Montreal, 1945.

Ravnitsky, Y. Ch. "Al 'milchemet mitzvah.'" *Ha'aretz*, May 18, 1927.

"Renowned Poet Shimshon Meltzer to be Commemorated on Tuesday." *Jerusalem Post*, May 18, 2009. http://www.jpost.com/Israel/Renowned-poet-Shimshon-Meltzer-to-be-commemorated-on-Tuesday.

"Report to His Britannic Majesty's Government to the Council of the League of Nations on the Administration of Palestine and Trans-Jordan." *UNISPAL Documents Collection*, 1927. http://unispal.un.org/UNISPAL.NSF/0/D0523C86855FAA6E052565E700693905.

Ribalow, Menachem. "Ha-sifrut ha-ivrit ba-amerika." In *Achisefer*, ed. Shmuel Niger and Menachem Ribalow, 93–182. New York: Louis LaMed Foundation for the Advancement of Hebrew and Yiddish literature, 1943.

Rimon, Helena. "Transformation of Solitudes: Chekhovian Plots in the Prose of Y. D. Berkowitz." In *Around the Point*, ed. Hillel Weiss, Roman Katsman, and Ber Kotlerman, 70–98. New Castle: Cambridge Scholars, 2014.

Rojanski, Rachel. "The Final Chapter in the Struggle for Cultural Autonomy." *Journal of Modern Jewish Studies* 6, no. 2 (2007): 185–204.

Rosenshine, Jay. "Louis LaMed, Jewish Culture His Hobby." *Michigan Jewish History* 3, no. 3 (1963): 18–24.

Rosenzweig, Franz. *Zweistromland.* Berlin: Philo Verlag, 1926.

Roskies, David. "The Holocaust According to Its Anthologists." In *The Anthology in Jewish Literature*, ed. David Stern, 95–113. New York: Oxford University Press, 2004.

Sadan, Dov. *Avnei bedek*. Tel Aviv: Ha-kibbutz ha-me'uchad, 1962.

———. "Ha-merchak ha-nora." In *Y. D. Berkovitz, mivchar ma'amarim al yetsirato*, ed. Avraham Holtz. Tel Aviv: Am oved, 1966.

Schachter, Allison. *Diasporic Modernisms: Hebrew and Yiddish Literature in the Twentieth Century*. New York: Oxford University Press, 2011.

Schocken, Shlomo Z. "Letter to Rachel Feygenberg," October 21, 1936. 602/45559-א. Gnazim Institute.

Schweid, Eliezer. "The Rejection of the Diaspora in Zionist Thought: Two Approaches." *Studies in Zionism* 5, no. 1 (1984): 43–70.

Segev, Tom. *The Seventh Million*. New York: Hill and Wang, 1993.

Seidman, Naomi. *A Marriage Made in Heaven: The Sexual Politics of Hebrew and Yiddish*. Berkeley: University of California Press, 1997.

Shaanan, Avraham. *Ha-sifrut ha-ivrit ha-chadasha le-zerameha*. Vol. 4. Tel Aviv: Masada, 1967.

Shacham, Natan, and Natan Yonatan, eds. *Sifriyat po'alim 50 shana*. Tel Aviv: Hotsa'at ha-kibbutz ha-artsi ha-shomer ha-tsa'ir, 1989.

Shaked, Gershon. *Ha-siporet ha-ivrit, 1880–1980*. Jerusalem: Keter, 1977.

———. *Modern Hebrew Fiction*. Bloomington: Indiana University Press, 2000.

———. "'Ve-halevai nitnah ha-yekholet le-hamshikh.'" *Tarbits* 51, no. 3 (1982): 479–90.

Shamri, Arye. *36 shirim al Leyzer Tsipres*. Trans. Avraham Shlonsky. Merhavya: Hotsa'at ha-kibbutz ha-artsi ha-shomer ha-tsa'ir, 1939.

Shamir, Yosef, ed. *Ha-shomer tsa'ir be-folin 1913–1950*. Tel Aviv: Sifriyat po'alim, 1991.

Shandler, Jeffrey. *Adventures in Yiddishland*. Berkeley: University of California Press, 2006.

Shavit, Ya'akov. "Ma'amadah shel ha-tarbut be-tahalikh yetsiratah shel chevrah le'umit be-erets yisra'el—emdot yesod u-musagei yesod." In *Toldot ha-yishuv ha-yehudi be-erets yisra'el me-az ha-aliyah ha-rishonah*, ed. Moshe Lisak, 3:9–29. Jerusalem: Mosad Bialik, 1999.

Shavit, Zohar. *Ha-chayim ha-sifrutiyim be-erets yisra'el, 1910–1933*. Tel Aviv: Ha-kibbutz ha-me'uchad, 1982.

———. "Mavo le-beniyatah shel tarbut ivrit be-erets yisra'el." In *Toldot ha-yishuv ha-yehudi be-erets yisra'el me-az ha-aliyah ha-rishonah*, ed. Moshe Lisak, 3:9–29. Jerusalem: Mosad Bialik, 1999.

———. "On the Hebrew Cultural Center in Berlin in the Twenties." *Gutenberg-Jahrbukh* 68 (1993): 371–80.

———. "The Status of Translated Literature in the Creation of Hebrew Literature in Pre-State Israel (the Yishuv period)." *Meta: Translators' Journal* 41, no. 1 (1998): 46–53.

Sherman, Joseph. "Sholem Asch." *The YIVO Encyclopedia of Jews in Eastern Europe*. Accessed December 28, 2014. http://www.yivoencyclopedia.org/article.aspx/Asch_Sholem.

Sherman, Joseph, and Gennady Estraikh, eds. *David Bergelson: From Modernism to Socialist Realism*. London: Modern Humanities Research Association and Maney Publishing, 2007.

[Shlonsky], A. Sh. "Chatoteret olam." *Hedim* 1, no. 4 (1922): 60–61.

Shlonsky, Avraham. "Al 'ha-shalom.'" *Ketuvim*, nos. 34–35 (1927): 1.

———. *Ba-galgal*. Tel Aviv: Davar, 1926.

———. *Le-aba-ima*. Tel Aviv: Ketuvim, 1927.

———. "Le-yovel Bialik." *Hedim* 1 (1923): 8–9.

———. "To'anot." *Davar*, November 13, 1925.

Shmeruk, Chone. "Hebrew-Yiddish-Polish: A Trilingual Jewish Culture." In *The Jews of Poland between the Two World Wars*, ed. Yisrael Gutman, Ezra Mendelsohn, Jehuda Reinharz, and Chone Shmeruk, 285–311. Hanover, NH: University Press of New England, 1989.

Shmeruk, Chone, and Yisrael Bartal. *Ha-keri'ah la-navi: mechkerei historyah ve-sifrut*. Jerusalem: Ha-universitah ha-ivrit bi-yerushalayim, 1999.

Shneer, David. *Yiddish and the Creation of Soviet Jewish Culture, 1918–1930*. Cambridge: Cambridge University Press, 2004.

Shneour, Zalman. "Af'n shlosbarg." In *Vilne*, ed. Yefim Yeshurin, 781–83. New York: Vilner Branch 367—Workmen's Circle, 1935.

———. *Anshei Shklov*. Tel Aviv: Dvir, 1999.

———. "Anshei Shklov." *Tekufoteinu* 1 (1933): 365–80.

———. *A toyt*. Warsaw: Ha-shachar, 1910.

———. *Chezyonot: shirim u-fo'emot 1912–1921*. Berlin: Ha-sefer, 1923.

———. *David Frishman va-acherim*. Tel Aviv: Dvir, 1959.

———. *Fertsik yor lider un poemen, 1903–1944*. New York: Yiddishn natsionalen arbeter-farband, 1945.

———. *Luchot genuzim*. Tel Aviv: Am oved, 1952.

———. *Min ha-chayim ve-ha-mavet*. Warsaw: Tushiya, 1910.

———. *Shklover yidn*. Vilna, Warsaw: Farlag B. Kletskin, 1929.

———. "Vilna." *Miklat* 1, no. 1 (1919): 1–14.

Shteinman, Eliezer. "Der goyrl fun a literat." *Der moment*, September 26, 1924.

———. *Duda'im*. Tel Aviv: Ketuvim, 1931.

———. *Esther Chayot*. Warsaw: A. Y. Stybel, 1923.

———. "Ha-lashon al ha-ovnayim." *Ketuvim*, no. 7 (1933).

———. "Hotsa'at Stybel." In *Erets*, 29–31. Odessa: Dos naye leben, 1919.

———. *Intim mit der velt*. Tel Aviv: Ha-menorah, 1971.

———. "Kol korei le-yehudei polin." *Ketuvim*, no. 13 (August 13, 1926): 1.

———. "Machshavot bi-zmanan." *Kolot* 1, no. 1 (1923): 31.

———. *Mi-dor el dor*. Tel Aviv: Neuman, 1950.

———. "Milu'im." *Ketuvim*, nos. 34–35 (1927): 2.

———. *Sefer ha-ma'amarim*. Warsaw: Derakhim, 1923.

———. *Tsu mentsh un folk*. Warsaw: Derakhim, 1922.

———. "Tvusat ha-sipur." *Moznayim* 4, no. 5 (1936): 467–77.

———. *Ukraine veynt*. Warsaw: Farlag alt-yung, 1923.

———. "Vegn film bikhlal un vegn yishn film." *Der moment*, October 28, 1927.

———. "Vegn iberike yudn." *Der moment*, July 22, 1927.

Shur, Shimon A. *Gdud meginei ha-safa*. Haifa: Haifa University, 2000.

Silberschlag, Eisig. *From Renaissance to Renaissance*. New York: Ktav, 1973.

Singer, Y. Y. *Mi-shnei evrei ha-visla*. Jerusalem: Ha-me'asef, 1945.

———. *Perl un andere dertseylungen*. Warsaw: Farlag kultur lige, 1922.

Soyer, Daniel. "Back to the Future: American Jews Visit the Soviet Union in the 1920s and 1930s." *Jewish Social Studies* 6, no. 3 (2000): 124–59.

Spengler, Oswald. *Der Untergang des Abendlandes*. Munich: Beck, 1922.

Stahl, Nanette. *Sholem Asch Reconsidered*. New Haven, CT: Beinecke Rare Book and Manuscript Library, 2004.

Stauber, Roni. *The Holocaust in Israeli Public Debate in the 1950s*. London and Portland, OR: Vallentine Mitchell, 2007.

Stein, Sarah Abrevaya. *Making Jews Modern: The Yiddish and Ladino Press in the Russian and Ottoman Empires*. Bloomington: Indiana University Press, 2004.

Steiner, George. *Extraterritorial*. New York: Atheneum, 1971.

Stencl, Avrum Nokhum. "Vider un vider." *Milgroym*, no. 6 (1924): 35.

Stybel, A. Y. "He'ara le-marat Rachel Feygenberg." *Davar*, January 1, 1926.

Swaan, A. de. *Words of the World: The Global Language System*. Cambridge: Polity, 2001.

Szeintuch, Yechiel, and Carrie Friedman-Cohen. *Be-reshut ha-rabim u-ve-reshut ha-yechid: Aharon Zeitlin ve-sifrut Yiddish*. Jerusalem: Magnes Press, Hebrew University, 2000.

Teich, Mikuláš, and Roy Porter. *The National Question in Europe in Historical Context*. Cambridge: Cambridge University Press, 1993.

"Te'udat ha-shiloach." *Ha-shiloach* 1, no. 1 (1896): 1.

Toury, Gideon. *Descriptive Translation Studies and Beyond*. Amsterdam and Philadelphia: J. Benjamins, 1995.

———. *Normot shel tirgum ve-ha-tirgum ha-sifruti le-ivrit ba-shanim 1930–1945*. Tel Aviv: Porter Institute of Poetics and Semiotics, University of Tel Aviv, 1977.

———. "Norms in Translation." In *The Translation Studies Reader*, ed. Lawrence Venuti, 198–211. London and New York: Routledge, 2012.

Tshaykov, Yoysef. "Milgroym." *Shtrom* 3 (1922): 78–79.

Tsiporni, A., A. Z. Rabinovitsh, and D. Shimonovitsh, eds. *Sefer ha-shana shel erets-yisra'el 1924–1925*. Tel Aviv: Hotsa'at agudat ha-sofrim ha-ivrim, 1926.

"Tsu di hebreishe shrayber: vos is ayer meynung vegn yidish in yisroyel?" *Heymish* 5, nos. 48–49 (1960): 3–6.

Tyrell, Ian. "What Is Transnational History?," 2007. http://iantyrrell.wordpress.com/what-is-transnational-history/.

Ungerfeld, Moshe. "Sicha im Z. Shneour." *Ketuvim*, no. 55 (1927): 2.

Vakser, Yisrael. "Di letste trer." *Milgroym*, no. 3 (1923): 37–39.

———. "Ha-dim'ah ha-achronah." *Rimon*, no. 3 (1923): 35–36.

———. "In zibn tog arum." *Milgroym*, no. 3 (1923): 35–37.

———. "Le-shivat ha-yamim." *Rimon*, no. 3 (1923): 37–38.

———. *Mayselekh far kinder*. Bessarabia: Yiddishe kultur-lige, 1923.

Valencia, Heather. *Else Lasker-Schüler und Abraham Nochem Stenzel: Eine Unbekannte Freundschaft*. Frankfurt am Main: Campus, 1995.

Venuti, Lawrence. "The Translator's Invisibility." *Criticism* 28, no. 2 (1986): 179–212.

———. *The Translator's Invisibility: A History of Translation*. London and New York: Routledge, 1995.

———. "Translation, Intertextuality, Interpretation." Lecture, Ohio State University, Columbus, OH, October 11, 2013.

Vertovec, Steven. "Conceiving and Researching Transnationalism." *Ethnic and Racial Studies* 22, no. 2 (1999): 447–62.

Vilfland, Yosef. "Letter from New York." *Al ha-mishmar*, December 9, 1943.

Voisine-Jechova, Hana. "Peut-on choisir sa langue?" *Revue de littérature comparée*, no. 69 (1995): 5–11.

Vokh. November 29, 1929.

Waldinger, Albert. "Abraham Cahan and Palestine." *Jewish Social Studies* 39, nos. 1/2 (1977): 75–92.

Walters, E. Garrison. *The Other Europe: Eastern Europe to 1945*. Syracuse: Syracuse University Press, 1987.

Wasserman, Henry. "How to Invent a Cultural Renaissance in Weimar Germany." *Katharsis* 2 (2004): 69–94.

Weinreich, Max. *History of the Yiddish Language*. Chicago: University of Chicago Press, 1980.

Weinreich, Uriel. *Languages in Contact*. The Hague and Paris: Mouton & Co., 1968.

Weiser, Keith, and Joshua A. Fogel. *Czernowitz at 100: The First Yiddish Language Conference in Historical Perspective*. Lanham, MD: Lexington Books, 2010.

Weissler, Chava. "For Women and Men Who Are Like Women: The Construction of Gender in Yiddish Devotional Literature." *Journal of Feminist Studies and Religion* 5, no. 2 (1989): 7–24.

Weitz, Eric D. *Weimar Germany: Promise and Tragedy*. Princeton: Princeton University Press, 2013.

Werses, Shmuel. "Kitvei-et ivriyim le-sifrut be-Polin ben shtei milchamot olam." In *Ben shtei milchamot olam*, 96–127. Jerusalem: Magnes Press, Hebrew University, 1997.

———. *Mi-lashon el lashon*. Jerusalem: Hotsa'at sefarim a. sh. Y. L. Magnes, ha-universita ha-ivrit, 1996.

———. "Sugiyat yidish be-masekhet Dov Sadan." *Sadan* 1 (1994): 9–33.

Wieseltier, Meir. "Dibur al Avot." In *Eikh nikra Avot Yeshurun*, ed. Lilach Lachman, 207–20. Tel Aviv: Ha-kibbutz ha-me'uchad, 2011.

Winford, Donald. *An Introduction to Contact Linguistics*. Malden, MA: Blackwell, 2003.

Wischnitzer, Rachel. "From My Archives." *Journal of Jewish Art* 6 (1979): 6.

Wischnitzer Bernstein, Rachel. "Di naye kunst un mir." *Milgroym*, no. 1 (1922): 2–7.

———. "Eine Selbst-Anzeige." *Soncino-Blatter* 1 1925–1926): 95

———. "Ha-omanut ha-chadasha va-anachnu." *Rimon*, no. 1 (1922): 2–6.

Wisse, Ruth. "Language as Fate." *Studies in Contemporary Jewry* 12 (1996): 129–47.

Wisse, Ruth R. *The Modern Jewish Canon*. New York: Free Press, 2000.

Wohlmann, Y. L. "Vos ikh her un zeh in Erets yisroel." *Der moment*, May 20, 1927.

Wolf-Monzon, Tamar. *Le-nogah nekudat ha-pele*. Haifa: Hotsa'at ha-sefarim shel universitat Haifa, 2005.

Wolitz, Seth. "Chagall's Last Soviet Performance: The Graphics for 'Troyer,' 1922." *Jewish Art* 21–22 (1995): 95–115.

———. "The Kiev-Grupe (1918–1920) Debate: The Function of Literature." *Studies in American Jewish Literature* 4, no. 2 (1978): 97–106.

Wolitz, Seth L. "Between Folk and Freedom: The Failure of the Yiddish Modernist Movement in Poland." *Yiddish* 8, no. 1 (1991): 26–51.

———. "The Jewish National Art Renaissance in Russia." In *Tradition and Revolution: The Jewish Renaissance in Russian Avant-Garde Art, 1912–1928*, ed. Ruth Apter-Gabriel, 21–41. Jerusalem: Israel Museum, 1987.

Yeshurin, Yefim, ed. *Vilne: a zamelbukh gevidmet der shtot vilne*. New York: Vilner brentsh 367 Arbeter ring, 1935.

Yeshurun, Avot. *Kol shirav*. Tel Aviv: Ha-kibbutz ha-me'uchad, 1995.

Yildiz, Yasemin. *Beyond the Mother Tongue*. New York: Fordham University Press, 2012.

Yishai, A. Z. Ben. "Milchamah be-tachanot-ruach." *Davar*, May 17, 1927.

Zeitlin, Aharon. "Dernenterung un noentkeyt tsvishn yidish un hebreish." In *Literarishe un filosofishe eseyen*, 194–203. New York: Altveltlekhn yiddishn kultur-kongres, 1980.

———. "Mendele ha-mekarev." In *Achisefer*, ed. Shmuel Niger and Menachem Ribalow, 74–80. New York: Louis LaMed Foundation for the Advancement of Hebrew and Yiddish Literature, 1943.

Zmora, Yisrael. "Birkat ha-shefa." *Moznayim* 14, no. 3 (1962): 185–89.

"Z. Shneour be-mechitsat ha-sofrim ha-ivrim." *Davar*, March 23, 1934.

"Z. Shneour yishtatef be-kvi'ut be-'Davar.'" *Davar*, November 14, 1935.

Zucker, Sheva. "Rokhl Faygnberg (Imri)." *Jewish Women: A Comprehensive Historical Encyclopedia*. Accessed November 26, 2014. http://jwa.org/encyclopedia/article/faygnberg-imri-rokhl.

Zuckermann, Ghil'ad. "A New Vision for Israeli Hebrew." *Journal of Modern Jewish Studies* 5, no. 1 (March 2006): 57–71.

Index

Italic page number denotes illustration.

Naomi Brenner is associate professor of Hebrew and Israeli Culture at The Ohio State University.

www.ingramcontent.com/pod-product-compliance
Lightning Source LLC
LaVergne TN
LVHW091108080826
845145LV00008B/1853

9780815634096